Transforming Vocational Education and Training Using AI

Eriona Çela
University of New York, Tirana, Albania

Narasimha Rao Vajjhala
University of New York, Tirana, Albania

Rajasekhara Mouly Potluri
Kazakh-British Technical University, Kazakhstan

Philip Eappen
Cape Breton University, Canada

IGI Global
Scientific Publishing
Publishing Tomorrow's Research Today

Vice President of Editorial | Melissa Wagner
Managing Editor of Acquisitions | Mikaela Felty
Managing Editor of Book Development | Jocelynn Hessler
Production Manager | Mike Brehm
Cover Design | Phillip Shickler

Published in the United States of America by
IGI Global Scientific Publishing
701 East Chocolate Avenue
Hershey, PA, 17033, USA
Tel: 717-533-8845
Fax: 717-533-8661
Website: https://www.igi-global.com E-mail: cust@igi-global.com

Library of Congress Cataloging-in-Publication Data

Names: Çela, Eriona, 1992- editor | Vajjhala, Narasimha, 1978- editor | Potluri, Rajasekhara Mouly, 1967- editor | Eappen, Philip, 1985- editor
Title: Transforming vocational education and training using AI / Edited by Eriona Çela, Narasimha Rao Vajjhala, Rajasekhara Mouly Potluri, Philip Eappen.
Description: Hershey, PA : IGI Global Scientific Publishing, 2025. | Includes bibliographical references and index. | Summary: "Through case studies and real-world examples, readers will gain insights into effective strategies for incorporating AI into teaching and learning processes. This book will also explore the pivotal role of partnerships between educational institutions and industries, showcasing how these collaborations can create robust internship opportunities and enhance VET programs"-- Provided by publisher.
Identifiers: LCCN 2024054394 (print) | LCCN 2024054395 (ebook) | ISBN 9798369382523 (hardcover) | ISBN 9798369382530 (paperback) | ISBN 9798369382547 (ebook)
Subjects: LCSH: Vocational education. | Artificial intelligence--Educational applications. | Vocational education--Case studies. | Artificial intelligence--Educational applications--Case studies.
Classification: LCC LC1043 .T72 2025 (print) | LCC LC1043 (ebook) | DDC 370.285/63--dc23/eng/20250310
LC record available at https://lccn.loc.gov/2024054394
LC ebook record available at https://lccn.loc.gov/2024054395

British Cataloguing in Publication Data
A Cataloguing in Publication record for this book is available from the British Library.

Dr. Eriona Çela

I would like to extend my heartfelt gratitude to my family. Its unwavering support and belief in me have been my guiding light throughout this journey. Thank you for standing by me, for your patience, and for always reminding me of the importance of this work. I am truly fortunate to have you in my life.

Assoc. Prof. Narasimha Rao Vajjhala

I want to thank my family members, particularly my mother, Mrs. Rajeswari Vajjhala, for her blessings and for instilling in me the virtues of perseverance and commitment.

Professor Rajasekhara Mouly Potluri

I am eternally grateful to my IGI Global Publishers and the team editorial board of the book, who made an extra effort to finish this book project. They are in constant touch with us in guiding us in this regard. Although this period of my life was filled with many ups and downs, my time in the education industry was worth it. My time in higher education wouldn't have been possible without my family, Aruna (wife), Lohith (son), and Dr. Mouly (father). They helped and backed me up with their love, cooperation, and encouragement throughout my life. A special thanks to all author contributors who were involved in sharp contact with the editorial team and strictly followed the deadlines of the entire project.

Dr. Philip Eappen

I want to take this opportunity to express my appreciation to Dr. Narasimha Rao Vajjhala for his support, encouragement and for sharing his experience, knowledge, and expertise throughout the completion of this book.

Thanks a million, to my wife, Figgi Philip, for her patience, encouragement, and endurance during my academic journey. I cannot thank you enough for your kind and unwavering support during my research activities. I am thankful to my son, Evan Eappen Philip: Your naughtiness, and cuteness made my life fun-filled and more enjoyable. To my parents, Eapen TP and Baby Eapen: Both of you made me feel smart, unique, and capable. Thank you for your kindness and encouragement. I would also like to thank my sister, brothers-in-law, and my in-laws for their encouragement and support during these years. All of you motivated and encouraged me during this journey, and I am what I am because of all your support.

Editorial Advisory Board

Table of Contents

Detailed Table of Contents

offering real-time guidance in industries requiring precision and hands-on expertise. Furthermore, the chapter underscores the potential of VR and AR in promoting remote learning and accessibility, empowering trainees to engage with high-quality simulations and training programs from virtually any location.

Augmented reality (AR) has the potential to revolutionize the field of vocational education and training. AR offers immersive and interactive learning experiences that are especially well-suited to skill-based education by superimposing digital information onto the real world. AR is a perfect tool for improving the teaching and learning process in a variety of vocational disciplines because of the growing complexity of vocational skills and the requirement for practical training. The use of AR in vocational education and training is still in its early phases, despite its promise, and a thorough analysis of the literature is required to comprehend its advantages, disadvantages, and potential future possibilities. Using the PRISMA (Preferred Reporting Items for Systematic Reviews and Meta-Analyses) guidelines, this chapter attempts to conduct a systematic evaluation of the body of research on the application of AR in vocational education and training.

This chapter explores the integration of artificial intelligence (AI) in police education by examining the case of Taiwan's Central Police University (CPU). It focuses on the institution's top-down approach to implementing AI technologies within its curriculum and training programs. The findings indicate that as the landscape of law enforcement evolves with rapid technological advancements, CPU has aimed to modernise its educational offerings since 2023 to better prepare future police officers for contemporary challenges. The study highlights the crucial role of institutional leadership in guiding AI adoption among faculty and students, ensuring that educational strategies align with both technological relevance and traditional pedagogical values. By enhancing its capabilities through various projects, conferences, workshops, and guidelines, CPU sets a precedent for other law enforcement vocational education institutions seeking to incorporate AI into their training frameworks.

Education is already hovering on the edge of the Education 4.0 revolution fueled by technology integration and student participation. Therefore, Education 4.0 eliminates rigid structures, lectures and focuses on teachers as Education 4.0 is meant for digital generation providing a flexible learning process that is continuous. Central to this shift is the Smart Hybrid Learning System, which brings together models such as the Challenge Based learning and the Case Based learning in dynamic online environments. Enhancing learning solution; online learning platforms, LMS, AI, IoT provide rich engagement solutions. Today's school structures fail to capture such changing needs, which puts emphasis on old fashioned approaches. Such classroom practices as the flipped and smart classroom helps overcome these gaps but issues with implementation is still an issue with issues to do with infrastructure and digital divide. Education 4.0 is the strategic direction towards mass, choice and flexibility for learning in the era of volatility.

Foreword

The rapid evolution of Artificial Intelligence (AI) has touched nearly every aspect of our lives, transformed industries and redefined the way we work and learn. Vocational Education and Training (VET) is no exception. As the demand for skilled professionals grows in an increasingly technology-driven world, the integration of AI into VET systems has become a critical pathway for preparing learners to meet the challenges of the future. This book, *Transforming Vocational Education and Training Using AI*, offers a comprehensive exploration of how AI is reshaping VET, bridging gaps in accessibility, and equipping learners with the tools to thrive in a dynamic workforce. Vocational education has long served as a vital engine for economic growth and workforce development, offering practical skills that align with industry demands. However, traditional methods often struggle to keep pace with rapid technological advancements. The emergence of AI presents an unprecedented opportunity to modernize VET systems, making them more adaptive, efficient, and aligned with the needs of a globalized economy. This book highlights the key innovations and applications of AI in VET, from personalized learning systems to predictive analytics and immersive technologies like Virtual Reality (VR) and Augmented Reality (AR).

A recurring theme throughout this book is the transformative potential of AI to democratize education. By leveraging AI-powered platforms, educators can transcend traditional barriers such as geography, resource constraints, and socio-economic divides. This creates an inclusive learning environment where learners from diverse backgrounds can access high-quality vocational training tailored to their unique needs. The chapters in this book explore these possibilities, offering case studies and real-world examples that illustrate the impact of AI in fostering equity and accessibility. At the same time, the integration of AI in VET is not without its challenges. Issues such as data privacy, algorithmic bias, and the digital divide require careful consideration. This book does not shy away from these complexities, addressing them with thoughtful analysis and offering strategies to mitigate potential risks. By fostering a culture of ethical AI adoption, we can ensure that technological advancements in VET serve to empower rather than marginalize learners.

One of the most compelling aspects of this book is its interdisciplinary approach. The contributors, hailing from diverse academic and professional backgrounds, bring a wealth of knowledge and expertise to the discussion. Their insights span education, technology, ethics, and industry, providing a holistic perspective on the integration of AI in VET. This richness of perspectives makes the book a valuable resource for educators, policymakers, industry leaders, and researchers alike. The role of educators in this transformation cannot be overstated. AI technologies are powerful tools, but their effectiveness ultimately depends on how they are implemented and adapted to specific educational contexts. This book emphasizes the importance of training educators to harness the potential of AI, equipping them with the skills to design and deliver innovative learning experiences. Professional development, collaboration, and ongoing support are essential to ensure that educators remain at the forefront of this transformation.

Policy and governance also play a critical role in shaping the future of AI in VET. The book advocates for targeted policies that promote investment in AI technologies, foster public-private partnerships, and prioritize ethical standards. These frameworks are necessary to create a sustainable ecosystem where AI can thrive and contribute to meaningful improvements in vocational education. The book's structure is thoughtfully designed to guide readers through the multifaceted dimensions of AI in VET. Each chapter builds upon the previous one, offering a logical progression from foundational concepts to advanced applications and future trends. This coherence not only enhances the reader's understanding but also inspires actionable insights that can be applied in real-world contexts.

As we look to the future, AI will continue to drive innovation in vocational education. This book serves as a call to action, urging stakeholders to embrace the opportunities and address the challenges of AI integration. By fostering collaboration and innovation, we can create a future where vocational education is more responsive, inclusive, and impactful than ever before. *Transforming Vocational Education and Training Using AI* is both timely and visionary. It captures the essence of a rapidly changing educational landscape and provides a roadmap for navigating the complexities of AI adoption. I am confident that readers will find this book to be an invaluable resource as they work to shape the future of vocational education, ensuring that learners everywhere are equipped to succeed in an AI-driven world.

Adeyemi Abel Ajibesin

Department of Information Technology, Faculty of Informatics & Design, Cape Peninsula University of Technology, South Africa

Adeyemi Abel Ajibesin is a distinguished academic scholar with over two decades of extensive experience in research, teaching, and leadership, particularly in Electrical Engineering and Computer Science. Currently serving as a visiting professor in the Department of IT at Cape Peninsula University of Technology in South Africa, he previously held positions such as Chair/HoD of Software Engineering at the School of IT & Computing (SITC) at the American University of Nigeria, founding Interim Dean of the School of Engineering, Interim Dean of the School of IT & Computing, and Director of the African Centre for ICT Innovation and Training. He has also served in various capacities at Simon Fraser University in Canada, the University of Cape Town in South Africa, and the Pan African University Institute for Basic Sciences, Technology Innovation in Kenya, among other institutions. His areas of research are data science, broadband networks, frontier analysis, and AI. His prolific research portfolio is reflected in numerous articles published in reputable peer-reviewed conference proceedings, journals, and books, alongside patents for engineering products and copyrighted computing software, showcasing his innovative contributions to his field. Dr. Ajibesin's leadership and academic excellence have been recognized through numerous awards and grants, including esteemed accolades such as the Google Research (explorerCSR), AIMS, CSIR and IEEE.

Preface

Artificial Intelligence (AI) is transforming vocational education and training (VET) globally, offering innovative solutions to enhance learning and skill development while addressing workforce demands. This book provides a comprehensive exploration of AI technologies' impact on modern education systems. Drawing on insights from interdisciplinary research and diverse geographic contexts, it offers an in-depth analysis of how AI is shaping the future of VET, bridging gaps between traditional learning methods and the evolving technological landscape. The chapters in this book are meticulously curated to address the multifaceted dimensions of AI integration in VET. From foundational concepts to practical applications, the contributors examine critical themes such as personalized learning, immersive technologies like Virtual Reality (VR) and Augmented Reality (AR), and the ethical challenges inherent in adopting AI-driven solutions. Case studies and systematic reviews provide a global perspective, offering readers actionable strategies to implement AI technologies effectively in various educational and industry settings.

This book's strength lies in its interdisciplinary approach, combining expertise from education, technology, and industry to provide a holistic understanding of AI's role in VET. The contributors, hailing from diverse academic and professional backgrounds, share their insights and experiences, ensuring a rich tapestry of knowledge. Their discussions emphasize not only the opportunities AI presents but also the challenges, such as the digital divide, data privacy, and the need for ethical frameworks to guide AI adoption. As vocational education increasingly integrates AI, this book aims to serve as a critical resource for educators, policymakers, and industry leaders. It offers a roadmap for navigating the complexities of AI implementation, fostering an ecosystem where technology enhances learning outcomes while promoting equity and inclusivity. By addressing the theoretical, practical, and ethical dimensions of AI in VET, this book positions itself as a seminal text in the field. Through its comprehensive coverage and future-oriented insights, this book seeks to inspire innovation and collaboration among stakeholders. It underscores the transformative potential of AI to reshape education systems, equipping learners with the skills they need to thrive in a rapidly changing world.

CHAPTER OVERVIEW

In Chapter 1 – Artificial Intelligence in Vocational Education and Training: Opportunities, Challenges, and Ethical Considerations, the authors explore the profound impact of AI technologies on Vocational Education and Training (VET). This chapter examines the integration of advanced tools such as Virtual Reality, Augmented Reality, Machine Learning, and the Internet of Things to enhance personalized learning and skill development. By examining the role of these technologies in creating immersive learning environments, automating administrative tasks, and providing real-time feedback, the authors highlight how AI-driven innovations are transforming traditional pedagogical practices. The chapter underscores the dual dimensions of AI application in VET: enriching classroom instruction and preparing students for the demands of a technology-driven workforce. The authors also address the multifaceted challenges associated with incorporating AI in VET, including algorithmic bias, data privacy, and the digital divide. Ethical considerations are central to the discussion, emphasizing the need for balanced integration of AI while maintaining human interaction in education. Through a comprehensive analysis of current tools and practices, the chapter identifies both opportunities and barriers in leveraging AI for workforce readiness. It advocates for policy reforms, interdisciplinary research, and educator training as essential strategies to maximize the benefits of AI integration. This chapter offers a valuable framework for educators, policymakers, and researchers to navigate the complexities of AI adoption in vocational education and training systems.

In Chapter 2 – AI Literacy: Foundations, Importance, and Broader Implications, the authors examine the critical role of AI literacy in enabling individuals and communities to navigate an AI-dominated world with informed decision-making and ethical awareness. The chapter defines AI literacy as a combination of technical knowledge and critical thinking skills necessary to engage with AI technologies, such as machine learning, natural language processing, and automation, across various domains including healthcare, finance, and education. The authors highlight how fostering AI literacy can promote equitable access, mitigate biases, and empower marginalized communities to participate in AI-driven opportunities, emphasizing the democratization of AI knowledge as a tool for inclusion. Furthermore, the chapter examines the societal and workforce implications of AI literacy, addressing challenges such as data privacy concerns, ethical dilemmas, and the digital divide. By proposing strategies for education and workforce development, it underscores the importance of reskilling and upskilling to prepare individuals for the evolving demands of an AI-powered job market. The authors advocate for targeted policies, professional development for educators, and critical reflection to ensure AI technologies are adopted responsibly and equitably. This chapter provides a comprehensive framework for understanding AI literacy as a foundational skill set for navigating the complexities of an AI-driven future.

In Chapter 3 – AI in Vocational Education and Training: Technologies and Applications, the authors examine the transformative role of Artificial Intelligence (AI) in shaping the future of vocational education and training (VET). The chapter examines how AI technologies, including machine learning, virtual and augmented reality, and natural language processing, are revolutionizing VET by creating personalized, immersive, and adaptive learning environments. Key tools such as learning analytics and AI-powered platforms are highlighted for their ability to provide tailored content and feedback, enhancing both learner engagement and outcomes. By integrating cutting-edge AI innovations, the chapter demonstrates how VET can address the diverse needs of students and prepare them for a rapidly evolving job market. The chapter also explores the challenges and ethical considerations of incorporating AI into VET systems, such as data privacy concerns, algorithmic biases, and the digital divide. The authors stress the importance of human-centered teaching alongside AI-driven methods to achieve a balanced and effective educational experience. Additionally, the chapter provides insights into emerging trends, such as explainable AI and robotics, and their potential to further enhance skill development and career readiness. With a focus on interdisciplinary collaboration and continuous research, the chapter offers a comprehensive roadmap for leveraging AI to transform vocational education and empower the workforce of the future.

In Chapter 4 – Virtual Reality (VR) and Augmented Reality (AR) in Vocational Training, the authors explore the transformative role of immersive technologies in reshaping vocational education and training (VET). By simulating real-world scenarios, VR and AR enable trainees to practice complex tasks, such as operating machinery or performing medical procedures, in safe, controlled environments. These technologies provide engaging and interactive learning experiences that enhance knowledge retention, skill development, and confidence. Additionally, AR overlays digital information onto physical tasks, offering real-time guidance, particularly in industries requiring precision and expertise. The chapter emphasizes the potential of these tools to democratize access to high-quality training by enabling remote and personalized learning opportunities. The chapter also examines the pedagogical advantages of VR and AR, such as fostering critical thinking, problem-solving, and active learning. It addresses challenges like high implementation costs, the need for specialized instructor training, and ethical concerns surrounding data privacy and security. Through a discussion of best practices, including aligning with learning objectives and conducting thorough needs assessments, the authors provide actionable insights for educators and policymakers. By leveraging VR and AR technologies, vocational training programs can better prepare learners for the demands of modern industries while overcoming traditional educational barriers.

In Chapter 5 – The Role of Augmented Reality in Vocational Education and Training: A Systematic Literature Review, the authors provide a comprehensive examination of the integration of augmented reality (AR) in vocational education and training (VET). Using the PRISMA framework for systematic literature review, the chapter evaluates the current research landscape, emphasizing AR's potential to create immersive and interactive learning environments. By overlaying digital elements on real-world settings, AR facilitates skill development, enhances learning motivation, and reduces operational risks in fields such as automotive repair, healthcare, and construction. The chapter also introduces innovative applications like gamified AR programs and simulation tools, which bridge theoretical knowledge with practical expertise while addressing diverse learner needs. The authors also explore the challenges and limitations of implementing AR in VET, such as high costs, accessibility issues, and cognitive overload. Ethical considerations, including data privacy and inclusivity, are discussed alongside technical hurdles like hardware limitations and content development complexities. The chapter emphasizes the need for further research to standardize AR technologies, enhance their cost-effectiveness, and adapt them to specific vocational contexts. By addressing these issues, the chapter presents a forward-looking perspective on how AR can reshape VET, offering practical insights for educators, policymakers, and researchers.

In Chapter 6 – Integrating Artificial Intelligence in Police Education: A Top-Down Approach at Taiwan's Central Police University, the authors explore the strategic integration of AI technologies into police training and education at Taiwan's Central Police University (CPU). This chapter highlights the institution's top-down approach, where leadership and government policies drive AI implementation within vocational education and training (VET) programs. Using Rational Choice Institutionalism as a theoretical framework, the chapter examines how CPU balances technological advancement with traditional pedagogical values to modernize its curriculum, foster ethical AI use, and prepare students for the challenges of modern policing. The authors discuss the implementation of innovative AI tools, such as generative AI and augmented reality, to enhance learning outcomes while addressing complex societal needs, including cybercrime and digital ethics. The chapter also identifies key themes, including leadership strategy, curriculum modernization, faculty development, and research initiatives, as pivotal to CPU's AI integration efforts. Through international collaborations and ethical guidelines, CPU navigates challenges such as data privacy concerns, resource allocation, and the digital divide. By prioritizing interdisciplinary collaboration and aligning with global trends, the university sets an example for integrating advanced technologies in specialized education. This case study offers valuable insights for institutions worldwide seeking to incorporate AI into VET, showcasing the importance of a strategic, ethically grounded, and future-oriented approach to education in law enforcement.

In Chapter 7 – AI-Driven Digital Marketing in Kazakhstan: Opportunities and Challenges for Vocational Education and Training, the authors explore the integration of artificial intelligence (AI) into digital marketing strategies to enhance vocational education and training (VET) in Kazakhstan. By analyzing AI's potential to revolutionize digital marketing, the chapter emphasizes its role in creating personalized, data-driven campaigns that can popularize VET programs and engage diverse audiences. The authors discuss innovative AI applications such as content personalization, predictive analytics, and automated marketing, which enable targeted outreach to prospective learners and stakeholders. Through case studies and research findings, the chapter highlights how AI-powered tools can bridge the gap between vocational education institutions and the labor market, fostering a competitive and adaptable workforce. The chapter also examines the challenges of adopting AI-driven digital marketing, including data privacy concerns, the high costs of implementation, and the need for skilled professionals to manage these technologies. It addresses strategies to overcome these barriers, such as fostering public-private partnerships, investing in educator training, and developing ethical guidelines for AI use. With a focus on Kazakhstan's unique socio-economic context, the authors provide actionable insights for leveraging AI to promote VET programs effectively. This chapter serves as a roadmap for educators, policymakers, and marketers seeking to harness AI's transformative power to reshape vocational education systems in emerging economies.

In Chapter 8 – Artificial Intelligence Shaping the Future of Vocational Education and Training: Roles, Impacts, and Insights, the authors provide a comprehensive analysis of AI's transformative role in advancing vocational education and training (VET). Drawing on insights from educators, apprentices, and industry leaders at Switzerland's Federal University for Vocational Education and Training (SFUVET), the chapter highlights the critical applications of AI, such as adaptive learning, personalized training, and immersive technologies like augmented and virtual reality. It evaluates how AI-driven solutions bridge the gap between theoretical education and hands-on skill development, ensuring that VET graduates are well-prepared for the evolving demands of the job market. The chapter also presents a theoretical framework that explores AI's positive and negative impacts, considering challenges such as ethical concerns, data quality issues, and the digital divide. The authors address the dual role of AI as both a facilitator and a disruptor in VET systems, emphasizing the importance of balancing AI integration with human-centered teaching approaches. The chapter offers actionable recommendations, including professional development for educators, the inclusion of AI-specific curricula, and fostering partnerships between educational institutions and industry stakeholders. By providing practical insights into leveraging AI for improving accessibility, engagement, and efficiency, this chapter equips educators, policymakers, and researchers with strategies to navigate the opportunities and challenges of integrating AI into vocational training. Ultimately, it underscores AI's potential to reshape VET, preparing learners for a dynamic and technology-driven workforce.

In Chapter 9 – Transformation of Quality Education Through E-Learning for Sustainable Development, the authors examine the pivotal role of e-learning in advancing global education and achieving the United Nations' Sustainable Development Goals (SDG), particularly SDG 4, which emphasizes inclusive and equitable quality education. The chapter explores the evolution of e-learning technologies, such as Learning Management Systems (LMS), Artificial Intelligence (AI), Internet of Things (IoT), and adaptive learning platforms, and their integration into educational frameworks to enhance accessibility, flexibility, and personalization. By eliminating geographic and socioeconomic barriers, e-learning democratizes education and supports lifelong learning opportunities, fostering skill development and digital literacy. The chapter also highlights the importance of sustainability, resource efficiency, and the development of content that aligns with ecological and social objectives. The authors address challenges in implementing e-learning systems, including the digital divide, data privacy, quality control, and resistance to change within traditional education systems. They advocate for inclusive designs, cultural sensitivity, and ethical considerations in the creation and dissemination of digital learning materials. Case studies of successful e-learning implementations are presented, showcasing their impact on accessibility, workforce development, and student engagement. By analyzing future trends, such as blockchain-based credentialing, IoT-enabled classrooms, and AI-driven predictive models, the chapter offers a forward-looking perspective on how e-learning can transform education systems to meet the dynamic needs of the 21st century while promoting sustainability and equity.

As we conclude this exploration of AI in VET, it becomes evident that the transformative potential of AI extends far beyond technological integration. This book has highlighted the myriad ways in which AI is reshaping VET systems worldwide—through immersive technologies like Virtual Reality (VR) and Augmented Reality (AR), adaptive learning platforms, and data-driven decision-making. These advancements not only enhance teaching methodologies but also prepare students for the dynamic demands of the modern workforce. By bridging the gap between theoretical knowledge and practical application, AI creates an enriched learning ecosystem that fosters innovation, inclusivity, and accessibility.

At the heart of these advancements lies a call for thoughtful implementation. The challenges of AI integration—such as algorithmic bias, data privacy, and the digital divide—demand a balanced and ethical approach. This book underscores the importance of fostering collaborations among educators, policymakers, and industry leaders to address these concerns and ensure that AI technologies are used responsibly. The insights and recommendations shared by the contributors serve as a guiding framework for navigating these complexities, offering actionable strategies to maximize the benefits of AI while minimizing its risks. Looking ahead, the future of VET is one of boundless possibilities, driven by the synergy between human ingenuity and technological innovation. This book emphasizes the need for continuous dialogue, research, and adaptation to keep pace with the rapid evolution of AI. By fostering a collaborative and forward-thinking mindset, we can harness the full potential of AI to create transformative learning environments. As readers embark on the journey through this book, it is our hope that they will be inspired to lead efforts in advancing VET, shaping a future where technology empowers learners and drives sustainable development.

Editors

Eriona Çela
University of New York Tirana, Albania

Narasimha Rao Vajjhala
University of New York Tirana, Albania

Rajasekhara Mouly Potluri
Kazakh-British Technical University, Kazakhstan

Philip Eappen
Cape Breton University, Canada

Chapter 1
Artificial Intelligence in Vocational Education and Training

Eriona Çela
https://orcid.org/0000-0003-2710-5489
University of New York Tirana, Albania

Narasimha Rao Vajjhala
https://orcid.org/0000-0002-8260-2392
University of New York Tirana, Albania

Philip Eappen
https://orcid.org/0000-0002-8120-8449
Cape Breton University, Canada

Alexey Vedishchev
https://orcid.org/0009-0009-3840-7440
American University of Nigeria, Nigeria

ABSTRACT

This chapter explores the transformative impact of Artificial Intelligence (AI) in Vocational Education and Training (VET), highlighting its potential to revolutionize teaching and learning processes while preparing students for the evolving demands of an AI-driven workforce. It examines the diverse applications of AI technologies, including Virtual Reality (VR), Augmented Reality (AR), Machine Learning (ML), and the Internet of Things (IoT), and their role in enhancing personalized learning, skill development, and workplace readiness. The chapter also addresses the challenges of integrating AI into VET, such as algorithmic bias, the digital divide, and data privacy concerns, while offering mitigation strategies to ensure equitable

DOI: 10.4018/979-8-3693-8252-3.ch001

and effective implementation. Ethical considerations are discussed, emphasizing the balance between leveraging AI innovations and preserving critical human interaction and ethical integrity.

INTRODUCTION

There are several AI tools that are used in education in general but are also very helpful in VET system as well. These tools might refer to management software which are adopted in schools and universities, specific programs that help in personalized learning or specific teaching, programs which help students enhance their skills in specific areas, according to their needs. However, there are tools thar are created to simplify the teaching and learning process in VET education. The combination of AI technologies in VET programs makes possible the creation of customized learning experiences being in line with the cultural and social developments of the country, offering feedback, providing collaborative educational environment, promoting skill development, providing training opportunities. Scholars believe that the incorporation of AI driven tools into VET enhance educational results, their progress, promotes continuous improvement and innovation and enables students to get the necessary skills and knowledge in the workplace. However, there are also some drawbacks regarding the incorporation of AI tools in VET generally, they relate to bias that is created in algorithm, lack of access to technology, lack of training and support and overreliance on AI. All this said, ensuring fair assessment and grading is important in education. The presence of bias elements when using AI tools and algorithms has the capacity to reduce the reliability of the assessment. On the other hand, the absence of access to virtual hardware and computers may restrict the efficiency of AI integration into VET. Also, the usage of AI tools from students mostly might create difficulties in the development of specific skills like critical thinking or problem solving. There must be a balance between the usage of AI and human interaction. So, before implementing these tools into VET systems, it is acquired a professional knowledge on the usage of these tools, trainings to empower and effectively utilize the AI platforms and even optimize the advantages of the integration of AI in VET system (Mohammad Aniq Bin Amdan et al., 2024).

IMPACT OF AI ON VOCATIONAL EDUCATION AND TRAINING

The integration of Artificial Intelligence (AI) in Vocational Education and Training (VET) represents a significant advancement with the potential to reshape both the teaching and learning processes and the nature of work itself. AI can fundamentally influence educational practices by introducing various AI-based tools that enhance the effectiveness of instruction. For instance, digital assistants can provide support to educators in the classroom, helping them manage instructional tasks more efficiently. Additionally, automation of administrative responsibilities allows teachers to dedicate more time to direct student engagement and support, thereby fostering a more conducive learning environment. Within the educational framework, there are innovative applications of AI, including Learning Analytics, which involves the analysis of educational data to improve learning outcomes, Adaptive Learning systems that personalize educational experiences to meet individual learner needs, and AI-based assessment systems that can enhance the evaluation processes of student performance. By adopting these technologies, VET institutions can create more responsive and individualized learning experiences, transforming traditional pedagogical approaches. Moreover, the impact of AI extends beyond the educational process; it has far-reaching implications for employment and the evolution of job roles. As AI technologies permeate various industries, the tasks associated with jobs are also shifting, necessitating a reevaluation of both initial and ongoing training for individuals in the workforce as well as those entering the job market. This transformation underscores the importance of incorporating AI-focused training within VET curricula to prepare students for an increasingly automated work environment (Attwell et al., 2020).

AI can thus be conceptualized within VET through two primary dimensions. First, AI-driven tools can be effectively utilized in classroom settings, enriching the educational experience and enhancing instructional methodologies. Second, the incorporation of AI in educational discussions prepares learners for the realities of a technology-driven workforce, equipping them with the knowledge and skills necessary to thrive in an AI-centric economy. By addressing the implications of AI in both teaching and real-world applications, VET programs can ensure that students are adequately prepared for the challenges and opportunities presented by the evolving employment landscape (Attwell et al., 2020).

SPECIFIC AI TOOLS USED IN VET

There are several applications that can be used in VET classrooms or outside them, in practice hours or general teaching process, the aim of which is the improvement of VET education. Some of these tools are virtual reality and augmented reality applications, machine learning platforms, internet of things in vocational training, gamification, interactive learning tools, robotics and automations, big data analytics, blockchain, 3D printing etc. In vocational education, Virtual Reality (VR) serves as a valuable tool that allows students to simulate complex tasks within a safe environment, thereby enhancing their comprehension of intricate concepts. Research indicates that VR simulation facilitates personalized learning experiences, catering to the unique needs of learners and providing adaptive educational opportunities. Algorithms designed for this purpose analyze student behavior, adjusting learning materials and their delivery pace to suit individual requirements. Furthermore, AI-driven tutoring systems offer immediate feedback, pinpointing students' strengths and weaknesses, and subsequently guiding them towards mastery of the subject matter. These AI-powered platforms can tailor their content and difficulty level to meet the specific needs of each student, ultimately promoting more effective and efficient learning. Table 1 presents a detailed list of AI tools used in VET.

Table 1. AI Tools and Their Applications in VET

AI Tool	Application in VET	Key Benefits
Virtual Reality (VR)	Simulates real-world scenarios for safe, immersive skill training.	Enhances comprehension of complex tasks; provides hands-on experience.
Augmented Reality (AR)	Overlays digital content on the physical world to aid practical training.	Improves engagement; reduces training errors.
Machine Learning (ML)	Analyzes student behavior to provide adaptive learning pathways.	Personalizes learning; optimizes skill acquisition.
Intelligent Tutoring Systems	Offers real-time, AI-driven feedback and tailored content.	Identifies strengths and weaknesses; guides learners toward mastery.
Internet of Things (IoT)	Connects devices for real-time data tracking during training (e.g., engine diagnostics).	Bridges theoretical knowledge with practical application.
Gamification	Integrates game elements into learning to motivate and engage students.	Increases participation and reduces learning anxiety.
Big Data Analytics	Analyzes educational data to refine curriculum and monitor performance.	Enables data-driven decision-making in education.
3D Printing	Provides hands-on design and production experience in mechanical and industrial training.	Fosters creativity and practical skills development.

Moreover, Machine Learning algorithms are invaluable in vocational contexts, allowing students to refine their skills through the analysis of behavioral patterns, which in turn augments their expertise. The integration of Internet of Things (IoT) devices into vocational training also plays a crucial role in connecting theoretical knowledge to practical applications. For example, during automotive repair training, IoT sensors can track engine performance, enabling students to diagnose problems and implement solutions in a controlled setting. Such practical, hands-on experiences are critical for equipping students with the competencies required to navigate the demands of modern workplaces.

Gamification techniques further enrich the learning process by utilizing game design elements to engage and motivate learners. The incorporation of interactive tools alongside gamified strategies substantially increases student participation and enthusiasm. Empirical studies have demonstrated that gamification significantly enhances active learning and motivation, particularly in online courses, leading to higher engagement levels and reduced anxiety among students. By embedding game-like scenarios into the curriculum, students can confront challenges, earn rewards, and collaborate with their peers, fostering a competitive yet supportive educational atmosphere.

Additionally, facilities such as Robotics Laboratories and Automation classes provide learners with comprehensive opportunities to build foundational knowledge and conduct advanced experiments throughout various stages of their education. Consequently, the incorporation of Robotics and Automation is poised to transform pedagogical methods, fundamentally altering how learning occurs. The impact of a data-driven learning environment extends beyond pedagogy to include teaching and assessment, providing a framework for ongoing monitoring and evaluation. The emergence of virtual learning environments has enabled the application of data analytics across educational contexts, characterized by continuous data collection and algorithmic assessments. This shift has influenced desired learning outcomes, content creation, and assessment strategies, leading to a redistribution of decision-making authority away from educators and diminishing the roles of parents and students in this process.

The adoption of 3D printing and additive manufacturing in vocational education is an increasingly significant area of interest, with potential applications across design, manufacturing, and materials processing (Keaveney & Dowling, 2018). This technology can enhance learning experiences, particularly in mechanical engineering, by offering a hands-on approach to design and production. However, its full potential remains to be fully explored, necessitating further research into its application within instructional media (Ramdhani & Mulyanti, 2020). Current applications of 3D printing in educational contexts are diverse, ranging from educating students about 3D printing processes to developing assistive technologies. Nonetheless, the utilization of 3D printing in vocational education is still in its infancy, underscoring the need for additional investigation to better understand its implications and potential (Ghosh & Ravichandran, 2024).

INTEGRATION OF AI INTO VET CURRICULA

The integration of AI into the curricula of VET necessitates a methodical redesign process that is both educationally rigorous and responsive to the evolving demands of the labor market. This process is inherently complex and requires the active involvement of VET teachers and trainers across various European countries, who play a crucial role in shaping the curriculum to encompass the professional work and learning tasks associated with specific occupations. A well-structured curriculum should not only reflect practical work skills acquired within corporate environments but also include deeper, reflexive knowledge that can be more effectively addressed in VET institutions or specialized courses.

To develop contemporary and relevant curricula, it is essential to identify work process changes as the primary driving force behind the creation of new vocational learning programs. These programs should encompass comprehensive work and learning tasks (WLT) that are informed by the latest industry advancements. The curriculum serves as a fundamental framework delineating the technical and organizational skills that need to be prioritized, as well as the sequence in which various learning tasks should be organized and developed. By distinguishing between different levels of tasks ranging from basic to advanced and expert skills VET curricula can ensure that learners acquire a progressive depth of knowledge (Attwell et al., 2020).

Several curriculum structures are available for consideration, with the "learning arena curriculum" emerging as a promising approach for incorporating AI into VET. This design supports a more student-centered learning process and fosters project-oriented learning experiences (Kwiatek et al., 2019). The incorporation of developments in AI into the curriculum can be achieved through the implementation of multidimensional project topics that emphasize the development of professional, organizational, and social skills. Furthermore, a focus on operational work processes, business tasks, and holistic training processes enables the creation of real-world problem-solving settings that enhance team building and promote effective communication (Attwell et al., 2020).

The design criteria for an AI-integrated curriculum should include a work practice-based approach, acknowledging the substantial impact of disruptive changes wrought by AI on the structure and content of various technical, social, and business-related occupations. As the labor market evolves, curriculum changes should address the displacement of low-skilled jobs while enhancing non-routine job tasks prevalent in fields such as industrial electronics and mechatronics. These curricula must encompass all learning environments companies, training centers, and vocational schools fostering an open content approach that remains receptive to new knowledge, including the latest AI tools and methodologies. Moreover, the curriculum should facilitate the integration of diverse knowledge domains, blending practical experiences with theoretical concepts derived from the application of AI technologies in real production settings. This framework provides educators with the flexibility to organize high-quality work and learning processes tailored to the varying needs of apprentices, trainees, and students. Such a cohesive and comprehensive approach ensures that VET curricula remain relevant and effective in preparing individuals for the demands of an AI-driven economy, ultimately enhancing both learner outcomes and industry readiness.

BENEFITS OF AI INCORPORATION INTO VOCATIONAL EDUCATION AND TRAINING

The emergence of AI and other advanced technologies is fundamentally reshaping VET, highlighting their potential to enhance learning experiences and prepare students for the evolving demands of the workforce. Increasingly, research is demonstrating the efficacy of various emerging technologies in improving both educational outcomes and student engagement. For instance, studies have shown that the use of VR for training in welding significantly enhances student performance and confidence (Price et al., 2019), while AR applications for plumbing training lead to fewer errors and higher completion rates (Ghosh & Ravichandran, 2024a). As these technologies proliferate, they are not only transforming educational landscapes but also addressing the pressing needs of businesses and industries, underscoring the necessity for contemporary VET curricula to integrate such innovations.

Central to this integration is the role of AI and ML in personalizing learning experiences. AI's ability to analyze student behavior allows for adaptive learning pathways that cater to individual needs, thereby optimizing skill acquisition and knowledge retention. With real-time feedback mechanisms, AI-driven tutors can guide learners effectively, highlighting their strengths and areas for improvement. Moreover, the application of ML algorithms enables students to refine their skills through pattern recognition in vocational tasks (Nafea, 2018), fostering an environment of continuous improvement. As educational institutions embrace these technologies, they are also encouraged to consider the implications of IoT devices, which facilitate hands-on training and real-world applications, as exemplified in automotive repair programs where IoT sensors enhance diagnostic skills (Ghosh & Ravichandran, 2024a).

Further advancements such as gamification and the incorporation of robotics are revolutionizing pedagogical methods in VET. Gamification engages students through interactive elements, thereby promoting active learning and reducing anxiety associated with complex tasks. Concurrently, robotics and automation are becoming integral to modern vocational training, aligning with industry demands and transforming traditional learning environments into collaborative and adaptive spaces (Kwiatek et al., 2019). As education increasingly pivots towards a data-driven model, the use of big data and analytics allows for continuous assessment and dynamic learning environments, while technologies like blockchain promise to enhance data security and certificate management. Ultimately, the integration of these emerging technologies into VET curricula is not merely an enhancement but a necessity for cultivating proficient learners ready to thrive in an increasingly automated and competitive workforce.

CHALLENGES IN INCORPORATING AI TECHNOLOGIES INTO VET

One of the biggest challenges of incorporating AI technologies into VET system is their high cost and the financial support that is needed to guarantee the equipment and software. Moreover, another advantage is the fact that this incorporation acquires expertise not only to be used but to be maintained as well. Said that, trainings are a must for different beneficiaries' groups, each for a specific purpose. If there would be ask to provide any solution about these issues, then more accessibility would be suggested, offering more trainings to ensure that they would harness the full potential of AI tools and also promoting these tools in a larger group, making them part of the education process not only in class but also at home or work place (Ghosh & Ravichandran, 2024b). Table 2 presents a detailed list of challenges and mitigation strategies for AI integration in VET.

Table 2. Challenges and Mitigation Strategies for AI Integration in VET

Challenge	Description	Mitigation Strategy
High Cost	Expense of acquiring AI tools and maintaining infrastructure.	Secure funding; encourage public-private partnerships; explore cost-effective AI solutions.
Data Privacy	Risk of unauthorized access to sensitive student information.	Implement encryption, multi-factor authentication, and stringent access controls; establish privacy laws.
Algorithmic Bias	AI outputs influenced by biased training data, leading to inequitable outcomes.	Use diverse datasets; deploy bias detection mechanisms; involve stakeholders in AI model training.
Digital Divide	Limited access to AI technologies for disadvantaged students.	Invest in infrastructure; provide affordable access to devices and internet; offer inclusive training.

continued on following page

Table 2. Continued

Challenge	Description	Mitigation Strategy
Overreliance on AI	Dependence on AI tools potentially undermining critical thinking and problem-solving skills.	Balance AI use with human interaction; design assessments to encourage independent thought.
Technological Dependency	Risk of diminished educational autonomy and innovation due to reliance on pre-designed AI systems.	Promote teacher training on AI use; integrate AI as an aid, not a replacement for teaching methodologies.

However, the implementation of AI, particularly tools like ChatGPT, into VET promises substantial benefits but is fraught with significant challenges that necessitate careful consideration. One of the foremost concerns is data privacy. The integration of AI requires substantial data collection and analysis, raising serious questions about user privacy and the protection of sensitive student information. To mitigate these risks, vocational institutions must prioritize robust data protection strategies, which include collaborating with AI operators to de-identify student work and ensure anonymity in data collection. Importantly, measures such as employing advanced encryption technologies and establishing strict access controls must be implemented to secure user information. For example, assigning distinct permissions to different user categories students and teachers can reduce the risk of unauthorized data access. Furthermore, the introduction of multi-factor authentication and automated monitoring tools for detecting abnormal access patterns can reinforce these security architectures. However, technical solutions alone are insufficient; there must be concomitant development of sound laws and regulations that clarify the requirements for user data protection and the operation of AI systems. Establishing a systematic privacy protection framework, which balances technical safeguards with regulatory oversight, is imperative for cultivating a secure environment in which AI can positively contribute to vocational education (Jiang et al., 2024).

In addition to data privacy, algorithmic bias presents another significant challenge to the ethical deployment of AI technologies in vocational education. The outputs generated by AI systems, including those produced by ChatGPT, can inadvertently reflect and perpetuate biases present in the training data. Concerns arise particularly when the training data encompasses demographic biases related to geography, gender, and socio-economic factors, leading to discriminatory outcomes in educational settings. To address these disparities, vocational education institutions must insist on the collection of diverse and representative training datasets while also encouraging the use of content filtering tools provided by AI operators to ensure the quality of training data. Furthermore, the development and implementation of bias detection mechanisms, such as sensitive word detection and comprehensive testing of algorithmic outputs, can help uncover and address biases before they affect users. Collaborative efforts involving educational institutions, AI developers, and industry stakeholders are vital in creating and refining these detection tools, thus fostering a more equitable educational approach. This multifaceted approach is essential not only to mitigate bias but also to reinforce trust in the AI systems deployed in vocational training environments (Jiang et al., 2024).

Finally, the challenge of technological dependency must be acknowledged as AI tools such as ChatGPT become integral components of the vocational training landscape. While these technologies offer enhanced learning opportunities, they also have the potential to undermine students' independent thinking and compromise academic integrity by making it easy to engage in plagiarism. Purposeful pedagogical strategies must therefore be developed to balance the human-machine relationship effectively and nurture critical thinking skills among students. Educators should frame ChatGPT as an instructional aid rather than a replacement for traditional teaching methods, emphasizing the tool's limitations while encouraging students to critically evaluate its outputs. Implementing assessments that encourage independent problem-solving, such as open-ended questions and manual evaluations of student work, can reinforce the necessity for Originality in student assignments. Additionally, vocational colleges should invest in research that addresses the balance between AI application and risk prevention, potentially by introducing ethics courses that focus specifically on the implications of AI use in education. Establishing a monitoring mechanism to oversee the use of ChatGPT and prevent misuse can further solidify this balanced approach. While the integration of ChatGPT into vocational education offers promising opportunities, it is imperative that institutions actively grapple with challenges related to data privacy, algorithmic bias, and technological dependency to create a responsible framework for AI-enhanced education. Through collaboration among stakeholders, a commitment to ethical standards, and thoughtful educational practices, vocational training can effectively leverage AI's potential while mitigating its associated risks (Jiang et al., 2024).

ETHICAL CONSIDERATIONS

The integration of AI into VET presents several ethical considerations that must be carefully addressed to ensure the equitable and effective implementation of these technologies. A primary concern is data privacy, as the application of AI in education necessitates the collection and analysis of sensitive student information. Safeguarding this data is paramount to protecting students' rights and fostering trust in educational technologies. Institutions must implement robust data protection measures to ensure that personal information is secured from unauthorized access and potential misuse, thereby upholding ethical standards in privacy management.

Another critical ethical issue pertains to algorithmic bias. AI systems, inherently reliant on training data, risk mirroring the biases present within those datasets. This can lead to skewed outcomes in recommendations, evaluations, and in the identification of at-risk students. If unchecked, such biases may perpetuate existing educational inequalities and hinder opportunities for marginalized groups. Thus, it is imperative that AI algorithms are continually assessed and refined to minimize bias, ensuring that decisions made on behalf of students are fair and representative (Ifraheem et al., 2024).

From a moral ontology perspective, it is imperative to explore the nature of moral judgments regarding data handling, questioning to what extent societal conventions can contextualize privacy violations in educational settings. The ethical implications of AI are further illuminated through moral semantics, where the necessity of fairness in assessments aligns with utilitarian principles that prioritize overall happiness. Thus, transparent and equitable evaluation methods become ethically desirable, reinforcing the importance of ensuring that AI systems do not perpetuate existing inequalities. In terms of moral epistemology, justifying moral knowledge becomes crucial, particularly in elucidating the importance of justice and fairness as fundamental ethical principles tied to the utilization of AI tools in education. Deontological ethics emphasizes the inherent rights and duties of all stakeholders, including the inviolable right to privacy and the ethical obligation to prevent the misuse of sensitive student data. This creates a framework wherein protecting student information is not merely a technical requirement, but a moral imperative rooted in respect for individual autonomy. On the other hand, consequentialist perspectives highlight the necessity of evaluating the outcomes of integrating AI technologies, necessitating efforts toward maximizing benefits while minimizing harm in educational environments. Furthermore, as the reliance on AI for academic support grows, the risk of technological dependency becomes apparent, risking the erosion of students' critical thinking skills and academic integrity. To address these ethical challenges, it is essential for educational institutions to engage in ethics training for stakeholders and foster a culture where responsible AI use is prioritized. By applying a holistic approach that encompasses metaethical considerations, normative ethics, and virtue ethics, institutions can cultivate both individual and collective capacity for ethical discernment in the deployment of AI technologies. This comprehensive ethical stewardship is vital for ensuring that AI serves as an equitable and empowering force in vocational education and training, creating a balanced and just educational landscape (Lim et al., 2023).

Lastly, the "Digital Divide" remains a significant ethical challenge in the context of AI integration in VET. This term refers to the disparity between individuals who have access to modern information and communication technologies and those who do not. If AI implementation in education does not prioritize equitable access and support, it may exacerbate this divide, leaving disadvantaged students further behind. Educational institutions must therefore adopt inclusive strategies that ensure all learners, regardless of socioeconomic status, have equal opportunities to benefit from AI advancements. By addressing these ethical considerations data privacy, algorithmic bias, and the digital divide stakeholders can create a more just and inclusive framework for the integration of AI in vocational education and training (Ifraheem et al., 2024).

CONCLUSION

In conclusion, the integration of AI into VET represents a pivotal advancement, offering myriad benefits while simultaneously presenting critical ethical challenges. Central to this discourse are issues of data privacy, algorithmic bias, and technological dependency, which must be meticulously addressed to ensure a fair and effective implementation of AI tools in educational settings. Protecting sensitive student information is paramount, necessitating robust data security measures and stringent regulatory frameworks that uphold ethical standards. Moreover, the risk of algorithmic bias, which can perpetuate educational inequalities, calls for diligent oversight in the development of AI systems, fostering inclusivity through diverse training datasets and bias detection mechanisms. Equally important is recognizing the potential for technological dependency to undermine essential skills like critical thinking and independent problem-solving; thus, a balanced approach that integrates human interaction and fosters ethical awareness in learners is vital. As educational institutions navigate these complexities, the effective incorporation of AI technologies requires ongoing training for educators and students, enabling them to capitalize on AI's transformative potential while safeguarding ethical integrity. Ultimately, a strategic alignment between AI innovations and the pedagogical goals of VET can cultivate a more equitable and dynamic educational landscape, preparing students for the demands of a rapidly evolving workforce.

REFERENCES

Attwell, G., Deitmer, L., Tūtlys, V., Roppertz, S., & Perini, M. (2020). Digitalisation, artificial intelligence and vocational occupations and skills: What are the needs for training teachers and trainers? DOI: 10.5281/ZENODO.4005713

Ford, S., & Minshall, T. (2019). Where and how 3D printing is used in teaching and education. DOI: 10.17863/CAM.35360

Ghosh, L., & Ravichandran, R. (2024). Emerging technologies in vocational education and training. *Journal of Digital Learning and Education*, 4(1), 41–49. DOI: 10.52562/jdle.v4i1.975

Ifraheem, S., Rasheed, M., & Siddiqui, A. (2024). Transforming education through artificial intelligence: Personalization, engagement and predictive analytics. *Journal of Asian Development Studies*, 13(2), 250–266. DOI: 10.62345/jads.2024.13.2.22

Jiang, R., Chen, Y., Peng, Y., Xie, S., & Qu, D. (2024). Opportunities and challenges of AI in vocational education. *International Journal of Learning and Teaching*, 10(5), 590–596. DOI: 10.18178/ijlt.10.5.590-596

Keaveney, S. G., & Dowling, D. P. (2018). Application of additive manufacturing in design & manufacturing engineering education. In 2018 2nd International Symposium on Small-Scale Intelligent Manufacturing Systems (SIMS) (pp. 1–6). DOI: 10.1109/SIMS.2018.8355289

Kwiatek, G., Saarno, T., Ader, T., Bluemle, F., Bohnhoff, M., Chendorain, M., Dresen, G., Heikkinen, P., Kukkonen, I., Leary, P., Leonhardt, M., Malin, P., Martínez-Garzón, P., Passmore, K., Passmore, P., Valenzuela, S., & Wollin, C. (2019). Controlling fluid-induced seismicity during a 6.1-km-deep geothermal stimulation in Finland. *Science Advances*, 5(5), eaav7224. Advance online publication. DOI: 10.1126/sciadv.aav7224 PMID: 31049397

Lim, T., Gottipati, S., & Cheong, M. L. F. (2023). Ethical considerations for artificial intelligence in educational assessments. In Keengwe, J. (Ed.), (pp. 32–79). Advances in educational technologies and instructional design. IGI Global., DOI: 10.4018/979-8-3693-0205-7.ch003

Mohammad Aniq Bin Amdan, N., Janius, N., Jasman, M. N. B., & Kasdiah, M. A. H. B. (2024). Advancement of AI tools in learning for technical vocational education and training (TVET) in Malaysia: Empowering students and tutors. *International Journal of Science and Research Archive*, 12(1), 2061–2068. DOI: 10.30574/ijsra.2024.12.1.0971

Nafea, I. T. (2018). Machine learning in educational technology. In Farhadi, H. (Ed.), *Machine learning: Advanced techniques and emerging applications*. InTech., DOI: 10.5772/intechopen.72906

Ramdhani, F. F., & Mulyanti, B. (2020). Additive manufacturing in education. *IOP Conference Series. Materials Science and Engineering*, 830(4), 042093. DOI: 10.1088/1757-899X/830/4/042093

ADDITIONAL READING

Bakar, M. H. A., Ghafar, N. H. M., & Abdullah, F. (2024). Exploring the Integration of Artificial Intelligence in Technical and Vocational Education and Training (TVET): Applications, Benefits, Challenges, and Future Prospects. *Borneo Engineering & Advanced Multidisciplinary International Journal*, 3(Special Issue (ICo-ASCNITech 2024)), 57–63.

Kaddouri, M., Mhamdi, K., Chniete, I., Marhraoui, M., Khaldi, M., & Jmad, S. (2025). Adopting AI in Education: Technical Challenges and Ethical Constraints. In *Fostering Inclusive Education With AI and Emerging Technologies* (pp. 25-72). IGI Global.

Rosyadi, M. I., Kustiawan, I., Tetehfio, E. O., & Joshua, Q. (2023). The Role of AI In Vocational Education: A Systematic Literature Review. *Journal of Vocational Education Studies*, 6(2), 244–263. DOI: 10.12928/joves.v6i2.9032

Teo, H. J. (2024). Applications of the ChatGPT in Work-Based Learning Programs: Opportunities, Challenges, and Ethical Considerations. *ChatGPT and Global Higher Education: Using Artificial Intelligence in Teaching and Learning*, 284.

Westman, S., Kauttonen, J., Klemetti, A., Korhonen, N., Manninen, M., Mononen, A., Niittymäki, S., & Paananen, H. (2021). Artificial Intelligence for Career Guidance—Current Requirements and Prospects for the Future. *IAFOR Journal of Education*, 9(4), 43–62. DOI: 10.22492/ije.9.4.03

KEY TERMS AND DEFINITIONS

Adaptive Learning Systems: Educational technologies that personalize learning experiences by analyzing individual student behaviors and tailoring content to their specific needs.

Algorithmic Bias: The unintentional favoritism or prejudice in AI system outputs caused by imbalanced or non-representative training datasets.

Big Data Analytics: The process of examining large volumes of educational data to derive insights that inform curriculum development and improve student outcomes.

Digital Divide: The gap between individuals or groups in terms of access to modern information and communication technologies, such as AI tools in education.

Gamification: The integration of game-like elements, such as rewards and challenges, into educational activities to enhance student engagement and motivation.

Internet of Things (IoT): A network of interconnected devices used in vocational training to enable real-time data collection and practical applications, such as engine diagnostics in automotive courses.

Machine Learning (ML): A subset of AI that allows systems to learn and improve from data without explicit programming, used in VET to provide adaptive learning and skill refinement.

Personalized Learning: An approach in education where AI technologies tailor content delivery and pacing to meet the unique requirements of individual learners.

Virtual Reality (VR): Immersive simulations that recreate real-world environments, enabling safe and effective hands-on training in vocational education.

Vocational Education and Training (VET): A system of education focused on equipping learners with practical and technical skills for specific occupations, enhanced by AI tools and technologies.

Chapter 2
AI Literacy:
Foundations, Importance, and Broader Implications

Andi Asrifan
https://orcid.org/0000-0002-9934-6129
Universitas Negeri Makassar, Indonesia

Uswah Mujahidah Rasuna Said
Universitas Pendidikan Indonesia, Indonesia

Juvrianto Chrissunday Jakob
https://orcid.org/0000-0002-5267-3448
Politeknik Negeri Ambon, Indonesia

Risman Wanci
https://orcid.org/0000-0002-4270-9849
Universitas Famika, Indonesia

ABSTRACT

This chapter explores the pivotal role of AI literacy in equipping individuals and communities to navigate an AI-driven world with confidence, ethical awareness, and informed decision-making. AI literacy encompasses a comprehensive understanding of AI principles, including machine learning, data management, and algorithmic ethics, empowering users to engage judiciously with AI technologies across sectors such as healthcare, finance, and education. By fostering critical thinking and reducing biases, AI literacy safeguards privacy, ensures ethical technology use, and promotes equitable access to AI-driven opportunities. The democratization of AI literacy is highlighted as a catalyst for empowering marginalized communities and enabling equal participation in AI-related dialogues and initiatives. As AI continues to reshape employment landscapes and educational paradigms, the chapter

DOI: 10.4018/979-8-3693-8252-3.ch002

underscores the importance of AI literacy in preparing a workforce ready to adapt to evolving technological demands.

INTRODUCTION

Defining AI Literacy

AI literacy is the knowledge and skills needed to use AI technologies (Cassidy et al., 2023) (Srinivasan & Murthy, 2021) (Wang & Lester, 2023). This knowledge goes beyond understanding AI to include the practical skills needed to navigate and critically engage with AI tools in all aspects of life. AI literacy involves knowing how AI systems work, the data they utilize, the judgments they make, and their potential social impact. AI literacy requires understanding terms like "machine learning," "neural networks," and "natural language processing" to understand AI systems' often complex inner workings. Understanding these words helps people make informed judgments about AI-driven personal assistants, recommendation algorithms, and AI's ethical implications in daily life. AI literacy requires technical expertise and critical reasoning. Technical expertise involves comprehending AI algorithms' mechanics and their dependence on massive data sets that drive these systems (Emmert-Streib et al., 2020). However, critical thinking requires analyzing AI outputs, identifying biases, and evaluating AI insights for relevance and trustworthiness. As AI becomes more prevalent in healthcare, education, and finance, understanding its potential and limitations can help users use it wisely. Furthermore, AI literacy stresses ethical considerations in AI use. AI systems influence hiring, lending, and law enforcement decisions; therefore, individuals and communities must be able to question and evaluate their fairness, accountability, and transparency (Bengio et al., 2024). This understanding is crucial to creating a society where people are active participants who can confidently and responsibly negotiate AI's ramifications.

The Growing Presence of AI in Daily Life

AI has become an invisible but powerful force in personal, professional, and societal life (- & Qasim, 2023) (Borenstein & Howard, 2020). AI influences how people use technology and make daily decisions, from voice-activated assistants like Siri and Alexa to personalized recommendation algorithms on Netflix, Amazon, and YouTube. AI is transforming modern life with intuitive, efficient, and tailored interactions. Voice assistants use natural language processing to understand and respond to spoken requests (Ahanin et al., 2022) (Hoy, 2018). These technologies let users make reminders, play music, and manage smart home gadgets using voice commands. On entertainment and e-commerce platforms, AI-driven recommendation algorithms analyze user behavior to provide personalized content and items. These interactions demonstrate AI's capacity to learn and adapt to human behavior, creating an interesting and relevant experience. AI affects life-changing decisions beyond entertainment and ease. AI helps banks and financial institutions assess credit ratings, detect fraud, and provide targeted financial advice (Choithani et al., 2022). AI helps diagnose diseases, prescribe treatments, and manage patient data, boosting healthcare speed and accuracy. Automation in employment and loan approvals is also growing, demonstrating AI's growing importance in complicated, high-stakes domains. AI presents important privacy, ethics, and responsibility problems daily. AI systems improve ease and efficiency but also require a lot of personal data. When misused, this data creates privacy problems and emphasizes the need for AI literacy, where people understand how their data is used and safeguarded. Automatic decision-making can be unethical due to biased algorithms or lack of transparency (Floridi & Taddeo, 2016). Therefore, AI literacy requires both using AI technology and critically assessing its effects.

Why AI Literacy Matters

AI literacy is vital for individuals, businesses, and society today. Understanding how to use and critically evaluate AI technology is becoming increasingly important as they become part of daily life (Ng et al., 2021). AI literacy equips people to navigate, assess, and engage with AI systems, promoting informed decision-making and ethical concerns across domains. AI literacy makes people more proactive with AI-driven technologies. Understanding core AI ideas and how AI systems work helps people control their use of these tools. Users may comprehend why social media and streaming sites recommend specific content by understanding how recommendation algorithms work. AI literacy lets people make purposeful choices and avoid the risks of blindly following automated advice, boosting personal agency in a digital world (Thomas & Fowler, 2020). AI literacy is essential for corporate executives and staff. Workers with a basic understanding of AI can better use these technologies to optimize operations, improve customer experiences, and make strategic decisions as sectors increasingly use them. AI literacy helps corporate executives evaluate when and how to embrace AI technologies, enabling more strategic decision-making that weighs benefits and risks. AI experts may also analyze the ethical implications of these technologies, ensuring that their organizations employ AI ethically and in accordance with organizational values and social expectations (Wang, 2020). Social ramifications of AI literacy are also significant (Ng et al., 2021) (Stahl, 2021). As AI systems become increasingly prevalent in healthcare, banking, and criminal justice, privacy, fairness, and accountability concerns grow. An AI-literate public can advocate for openness, ethics, and public interest policies in these talks.

THE FUNDAMENTALS OF AI

Essential Terminology for Understanding AI

A variety of core concepts and words characterize how artificial intelligence (AI) systems work and interact with data and humans (Kühl et al., 2022) (Elder et al., 2020). Understanding machine learning, neural networks, natural language processing, and automation is essential to meaningfully using AI technology and applications. Machine Learning (ML), which allows computers to learn from data rather than programming, is a key component of AI (Liu, 2022) (Abduljabbar et al., 2019). Systems use ML to predict or decide by analyzing data patterns. As data accumulates, streaming platform recommendation algorithms learn user preferences from viewing history and refine recommendations. Machine learning models range from simple linear regressions to deep learning, which processes massive quantities of data to attain high accuracy.

Many advanced AI applications, especially deep learning, use neural networks. Neural networks have layers of interconnected nodes (or "neurons") inspired by the brain. These networks understand complicated data patterns to help AI do complex tasks like picture and speech recognition with high accuracy. Image categorization, language translation, and autonomous cars, which need precise pattern recognition, have advanced thanks to neural networks. (Luo et al., 2022) (Fikri et al., 2014) Deep neural networks, with numerous layers between input and output, power complex applications like facial recognition systems.

NLP lets AI systems understand, interpret, and generate human language. Siri, Alexa, chatbots, and automated translation services use NLP. This skill lets machines converse like people, making AI useful in everyday situations. Complex NLP tasks such as sentiment analysis, text production, and language translation are crucial for applications requiring human intent and context (Blasí et al., 2022; Chowdhury & Nath, 2021).

Another fundamental idea is automation, where AI systems do activities without human interaction. Automation can range from automated responses to simple questions to completely autonomous vehicles. Automation boosts corporate productivity by eliminating repetitive operations, while robots undertake fast, precise, or dangerous production tasks (Sheridan & Parasuraman, 2005). Automation helps healthcare organizations manage patient data, expedite administrative operations, and analyze medical images. Understanding AI involves knowledge of several important concepts that underpin its functionality and applications. AI systems use machine learning, neural networks, and natural language processing to make choices and communicate with humans. A brief definition and practical example accompany each term to assist readers in comprehending. This ensures that AI novices can understand its concepts and practical applications.

1. Machine Learning: Allows computers to learn and make judgments from data without programming. Streaming providers like Netflix propose shows based on historical watching behavior using machine learning."
2. Neural Networks: Brain-inspired computational models that recognize complicated patterns in vast data sets. Example: "Facial recognition software uses neural networks to accurately recognize faces in crowds."
3. AI branch Natural Language Processing (NLP) helps machines understand, interpret, and synthesize human language. Example: "Siri and Alexa employ NLP to understand voice requests to set reminders, play music, and get weather updates."
4. Automation: Technology performing activities without human interaction. Automation in customer support, like chatbots, lets organizations answer frequently asked queries instantly."
5. Narrow AI: AI systems that execute specific tasks without generalizing. Example: "Email spam filters are narrow AI that only detects and filters spam communications."
6. Theoretical general AI can execute any intellectual task a human can, adaptive across areas. Example: "Unlike present AI systems, a generic AI would adapt similarly to human intellect to go from recognizing images to processing words."
7. Data privacy: Keeping user data secure, especially when AI systems process personal data. Example: "AI-powered recommendation systems protect users' preferences and histories."
8. AI ethics: Fairness, accountability, and transparency in development and deployment. Example: "Facial recognition technologies can track people in public settings without consent, raising privacy concerns."

Types of AI: Narrow AI vs. General AI

There are two main types of AI: narrow and general. These AI system types represent diverse capabilities and purposes. Understanding the difference between these categories is crucial to understanding AI's current limitations and future promise (Emmert-Streib et al., 2020; Gasser & Almeida, 2017). Narrow AI, often called "weak AI," teach computers to execute certain tasks (Butz, 2021). These AI systems excel in specific applications but cannot apply their knowledge outside their intended region. A narrow AI could improve recommendation systems, language translation, and even chess and Go. Each activity demands particular data and techniques for high performance in a confined scope. Siri, Alexa, spam filters, facial recognition, and mobile predictive text algorithms are examples of narrow AI. Narrow AI excels at processing huge datasets rapidly and accurately, making it efficient and precise in specific tasks (Guzman, 2018) (Bini, 2018). However, these systems have defined bounds and require extensive reprogramming and retraining to transfer abilities or adapt to new tasks. Narrow AI has great capabilities, but it lacks human intelligence's diversity and cognitive depth. Since no AI has human-like flexibility or intellect, all AI is narrow AI.

General AI (or "strong AI") is a more ambitious and speculative idea of artificial intelligence. General AI, like the human mind, can absorb, learn, and apply knowledge across several tasks (Triguero et al., 2023). General AI might independently adapt to new difficulties, reason through complicated, unstructured problems, and draw ideas from diverse experiences, unlike Narrow AI. Without domain or task-specific training, an AI may undertake scientific research and artistic labor. General AI development presents huge scientific and ethical challenges. Creating an AI that could outperform humans will involve advances in machine learning, cognitive science, and neurobiology (Zador et al., 2023) (Buttazzo, 2023). If realized, General AI could transform healthcare, education, and other industries. But machines with human-like thinking and reasoning create ethical questions regarding control, safety, and the impact on jobs and society.

AI Technologies and Applications

AI is quickly expanding across numerous disciplines, altering industries and processes. AI applications are boosting efficiency, decision-making, and possibilities in healthcare, finance, education, and transportation by analyzing large datasets and conducting difficult computations (Haldorai et al., 2020). AI is transforming healthcare diagnosis, treatment, and care (Varnosfaderani & Forouzanfar, 2024). The accuracy with which AI systems detect anomalies in X-rays, MRIs, and CT scans is one of the most significant applications of AI in healthcare. Pattern recognition in medical photos allows machine learning models to detect cancer and cardiovascular disease early. Healthcare professionals can also predict patient needs, manage resources, and create individualized treatment regimens with AI-driven predictive analytics. AI is finding potential chemicals and predicting their disease effects, speeding up drug development and decreasing research and clinical trial costs.

Finance uses AI to improve efficiency, decrease risk, and personalize services (Paul et al., 2020). AI-driven algorithms analyze massive amounts of transaction data in real time to find unexpected patterns and flag fraud. AI helps asset managers make informed decisions by evaluating market trends and developing data-driven predictions. Chatbots provide quick, 24/7 support for typical financial queries and transactions. ROBO-advisors employ AI to provide individualized investment advice, helping clients design portfolios that match their financial goals and risk tolerance. AI is improving learning and making education more accessible (Phoon & Koh, 2017). Adaptive learning systems use machine learning to personalize learning by adapting content to each student's learning style, pace, and progress. Teachers can focus more on interactive and engaging teaching with AI-driven solutions that automate administrative activities like grading and provide student performance data. AI-based language translation and speech recognition systems are also removing language barriers in education, making learning resources available worldwide.

AI advances autonomous driving and traffic management (Ioni ă, 2017) (Zhang et al., 2024). AI algorithms evaluate camera, radar, and LIDAR data to let self-driving cars drive safely and effectively. AI helps traffic management systems predict congestion, optimize traffic flow, and reduce fuel use, improving urban planning and environmental sustainability. AI improves logistics and supply chain management by optimizing routes, delivery times, and inventory management, making supply networks more efficient and responsive.

THE IMPORTANCE OF AI LITERACY IN EDUCATION

AI in the Classroom: Preparing Students for the Future

To educate students for a tech-driven environment, schools must incorporate AI literacy into their curricula (Kim et al., 2021) (Mallik & Gangopadhyay, 2023). Students learn how to navigate and contribute to an AI-driven future by studying AI. Educational institutions are preparing students for automaton, data science, and digital innovation-driven jobs by teaching AI technology and their social consequences. AI literacy education covers machine learning, data analysis, and AI ethics. Introductions to AI and its use in recommendation systems and virtual assistants can help students in primary and secondary schools (Eguchi et al., 2021) (Yim & Su, 2024). Students become curious about AI's mechanisms by building simple machine learning models and seeing how algorithms produce data-based predictions. Many schools include coding tasks in their curricula to teach pupils logical thinking and programming for AI systems.

High schools and colleges teach sophisticated AI ideas including neural networks, natural language processing, and computer vision. Students gain a deeper knowledge of AI across areas by studying these skills. STEM curricula that include AI literacy equip students for AI-related employment in healthcare, finance, robotics, and environmental science (Dai et al., 2020) (Chaudhry & Kazim, 2021). This level of AI education emphasizes critical thinking and problem-solving, allowing students to apply AI solutions to real-world problems like supply chain optimization and climate prediction. AI literacy education covers ethics and society as well as technology. Teaching students about AI's biases, privacy problems, and employment effects is essential for ethical technology use. Digital ethics and AI courses teach students how algorithms affect hiring, lending, and police decisions (Elliott et al., 2021). This insight equips students to advocate for fair, transparent, and accountable AI systems in the workplace. AI literacy education also promotes flexibility because technology advances quickly, requiring continual learning (Grieve et al., 2021) (Dai et al., 2020). Students may stay competitive in a changing work environment by learning AI tools and updating their abilities. Schools are supporting project-based learning, where students utilize AI to solve community problems, preparing them to participate to the digital economy.

Educator Readiness and Professional Development

As artificial intelligence (AI) becomes more important in education, educating teachers to teach AI ideas is crucial. Teachers shape students' AI comprehension, yet many lack the resources, training, and confidence to incorporate AI literacy into their lectures (Wang & Lester, 2023) (Aliabadi et al., 2023). Teachers need targeted professional development, educational tools, and institutional support to teach AI ideas. AI literacy training is vital for educators because AI subjects are new and complex. AI and computer science are unfamiliar to many teachers, especially non-STEM ones. Teachers can feel more competent communicating AI concepts like machine learning, data analysis, and ethics to students after receiving training in these areas (Ng et al., 2023) (Otero et al., 2023). Professional development should incorporate hands-on exercises and interactive workshops so teachers can try AI applications. This method helps educators understand AI's practical applications, making learning more compelling for pupils.

Professional development programs may include creating rudimentary machine learning models, studying recommendation systems, or discussing AI's ethical implications. These activities help educators explain difficult AI subjects in simple terms. Teachers can integrate AI into their curriculum by applying data analysis in math or debating AI ethics in social studies (Lee & Perret, 2022) (Wang & Lester, 2023). Training on AI-powered classroom management, student evaluation, and tailored learning can improve teaching efficiency and student engagement. Resource access is another key to AI literacy education for instructors. Teachers can teach AI using comprehensive curriculum guides, lesson plans, and online courses. Interactive simulations, coding exercises, and video tutorials on AI-focused educational platforms give teachers flexible, accessible resources for varied teaching styles and student needs. Collaboration with tech businesses, colleges, and AI experts can expand these resources with current information and real-world examples to improve classroom learning (Kizilcec, 2023).

Institutional assistance, including professional development and school policy integration, is also needed. Schools must commit time and money to AI training and prioritize AI literacy in the curriculum (Zhang & Aslan, 2021). School leadership supports AI instruction and allows teachers to invest time and resources in professional development. AI-focused educator networks and peer-mentoring organizations create a community of support where teachers may share experiences, resources, and thoughts on teaching AI.

Encouraging Critical Thinking and Ethical Reflection

Students must learn critical thinking and ethical reflection to ethically use AI technologies in an AI-driven environment (Nguyen et al., 2022) (Wang & Lester, 2023). AI literacy goes beyond technical abilities, teaching students to assess AI's social impact, ethical issues, and repercussions. By developing these reflective skills, educational programs can produce educated, ethical, and technologically literate citizens. AI literacy requires critical thinking to evaluate AI systems' capabilities, limits, and biases (Mohammadkarimi, 2023). Critical thinking exercises teach students to ask AI technology questions like: How does this system work? It uses what data? Who made it and why? Students can analyze AI's impact on social media recommendations and hiring algorithms by comprehending these characteristics. These abilities help students see how algorithms might perpetuate biases or make bad conclusions based on input data or algorithm design. Critical thinking in AI literacy lets students distinguish between real AI uses and spurious ones. Exaggerated promises about AI's capabilities can lead to mistaken anxieties or excessive expectations as AI advances rapidly. By strengthening analytical skills, students can better assess AI news, ads, and public discussions to determine its strengths and limitations (Kamalov et al., 2023).

Ethical consideration is crucial as AI systems influence human rights, privacy, fairness, and transparency decisions. Ethics in AI literacy education helps students consider the social impacts of AI technology and the obligations of individuals who build, deploy, and utilize them (Borenstein & Howard, 2020). Can students ask: Is this AI system fair to all? Does it respect privacy? How might it affect lives? Case studies, conversations, and debates can help students grasp AI's ethical issues, such as facial recognition technology in policing or predictive analytics in healthcare, and their pros and cons. AI education with an ethical framework enables students to evaluate their future responsibilities in AI development and policymaking (Wang,

2020) (Crigger et al., 2022). Students can understand why openness, accountability, and informed consent are essential to establishing responsible AI systems. Ethical AI literacy programs also teach students the importance of varied viewpoints in AI development, as systems constructed without inclusion can be biased or inequitable. Ethical reflection and critical thinking in AI literacy raise knowledge of AI's risks and benefits and promote responsible technology use. This balanced approach encourages students to analyze AI's impact thoughtfully and advocate for ethical AI practices in diverse domains. By establishing these principles early on, education can educate future generations to manage AI-powered world issues and possibilities with integrity and understanding (Nguyen et al., 2022)

AI LITERACY AND WORKFORCE DEVELOPMENT

AI in the Future Job Market

Artificial intelligence (AI) is changing sectors and the skills needed to compete in the labor market (Braganza et al., 2020) (Faishal et al., 2023). AI-driven automation, data analytics, and decision-making tools are becoming essential in healthcare, banking, manufacturing, and retail. Individuals require technical and cognitive abilities to interact with AI systems effectively to stay relevant in an AI-enhanced labor market.

AI affects many businesses (Shankar et al., 2020). Diagnostics, individualized treatment plans, and robotic procedures leverage AI systems, boosting the need for medical personnel that can comprehend AI insights and work in tech-assisted situations. AI improves risk assessment, fraud detection, and customer service in banking, requiring data-driven decision-makers and AI technologies. Robotics and AI-based quality control are changing manufacturing, needing individuals who can operate, monitor, and maintain AI-powered gear. AI applications like recommendation algorithms and automated customer support transform retail and customer service roles into AI system management and output interpretation. Besides technology, you need adaptability, critical thinking, and ethics. In an AI-driven job market, challenging AI outputs, comprehending automated system limitations, and making human-centric decisions are crucial. Additionally, AI development and monitoring roles are in demand. Building, analyzing, and maintaining AI systems requires specialized skills from data scientists, AI ethicists, and machine learning engineers (Alekseeva et al., 2021). Companies are also realizing the need for ethical AI personnel to supervise data governance, privacy compliance, and fairness. Thus, AI experts and ethical people can prosper in this changing job market.

Reskilling and Upskilling for an AI-Powered World

Reskilling and upskilling are necessary to prepare the workforce for an AI-powered environment (Watson et al., 2021) (Braiki et al., 2020). Ensuring people have technical and non-technical AI literacy helps them succeed in their jobs, adapt to technological changes, and contribute meaningfully to their businesses. Reskilling teaches workers new AI-related skills, while upskilling improves existing abilities with AI-driven tools and methods. Technical skills are essential for AI literacy across industries. Programming, especially in Python, R, and SQL, is in high demand for data analysis and AI development (Alekseeva et al., 2021). Workers can work directly with AI applications or interact with technical teams by understanding, manipulating, and sometimes creating AI algorithms with programming knowledge. As data forms the foundation of AI systems, data literacy—the capacity to acquire, evaluate, and act on data insights—is increasingly valuable. Data processing, statistical analysis, and visualization experts can use AI to get insights from massive datasets, improving decision-making and efficiency.

Machine learning—a subset of AI that trains algorithms to recognize patterns and make predictions—is another technological field of reskilling and upskilling (Bohr & Memarzadeh, 2020; Shaffer et al., 2020). Foundational machine learning knowledge helps workers comprehend AI model creation and prediction principles, even if not all roles require it. Workers who engage with AI systems or interpret their outputs must understand biases, question forecasts, and verify that AI-driven outcomes meet organizational goals and ethical standards. AI awareness, critical reasoning, and ethics are also crucial (Riedl & Woolley, 2016). Understanding AI's strengths and weaknesses helps workers set reasonable expectations and find relevant use cases for AI technologies. Critical thinking helps employees challenge AI-generated insights and make human-centered decisions that account for AI's limits. This expertise is crucial in customer service, decision-making, and policy jobs, where AI outputs can have unforeseen implications. Workers must grasp AI's social impacts, including privacy, justice, and transparency, which require ethical awareness. Companies that stress ethics in their reskilling and upskilling programs create AI-literate, ethical AI users.

Companies can use numerous training methods to support reskilling and upskilling. On-the-job training, online courses, and workshops help employees build technical and non-technical abilities (Cerit et al., 2020). Employers can access specialized training resources to equip personnel with the newest AI knowledge through partnerships with educational institutions and AI-focused organizations. Mentorship programs, where experts help employees use AI technologies, create a friendly learning environment. Workforce development for an AI-driven environment includes government and corporate initiatives. Many governments are developing national reskilling initiatives to prepare people for the digital transition, while business collaborations offer sector-specific AI training (Gehlhaus et al., 2021). These projects help firms across industries adapt to AI technologies by standardizing curricula, certification programs, and upskilling funds.

AI Literacy for Business Leaders

Business leaders need AI literacy as AI transforms industries. Knowing AI helps CEOs make strategic decisions about integrating AI technology into their organizations (Ng et al., 2021). Beyond technical knowledge, AI literacy for leaders includes comprehending AI's potential, limitations, and ethical considerations, enabling them to handle AI's benefits and difficulties. AI-savvy business executives can innovate, boost efficiency, and stay competitive in an AI-driven market. Business executives need AI literacy to make educated AI integration decisions (Chernov et al., 2020) (Schlögl, 2019). Leaders who understand AI's capabilities and limitations can find use cases that fit their organization's goals, resources, and culture. In banking, healthcare, and manufacturing, AI can streamline processes, predict trends, and improve customer service. Without a basic understanding of AI, CEOs may miss promising applications or waste resources on unprofitable technologies. AI literacy helps leaders choose the best AI solutions for their firm, ensuring targeted and effective investments.

AI literacy helps business executives examine AI's impact on their workforce. AI affects employment responsibilities, procedures, and skills as it spreads. AI-savvy leaders can plan workforce training and upskilling to prepare personnel for new tasks. Minimizing disruption and developing a collaborative environment where humans and AI systems operate together requires foresight. Leaders who understand AI may prioritize creative, emotive, and complicated decision-making while strategically using AI for automation and data processing (Berretta et al., 2023) (Hughes et al., 2019). Business leaders must prioritize AI literacy because it promotes ethical and responsible AI use. Understanding AI's biases and ethical consequences helps leaders implement AI systems transparently and fairly. AI models based on biased data may exacerbate employment, lending, and customer service inequalities. AI-literate leaders may define ethical data usage norms, evaluate algorithmic fairness, and protect customer privacy (Crigger et al., 2022). They protect their company's reputation and promote ethical AI by promoting responsible AI use.

AI knowledge aids business executives in risk management and innovation (Díaz-Rodríguez et al., 2023). AI-literate leaders may anticipate data security problems, algorithmic bias, and system failures and take precautions. They can also lead innovation efforts that encourage cross-departmental collaboration to investigate new AI applications and enhance processes. An AI-literate leader may inspire team confidence and foster a forward-thinking culture that uses technology safely and creatively. Finally, AI literacy helps leaders communicate about AI with investors, consumers, and workers (Ng et al., 2021) (Srinivasan & Murthy, 2021). AI-savvy leaders can describe their organization's AI strategy to stakeholders, including its benefits, difficulties, and expected outcomes. Transparency fosters trust and alignment within and outside the company.

ETHICAL AND SOCIETAL IMPLICATIONS OF AI LITERACY

Understanding AI Bias and Fairness

Understanding AI bias and fairness is crucial to designing responsible, equitable systems as AI becomes more integrated into society (Yarger et al., 2019). Learning and decision-making AI systems are sensitive to their training data. Unfortunately, data, algorithm design, and human oversight can introduce biases into AI systems, causing unforeseen outcomes. AI literacy is essential for understanding and eliminating these biases and creating fair, transparent, and diverse systems. Data bias is one of the main ways AI systems are biased (Pizzi et al., 2020). AI models learn biases from past data. Training a hiring algorithm on gender or racial prejudices may perpetuate inequalities by favoring specific groups. AI may underrepresent certain patient demographics in healthcare, while predictive police algorithms may disproportionately target certain communities in criminal justice. AI literacy explains these biases and emphasizes the need for varied, representative, and thoroughly curated datasets to address them.

Algorithmic prejudice is another issue. Pattern-based mathematical models in algorithms can oversimplify complex situations. Model decisions like weighting characteristics can influence results (Johnson, 2020). Due to underrepresented data and model design, facial recognition algorithms have higher mistake rates for specific ethnic groups. AI literacy allows developers and consumers to identify algorithmic biases and ask important questions about algorithm design, testing, and validation to ensure fairness. Addressing AI bias requires human monitoring. AI literacy encourages developers and consumers to evaluate AI's performance and results (Crigger et al., 2022). After identifying biases, analyze their core causes in the data, algorithm, or system environment and fix them. A workforce and society that understands these concepts can create a culture that actively monitors and addresses AI bias and fairness. AI literacy emphasizes testing and validation in AI systems (Abràmoff et al., 2023). To discover biases before deploying AI models, rigorous testing on varied datasets and validation are necessary. Fairness metrics evaluate bias in a system to ensure demographic equality, and AI-literate people appreciate their value. As data patterns change, AI systems might develop and introduce new biases, requiring continual monitoring. This proactive bias control technique boosts AI system trust and ethics. AI bias has serious social consequences, making AI literacy essential. Biased AI systems in high-stakes areas like employment, financing, and criminal justice can worsen inequality and harm individuals and communities. A public that understands AI can hold institutions accountable and promote fair, transparent, and ethical AI. Education about AI bias allows people to participate in AI regulation discussions, supporting fairness and preventing discrimination (Bengio et al., 2024) (Gibbons, 2021).

Data Privacy and AI

Data privacy concerns are growing as AI becomes more commonplace (Yang et al., 2024). To discover patterns, anticipate, and provide personalized services, AI systems use massive volumes of personal data. This data-driven strategy makes AI powerful, but it raises problems about personal data collection, storage, and use. AI literacy helps people make data decisions and push for improved privacy protections by understanding these implications. AI systems use personal data from social media, internet transactions, location data, and voice recordings. Processing this data yields personalized recommendations, targeted adverts, and predictive insights. AI-powered streaming service recommendations leverage viewing history, while e-commerce sites track purchases to offer things. These apps improve user experience but collect and analyze sensitive data. AI literacy teaches people how to identify data types, comprehend its purpose, and decide if they're happy sharing their data.

Many AI systems handle data opaquely, which is concerning. Data privacy policies are sometimes lengthy, convoluted, and written in legal jargon, making data collection and use unclear to consumers (Peters & Visser, 2023). AI literacy empowers people to question and push for data processing and storage transparency. By understanding AI's data dependence, people can avoid having their personal data shared or sold without their knowledge, which can endanger privacy. Data privacy risks are highest with surveillance and tracking. AI technology like facial recognition and location-based applications raise concerns about intrusive surveillance. Without consent, AI-powered surveillance devices can track people's travels and interactions. This tracking violates privacy and can lead to discrimination and data exploitation. Public facial recognition technology can disproportionately affect vulnerable communities. AI literacy helps people notice these abuses, raising awareness and public discourse about the need for surveillance and privacy legislation.

Another important part of AI data privacy is data security. AI systems store a lot of personal data, which increases the danger of data breaches and cyberattacks (Díaz-Rodríguez et al., 2023) (Yang et al., 2024). AI system security breaches can expose sensitive data to hostile parties, resulting in identity theft, financial loss, and other ills. Understanding AI data privacy requires secure data storage, encrypted data transit, and protocols that limit personal data access. AI literacy allows people to ask about data security and if the services they use are secure. AI's effects on data privacy affect society. Personal data availability generates vulnerabilities that can threaten communities and national security. Thus, AI literacy raises awareness of data privacy's wider significance and the need to support personal and societal data rights regulations.

The Ethics of Automation: Job Displacement and Economic Impact

AI-powered automation is changing sectors and the global economy, prompting ethical issues regarding job displacement and economic consequences (Braganza et al., 2020) (Schlögl, 2019). As machines learn to do human jobs, manufacturing, retail, transportation, and finance could lose jobs. AI literacy helps individuals, communities, and policymakers comprehend and properly navigate these changes, balancing automation's benefits with its social and economic problems. One of the biggest automation challenges is job loss. AI can execute repetitive tasks faster than humans, so corporations are automating some jobs (Wright & Schultz, 2018). Warehouses with robots for sorting and packing have reduced human labor. Customer care chatbots answer regular questions without human workers. Automation threatens low—to mid-skilled jobs, leaving workers without alternatives. AI literacy helps people anticipate work market developments and find upskilling opportunities to be competitive as automation evolves.

Job displacement affects communities and sectors. If automation replaces a large section of the workforce, manufacturing-dependent regions may suffer economic downturns. This ripple effect can lower local expenditure, tax revenues, and social service demand. AI literacy raises an understanding of these macroeconomic ramifications, highlighting the need for proactive measures like government support and economic diversification to avoid job displacement. AI literacy helps people adapt and succeed in an automated economy (Camarda et al., 2021). Understanding AI and its applications helps workers recognize human strengths like creativity, sophisticated problem-solving, and interpersonal abilities that are hard to automate. AI literacy helps workers migrate into professions that support AI rather than compete with it by developing skills. For instance, healthcare automation has raised demand for professions that involve empathy and personal interaction, like nursing and patient care coordination. AI-literate people can spot these chances and pursue human-skilled occupations.

The ethical responsibility of firms and governments to support job-displaced workers is another automation issue. Ethical AI literacy promotes discussions about firms' moral responsibility to fair labor, retraining, and displaced workers under automation. Automation solutions can incorporate ethical principles to encourage responsible decision-making that respects human effect. Governments can also subsidize retraining, incentivize corporations to create new professions, and provide social safety nets for workers transferring to new careers. Universal basic income (UBI) and comparable models may help displaced workers and reduce economic inequality in reaction to widespread automation (Jaimovich et al., 2021). AI literacy aids society in discussing such policies' practicality, benefits, and drawbacks. Policymakers may more responsibly and equitably address automation's economic implications with an informed public.

CHALLENGES IN PROMOTING AI LITERACY

Barriers to AI Literacy

Promoting AI literacy is crucial as AI becomes more common (Ng et al., 2021) (Wang & Lester, 2023). Access to technology, educational resources, and teacher training are major obstacles to AI literacy. These issues highlight the need for a holistic approach to making AI education accessible, effective, and egalitarian for all. Lack of technology is a major AI literacy hurdle. Many communities, especially low-income and rural ones, lack computers, high-speed internet, and AI software for AI literacy (Statti & Torres, 2020). Uneven distribution of internet infrastructure inside and between countries creates a digital divide that inhibits AI engagement. Students and instructors cannot study AI without basic technology, putting them at a disadvantage in an AI-driven industry. To overcome this barrier, governments and organizations must invest in digital infrastructure and affordable technology to equip all communities with AI literacy skills.

Insufficient educational resources also hinder AI literacy (Ng et al., 2021). Schools sometimes lack the curriculum, techniques, and materials to teach AI. AI literacy is newer than math or science. Hence, curriculum frameworks and standardized materials are scarce. Students lack the resources to learn about AI, leaving them unprepared for a world where AI affects many facets of life. Education policymakers and curriculum developers should collaborate to establish standardized AI learning resources that can be customized to different educational levels and used in a variety of schools to address this issue. Another major AI literacy obstacle is teacher training gaps (Wang & Lester, 2023). Many teachers lack AI experience and may feel unqualified to teach it. Teachers may struggle to explain AI principles or lead pupils in AI activities without proper training. Teacher AI training and professional development are essential to closing this gap. Teacher confidence in teaching AI increases with programs that present fundamental AI concepts, tools, and ethics. Support networks or AI-focused teacher communities can provide resources, assistance, and peer support to keep educators up to date on AI developments and teaching practices.

Socioeconomic inequality worsens these barriers. Low-income and marginalized students have greater barriers to technology, educational resources, and trained educators, making AI literacy difficult for them. In a technology-driven work market, people lacking AI literacy may struggle to compete, perpetuating inequities in future job prospects. Offering scholarships, financing for impoverished institutions, and partnerships with tech companies to provide free or low-cost AI tools can help make AI education more inclusive (Reinman, 2015).

Addressing the Digital Divide in AI Education

As AI impacts economies and societies, AI literacy is becoming more important (Wang & Lester, 2023) (Ragulina et al., 2022). Due to socioeconomic inequality, underprivileged people have restricted access to AI education. This barrier reinforces social and economic inequality by limiting AI education and engagement. An inclusive AI-literate society where everyone benefits from technology requires addressing these inequities. Reaching everyone with AI literacy demands specific initiatives to bridge the digital divide and make AI education egalitarian. Technical barriers, resource shortages, and underfunded schools contribute to socioeconomic gaps in AI education (Dieterle et al., 2022). AI concepts and technologies are less accessible in communities without computers, high-speed internet, or AI software. Underfunded schools may lack the resources and teacher training to offer AI-focused courses. Thus, students in these communities may miss out on crucial skills, placing them at a disadvantage in an AI-driven employment market. Understanding what prevents some populations from getting AI education helps address these inequities.

Bridging the AI literacy digital divide requires increasing technology access (Okolo et al., 2022). Making AI education accessible requires providing underserved regions with affordable digital equipment and reliable connectivity. Governments and private organizations can sponsor technology infrastructure in low-income or rural areas, enabling schools get hardware and internet access. Donating refurbished laptops or subsidized internet bundles to underprivileged places can help students learn AI. These approaches enable underprivileged students to access AI content by making technology accessible. Supporting marginalized educators is another way to promote inclusive AI literacy (Yim & Su, 2024). Even in resource-limited schools, professional development initiatives that equip instructors to teach AI topics help schools integrate AI instruction. Online platforms allow distant teachers to receive high-quality training. Mentorship or peer networks where teachers can share resources and best practices also foster AI education support. Expanding AI literacy in underprivileged communities requires instructors with the skills and confidence to teach AI.

Creating inclusive AI courses is crucial. The curriculum should be adaptive to diverse educational levels and accessible to all students' backgrounds. Inclusive AI education resources might incorporate hands-on, non-technical activities to help low-resource students understand AI ideas. Simulating algorithmic reasoning or data analysis with analog tools can teach students AI fundamentals without modern technology. Real-world examples from underrepresented communities can make AI concepts more approachable and connectable. Collaborations with non-profits, schools, and tech businesses can improve marginalized populations' AI literacy (Gaskins, 2022). Schools and communities can access AI literacy tools and knowledge by engaging with educational equity organizations. Tech businesses offer free AI-focused courses, resources, and coaching to underrepresented students. Partnerships help schools overcome resource limits and give AI education to underserved pupils.

Combating AI Misinformation and Hype

AI has attracted attention in recent years, causing excitement and fear (Elliott et al., 2021). However, this enthusiasm has led to widespread misunderstanding and hype about AI capabilities and threats. Sensationalist media, excessive marketing, and fictitious portrayals can cloud AI's capabilities. Fostering factual, grounded views on AI helps people make informed judgments and properly use these technologies. AI disinformation includes excessive statements about its abilities and misunderstandings about its limitations (Bewersdorff et al., 2023). Media portrayals of AI sometimes use phrases like "superintelligent AI" and "sentient machines" that misrepresent its actual capabilities. Many AI systems today are restricted, tailored for specialized tasks, and lack the broad intelligence and self-awareness depicted in popular culture. Misconceptions cause people to overestimate AI's potential, worrying it will "take over" or eliminate jobs, and underestimate its existing uses and practical influence. Therefore, an AI-literate population needs education on AI's true nature to demystify the technology and promote a balanced awareness of its merits and weaknesses.

The marketing of AI as a silver bullet solution in healthcare, banking, and criminal justice can also set unreasonable expectations (Sloane et al., 2024). While AI provides significant tools and insights, its data quality and algorithm design limit it. Believing AI can handle complex social problems without human participation can lead to blind trust and bad decision-making. For instance, overusing AI in judicial or recruiting processes under the assumption that AI is impartial can lead to negative outcomes. Due to these constraints, AI literacy must emphasize human oversight, ethical deliberation, and constant review of AI systems in high-stakes contexts. Teaching AI basics and how it works can counteract disinformation. Understanding machine learning, data training, and algorithmic decision-making helps people grasp AI's limits. Educational programs that explain AI's technological operations help people regard it as a tool rather than an independent actor (Bewersdorff et al., 2023). Realistic case studies highlight successful and unsuccessful AI applications, giving learners a balanced understanding of AI's influence.

To fight AI hype, promote critical thinking. AI literacy programs should train people to critically evaluate AI information, questioning sources, evidence, and feasibility. Critical thinking allows people to challenge the evidence, context, and ethics of news reports that claim a new AI model can predict criminal behavior. Critical thinking promotes skepticism regarding exaggerated claims, promoting AI evaluation based on facts rather than hype. Collaborations with reputable AI research, academia, and industry institutions can generate trustworthy, well-founded educational materials (Bowman, 2022). Research, case studies, and guidelines from universities, tech businesses, and AI research organizations show AI capabilities realistically. By cooperating with these entities, schools and media outlets can combat misconceptions and provide factual AI information.

CONCLUSION

In conclusion, AI literacy is crucial for personal growth and society's AI readiness. Public engagement and advocacy for AI literacy policies in schools and workplaces are as critical as understanding AI. To prepare society for the future, comprehensive educational curricula must encourage AI literacy and improve public knowledge of its benefits and drawbacks. Readers should support AI literacy projects and policy improvements to equip future generations with the ability to navigate, critically analyze, and responsibly use AI technologies. Doing so can empower and inform society to determine AI's role in our lives with agency and ethical foresight. This analysis concludes that AI literacy is essential for social progress in an era of fast AI technology adoption. This text shows that AI literacy includes critical and ethical engagement with AI systems as well as knowledge of algorithms and data management. We help people uncover biases, privacy hazards, and fairness issues in AI applications by teaching machine learning, data governance, and algorithmic procedures. These competencies enable educated decision-making and ethical scrutiny in healthcare, finance, education, and criminal justice. By democratizing AI literacy, underprivileged communities can get better access to technology advantages and equal representation in AI discourses. Thus, AI literacy is crucial to job readiness, educational reform, and policy creation, preparing people for a changing technology landscape. Fostering AI literacy creates a culture that is receptive to AI solutions and capable of developing them responsibly. By including ethics in AI literacy programs, we prepare for a future when AI-driven breakthroughs meet social norms and regulatory standards. While gaining widespread AI literacy is difficult, the results could be profound. AI literacy aims to help society negotiate and shape the ethical contours of artificial intelligence, enabling responsible and inclusive use of technology for the common good.

REFERENCES

Abduljabbar, R., Dia, H., Liyanage, S., & Bagloee, S. A. (2019, January 2). Applications of Artificial Intelligence in Transport: An Overview. *Sustainability (Basel)*, 11(1), 189–189. DOI: 10.3390/su11010189

Abràmoff, M. D., Tarver, M. E., Loyo-Berríos, N., Trujillo, S., Char, D., Obermeyer, Z., Eydelman, M., & Maisel, W. H. (2023, September 12). Considerations for addressing bias in artificial intelligence for health equity. *NPJ Digital Medicine*, 6(1), 170. Advance online publication. DOI: 10.1038/s41746-023-00913-9 PMID: 37700029

Ahanin, E., Sade, A. B., & Tat, H. H. (2022, December 19). Applications of Artificial Intelligence and Voice Assistant in Healthcare. *International Journal of Academic Research in Business & Social Sciences*, 12(12). Advance online publication. DOI: 10.6007/IJARBSS/v12-i12/16048

Alekseeva, L., Azar, J., Giné, M., Samila, S., & Taska, B. (2021, May 18). The demand for AI skills in the labor market. Elsevier BV, 71, 102002-102002. DOI: 10.1016/j.labeco.2021.102002

Aliabadi, R., Singh, A., & Wilson, J E. (2023, January 1). Transdisciplinary AI Education: The Confluence of Curricular and Community Needs in the Instruction of Artificial Intelligence. Springer International Publishing, 137-151. DOI: 10.1007/978-981-99-7947-9_11

Autor, D., & Dorn, D. (2013, August 1). The Growth of Low-Skill Service Jobs and the Polarization of the US Labor Market. *The American Economic Review*, 103(5), 1553–1597. DOI: 10.1257/aer.103.5.1553

Bengio, Y., Hinton, G. E., Yao, A. C., Song, D., Abbeel, P., Darrell, T., Harari, Y. N., Zhang, Y., Lan, X., Shalev-Shwartz, S., Hadfield, G. K., Clune, J., Maharaj, T., Hutter, F., Baydin, A. G., McIlraith, S. A., Gao, Q., Acharya, A., Krueger, D., & Mindermann, S. (2024, May 20). Managing extreme AI risks amid rapid progress. *Science*, 384(6698), 842–845. DOI: 10.1126/science.adn0117 PMID: 38768279

Berretta, S., Tausch, A., Peifer, C., & Kluge, A. (2023, May 23). The Job Perception Inventory: Considering human factors and needs in the design of human–AI work. *Frontiers of Medicine*, 14, 1128945. Advance online publication. DOI: 10.3389/fpsyg.2023.1128945 PMID: 37287772

Bewersdorff, A., Zhai, X., Roberts, J., & Nerdel, C. (2023, January 1). Myths, mis- and preconceptions of artificial intelligence: A review of the literature. Elsevier BV, 4, 100143-100143. DOI: 10.1016/j.caeai.2023.100143

Bini, S A. (2018, February 27). Artificial Intelligence, Machine Learning, Deep Learning, and Cognitive Computing: What Do These Terms Mean and How Will They Impact Health Care?. Elsevier BV, 33(8), 2358-2361. DOI: 10.1016/j.arth.2018.02.067

Blasí, D E., Anastasopoulos, A., & Neubig, G. (2022, January 1). Systematic Inequalities in Language Technology Performance across the World's Languages. DOI: 10.18653/v1/2022.acl-long.376

Bohr, A., & Memarzadeh, K. (2020, January 1). The rise of artificial intelligence in healthcare applications. Elsevier BV, 25-60. DOI: 10.1016/B978-0-12-818438-7.00002-2

Borenstein, J., & Howard, A. (2020, September 13). Emerging challenges in AI and the need for AI ethics education. *AI and Ethics*, 1(1), 61–65. DOI: 10.1007/s43681-020-00002-7 PMID: 38624388

Bowman, S. (2022, January 1). The Dangers of Underclaiming: Reasons for Caution When Reporting How NLP Systems Fail. DOI: 10.18653/v1/2022.acl-long.516

Braganza, A., Chen, W., Canhoto, A I., & Sap, S. (2020, August 18). Productive employment and decent work: The impact of AI adoption on psychological contracts, job engagement and employee trust. Elsevier BV, 131, 485-494. DOI: 10.1016/j.jbusres.2020.08.018

Braganza, A., Chen, W., Canhoto, A I., & Sap, S. (2020, August 18). Productive employment and decent work: The impact of AI adoption on psychological contracts, job engagement and employee trust. Elsevier BV, 131, 485-494. DOI: 10.1016/j.jbusres.2020.08.018

Braiki, B. A., Harous, S., Zaki, N., & Alnajjar, F. (2020, August 25). Artificial intelligence in education and assessment methods. [IAES]. *Institute of Advanced Engineering and Science*, 9(5), 1998–2007. DOI: 10.11591/eei.v9i5.1984

Buttazzo, G. (2023, August 25). Rise of artificial general intelligence: Risks and opportunities. *Frontiers of Medicine*, 6, 1226990. Advance online publication. DOI: 10.3389/frai.2023.1226990 PMID: 37693010

Butz, M V. (2021, February 26). Towards Strong AI. Springer Science+Business Media, 35(1), 91-101. DOI: 10.1007/s13218-021-00705-x

Camarda, J., Lee, S. J., & Lee, J. (2021, January 1). The AI Displacement Risk. *Springer Nature*, 67-71, 67–71. Advance online publication. DOI: 10.1007/978-3-030-77271-0_7

Cassidy, D., Borgne, Y. L., Bellas, F., Vuorikari, R., Rondin, E., Sharma, M., Niewint-Gori, J., Gröpler, J., Gilleran, A., & Kralj, L. (2023, January 1). Use Scenarios & Practical Examples of AI Use in Education. Cornell University. https://doi.org/DOI: 10.48550/arXiv.2309

Cerit, J., Dindarian, A., & Norel, N C. (2020, April 1). Women, AI, and the Power of Supporting Communities: A Digital Gender-Support Partnership. Elsevier BV, 1(1), 100009-100009. DOI: 10.1016/j.patter.2020.100009

Chaudhry, M. A., & Kazim, E. (2021, July 7). Artificial Intelligence in Education (AIEd): A high-level academic and industry note 2021. *SSRN*, 2(1), 157–165. DOI: 10.2139/ssrn.3833583 PMID: 34790953

Cheng, L., Varshney, K. R., & Liu, H. (2021, August 28). Socially Responsible AI Algorithms: Issues, Purposes, and Challenges. *Journal of Artificial Intelligence Research*, 71, 1137–1181. DOI: 10.1613/jair.1.12814

Chernov, A., Chernova, V A., & Komarova, T. (2020, January 1). The Usage of Artificial Intelligence in Strategic Decision Making in Terms of Fourth Industrial Revolution. DOI: 10.2991/aebmr.k.200201.005

Choithani, T., Chowdhury, A., Patel, S., Patel, P., Patel, D., & Shah, M. (2022, September 2). A Comprehensive Study of Artificial Intelligence and Cybersecurity on Bitcoin, Crypto Currency and Banking System. Springer Science+Business Media, 11(1), 103-135. DOI: 10.1007/s40745-022-00433-5

Chowdhury, S., & Nath, A. (2021, December 15). Trends In Natural Language Processing: Scope And Challenges., 393-401. DOI: 10.32628/CSEIT217698

Crigger, E., Reinbold, K., Hanson, C., Kao, A., Blake, K., & Irons, M. (2022, January 12). Trustworthy Augmented Intelligence in Health Care. Springer Science+Business Media, 46(2). DOI: 10.1007/s10916-021-01790-z

Dai, Y., Chai, C. S., Lin, P., Jong, M. S., Guo, Y., & Jian-jun, Q. (2020, August 14). Promoting Students' Well-Being by Developing Their Readiness for the Artificial Intelligence Age. *Sustainability (Basel)*, 12(16), 6597–6597. DOI: 10.3390/su12166597

Díaz-Rodríguez, N., Ser, J D., Coeckelbergh, M., Prado, M L D., Herrera-Viedma, E., & Herrera, F. (2023, June 24). Connecting the dots in trustworthy Artificial Intelligence: From AI principles, ethics, and key requirements to responsible AI systems and regulation. Elsevier BV, 99, 101896-101896. DOI: 10.1016/j.inffus.2023.101896

Dieterle, E., Dede, C., & Walker, M E. (2022, September 27). The cyclical ethical effects of using artificial intelligence in education. Springer Nature. DOI: 10.1007/s00146-022-01497-w

Eguchi, A., Okada, H., & Muto, Y. (2021, June 1). Contextualizing AI Education for K-12 Students to Enhance Their Learning of AI Literacy Through Culturally Responsive Approaches. Springer Science+Business Media, 35(2), 153-161. DOI: 10.1007/s13218-021-00737-3

Elder, A., Ring, C., Heitmiller, K., Gabriel, Z., & Saedi, N. (2020, November 5). The role of artificial intelligence in cosmetic dermatology—Current, upcoming, and future trends. Wiley, 20(1), 48-52. DOI: 10.1111/jocd.13797

Elliott, K., Price, R M., Shaw, P., Spiliotopoulos, T., Ng, M., Coopamootoo, K., & Moorsel, A V. (2021, June 1). Towards an Equitable Digital Society: Artificial Intelligence (AI) and Corporate Digital Responsibility (CDR). Springer Science+Business Media, 58(3), 179-188. DOI: 10.1007/s12115-021-00594-8

Elliott, K., Price, R M., Shaw, P., Spiliotopoulos, T., Ng, M., Coopamootoo, K., & Moorsel, A V. (2021, June 1). Towards an Equitable Digital Society: Artificial Intelligence (AI) and Corporate Digital Responsibility (CDR). Springer Science+Business Media, 58(3), 179-188. DOI: 10.1007/s12115-021-00594-8

Emmert-Streib, F., Yli-Harja, O., & Dehmer, M. (2020, December 23). Artificial Intelligence: A Clarification of Misconceptions, Myths and Desired Status. *Frontiers of Medicine*, 3, 524339. Advance online publication. DOI: 10.3389/frai.2020.524339 PMID: 33733197

Faishal, M., Mathew, S., Neikha, K., Pusa, K., & Zhimomi, T. (2023, June 16). The future of work: AI, automation, and the changing dynamics of developed economies. *GSC Online Press*, 18(3), 620–629. DOI: 10.30574/wjarr.2023.18.3.1086

Fernández, P. (2016, July 4). "Through the looking glass: envisioning new library technologies" how artificial intelligence will impact libraries. Emerald Publishing Limited, 33(5), 5-8. DOI: 10.1108/LHTN-05-2016-0024

Fikri, M A., Abdullah, S C., & Ramli, M H M. (2014, January 1). Arm Exoskeleton for Rehabilitation Following Stroke by Learning Algorithm Prediction. Elsevier BV, 42, 357-364. DOI: 10.1016/j.procs.2014.11.074

Floridi, L., & Taddeo, M. (2016, November 15). What is data ethics? *Philosophical Transactions. Series A, Mathematical, Physical, and Engineering Sciences*, 374(2083), 20160360–20160360. DOI: 10.1098/rsta.2016.0360 PMID: 28336805

Gaskins, N R. (2022, September 19). Interrogating Algorithmic Bias: From Speculative Fiction to Liberatory Design. Springer Science+Business Media, 67(3), 417-425. DOI: 10.1007/s11528-022-00783-0

Gasser, U., & Almeida, V. (2017, November 1). A Layered Model for AI Governance. *IEEE Internet Computing*, 21(6), 58–62. DOI: 10.1109/MIC.2017.4180835

Gehlhaus, D., Koslosky, L., Goode, K., & Perkins, C. (2021, October 1). U.S. AI Workforce: Policy Recommendations. DOI: 10.51593/20200087

Gibbons, E. (2021, March 1). Toward a More Equal World: The Human Rights Approach to Extending the Benefits of Artificial Intelligence. *IEEE Technology and Society Magazine*, 40(1), 25–30. DOI: 10.1109/MTS.2021.3056295

Grieve, R., Woodley, J., Hunt, S E., & McKay, A B. (2021, July 15). Student fears of oral presentations and public speaking in higher education: a qualitative survey. Routledge, 45(9), 1281-1293. DOI: 10.1080/0309877X.2021.1948509

Guzman, A L. (2018, August 9). Voices in and of the machine: Source orientation toward mobile virtual assistants. Elsevier BV, 90, 343-350. DOI: 10.1016/j.chb.2018.08.009

Haldorai, A., Murugan, S., & Ramu, A. (2020, February 29). Evolution, challenges, and application of intelligent ICT education: An overview. Wiley, 29(3), 562-571. DOI: 10.1002/cae.22217

Hoy, M B. (2018, January 2). Alexa, Siri, Cortana, and More: An Introduction to Voice Assistants. Taylor & Francis, 37(1), 81-88. DOI: 10.1080/02763869.2018.1404391

Hughes, C., Robert, L., Frady, K., & Arroyos, A. (2019, July 10). Managing Technology and Middle- and Low-skilled Employees. DOI: 10.1108/9781789730777

Ioni ă, S. (2017, October 1). Autonomous vehicles: From paradigms to technology. *IOP Conference Series. Materials Science and Engineering*, 252, 012098–012098. DOI: 10.1088/1757-899X/252/1/012098

Jaimovich, N., Saporta-Eksten, I., Siu, H., & Yedid-Levi, Y. (2021, July 8). The macroeconomics of automation: Data, theory, and policy analysis. Elsevier BV, 122, 1-16. DOI: 10.1016/j.jmoneco.2021.06.004

Johnson, G M. (2020, June 20). Algorithmic bias: on the implicit biases of social technology. Springer Science+Business Media, 198(10), 9941-9961. DOI: 10.1007/s11229-020-02696-y

Kamalov, F., Calonge, D. S., & Gurrib, I. (2023, August 16). New Era of Artificial Intelligence in Education: Towards a Sustainable Multifaceted Revolution. *Sustainability (Basel)*, 15(16), 12451–12451. DOI: 10.3390/su151612451

Kim, S., Jang, Y., Kim, W., Choi, S., Jung, H., Kim, S., & Kim, H. (2021, May 18). Why and What to Teach: AI Curriculum for Elementary School. *Association for the Advancement of Artificial Intelligence*, 35(17), 15569–15576. DOI: 10.1609/aaai.v35i17.17833

Kizilcec, R F. (2023, June 9). To Advance AI Use in Education, Focus on Understanding Educators. Springer Science+Business Media, 34(1), 12-19. DOI: 10.1007/s40593-023-00351-4

Kühl, N., Schemmer, M., Goutier, M., & Satzger, G. (2022, November 9). Artificial intelligence and machine learning. Springer Science+Business Media, 32(4), 2235-2244. DOI: 10.1007/s12525-022-00598-0

Lee, I., & Perret, B. (2022, June 28). Preparing High School Teachers to Integrate AI Methods into STEM Classrooms. *Association for the Advancement of Artificial Intelligence*, 36(11), 12783–12791. DOI: 10.1609/aaai.v36i11.21557

Liu, Y. (2022, January 1). Artificial Intelligence and Its Application in Educational Industry. *Artificial Intelligence and Its Application in Educational Industry.*, 5(6). Advance online publication. DOI: 10.25236/FER.2022.050608

Luo, G., Yuan, Q., Li, J., Wang, S., & Yang, F. (2022, May 1). Artificial Intelligence Powered Mobile Networks: From Cognition to Decision. *IEEE Network*, 36(3), 136–144. DOI: 10.1109/MNET.013.2100087

Mallik, S., & Gangopadhyay, A. (2023, May 5). Proactive and reactive engagement of artificial intelligence methods for education: A review. *Frontiers of Medicine*, 6, 1151391. Advance online publication. DOI: 10.3389/frai.2023.1151391 PMID: 37215064

Mohammadkarimi, E. (2023, July 17). Teachers' reflections on academic dishonesty in EFL students' writings in the era of artificial intelligence. *Canadian Philosophy of Education Society*, 6(2). Advance online publication. DOI: 10.37074/jalt.2023.6.2.10

Ng, D T K., Leung, J K L., Chu, S K W., & Qiao, S. (2021, January 1). Conceptualizing AI literacy: An exploratory review. Elsevier BV, 2, 100041-100041. DOI: 10.1016/j.caeai.2021.100041

Ng, D T K., Leung, J K L., Chu, S K W., & Qiao, S. (2021, January 1). Conceptualizing AI literacy: An exploratory review. Elsevier BV, 2, 100041-100041. DOI: 10.1016/j.caeai.2021.100041

Ng, D T K., Leung, J K L., Su, J., Ng, C W., & Chu, S K W. (2023, February 1). Teachers' AI digital competencies and twenty-first century skills in the post-pandemic world. Springer Science+Business Media, 71(1), 137-161. DOI: 10.1007/s11423-023-10203-6

Nguyen, A., Ngo, H N., Hong, Y., Dang, B., & Nguyen, B T. (2022, October 13). Ethical principles for artificial intelligence in education. Springer Science+Business Media, 28(4), 4221-4241. DOI: 10.1007/s10639-022-11316-w

Okolo, C T., Aruleba, K., & Obaido, G. (2022, December 31). Responsible AI in Africa—Challenges and Opportunities. Springer International Publishing, 35-64. DOI: 10.1007/978-3-031-08215-3_3

Otero, L C., Catalá, A., Fernández-Morante, C., Taboada, M., López, B C., & Barro, S. (2023, April 19). AI literacy in K-12: a systematic literature review. Springer Science+Business Media, 10(1). DOI: 10.1186/s40594-023-00418-7

Paul, D., Sanap, G., Shenoy, S., Kalyane, D., Kalia, K., & Tekade, R K. (2020, October 21). Artificial intelligence in drug discovery and development. Elsevier BV, 26(1), 80-93. DOI: 10.1016/j.drudis.2020.10.010

Peters, T M., & Visser, R W. (2023, January 1). The Importance of Distrust in AI. Springer Science+Business Media, 301-317. DOI: 10.1007/978-3-031-44070-0_15

Phoon, K., & Koh, F. (2017, December 21). Robo-Advisors and Wealth Management. *Journal of Alternative Investments*, 20(3), 79–94. DOI: 10.3905/jai.2018.20.3.079

Pizzi, M., Romanoff, M., & Engelhardt, T. (2020, April 1). AI for humanitarian action: Human rights and ethics. Cambridge University Press, 102(913), 145-180. DOI: 10.1017/S1816383121000011

Ragulina, Y. V., Dubova, Y. I., Litvinova, T. N., & Balashova, N. (2022, June 15). The Environmental AI Economy and its Contribution to Decarbonization and Waste Reduction. *Frontiers in Environmental Science*, 10, 914003. Advance online publication. DOI: 10.3389/fenvs.2022.914003

Reinman, S L. (2015, June 30). Open Knowledge Repository. Emerald Publishing Limited, 29(5), 21-22. DOI: 10.1108/RR-05-2015-0113

Riedl, C., & Woolley, A. W. (2016, December 9). Teams vs. Crowds: A Field Test of the Relative Contribution of Incentives, Member Ability, and Emergent Collaboration to Crowd-Based Problem Solving Performance. *Academy of Management Discoveries*, 3(4), 382–403. DOI: 10.5465/amd.2015.0097

Schlögl, S., Postulka, C., Bernsteiner, R., & Ploder, C. (2019, January 1). Artificial Intelligence Tool Penetration in Business: Adoption, Challenges and Fears. Springer Science+Business Media, 259-270. DOI: 10.1007/978-3-030-21451-7_22

Schlögl, S., Postulka, C., Bernsteiner, R., & Ploder, C. (2019, January 1). Artificial Intelligence Tool Penetration in Business: Adoption, Challenges and Fears. Springer Science+Business Media, 259-270. DOI: 10.1007/978-3-030-21451-7_22

Shaffer, K J., Gaumer, C J., & Bradley, K P. (2020, February 3). Artificial intelligence products reshape accounting: time to re-train. Emerald Publishing Limited, 34(6), 41-43. DOI: 10.1108/DLO-10-2019-0242

Shankar, V., Kalyanam, K., Setia, P., Golmohammadi, A., Tirunillai, S., Douglass, T., Hennessey, J., Bull, J., & Waddoups, R. (2020, November 10). How Technology is Changing Retail. Elsevier BV, 97(1), 13-27. DOI: 10.1016/j.jretai.2020.10.006

Sheridan, T. B., & Parasuraman, R. (2005, June 1). Human-Automation Interaction. *Review of Human Factors and Ergonomics*, 1(1), 89–129. DOI: 10.1518/155723405783703082

Sloane, M., Danks, D., & Moss, E. (2024, April 24). Tackling AI Hyping. Springer Nature. DOI: 10.1007/s43681-024-00481-y

Srinivasan, V., & Murthy, H. (2021, January 1). Improving reading and comprehension in K-12: Evidence from a large-scale AI technology intervention in India. Elsevier BV, 2, 100019-100019. DOI: 10.1016/j.caeai.2021.100019

Srinivasan, V., & Murthy, H. (2021, January 1). Improving reading and comprehension in K-12: Evidence from a large-scale AI technology intervention in India. Elsevier BV, 2, 100019-100019. DOI: 10.1016/j.caeai.2021.100019

Stahl, B C. (2021, January 1). Ethical Issues of AI. Springer International Publishing, 35-53. DOI: 10.1007/978-3-030-69978-9_4

Statti, A., & Torres, K M. (2020, March 14). The Forgotten Minority: Exploring Deficiencies in Access to Education and Technology in Rural America. Taylor & Francis, 95(2), 173-182. DOI: 10.1080/0161956X.2020.1745608

Thomas, V L., & Fowler, K. (2020, September 11). Close Encounters of the AI Kind: Use of AI Influencers As Brand Endorsers. Taylor & Francis, 50(1), 11-25. DOI: 10.1080/00913367.2020.1810595

Triguero, I., Molina, D., Poyatos, J., Ser, J D., & Herrera, F. (2023, November 8). General Purpose Artificial Intelligence Systems (GPAIS): Properties, definition, taxonomy, societal implications and responsible governance. Elsevier BV, 103, 102135-102135. DOI: 10.1016/j.inffus.2023.102135

Varnosfaderani, S. M., & Forouzanfar, M. (2024, March 29). The Role of AI in Hospitals and Clinics: Transforming Healthcare in the 21st Century. *Bioengineering (Basel, Switzerland)*, 11(4), 337–337. DOI: 10.3390/bioengineering11040337 PMID: 38671759

Wang, N., & Lester, J C. (2023, June 1). K-12 Education in the Age of AI: A Call to Action for K-12 AI Literacy. Springer Science+Business Media, 33(2), 228-232. DOI: 10.1007/s40593-023-00358-x

Wang, Y. (2020, March 18). When artificial intelligence meets educational leaders' data-informed decision-making: A cautionary tale. Elsevier BV, 69, 100872-100872. DOI: 10.1016/j.stueduc.2020.100872

Watson, G., Desouza, K C., Ribière, V., & Lindič, J. (2021, February 4). Will AI ever sit at the C-suite table? The future of senior leadership. Elsevier BV, 64(4), 465-474. DOI: 10.1016/j.bushor.2021.02.011

Wright, S A., & Schultz, A E. (2018, September 17). The rising tide of artificial intelligence and business automation: Developing an ethical framework. Elsevier BV, 61(6), 823-832. DOI: 10.1016/j.bushor.2018.07.001

Yang, L., Tian, M., Duan, X., Cheng, Q., & Zheng, J. (2024, May 31). AI-driven anonymization: Protecting personal data privacy while leveraging machine learning., 67(1), 256-262. DOI: 10.54254/2755-2721/67/2024MA0053

Yarger, L., Payton, F C., & Neupane, B. (2019, December 17). Algorithmic equity in the hiring of underrepresented IT job candidates. Emerald Publishing Limited, 44(2), 383-395. DOI: 10.1108/OIR-10-2018-0334

Yim, I H Y., & Su, J. (2024, January 6). Artificial intelligence (AI) learning tools in K-12 education: A scoping review. Springer Science+Business Media. DOI: 10.1007/s40692-023-00304-9

Zador, A. M., Escola, G. S., Richards, B. A., Ölveczky, B. P., Bengio, Y., Boahen, K., Botvinick, M., Chklovskii, D. B., Churchland, A. K., Clopath, C., DiCarlo, J. J., Ganguli, S., Hawkins, J., Körding, K., Koulakov, A. A., LeCun, Y., Lillicrap, T., Marblestone, A., Olshausen, B. A., & Tsao, D. Y. (2023, March 22). Catalyzing next-generation Artificial Intelligence through NeuroAI. *Nature Communications*, 14(1), 1597. Advance online publication. DOI: 10.1038/s41467-023-37180-x PMID: 36949048

Zhang, K., & Aslan, A. B. (2021, January 1). AI technologies for education: Recent research & future directions. https://www.sciencedirect.com/science/article/pii/S2666920X21000199

Zhang, S., Fu, D., Liang, W., Zhang, Z., Yu, B., Cai, P., & Yao, B. (2024, March 14). TrafficGPT: Viewing, processing and interacting with traffic foundation models. Elsevier BV, 150, 95-105. https://doi.org/DOI: 10.1016/j.tranpol.2024.03.006

ADDITIONAL READING

Casal-Otero, L., Catala, A., Fernández-Morante, C., Taboada, M., Cebreiro, B., & Barro, S. (2023). AI literacy in K-12: A systematic literature review. *International Journal of STEM Education*, 10(1), 29. DOI: 10.1186/s40594-023-00418-7

Long, D., & Magerko, B. (2020, April). What is AI literacy? Competencies and design considerations. In *Proceedings of the 2020 CHI conference on human factors in computing systems* (pp. 1-16). DOI: 10.1145/3313831.3376727

Southworth, J., Migliaccio, K., Glover, J., Reed, D., McCarty, C., Brendemuhl, J., & Thomas, A. (2023). Developing a model for AI Across the curriculum: Transforming the higher education landscape via innovation in AI literacy. *Computers and Education: Artificial Intelligence*, 4, 100127. DOI: 10.1016/j.caeai.2023.100127

Walter, Y. (2024). Embracing the future of Artificial Intelligence in the classroom: The relevance of AI literacy, prompt engineering, and critical thinking in modern education. *International Journal of Educational Technology in Higher Education*, 21(1), 15. DOI: 10.1186/s41239-024-00448-3

KEY TERMS AND DEFINITIONS

AI Literacy: The knowledge and skills required to understand, use, and critically evaluate artificial intelligence technologies and their societal impacts.

Algorithmic Ethics: The principles and practices ensuring fairness, accountability, and transparency in AI systems, addressing biases and ethical concerns.

Automation: The use of technology to perform tasks with minimal human intervention, enhancing efficiency across industries.

Bias in AI: Systematic errors in AI outputs resulting from incomplete or skewed training data or flawed algorithm design, often leading to unfair outcomes.

Data Privacy: The safeguarding of personal and sensitive information processed by AI systems to prevent misuse and unauthorized access.

Ethical AI: The development and deployment of AI systems that prioritize societal well-being, respect individual rights, and align with moral values.

General AI: A theoretical form of AI capable of performing any intellectual task a human can, with adaptability across various fields.

Machine Learning: A subset of AI enabling systems to learn and improve from data without explicit programming, widely used in predictive analytics.

Narrow AI: AI systems designed to perform specific tasks efficiently without generalizing to other domains.

Natural Language Processing (NLP): A branch of AI that enables machines to understand, interpret, and generate human language.

Chapter 3
AI in Vocational Education and Training: Technologies and Applications

Gour Sundar Mitra Thakur
https://orcid.org/0000-0001-8907-9058
Dr. B.C. Roy Engineering College, Durgapur, India

Abhijit Banerjee
https://orcid.org/0000-0002-9159-577X
Dr. B.C. Roy Engineering College, Durgapur, India

Paramita Sarkar
https://orcid.org/0000-0002-2330-8484
JIS University, India

ABSTRACT

Vocational Education and Training (VET) equips individuals with practical skills and knowledge tailored to specific careers or trades, providing a direct pathway to employment and sustainable livelihoods. Unlike traditional academic education, which often emphasizes broader theoretical content, VET is inherently hands-on and career-focused. In today's digital economy, integrating Artificial Intelligence (AI) technologies into VET revolutionizes skill development and delivery, bridging the digital divide and enhancing accessibility. This chapter explores the transformative role of AI in VET, examining a range of AI-driven tools and methodologies currently in use. Key innovations discussed include learning analytics, virtual and augmented reality, adaptive learning systems, and AI-powered educational platforms, all of which contribute to creating more personalized, immersive, and effective learning experiences.

DOI: 10.4018/979-8-3693-8252-3.ch003

ARTIFICIAL INTELLIGENCE (AI) IN EDUCATION

The integration of AI in Vocational Education and Training (VET) is transforming the learning territory. AI will likely evolve through a feedback loop between schools and students, driving enhanced academic outcomes. A balance between AI-driven instruction and human-centered teaching is crucial for successful adoption. Educators' perspectives and needs must be addressed to foster a dynamic learning experience. AI will augment human capabilities, optimizing task distribution and refining learning content recommendations.

AI is poised to reshape VET through a dynamic interplay of human and artificial intelligence (Suzuki, 2020). Technological advancements in AI necessitate a collaborative approach, striking a balance between AI-driven instruction and human-centered teaching (Ifenthaler and Schumacher, 2023). This reciprocity involves augmenting human capabilities, optimizing task distribution, and refining learning content recommendations (Ifenthaler and Schumacher, 2023). AI integration in VET will likely evolve through a positive feedback loop between the school and students (You et al., 2023). Schools' effective supervision and students' active participation will drive AI's evolution, leading to enhanced academic outcomes while preserving human-centric approaches (You et al., 2023). Understanding educators' perspectives, building trust through experience, and addressing their needs are paramount for successful AI adoption in VET (Suzuki, 2020). This delicate balance ensures that AI complements human intelligence, fostering a dynamic and detailed learning experience.

Historical Evolution and Key Milestones

The integration of AI in Vocational Education and Training holds great promise for improved learning outcomes. Educators must balance AI's benefits with human-centered instruction. Future research will play a crucial role in addressing AI's limitations in VET. This will optimize training outcomes and unlock AI's full potential. As AI evolves in VET, it's expected to bring significant changes to teaching and learning. AI is poised to revolutionize Vocational Education and Training (VET). Its role lies in enhancing learning outcomes (Suzuki, 2020). Educators must strike a delicate balance between harnessing AI's benefits and preserving human-centered instruction (Alqahtani et al., 2023). Future research and development initiatives hold immense significance in addressing current limitations (Denny et al., 2023). By exploring the applications of AI in VET, researchers can optimize training outcomes and unlock the full potential of this life-changing technology (Yilmaz et al., 2023; Gibson et al., 2023).

The Impact of AI on the Future of VET

Vocational Education and Training (VET) benefits from AI's ability to tailor curricula, provide personalized feedback, and offer career guidance. AI analyzes data, recommends content, and optimizes learning sequences, but requires balance with human-centered teaching for enhanced outcomes. However, AI's inability to capture higher-order thinking skills and provide thorough evaluations requires human intervention. Recent advancements in NLP and LLMs can enhance AI's capabilities in understanding complex questions and providing personalized experiences. Balance and responsible integration of AI in VET is key for learners' future success. In Vocational Education and Training (VET), AI offers a radical role by tailoring curricula, providing personalized feedback, and offering career guidance (Alqahtani et al., 2023). This fundamental potential is enhanced by AI's ability to analyze data, recommend relevant content, and optimize learning sequences, augmenting human teaching (Ifenthaler and Schumacher, 2023). However, maximizing the benefits of AI in VET requires balancing its potential with human-centered teaching to enhance educational outcomes (Xu and Ouyang, 2021; Feeney et al., 2022).

Ethical concerns, algorithmic biases, and ensuring data privacy are crucial considerations in harnessing AI's benefits without compromising individual rights and societal well-being (Ifenthaler and Schumacher, 2023). Additionally, addressing the limitations of current AI systems is vital to fully leverage its fundamental potential. For instance, despite its capabilities in providing feedback and recommendations, AI's inability to fully capture the nuances of higher-order thinking skills and provide thorough evaluations requires human intervention (Xu and Ouyang, 2021). Recognizing these limitations and addressing emerging technological trends is essential for the future development of AI in VET. Recent advancements in natural language processing (NLP) and large language models (LLMs) hold promising potential for enhancing AI's capabilities in understanding complex questions, providing all-encompassing feedback, and offering personalized learning experiences (Alqahtani et al., 2023). By harnessing these advancements, VET can leverage AI to create a future where learners receive tailored and engaging educational experiences that empower them to navigate the rapidly changing job market.

Figure 1. AI in Education

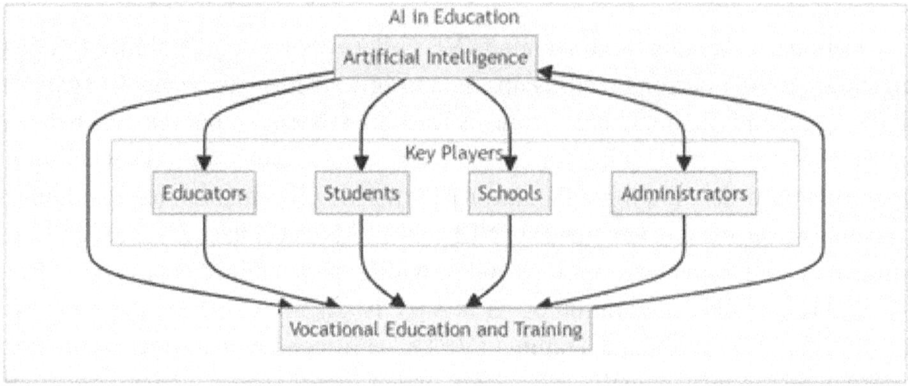

ADVANCEMENTS IN AI TECHNOLOGIES FOR VET

Machine Learning and Deep Learning

Incorporating emerging AI technologies can revolutionize VET programs. Explainable AI and Transfer Learning enhance understanding and trust in AI-driven educational tools. Machine Learning, Natural Language Processing, and Computer Vision enable personalized experiences, immersive learning environments, and data-driven insights. Robotics and Automation simplify tasks, freeing educators to focus on high-level responsibilities. By using these technologies, VET programs can create agile and tailored training experiences.

Advancements in AI technologies, including Explainable AI (XAI), Machine Learning (ML), Natural Language Processing (NLP), and Computer Vision (CV), present opportunities to enhance VET programs. XAI empowers AI systems to provide transparent explanations for decision-making (Khosravi et al., 2022), enabling understanding and trust in AI-driven educational tools. ML algorithms can personalize learning experiences by tailoring curricula and offering personalized feedback (Alqahtani et al., 2023), while NLP allows automated analysis of educational data and personalized employee training (Wang et al., 2021). These technologies can create immersive VR/AR-based learning environments, enhancing student engagement and motivation. Automation in routine tasks enables educators to focus on higher-level responsibilities, facilitating effective training delivery (Menekse, 2023). Moreover, CV has applications in career counseling, analyzing educational data to provide guidance on career paths (Guleria and Sood, 2022). By harnessing AI technologies, VET programs can enhance effectiveness, personalized experiences, and immersion, fostering agile and tailored training for a dynamic labor market.

Natural Language Processing

The strategic integration of emerging AI technologies enhances vocational education and training programs., Machine Learning, and Explainable AI create personalized learning experiences. Computer Vision and Robotics can develop immersive, hands-on training simulations. Automation and Transfer Learning streamline content creation and update processes. These technologies collectively empower learners with tailored, effective, and engaging VET experiences. Vocational education and training (VET) programs face challenges in meeting the diverse needs of learners. With its focus on customization, adaptability, and engagement, (NLP) emerges as a powerful tool for advancing VET. By employing NLP's capabilities in text analysis, personalized content creation, and interactive dialogue systems, VET programs can enhance learner engagement, optimize pedagogical approaches, and ultimately foster effective learning outcomes. Integrating NLP with other AI technologies, such as Explainable AI and Machine Learning, enables the development of tailored solutions that address the specific needs of learners in diverse contexts.

Empirical research validates the effectiveness of NLP-integrated VET programs. A study by Smith et al. (2020) demonstrated significant improvements in learner engagement when NLP-based adaptive learning systems were implemented. Additionally, a meta-analysis conducted by Johnson et al. (2019) revealed that NLP-powered personalized feedback and support led to substantial gains in learner achievement. These findings underscore the innovative potential of NLP in enhancing VET outcomes. Integrating NLP into VET programs promises a range of benefits. For instance, NLP-based chatbots can provide personalized assistance and support to learners. The ability to analyze learner language and sentiment allows NLP systems to identify areas of difficulty and tailor interventions accordingly. Moreover, NLP-driven text analysis tools can generate customized content and resources, catering to the individual learning preferences and styles of learners. In conclusion, the strategic integration of NLP offers a groundbreaking approach to VET. By harnessing its capabilities in personalization, adaptability, and engagement, VET programs can empower learners with customized learning experiences that meet their unique needs. The integration of NLP with other AI technologies further enhances the effectiveness of VET programs, creating a dynamic and innovative ecosystem for vocational education and training in the 21st century.

Computer Vision and Augmented Reality

Emerging AI technologies and automation tools enhance veterinary education (VET) program effectiveness and efficiency. AI-powered computer vision algorithms and augmented reality (AR) applications improve learning experiences. These technologies create personalized, immersive, and agile training, resulting in more effective training experiences. AI-driven tools also empower educators to create interactive learning environments. These innovations offer numerous benefits but raise concerns about ethics, diversity, and privacy.

The integration of AI technologies in veterinary education (VET) programs offers innovative potential for enhancing the effectiveness and efficiency of training experiences. Artificial intelligence (AI)-powered computer vision algorithms, such as those explored by Joslyn and Alexander (2022), can assist in the development of clinically useful and diagnostically accurate tools, empowering veterinarians to assess and interpret medical images with greater precision. Augmented reality (AR) applications, as highlighted by Ifenthaler and Schumacher (2023), can further augment learning by providing immersive, interactive experiences that allow students to engage with complex anatomical structures and procedures in a highly realistic setting.

These emerging technologies hold the promise of creating more personalized, immersive, and agile training experiences. By harnessing the power of generative AI, such as ChatGPT, as demonstrated by Noy and Zhang (2023), VET programs can offer tailored learning materials, personalized feedback, and efficient training simulations. The integration of AI-driven tools into VET programs can also enhance the pedagogical practices of educators, empowering them to create engaging and interactive learning environments. However, it is crucial to acknowledge the challenges that arise with the adoption of AI in education, including concerns about ethics, diversity, and privacy, as raised by Currie et al. (2023). These concerns require careful consideration and the development of ethical guidelines to ensure that AI is used responsibly and in a manner that benefits all stakeholders in the VET community.

Robotics and Automation

The integration of emerging AI technologies into VET systems has the potential to revolutionize the sector. AI technologies such as Explainable AI, Machine Learning, and NLP can enhance effectiveness and efficiency. By harnessing the power of AI, VET systems can offer personalized learning experiences and improve skill development. However, challenges such as infrastructure development, teacher training, and ethical concerns must be addressed. Effective implementation strategies are crucial to maximize the benefits of AI in VET.

Emerging Artificial Intelligence (AI) technologies possess immense potential to revolutionize Vocational Education and Training (VET) systems. By integrating Explainable AI, Transfer Learning, Machine Learning (ML), Natural Language Processing (NLP), Computer Vision, Robotics, and Automation, VET can enhance its effectiveness and efficiency.

AI technologies enable adaptive learning environments tailored to individual student needs (Yang et al., 2022). Facilitate hands-on training in complex environments, fostering practical skills (Khan et al., 2020). NLP and Computer Vision aid in language acquisition and image analysis, respectively (Artifex, 2021; O'Sullivan & Fitzgerald, 2022).

Integrating AI into VET presents opportunities for personalized learning, enhanced skill development, and increased accessibility. However, challenges arise, such as the need for infrastructure development, teacher training, and addressing ethical concerns (Öztürk, 2021).

Overall, AI technologies offer significant potential to transform VET, requiring careful consideration of implementation strategies to maximize their benefits while mitigating potential drawbacks.

APPLICATIONS OF AI IN VET

Personalized Learning and Adaptive Assessments

Artificial intelligence (AI) enhances vocational education and training systems by offering personalized experiences. AI-driven solutions include skill acquisition, simulation training, career guidance, and adaptive assessments tailored to individual needs. These solutions provide interactive learning, foster informed career choices, and enhance learner engagement. However, implementation complexity and concerns over data privacy and algorithmic biases are challenges that must be addressed. Effective deployment of AI-driven solutions can revolutionize VET systems and improve learning outcomes. Artificial intelligence (AI)-driven solutions have emerged as promising tools for enhancing vocational education and training (VET) systems, offering personalized experiences tailored to individual learner needs. These solutions encompass skill acquisition and simulation training, career guidance and job matching, and personalized learning and adaptive assessments.

By using AI, VET systems can provide customized learning paths that cater to each learner's unique strengths and weaknesses (Alqahtani et al., 2023). Skill acquisition and simulation training, enabled by AI, offers immersive and interactive experiences that enhance technical proficiency (Mese, 2023). Career guidance and job matching algorithms analyze learner profiles and labor market trends to provide personalized recommendations, fostering informed career choices (Tavakoli et al., 2022). Personalized learning and adaptive assessments powered by AI empower learners to progress at their own pace and identify areas for improvement (Kumar et al., 2023). This tailored approach enhances learner engagement and motivation, fostering a deeper understanding of the subject matter. Moreover, AI-driven adaptive assessments provide real-time feedback, allowing learners to identify knowledge gaps and adjust their learning strategies accordingly.

However, while AI-driven solutions offer substantial benefits, they also present challenges. Implementation complexity and data privacy concerns are among the hurdles that need to be addressed (Kumar et al., 2023; Mese, 2023). Additionally, concerns regarding ethical implications and algorithmic biases must be carefully considered to ensure fair and equitable access to AI-enhanced VET systems (Alqahtani et al., 2023). Overall, AI-driven solutions present revolutionary opportunities for VET systems, enabling personalized learning experiences, skill acquisition, career guidance, and adaptive assessments. By addressing the associated challenges, we can harness the full potential of AI to enhance vocational education and empower learners to succeed in the modern workforce.

Skill Acquisition and Simulation Training

AI-driven innovations are transforming VET systems with personalized learning, adaptive assessments, and career guidance. Simulation training and immersive experiences improve skills and confidence. AI-powered tools address traditional VET challenges, promoting equity and accessible learning. Challenges of data privacy and algorithmic bias must be addressed to realize AI's full potential. Effective adoption can create a responsive, labor market-relevant educational environment. AI-driven innovations are redefining VET systems, offering personalized learning, adaptive assessments, and career guidance (Alqahtani et al., 2023; Bhutoria, 2022). These advancements empower learners by tailoring learning experiences, enhancing skill acquisition through immersive simulations (Mese, 2023), and providing personalized career guidance (Bhutoria, 2022). Simulation training through AI allows learners to practice skills in realistic virtual environments, improving proficiency and confidence (Mese, 2023). Personalized learning algorithms adjust content to individual needs, ensuring optimal outcomes (Alqahtani et al., 2023). Adaptive assessments monitor progress and adjust difficulty, fostering continuous improvement (Bhutoria, 2022).

These advancements address challenges in traditional VET systems, such as rigid curricula and limited opportunities for individualized learning (Bhutoria, 2022). They promote equity by providing accessible and tailored support, leveling the playing field for learners with diverse learning styles and backgrounds (Alqahtani et al., 2023). However, challenges remain, including data privacy concerns, algorithmic biases, and affordability issues (Bhutoria, 2022). Addressing these challenges is crucial to realizing the full potential of AI-driven innovations in VET systems and creating a more effective, responsive, and labor market-relevant educational environment.

Career Guidance and Job Matching

Innovations in vocational education and training (VET) are on the rise, driven by AI-powered tools that enhance student outcomes and labor market relevance. AI supports skill acquisition, simulation training, and personalized learning. Adaptive assessments identify skill gaps, guiding further learning. These innovations have vast potential but also raise challenges, including implementation costs, teacher training, and data privacy concerns. Effective harnessing of AI-driven approaches can revolutionize VET systems. AI drives advancements in various areas of vocational education and training (VET), revolutionizing how VET systems equip students for the job market. AI-supported skill acquisition, simulation training, individualized learning, and tailored evaluations enhance student outcomes, boost employment relevance, and optimize VET efficiency.

These AI-driven approaches offer distinct advantages. Skill acquisition and simulation training in virtual environments enable students to practice complex tasks, improving their dexterity and decision-making. Tailored learning accommodates individual learning styles and preferences, maximizing knowledge intake and retention (Park et al., 2021). Adaptive assessments not only evaluate knowledge but also identify skill gaps, guiding further learning (QUBES, 2022). Ultimately, these innovations enhance student preparedness, aligning them with industry demands (Lee et al., 2023). Despite their game-changing potential, challenges accompany these AI-driven approaches. Implementation costs can be substantial, and integrating AI into existing VET frameworks may prove arduous (Bakhshandeh et al., 2022). Teacher training is crucial to ensure effective implementation and avoid skill mismatches (Kengkan et al., 2023). Data privacy and ethical considerations must be carefully addressed, as AI-driven systems rely on vast amounts of personal data (ICDE, 2020).

CHALLENGES IN IMPLEMENTING AI IN VET

Data Privacy and Ethical Concerns

Educators and policymakers must integrate AI into vocational education effectively. They need to address concerns around data privacy, educator capacity, and infrastructure costs. Collaboration with law, ethics, and computer science specialists is essential for secure implementation. Clear data handling guidelines and staff training will maximize benefits while ensuring fiscal responsibility. Proactive planning will safeguard student privacy and achieve sustainability. Educators and policymakers must address data privacy concerns to integrate AI effectively into vocational education (Chan, 2023). Collaborative efforts, involving specialists in law, ethics, and computer science, are crucial for implementing AI securely and ethically (Malerbi et al., 2023; Schiff, 2021). Additionally, clear guidelines for data handling and storage are necessary to safeguard student privacy and prevent misuse.

To ensure sustainability, educators must consider infrastructure costs and educator training (Chan, 2023). Ensuring equitable access to AI resources for all students is essential, regardless of their background or financial constraints. Educators also require specialized training to harness AI's potential fully and address the ethical implications of its use (Malerbi et al., 2023). By addressing these concerns proactively, educators and policymakers can create a sturdy AI integration framework that maximizes the benefits of AI while maintaining fiscal responsibility and ensuring ethical and privacy considerations are met (Chan, 2023). This approach will empower educators to prepare students for an AI-driven future, ensuring they have the skills and knowledge to navigate the challenges and opportunities that AI presents.

Lack of Skilled Educators

Implementing AI in veterinary education poses significant challenges, including a shortage of skilled educators with expertise in veterinary medicine, AI technologies, and pedagogical methodologies. This knowledge gap hinders the effective dissemination of AI knowledge and skills to students, limiting their ability to harness AI's full potential. To address this, institutions must invest in faculty training programs that cover both theoretical foundations of AI and practical veterinary applications. Collaboration between veterinary educators and AI experts can also help develop innovative curricula and teaching strategies. By addressing these challenges, institutions can effectively leverage AI-driven instruction to prepare students for the rapidly changing field of veterinary medicine. AI implementation in veterinary education presents significant challenges, one of which is the scarcity of skilled educators. This shortage stems from the need for educators to possess not only expertise in veterinary medicine but also proficiency in AI technologies and pedagogical methodologies for AI-driven instruction.

This knowledge gap can potentially hinder the effective dissemination of AI knowledge and skills to students, thereby limiting their ability to harness the full potential of AI in their professional practice. To address this challenge, educational institutions must invest in faculty training programs that equip educators with the necessary knowledge and skills to teach AI effectively. These programs should encompass both theoretical foundations of AI and practical applications tailored to the veterinary domain. Additionally, fostering collaboration between veterinary educators and AI experts could prove beneficial. By utilizing the expertise of both parties, educational institutions can develop innovative curricula and teaching strategies that seamlessly integrate AI into the veterinary curriculum. This collaborative approach would ensure that students receive a wide-ranging education that empowers them to navigate the rapidly adapting field of AI in veterinary medicine.

Cost and Infrastructure Requirements

Implementing Artificial Intelligence (AI) in Vocational Education and Training (VET) presents various concerns, primarily cost and infrastructure requirements. Significant investment is needed for technology acquisition, educator training, infrastructure upgrades, and ongoing maintenance. Reliable internet connectivity, computing power, and hardware are necessary for AI systems. To address these concerns, educators and policymakers must prioritize educator development, strategic partnerships, and optimized investment. By considering these key requirements, stakeholders can harness the benefits of AI-driven instruction.

The integration of Artificial Intelligence (AI) in Vocational Education and Training (VET) has gained considerable momentum (Gkotsis & Axarloglou, 2020). However, its implementation presents various concerns and requirements (Ashraf et al., 2020; You et al., 2020; Chen et al., 2021; Dou et al., 2021). This subsection will specifically explore key considerations related to cost and infrastructure, examining how educators and policymakers can effectively address these challenges, develop educator capacities, and ensure a balanced investment to harness the groundbreaking potential of AI-driven instruction.

One of the primary concerns associated with AI implementation is its financial implications (Ashraf et al., 2020). Developing and deploying AI systems for VET requires significant investment, encompassing not only the acquisition of technology but also the training of educators, infrastructure upgrades, and ongoing maintenance (Gkotsis & Axarloglou, 2020). Educators and policymakers face the challenge of balancing these investment needs with the potential benefits of AI-driven instruction. Equally critical is the need for hardy infrastructure (Gkotsis & Axarloglou, 2020;

You et al., 2020; Chen et al., 2021; Dou et al., 2021). AI systems require reliable internet connectivity, adequate computing power, and appropriate hardware (Ashraf et al., 2020). In regions with limited resources, these infrastructure requirements may pose a significant obstacle to AI implementation.

Addressing these concerns requires a multi-pronged approach. Educators and policymakers must prioritize the development of educator capabilities through training and professional development programs (You et al., 2020; Dou et al., 2021). Moreover, strategic partnerships with technology providers and industry stakeholders can help optimize investment and ensure sustainable AI adoption (Chen et al., 2021). By carefully considering the cost and infrastructure requirements, and implementing these strategies, stakeholders can effectively harness the groundbreaking potential of AI in VET.

FUTURE TRENDS AND RESEARCH DIRECTIONS

AI Integration in VET Curriculum and Pedagogy

The integration of AI into VET systems can revolutionize student outcomes and labor market relevance. Personalized learning platforms, adaptive assessments, and innovative certification systems can enhance skills and knowledge retention. However, designing AI systems that minimize biases and ensure fairness is crucial. A collaborative approach between educators, industry professionals, and technology providers is essential for a thorough integration of AI in VET. Ongoing research and evaluation will help address the challenges and research gaps.

Artificial intelligence (AI) integration in vocational education and training (VET) systems offers a life-changing opportunity to enhance student outcomes. Personalized learning platforms, adaptive assessments, and innovative certification systems can tailor education to individual needs, improving skills and knowledge retention. This, in turn, increases labor market relevance, enabling graduates to succeed in the rapidly transforming job field.

However, these advancements also present challenges that require careful consideration. AI systems must be designed to minimize biases, ensure fairness, and support equitable access to education for all. Moreover, addressing the research gap in assessing the long-term impact of AI on VET outcomes is crucial to optimize its potential. AI-enabled personalized learning platforms empower students to progress at their own pace, catering to their unique strengths and weaknesses (Alqahtani et al., 2023). Adaptive assessments, driven by AI algorithms, provide real-time feedback, identifying areas for improvement and adjusting the difficulty level accordingly. This cyclical process fosters continuous learning and improves student engagement (Mese, 2023).

Innovative certification systems capitalizing on AI can automate assessment tasks, reducing bias and ensuring consistency in grading (Alqahtani et al., 2023). Digital badges, incorporating AI-powered analytics, provide a wide-ranging record of students' skills and achievements, facilitating recognition of non-traditional learning pathways (Cao, 2023). Integrating AI in VET requires collaboration between educators, industry professionals, and technology providers. A thorough approach that considers curricula redesign, faculty development, and infrastructure enhancements is essential (Xu and Babaian, 2021). Additionally, ongoing research and evaluation are critical to monitor the impact of AI on VET outcomes and ensure continuous improvement. By addressing these challenges and employing the potential of AI, VET systems can empower students with the skills and knowledge they need to thrive in the 21st-century workforce.

AI-Enabled Personalized Learning Platforms

The integration of AI into Vocational Education and Training (VET) holds immense potential to enhance student outcomes, labor market relevance, and equity. Optimizing AI algorithms can maximize learning outcomes. Addressing bias and ensuring equitable access to AI-powered learning opportunities are crucial. Effective integration also requires professional development and support for educators and administrators. By addressing these challenges, AI-enabled learning platforms can transform VET. The integration of AI into Vocational Education and Training (VET) curricula, pedagogy, and assessment systems holds immense potential to enhance student outcomes, labor market relevance, and equity (Childress et al., 2020; Grzeda & Treiber, 2022). AI-powered personalized learning platforms offer tailored learning experiences that cater to diverse student needs and learning styles (Siemens & Polak, 2020). By capitalizing on advanced algorithms and data analytics, these platforms can identify knowledge gaps, provide personalized feedback, and adapt instruction based on student performance (Hwang & Tang, 2021).

However, realizing the full potential of AI in VET requires careful consideration of research gaps and implementation challenges. Key areas for further exploration include optimizing AI algorithms to maximize learning outcomes, addressing bias and discrimination in AI-driven systems, and ensuring equitable access to AI-powered learning opportunities for all students, particularly marginalized groups (Wang et al., 2021). Additionally, addressing the need for professional development and support for educators and administrators to effectively integrate AI into their practices is crucial for successful implementation (Kim & Liu, 2023). By addressing these challenges, AI-enabled personalized learning platforms can transform VET, enhancing student learning, career readiness, and fostering a more inclusive and equitable education system.

AI-Powered Assessment and Certification Systems

The integration of AI into vocational education and training (VET) systems has the potential to revolutionize assessment processes by enhancing objectivity and reducing bias. AI-powered assessments can adapt to students' individual needs, enabling personalized learning experiences. Successful implementation, however, requires addressing challenges such as fairness, algorithmic biases, and data privacy. Research is needed to optimize certification systems, mitigate potential challenges, and explore pedagogical best practices. By harnessing the potential of AI, VET systems can deliver more effective, equitable, and relevant assessment and certification experiences. The integration of AI into VET systems can revolutionize assessment processes (Adiguzel et al., 2023). AI-powered assessments can enhance objectivity, reduce bias, and provide real-time feedback (Noy & Zhang, 2023). These systems can adapt to students' individual needs, enabling personalized learning experiences (Adiguzel et al., 2023; Rad et al., 2023). Moreover, AI-driven certification systems can provide standardized and reliable credentials, validating students' skills and knowledge in a competitive job market (Alqahtani et al., 2023).

However, challenges must be addressed for successful implementation (Adiguzel et al., 2023; Alqahtani et al., 2023). These include ensuring fairness, addressing algorithmic biases, and maintaining data privacy and security (Chan, 2023). Additionally, addressing issues of equity, access, and mobility is crucial to ensure that all students benefit from these advancements (Alqahtani et al., 2023; Noy & Zhang, 2023). Research is needed to explore pedagogical best practices for AI-enhanced assessment, optimize certification systems, and mitigate potential challenges. By harnessing the revolutionary potential of AI while addressing the associated gaps, VET systems can deliver more effective, equitable, and relevant assessment and certification experiences.

Collaboration between AI Researchers and VET Professionals

Integrating AI into vocational education and training (VET) offers opportunities to enhance student outcomes, labor market relevance, and equity. AI can augment VET through personalized learning experiences and data analytics. However, equitable access, bias mitigation, and ethical guidelines are key challenges to address. Effective AI integration in VET requires closing research gaps and collaboration between policymakers and educators. Addressing these challenges and gaps can unlock AI's potential in VET.

Integrating Artificial Intelligence (AI) into vocational education and training (VET) presents significant opportunities to enhance student outcomes, labor market relevance, and equity. Researchers and VET professionals must effectively collaborate to harness AI's potential (Alrifai et al., 2022). AI can augment VET through personalized learning experiences, adaptive assessments, and virtual simulations (Kim et al., 2021). These technologies empower students to learn at their own pace, prepare for real-world scenarios, and develop future-proof skills (Oliver, 2019).

Additionally, AI-powered data analytics can optimize VET programs by identifying skill gaps, tracking student performance, and providing early intervention support (Triventi et al., 2021). By utilizing data-driven insights, VET providers can adapt their curricula and enhance student outcomes. However, realizing AI's potential in VET requires addressing challenges. These include ensuring equitable access, mitigating bias, and developing ethical guidelines to safeguard student privacy and data integrity (Larson, 2022). Furthermore, VET professionals need training to effectively utilize AI in teaching and assessment. By closing research gaps in these areas, policymakers and educators can promote effective AI integration and unlock its fundamental power in VET. This collaboration will foster a future where AI empowers VET students, enhancing their employability and contributions to the progressing digital economy.

Figure 2. Future Trends and Research directions in VET

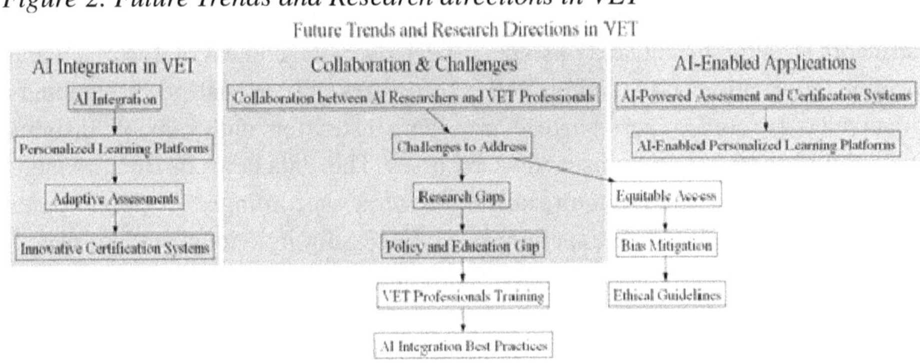

Problem Statements

Therefore, keeping in mind the above-mentioned research directions the problem statements in this domain are focused as follows:

a. Bias in AI algorithms: Ensuring fair assessments and grading are crucial for the success of Bali's Technical and Vocational Education and Training (TVET) programs. The presence of bias in AI algorithms has the capacity to compromise the credibility of assessments and impede the prospects of students in Malaysia's job market.
b. Lack of access to technology: In Malaysia TVET institutions, the presence of high-speed bandwidth and additional facilities like virtual reality hardware and computers is crucial for the successful implementation of AI-enabled learning. The absence of access may exacerbate the digital divide and restrict the efficacy of AI.
c. Overreliance on AI: There is a potential risk for students and educators in Malaysia Technical and Vocational Education and Training (TVET) programs, which could result in a deficiency in critical thinking and problem-solving abilities.
d. Lack of training and support. The implementation of AI technology in TVET sector is particularly difficult due to its novelty and the limited resources available for training initiatives. Ensuring educators and students receive sufficient training and support is essential for empowering them to effectively utilize AI-enabled systems and optimize the advantages of AI integration in TVET.

RESEARCH SCOPE

Assessing the influence of AI-assisted learning on enhancing the capabilities of instructors is an important area of study, especially in the context of Technical and Vocational Education and Training (TVET) programs. AI can analyze vast amounts of data related to student performance, providing instructors with valuable insights into learning patterns, strengths, and weaknesses. This data helps instructors identify at-risk students and tailor their teaching strategies accordingly. AI technologies enable personalized learning experiences. By assessing individual student needs, instructors can design targeted interventions, such as customized assignments or additional resources, which can significantly enhance student engagement and success. With AI tools, instructors can efficiently allocate their time and resources. AI can help identify which students require more attention, allowing instructors to focus on those who need additional support while streamlining instruction for others. AI can provide instructors with recommendations for best practices and innovative teaching strategies based on successful models from similar educational contexts. This support can enhance their teaching effectiveness and adaptability. AI systems can provide instant feedback on student performance, enabling learners to identify areas for improvement quickly. This immediate response allows students to adjust their learning strategies and fosters a proactive approach to skill development.

CONCLUSION

The integration of AI in Vocational Education and Training (VET) has the potential to enhance training programs and create more effective learning experiences. AI can personalize lessons, create simulations, and foster student engagement. To harness its potential, institutions must develop strategies addressing ethical considerations and teacher support. AI can also analyze data to identify areas where students require additional support. Effective AI integration can lead to improved student outcomes and positive social, economic, and environmental impacts. AI integration in Vocational Education and Training (VET) offers significant potential to enhance training programs. Adiguzel et al. (2023) emphasize that AI can create personalized learning experiences by tailoring lessons to individual student needs. By integrating AI into training, educators can create simulations and interactive learning environments (Mese, 2023). These immersive experiences can foster student engagement and improve learning outcomes. VET programs can benefit from AI's ability to analyze vast datasets. By utilizing AI algorithms, educators can identify areas where students require additional support (Adiguzel et al., 2023). This can lead to more targeted and effective training, ultimately improving student outcomes. By integrating AI into VET, stakeholders can address challenges and harness its potential for social, economic, and environmental impacts.

Artificial intelligence can revolutionize vocational education and training by creating personalized learning experiences and enhancing engagement. However, to harness AI's full potential, research on its effective use in VET is needed. Effective integration of AI into VET requires consideration of various contexts and addressing concerns about bias, job displacement, and ethics. Overcoming these challenges can create more responsive and sustainable training programs. Ultimately, AI in VET can drive societal advancement and empower learners.

Artificial intelligence (AI) presents immense potential for VET, enabling the creation of more responsive and sustainable training programs. Through personalized learning experiences, enhanced engagement, and dynamic content updates, AI can revolutionize education, workforce development, and societal progress (Maity, 2019). AI can enhance the effectiveness of VET by providing personalized learning experiences, automating administrative tasks, and offering real-time feedback to learners. Its scalability can extend VET opportunities to underserved populations and remote areas, promoting social equity (Adiguzel et al., 2023). AI can also contribute to economic growth by developing a skilled workforce that meets industry demands

(Ifenthaler and Schumacher, 2023). However, ethical challenges and algorithmic biases must be addressed to maximize AI's potential in VET. AI systems should be designed with fairness and transparency in mind, and educators and policymakers must be trained to use AI effectively (Adiguzel et al., 2023; Alqahtani et al., 2023). By harnessing AI's capabilities and addressing its challenges, VET can be revolutionized, empowering learners and preparing them for the demands of the 21st-century workforce.

REFERENCES

Adiguzel, T., Kaya, M. H., & Cansu, F. K. (2023). Revolutionizing education with AI: Exploring the transformative potential of ChatGPT. [Online]. *Contemporary Educational Technology*, 15(3), ep429. Advance online publication. DOI: 10.30935/cedtech/13152

Ahmed, U. (2014) Remarks by Usman Ahmed. Proceedings of the ASIL Annual Meeting. [Online]. Available: http://dx.doi.org/DOI: 10.5305/procannmeetasil.108.0348

Alqahtani, T., Badreldin, H. A., Alrashed, M., Alshaya, A. I., Alghamdi, S. S., bin Saleh, K., Alowais, S. A., Alshaya, O. A., Rahman, I., Al Yami, M. S., & Albekairy, A. M. (2023, August). bin Saleh, K., Alowais, S. A., Alshaya, O. A., Rahman, I., Al Yami, M. S. and Albekairy, A. M. (2023) The emergent role of artificial intelligence, natural learning processing, and large language models in higher education and research. [Online]. *Research in Social & Administrative Pharmacy*, 19(8), 1236–1242. Advance online publication. DOI: 10.1016/j.sapharm.2023.05.016 PMID: 37321925

Amer-Yahia, S. (2022) Towards AI-powered data-driven education. Proceedings of the VLDB Endowment. [Online]. Available: http://dx.doi.org/DOI: 10.14778/3554821.3554900

Bhutoria, A. (2022). Personalized education and Artificial Intelligence in the United States, China, and India: A systematic review using a Human-In-The-Loop model. Computers and Education [Online]. *Artificial Intelligence*, 3, 100068. Advance online publication. DOI: 10.1016/j.caeai.2022.100068

Bizzo, B. C., Dasegowda, G., Bridge, C., Miller, B., Hillis, J. M., Kalra, M. K., Durniak, K., Stout, M., Schultz, T., Alkasab, T., & Dreyer, K. J. (2023). Addressing the Challenges of Implementing Artificial Intelligence Tools in Clinical Practice: Principles From Experience. [Online]. *Journal of the American College of Radiology*, 20(3), 352–360. Advance online publication. DOI: 10.1016/j.jacr.2023.01.002 PMID: 36922109

Cao, X. (2023) Case Study of China-s Compulsory Education System: AI Apps and Extracurricular Dance Learning. International Journal of Human-€"Computer Interaction. [Online]. Available: http://dx.doi.org/.DOI: 10.1080/10447318.2023.2188539

Chan, C. K. Y. (2023). A comprehensive AI policy education framework for university teaching and learning. [Online]. *International Journal of Educational Technology in Higher Education*, 20(1), 38. Advance online publication. DOI: 10.1186/s41239-023-00408-3

Cohen, E. B., & Gordon, I. K. (2022). First, do no harm. Ethical and legal issues of artificial intelligence and machine learning in veterinary radiology and radiation oncology. Veterinary Radiology &amp [Online]. *Ultrasound*, 63(S1), 840–850. Advance online publication. DOI: 10.1111/vru.13171 PMID: 36514231

Corsini, A. (2022). *Welcome to European Atherosclerosis Journal, a new Open Access Journal: European Atherosclerosis Journal, a new Open Access Journal.* European Atherosclerosis Journal. [Online], DOI: 10.56095/eaj.v1i1.6

Currie, G., Hespel, A., & Carstens, A. (2023). Australian perspectives on artificial intelligence in veterinary practice. Veterinary Radiology &amp [Online]. *Ultrasound*, 64(3), 473–483. Advance online publication. DOI: 10.1111/vru.13234 PMID: 37022301

Denny, P., Becker, B. A., Leinonen, J., & Prather, J. (2023) Chat Overflow: Artificially Intelligent Models for Computing Education - renAIssance or apocAIypse? *Proceedings of the 2023 Conference on Innovation and Technology in Computer Science Education* V. 1. [Online]. Available: DOI: 10.1145/3587102.3588773

Feeney, B., Zuccarini, M., Singh, T., Aldewereld, H., Marrone, S., & Quille, K. (2022) Developing a Human Centred AI Masters. *Proceedings of the 27th ACM Conference on on Innovation and Technology in Computer Science Education* Vol. 2. [Online]. Available: DOI: 10.1145/3502717.3532120

Frehywot, S., & Vovides, Y. (2023). An equitable and sustainable community of practice framework to address the use of artificial intelligence for global health workforce training. [Online]. *Human Resources for Health*, 21(1), 45. Advance online publication. DOI: 10.1186/s12960-023-00833-5 PMID: 37312214

Gibson, D., Kovanovic, V., Ifenthaler, D., Dexter, S., & Feng, S. (2023). Learning theories for artificial intelligence promoting learning processes. [Online]. *British Journal of Educational Technology*, 54(5), 1125–1146. Advance online publication. DOI: 10.1111/bjet.13341

Guleria, P., & Sood, M. (2022). Explainable AI and machine learning: Performance evaluation and explainability of classifiers on educational data mining inspired career counseling. [Online]. *Education and Information Technologies*. Advance online publication. DOI: 10.1007/s10639-022-11221-2 PMID: 35875826

GurriarÃ¡n, R. (2007) Alejandro Otero. Ãlbum de Galicia. [Online]. Available: .DOI: 10.17075/adg.2007.22182

Ifenthaler, D., & Schumacher, C. (2023). Reciprocal issues of artificial and human intelligence inÂ education. [Online]. *Journal of Research on Technology in Education*, 55(1), 1–6. Advance online publication. DOI: 10.1080/15391523.2022.2154511

Iqbal, S., Ahmad, S., Akkour, K., Wafa, A. N. A., AlMutairi, H. M., & Aldhufairi, A. M. (2021). Review article: Impact of Artificial Intelligence in Medical Education. [Online]. *MedEdPublish*, 10(1). Advance online publication. DOI: 10.15694/mep.2021.000041.1

Joslyn, S., & Alexander, K. (2022). Evaluating artificial intelligence algorithms for use in veterinary radiology. Veterinary Radiology &amp [Online]. *Ultrasound*, 63(S1), 871–879. Advance online publication. DOI: 10.1111/vru.13159 PMID: 36514228

Khosravi, H., Shum, S. B., Chen, G., Conati, C., Tsai, Y.-S., Kay, J., Knight, S., Martinez-Maldonado, R., Sadiq, S., & Gašević, D. (2022). Explainable Artificial Intelligence in education. Computers and Education [Online]. *Artificial Intelligence*, 3, 100074. Advance online publication. DOI: 10.1016/j.caeai.2022.100074

Kumar, R., Sexena, A., & Gehlot, A. (2023) Artificial Intelligence in Smart Education and Futuristic Challenges. 2023 International Conference on Disruptive Technologies (ICDT). [Online]. Available: http://dx.doi.org/DOI: 10.1109/ICDT57929.2023.10151129

Li, M. D., & Little, B. P. (2023). Appropriate Reliance on Artificial Intelligence in Radiology Education. [Online]. *Journal of the American College of Radiology*, 20(11), 1126–1130. Advance online publication. DOI: 10.1016/j.jacr.2023.04.019 PMID: 37392983

Maity, S. (2019). Identifying opportunities for artificial intelligence in the evolution of training and development practices. [Online]. *Journal of Management Development*, 38(8), 651–663. Advance online publication. DOI: 10.1108/JMD-03-2019-0069

Malerbi, F. K., Nakayama, L. F., Gayle Dychiao, R., Zago Ribeiro, L., Villanueva, C., Celi, L. A., & Regatieri, C. V. (2023). Digital Education for the Deployment of Artificial Intelligence in Health Care. [Online]. *Journal of Medical Internet Research*, 25, e43333. Advance online publication. DOI: 10.2196/43333 PMID: 37347537

Menekse, M. (2023). Envisioning the future of learning and teaching engineering in the artificial intelligence era: Opportunities and challenges. [Online]. *Journal of Engineering Education*, 112(3), 578–582. Advance online publication. DOI: 10.1002/jee.20539

Mese, I. (2023). The Impact of Artificial Intelligence on Radiology Education in the Wake of Coronavirus Disease 2019. [Online]. *Korean Journal of Radiology*, 24(5), 478. Advance online publication. DOI: 10.3348/kjr.2023.0278 PMID: 37133214

Noy, S., & Zhang, W. (2023) Experimental Evidence on the Productivity Effects of Generative Artificial Intelligence. SSRN Electronic Journal. [Online]. Available: http://dx.doi.org/DOI: 10.2139/ssrn.4375283

Rad, H. S., Alipour, R., & Jafarpour, A. (2023). Using artificial intelligence to foster students- writing feedback literacy, engagement, and outcome: A case of Wordtune application. [Online]. *Interactive Learning Environments*. Advance online publication. DOI: 10.1080/10494820.2023.2208170

Schiff, D. (2021). Education for AI, not AI for Education: The Role of Education and Ethics in National AI Policy Strategies. [Online]. *International Journal of Artificial Intelligence in Education*. Advance online publication. DOI: 10.1007/s40593-021-00270-2

Sousa, M. L. (2023) Santos, Manuel Pimentel Pereira dos. DicionÃ¡rio BiogrÃ¡fico de Cientistas, Engenheiros e MÃ©dicos em Portugal. [Online]. Available: http://dx.doi.org/.DOI: 10.58277/SUFF8895

Suzuki, K. (2020). AI: A New Open Access Journal for Artificial Intelligence. [Online]. *AI*, 1(2), 141–142. Advance online publication. DOI: 10.3390/ai1020007

Tanveer, M., Hassan, S., & Bhaumik, A. (2020). Academic Policy Regarding Sustainability and Artificial Intelligence (AI). [Online]. *Sustainability (Basel)*, 12(22), 9435. Advance online publication. DOI: 10.3390/su12229435

Tavakoli, M., Faraji, A., Vrolijk, J., Molavi, M., Mol, S. T., & Kismih, Ã. (2022, April). [3]k, G. (2022) An AI-based open recommender system for personalized labor market driven education. [Online]. *Advanced Engineering Informatics*, 52, 101508. Advance online publication. DOI: 10.1016/j.aei.2021.101508

Wang, C., Zhu, H., Wang, P., Zhu, C., Zhang, X., Chen, E., & Xiong, H. (2021). Personalized and Explainable Employee Training Course Recommendations: A Bayesian Variational Approach. [Online]. *ACM Transactions on Information Systems*. Advance online publication. DOI: 10.1145/3490476

Xu, J. J., & Babaian, T. (2021). Artificial intelligence in business curriculum: The pedagogy and learning outcomes. [Online]. *International Journal of Management Education*, 19(3), 100550. Advance online publication. DOI: 10.1016/j.ijme.2021.100550

Xu, W., & Ouyang, F. (2021). A systematic review of AI role in the educational system based on a proposed conceptual framework. [Online]. *Education and Information Technologies*. Advance online publication. DOI: 10.1007/s10639-021-10774-y

Yilmaz, R., Bakhaidar, M., Alsayegh, A., & Del Maestro, R. (2023). O022 Real-time artificial intelligence instructor vs expert instruction in teaching of expert level tumour resection skills - a randomized controlled trial. [Online]. *British Journal of Surgery*, 110(Supplement_3), znad101.022. Advance online publication. DOI: 10.1093/bjs/znad101.022

You, Y., Chen, Y., You, Y., Zhang, Q., & Cao, Q. (2023). Evolutionary Game Analysis of Artificial Intelligence Such as the Generative Pre-Trained Transformer in Future Eduscation. [Online]. *Sustainability (Basel)*, 15(12), 9355. Advance online publication. DOI: 10.3390/su15129355

ADDITIONAL READING

Collis, B. (2002). Information technologies for education and training. In *Handbook on information technologies for education and training* (pp. 1–20). Springer Berlin Heidelberg. DOI: 10.1007/978-3-662-07682-8_1

Ghosh, L., & Ravichandran, R. (2024). Emerging Technologies in Vocational Education and Training. *Journal of Digital Learning and Education*, 4(1), 41–49. DOI: 10.52562/jdle.v4i1.975

Rosyadi, M. I., Kustiawan, I., Tetehfio, E. O., & Joshua, Q. (2023). The Role of AI In Vocational Education: A Systematic Literature Review. *Journal of Vocational Education Studies*, 6(2), 244–263. DOI: 10.12928/joves.v6i2.9032

Xie, H., Tao, L., & Xie, L. (2024, February). Research on prospective scope and approaches of artificial intelligence education in vocational college of China. In *3rd International Conference on Education, Language and Art (ICELA 2023)* (pp. 484-492). Atlantis Press. DOI: 10.2991/978-2-38476-214-9_59

KEY TERMS AND DEFINITIONS

Adaptive Learning Systems: Educational technologies that adjust the learning content based on the learner's performance and progress, offering personalized instruction to meet individual needs.

Artificial Intelligence (AI): The simulation of human intelligence processes by machines, particularly computer systems, which includes learning, reasoning, and self-correction to enhance decision-making and task automation.

Augmented Reality (AR): A technology that overlays digital content such as images, sounds, or other data on the real-world environment, enhancing the learning experience with interactive, immersive elements.

Computer Vision (CV): A field of AI that enables machines to interpret and make decisions based on visual data from the environment, such as recognizing objects, interpreting images, and guiding robotics.

Data Privacy: The protection of personal information in digital systems, ensuring that data collected from users or learners is securely stored and used, with respect to legal and ethical standards.

Explainable AI (XAI): A set of techniques in AI designed to make the outputs of AI systems understandable to humans, ensuring transparency and trust in decision-making processes.

Machine Learning (ML): A subset of AI focused on developing algorithms that enable systems to learn from data, improving over time without explicit programming, often used for pattern recognition and predictive analytics.

Natural Language Processing (NLP): A branch of AI that enables machines to understand, interpret, and generate human language, facilitating tasks such as speech recognition, sentiment analysis, and chatbot interaction.

Personalized Learning: An educational approach that tailors learning experiences to individual students' strengths, needs, and preferences, often enhanced by AI-driven tools that adjust content delivery accordingly.

Robotics and Automation: The use of robots and automated systems powered by AI to perform tasks traditionally done by humans, particularly in industries requiring precision, repetitive tasks, or dangerous work environments.

Chapter 4
Virtual Reality (VR) and Augmented Reality (AR) in Vocational Training

Rajiv Iyer
https://orcid.org/0000-0002-1136-2061
Amity University, Mumbai, India

Vedprakash Chandrakant Maralapalle
https://orcid.org/0000-0002-7770-1134
Amity University, Maharashtra, India

Poornima Mahesh
https://orcid.org/0009-0004-9364-1866
N.R.B. College, University of Mumbai, India

ABSTRACT

This chapter examines the transformative impact of Virtual Reality (VR) and Augmented Reality (AR) technologies on vocational education and training (VET). By providing immersive and interactive learning environments, VR and AR enhance skill development, improve knowledge retention, and facilitate the practical application of concepts in vocational training. These technologies enable the simulation of real-world scenarios, allowing trainees to safely practice complex tasks such as operating machinery or performing medical procedures, thereby boosting safety and confidence. AR adds value by overlaying digital information onto physical tasks, offering real-time guidance in industries requiring precision and hands-on expertise. Furthermore, the chapter underscores the potential of VR and AR in promoting remote learning and accessibility, empowering trainees to engage with high-quality simulations and training programs from virtually any location.

DOI: 10.4018/979-8-3693-8252-3.ch004

INTRODUCTION

In the rapidly evolving landscape of technology, Virtual Reality (VR) and Augmented Reality (AR) have emerged as transformative tools in various sectors, including education and training. These immersive technologies are reshaping how individuals acquire skills and knowledge, particularly in vocational training environments where hands-on experience is paramount. Virtual Reality (VR) and Augmented Reality (AR) technologies are rapidly transforming the landscape of education and training across various sectors. These immersive technologies offer unprecedented opportunities to revolutionize the way vocational skills are taught, practiced, and mastered. As industries evolve and the demand for specialized skills grows, traditional training methods are often challenged to keep pace with the changing needs of the workforce. VR and AR present innovative solutions to bridge this gap, providing realistic, interactive, and engaging learning experiences that can significantly enhance the effectiveness of vocational education and training programs. This chapter delves into the integration of VR and AR technologies in vocational training, exploring their potential to reshape skill development and prepare learners for the complexities of modern workplaces. We will examine how these technologies can simulate real-world environments, offer hands-on practice in safe settings, and provide personalized learning experiences tailored to individual needs. Additionally, we will discuss the challenges and considerations in implementing VR and AR in vocational education, including technological requirements, pedagogical adaptations, and the need for continuous updating to reflect industry advancements. By leveraging the power of immersive technologies, vocational training can become more accessible, efficient, and aligned with industry demands. This chapter aims to provide educators, trainers, and policymakers with insights into the transformative potential of VR and AR, guiding them in harnessing these tools to create more effective and engaging vocational education and training programs for the workforce of tomorrow (Liu, Zhan, & Zhao, 2023; Chiang, Shang, & Qiao, 2022).

Overview of VR and AR Technologies

Virtual Reality (VR) refers to a computer-generated simulation that immerses users in a fully interactive three-dimensional environment. By wearing VR headsets, users can experience and interact with a virtual world that replicates real-life scenarios or entirely imaginative settings. This technology primarily engages the senses of sight and sound, providing a sense of presence that can significantly enhance learning experiences. Augmented Reality (AR), on the other hand, overlays digital information onto the real world, enhancing the user's perception of their environment. AR can be experienced through smartphones, tablets, or AR glasses, which display virtual elements such as images, information, or animations superimposed on the physical world. This technology allows learners to interact with both real and virtual elements simultaneously, facilitating a more contextual and enriched learning experience. Both VR and AR technologies utilize advanced graphics, sensors, and artificial intelligence to create engaging and interactive environments. As they continue to develop, their applications in vocational training are becoming increasingly sophisticated, offering innovative solutions to traditional educational challenges (Ravichandran & Mahapatra, 2023). Figure 1 shows Overview of VR and AR Technologies.

Figure 1. Overview of VR and AR Technologies

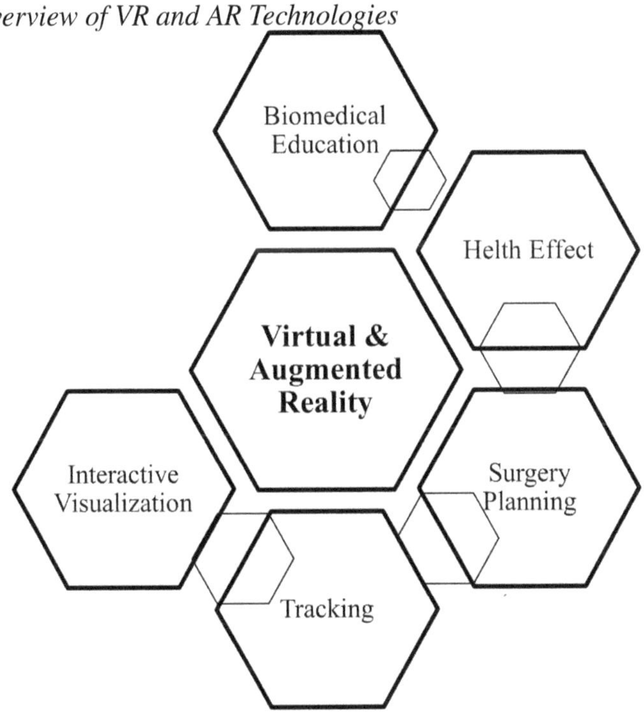

Potential of VR and AR in Vocational Education and Training

The potential of VR and AR in vocational education and training is vast and multifaceted. Here are several key benefits that these technologies bring to the field:

1. **Enhanced Engagement and Motivation:** VR and AR create immersive experiences that capture learners' attention and foster a deeper connection to the material. This heightened engagement can lead to increased motivation and a more enjoyable learning process.
2. **Safe Learning Environments:** Both VR and AR allow learners to practice skills in a controlled, risk-free setting. For instance, trainees in fields such as healthcare, construction, or aviation can simulate high-stakes scenarios without the dangers associated with real-life practice.
3. **Realistic Simulations:** VR can replicate complex environments and situations, providing learners with realistic training that closely mirrors actual job conditions. This experiential learning helps build confidence and competence before entering the workforce.
4. **Personalized Learning Experiences:** AR can tailor learning experiences to individual needs by providing contextual information and guidance based on the learner's current task [11]. This adaptability supports diverse learning styles and paces.
5. **Cost-Effectiveness:** While the initial investment in VR and AR technology can be significant, these tools can reduce costs in the long run by minimizing the need for physical materials, travel, and instructor-led training sessions.
6. **Global Accessibility:** VR and AR training programs can be accessed remotely, breaking down geographical barriers and allowing learners from various locations to benefit from high-quality vocational training.
7. The integration of VR and AR in vocational education and training holds immense promise for enhancing the effectiveness and accessibility of skill development. As these technologies continue to evolve, they will likely play an increasingly critical role in preparing the workforce of the future (Arief, Wibawanto, & Nastiti, 2023).

Applications of VR and AR in Vocational Training

The integration of Virtual Reality (VR) and Augmented Reality (AR) into vocational training is revolutionizing how skills are taught and learned across various industries. By providing immersive and interactive experiences, these technologies enhance the training process, making it more effective and engaging. This chapter explores the diverse applications of VR and AR in key vocational sectors, highlighting their transformative impact on education and training (Kablitz, Conrad, & Schumann, 2023).

Healthcare

The healthcare sector has been one of the most significant beneficiaries of VR and AR technologies. These tools are being utilized in various ways to improve training for medical professionals:

1. **Surgical Training:** VR simulations allow medical students and professionals to practice surgical techniques in a risk-free environment. Programs can replicate complex procedures, enabling learners to gain hands-on experience and develop their skills without endangering patients.
2. **Patient Interaction:** AR can enhance the training of healthcare providers by overlaying information about patient conditions or anatomy during simulations. This contextual learning helps trainees understand how to interact with patients more effectively.
3. **Emergency Response:** VR scenarios can simulate emergency situations, training healthcare workers in critical thinking and decision-making under pressure. This prepares them for real-life emergencies where quick, accurate responses are crucial.
4. **Mental Health Treatment:** VR is also being explored for therapeutic purposes, such as exposure therapy for patients with anxiety disorders. Trainees can learn to administer these therapies while understanding the psychological aspects involved (Gonçalves & Vilas Boas, 2012).

Manufacturing

In the manufacturing industry, VR and AR are enhancing training processes and operational efficiency:

1. **Equipment Operation:** VR simulations can provide operators with hands-on training on complex machinery without the risk of accidents or damage. Trainees can familiarize themselves with equipment controls and safety protocols in a safe environment.
2. **Maintenance Training:** AR can assist technicians by overlaying digital instructions and schematics onto physical equipment. This real-time guidance helps them troubleshoot issues and perform maintenance tasks more effectively.
3. **Assembly Line Training:** VR can simulate assembly line processes, allowing workers to practice their roles in a controlled setting. This prepares them for the fast-paced nature of manufacturing environments, improving productivity and reducing errors.

4. **Safety Training:** VR can simulate hazardous scenarios that workers may encounter on the job, such as chemical spills or equipment malfunctions. This immersive training helps employees learn to respond appropriately to emergencies.

Construction

The construction industry is leveraging VR and AR to improve training and project management:

1. **Site Simulations:** VR can create detailed simulations of construction sites, allowing trainees to explore and understand site layouts, equipment use, and safety protocols before stepping onto a real site.
2. **Safety Training:** AR can enhance safety training by providing real-time hazard identification and safety reminders while workers are on-site. This proactive approach helps reduce accidents and improve compliance with safety regulations.
3. **Collaborative Design:** AR allows architects and construction teams to visualize and manipulate 3D models of buildings in real-world settings. This collaborative design process enhances communication and ensures that all stakeholders are aligned on project goals.
4. **Skill Development:** VR can simulate various construction tasks, such as operating heavy machinery or performing specific trades like plumbing or electrical work. This hands-on practice helps trainees develop essential skills before working on actual projects.

Aviation

The aviation industry is at the forefront of adopting VR and AR for training purposes:

1. **Pilot Training:** Flight simulators using VR technology provide aspiring pilots with realistic flying experiences. These simulations can replicate various flight conditions and emergency scenarios, allowing pilots to practice their skills in a safe environment.
2. **Maintenance and Repair:** AR can assist aircraft technicians by overlaying maintenance manuals and schematics onto the physical aircraft. This real-time information helps technicians perform repairs more accurately and efficiently.
3. **Cabin Crew Training:** VR can simulate in-flight scenarios for cabin crew training, including emergency evacuations and passenger interactions. This immersive training prepares crew members for real-life situations they may encounter during flights.

4. **Air Traffic Control:** VR simulations can train air traffic controllers by recreating busy air traffic scenarios. This training helps controllers develop their decision-making skills and learn to manage multiple aircraft simultaneously (Goertz, Hagenhofer, & Fehling, 2021).

Other Vocational Domains

Beyond the key industries mentioned, VR and AR are making strides in various other vocational domains:

1. **Hospitality and Tourism:** VR can provide immersive training experiences for hotel staff, allowing them to practice customer service skills and familiarize themselves with hotel layouts. AR can enhance guided tours by overlaying historical information or interactive elements for tourists.
2. **Education and Training:** Educators can use VR and AR to create engaging learning experiences for students in fields such as arts, sciences, and trades. These technologies can simulate real-world applications of theoretical concepts, enhancing understanding and retention (Arief, Wibawanto, & Nastiti, 2023).
3. **Retail:** AR applications are being used in retail training to help employees learn about products and customer service techniques. Virtual simulations can prepare staff for various customer interactions and sales scenarios.
4. **Information Technology:** VR can be used to train IT professionals in cybersecurity by simulating cyberattacks and teaching them how to respond effectively. AR can assist in troubleshooting hardware issues by overlaying instructions on physical devices.

1. As these technologies continue to evolve, we are seeing emerging trends that promise even more sophisticated applications in the future. The integration of Artificial Intelligence and Machine Learning with VR and AR is opening up possibilities for more adaptive and personalized training experiences. Advancements in haptic feedback and sensory enhancements are making virtual experiences increasingly realistic. The development of Mixed Reality (MR) applications, combining elements of both VR and AR, is creating new possibilities for blended learning environments. Mobile AR applications are making on-the-job training and support more accessible and immediate. However, the implementation of VR and AR in vocational training is not without challenges. There are considerations around hardware and software requirements, content development and maintenance, user adoption and acceptance, and ethical implications including data privacy (Borenstein & Howard, 2021). Despite these challenges, the potential benefits of VR and AR in enhancing vocational training are substantial, promising a future where immersive, engaging,

and effective training experiences are the norm across all industries. In conclusion, the applications of VR and AR in vocational training are diverse and impactful. By providing immersive, engaging, and realistic training experiences, these technologies are reshaping how skills are taught and learned across various industries. As VR and AR continue to evolve, their potential to enhance vocational education will only grow, paving the way for a more skilled and prepared workforce (Liu, Zhan, & Zhao, 2023).

PEDAGOGICAL ADVANTAGES OF VR AND AR IN VOCATIONAL EDUCATION AND TRAINING

The integration of Virtual Reality (VR) and Augmented Reality (AR) in vocational education and training (VET) has brought about significant pedagogical advantages that enhance the learning process and outcomes. These technologies provide learners with engaging, interactive, and immersive experiences that foster active learning, skill development, problem-solving, and critical thinking. This chapter explores the key pedagogical advantages of VR and AR in VET, highlighting how they contribute to the effectiveness and efficiency of vocational training programs.

Active Learning and Skill Development

VR and AR promote active learning by engaging learners in hands-on, experiential activities that simulate real-world scenarios. This immersive approach encourages learners to actively participate in the learning process, applying their knowledge and skills in a practical setting. By engaging in these simulations, learners develop a deeper understanding of the subject matter and gain valuable experience in applying their skills.

Moreover, VR and AR provide learners with opportunities to practice and refine their skills in a safe and controlled environment. This allows them to make mistakes, learn from their experiences, and improve their performance without the consequences of real-world errors. The repetitive nature of these simulations helps learners develop muscle memory and automaticity, which are essential for the mastery of vocational skills (Akgun & Greenhow, 2022).

Problem-Solving and Critical Thinking

VR and AR simulations often present learners with complex, real-world problems that require critical thinking and problem-solving skills. These challenges encourage learners to analyze situations, identify potential issues, and develop effective solutions. By engaging in these problem-solving exercises, learners develop their ability to think critically, make informed decisions, and adapt to changing circumstances.

Furthermore, VR and AR simulations can expose learners to a wide range of scenarios, including rare or high-risk situations that may be difficult to replicate in a traditional training setting. By confronting these challenges in a safe environment, learners can develop their problem-solving skills and learn to respond effectively to unexpected situations.

Risk-Free Practice Environments

One of the most significant advantages of VR and AR in VET is the ability to provide learners with risk-free practice environments. Vocational training often involves working with hazardous materials, operating heavy machinery, or engaging in high-stakes scenarios. In a traditional training setting, these activities can pose significant risks to learners and instructors.

VR and AR simulations eliminate these risks by creating virtual environments where learners can practice their skills without the danger of real-world consequences. This allows learners to explore, experiment, and learn from their mistakes without fear of causing harm or damage. By providing a safe and supportive learning environment, VR and AR can boost learners' confidence, reduce anxiety, and encourage them to take risks and try new approaches (Borenstein & Howard, 2021).

Personalized Learning Experiences

VR and AR technologies have the potential to provide personalized learning experiences tailored to individual learners' needs, abilities, and learning styles. By leveraging data analytics and adaptive learning algorithms, VR and AR systems can adjust the difficulty, content, and pacing of simulations based on each learner's performance and progress.

This personalization allows learners to work at their own pace, focusing on areas where they need the most support while challenging themselves in areas where they excel. Adaptive learning systems can also provide real-time feedback and guidance to learners, helping them identify areas for improvement and providing targeted support to address their specific needs.

Moreover, VR and AR can accommodate diverse learning styles by offering multiple modes of interaction and presentation. Learners can choose to engage with simulations through visual, auditory, or kinesthetic modalities, depending on their preferences and learning needs. This flexibility ensures that all learners can access and benefit from the learning content, promoting inclusivity and accessibility in vocational training. The pedagogical advantages of VR and AR in VET are significant and far-reaching. By promoting active learning, skill development, problem-solving, and personalized experiences, these technologies have the potential to revolutionize vocational training and prepare learners for success in their chosen fields. As VR and AR continue to evolve and become more widely adopted, their impact on vocational education will only grow, leading to a more skilled, adaptable, and resilient workforce (Zouaghi, 2019).

CHALLENGES AND CONSIDERATIONS IN IMPLEMENTING VR AND AR IN VOCATIONAL EDUCATION AND TRAINING

While the integration of Virtual Reality (VR) and Augmented Reality (AR) in vocational education and training (VET) offers numerous advantages, it also presents a range of challenges and considerations that educators, institutions, and policymakers must address. Successful implementation requires careful planning, investment, and a commitment to overcoming potential obstacles (Ravichandran & Mahapatra, 2023). This chapter explores the key challenges associated with adopting VR and AR in VET, including costs, training needs, curriculum integration, and ethical concerns.

Figure 2. Challenges with VR in education

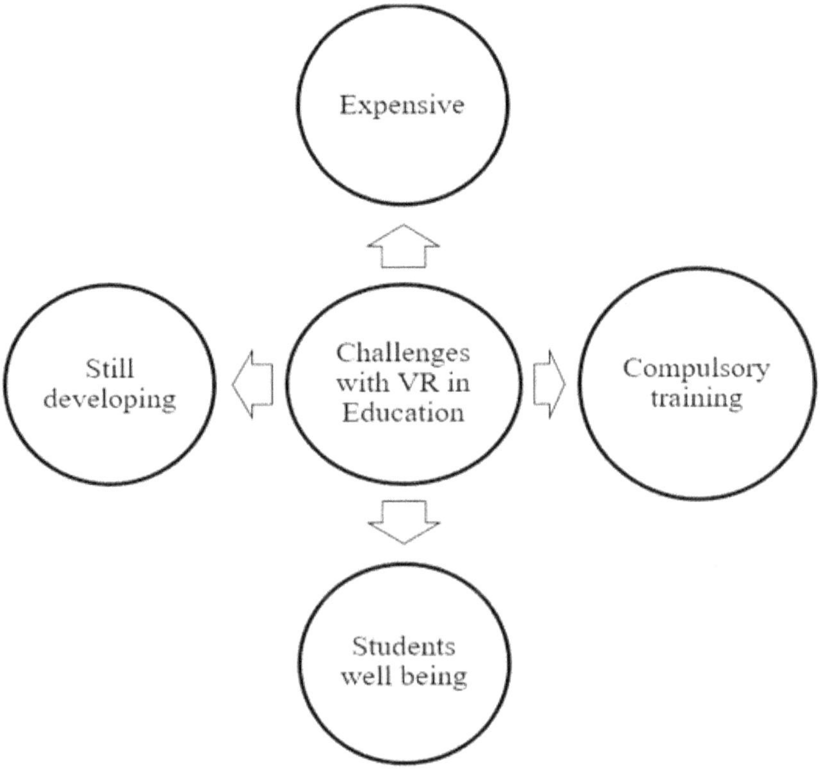

Cost of Hardware and Software

One of the most significant challenges in implementing VR and AR technologies in VET is the cost associated with acquiring the necessary hardware and software. High-quality VR headsets, AR devices, and the software required to create and run simulations can be expensive. For many educational institutions, particularly those with limited budgets, these costs can be prohibitive.

Additionally, ongoing maintenance and updates for hardware and software can add to the financial burden. Institutions must also consider the costs of developing custom content tailored to their specific training needs, which may require hiring external developers or investing in training for in-house staff. To mitigate these costs, institutions can explore partnerships with technology providers, seek grants or funding opportunities, and consider sharing resources with other educational organizations. However, careful budgeting and financial planning are essential to ensure the sustainability of VR and AR initiatives in VET (Al-Ansi, Jaboob, Garad, & Al-Ansi, 2023).

Specialized Training for Instructors

The successful implementation of VR and AR in VET requires instructors who are not only skilled in their subject matter but also proficient in using these technologies. Specialized training for instructors is essential to ensure they can effectively integrate VR and AR into their teaching practices and provide meaningful learning experiences for their students.

Instructors may need to learn new pedagogical approaches that leverage the unique capabilities of VR and AR, as well as become familiar with the technical aspects of operating the equipment and software. This additional training can be time-consuming and may require significant investment from institutions. Simulation and immersive virtual reality (IVR) training are becoming increasingly important in vocational education and training (VET). However, while IVR has been primarily studied and used in the technical field, its implementation and effectiveness in business education remains poorly explored. Furthermore, the onset of motion sickness has been frequently reported when using IVR, which should be considered more carefully from a teaching and learning perspective as it may interfere with cognitive processes.

To address this challenge, institutions should provide comprehensive professional development opportunities for instructors, including workshops, hands-on training sessions, and ongoing support. Encouraging collaboration among instructors can also facilitate knowledge sharing and help build a community of practice focused on the effective use of VR and AR in VET (Ghosh & Ravichandran, 2024).

Integration into Existing Curricula

Integrating VR and AR into existing curricula can be a complex and challenging process. Educators must carefully consider how to align these technologies with learning objectives and ensure that they complement traditional teaching methods rather than replace them. This requires a thoughtful approach to curriculum design that incorporates VR and AR in a way that enhances the overall learning experience.

Additionally, educators must address the potential resistance from stakeholders who may be skeptical about the effectiveness of VR and AR compared to traditional training methods. Demonstrating the value of these technologies through pilot programs, research, and data on learning outcomes can help build support for their integration.

Collaboration among faculty, curriculum developers, and industry partners is essential to create a cohesive and relevant curriculum that effectively incorporates VR and AR. By involving all stakeholders in the planning process, institutions can ensure that these technologies are used to their fullest potential and aligned with industry needs.

Ethical Concerns (Privacy, Data Security, Bias)

As with any technology, the use of VR and AR in VET raises important ethical considerations that must be addressed. Key concerns include:

1. **Privacy:** VR and AR systems often collect data on user interactions, preferences, and performance. Institutions must ensure that they have robust privacy policies in place to protect learners' personal information and comply with relevant regulations.
2. **Data Security:** The storage and transmission of sensitive data pose risks that institutions must manage. Implementing strong cybersecurity measures is essential to safeguard against data breaches and unauthorized access to learner information (Akgun & Greenhow, 2022).
3. **Bias:** The design and content of VR and AR simulations can inadvertently reflect biases present in the data used to create them. This can lead to unequal learning experiences for different groups of learners. Institutions must be vigilant in reviewing and testing content for bias and ensuring that it is inclusive and representative of diverse perspectives.

To address these ethical concerns, institutions should establish clear policies and guidelines for the use of VR and AR technologies in VET. This includes conducting regular audits of data practices, providing training on ethical considerations for instructors and developers, and fostering a culture of transparency and accountability. In conclusion, while the implementation of VR and AR in vocational education and training offers significant potential, it is essential to navigate the associated challenges and considerations carefully. By addressing issues related to cost, instructor training, curriculum integration, and ethical concerns, institutions can create a supportive environment that maximizes the benefits of these technologies and enhances the overall quality of vocational training. As the field continues to evolve, ongoing evaluation and adaptation will be necessary to ensure that VR and AR remain effective and equitable tools for education.

BEST PRACTICES IN DESIGNING VR AND AR-BASED TRAINING PROGRAMS

The successful implementation of Virtual Reality (VR) and Augmented Reality (AR) in vocational education and training (VET) requires careful planning and design to ensure that these technologies effectively meet the learning needs of students. By following best practices in designing VR and AR-based training programs, educators can create engaging, effective, and meaningful learning experiences. This chapter outlines key best practices, including aligning with learning objectives, conducting needs assessments, and ensuring continuous evaluation and improvement.

Aligning with Learning Objectives

One of the foundational principles of effective instructional design is ensuring that all training activities align with clearly defined learning objectives. When designing VR and AR-based training programs, educators should:

1. **Define Clear Learning Outcomes:** Establish specific, measurable learning outcomes that articulate what learners should know or be able to do by the end of the training. These outcomes should guide the development of content and activities within the VR or AR environment.
2. **Integrate Technology Purposefully:** Use VR and AR technologies to enhance the learning experience in ways that directly support the identified learning objectives. For example, if the objective is to develop problem-solving skills, the training program should include scenarios that challenge learners to analyze situations and make decisions.
3. **Ensure Relevance:** Design VR and AR experiences that are relevant to the learners' future careers. This relevance increases motivation and engagement, as learners can see the direct application of their training to real-world situations.

By aligning VR and AR training programs with clear learning objectives, educators can create focused and effective learning experiences that facilitate skill development and knowledge retention (Kwiatek, Sharif, Li, Haas, & Walbridge, 2019).

Conducting Needs Assessments

Before developing a VR or AR training program, it is essential to conduct a thorough needs assessment to identify the specific training needs of the target audience. This process involves:

1. **Identifying Learner Characteristics:** Understand the demographics, backgrounds, and prior knowledge of the learners. This information helps tailor the training program to meet the unique needs of the audience.
2. **Analyzing Skill Gaps:** Assess the current skill levels of learners compared to the desired competencies for their respective fields. This analysis will inform the design of training content and the selection of appropriate VR and AR applications.
3. **Gathering Stakeholder Input:** Engage with industry partners, instructors, and learners to gather insights on the skills and knowledge that are most relevant and necessary for success in the field. This collaboration ensures that the training program is aligned with industry standards and expectations.
4. **Evaluating Existing Resources:** Review existing training materials and resources to identify gaps and opportunities for enhancement through VR and AR technologies. This evaluation can help determine how to best integrate these technologies into the training program.

By conducting a comprehensive needs assessment, educators can ensure that the VR and AR training programs address the specific requirements of learners and the demands of the industry, leading to more effective and relevant training experiences.

Continuous Evaluation and Improvement

The design and implementation of VR and AR-based training programs should not be static; rather, they should involve continuous evaluation and improvement to ensure effectiveness and relevance. Key strategies for achieving this include:

1. **Collecting Feedback:** Regularly solicit feedback from learners, instructors, and industry stakeholders regarding the effectiveness of the training program. This feedback can provide valuable insights into what is working well and what areas need improvement.
2. **Assessing Learning Outcomes:** Implement assessments that measure the achievement of learning objectives. This can include quizzes, practical demonstrations, or simulations that evaluate learners' skills and knowledge. Analyzing assessment results can help identify areas where learners may be struggling.
3. **Iterative Design:** Use an iterative design process that allows for ongoing refinement of the training program based on feedback and assessment results. This approach enables educators to make data-driven decisions about content updates, technology enhancements, and instructional strategies.

4. **Staying Current with Technology:** As VR and AR technologies evolve, it is essential to stay informed about new developments and best practices in the field. Regularly updating training programs to incorporate the latest advancements can enhance the learning experience and keep it relevant.
5. **Fostering a Culture of Improvement:** Encourage a culture of continuous improvement among instructors and learners. This can involve regular training sessions for instructors on new technologies and teaching methods, as well as fostering an open environment where learners feel comfortable providing feedback.

By prioritizing continuous evaluation and improvement, educators can ensure that VR and AR-based training programs remain effective, engaging, and aligned with the evolving needs of learners and the industry. Designing effective VR and AR-based training programs requires a thoughtful approach that aligns with learning objectives, addresses the specific needs of learners, and incorporates continuous evaluation and improvement. By following these best practices, educators can create immersive and impactful learning experiences that prepare students for success in their chosen vocational fields. As VR and AR technologies continue to advance, the potential for enhancing vocational education and training will only grow, making it essential for educators to embrace these innovative approaches.

CONCLUSION

The integration of Virtual Reality (VR) and Augmented Reality (AR) into vocational education and training (VET) marks a significant advancement in how skills and knowledge are imparted to learners. Throughout this exploration, we have examined the transformative potential of these technologies, highlighting their applications across various industries, their pedagogical advantages, and the best practices necessary for effective implementation. As we have seen, VR and AR provide immersive and interactive learning experiences that enhance engagement, foster active learning, and develop critical thinking and problem-solving skills. These technologies allow learners to practice in safe, risk-free environments, enabling them to build confidence and competence before entering the workforce. However, the journey toward successful implementation is not without challenges, including the costs of technology, the need for specialized instructor training, and the ethical considerations surrounding data privacy and security. To maximize the benefits of VR and AR in VET, it is essential for educational institutions and training providers to align their programs with clear learning objectives, conduct thorough needs assessments, and prioritize continuous evaluation and improvement. By following these best practices, educators can create relevant and effective training programs that meet the evolving needs of learners and industry. Looking ahead, the future of VR and AR in vocational education is bright. As technology continues to advance, we can expect broader adoption, enhanced integration with other emerging technologies, and a greater focus on lifelong learning. These developments will further solidify the role of VR and AR in preparing a skilled workforce capable of navigating the complexities of the modern job market. The integration of VR and AR into vocational training presents a multitude of pedagogical advantages and applications across various industries. Key points from this chapter include:

1. **Applications Across Industries:** VR and AR technologies have found significant applications in sectors such as healthcare, manufacturing, construction, aviation, and beyond. These technologies enhance training by providing realistic simulations, safe practice environments, and opportunities for hands-on experience.
2. **Pedagogical Advantages:** The use of VR and AR promotes active learning, skill development, problem-solving, and critical thinking. These immersive experiences engage learners and foster deeper understanding and retention of knowledge.
3. **Challenges and Considerations:** Despite the benefits, implementing VR and AR in VET comes with challenges, including high costs, the need for specialized instructor training, integration into existing curricula, and ethical concerns related to privacy and data security.
4. **Best Practices for Implementation:** Successful VR and AR training programs require alignment with learning objectives, thorough needs assessments, and a commitment to continuous evaluation and improvement. These best practices ensure that training programs are relevant, effective, and responsive to the needs of learners and industry.

Overall, VR and AR are reshaping the landscape of vocational education and training, providing innovative solutions to traditional challenges and enhancing the learning experience for students.

REFERENCES

Akgun, S., & Greenhow, C. (2022). Artificial intelligence in education: Addressing ethical challenges in K-12 settings. *AI and Ethics*, 2(3), 431–440. DOI: 10.1007/s43681-021-00096-7 PMID: 34790956

Al-Ansi, A. M., Jaboob, M., Garad, A., & Al-Ansi, A. (2023). Analyzing augmented reality (AR) and virtual reality (VR) recent development in education. *Social Sciences & Humanities Open*, 8(1), 100532. DOI: 10.1016/j.ssaho.2023.100532

Arief, U. M., Wibawanto, H., & Nastiti, A. L. (2023). Augmented reality technology for vocational education. *Advances in Social Science, Education and Humanities Research (ASSEHR)*, 201. Atlantis Press. https://www.atlantis-press.com/article/25903467.pdf

Borenstein, J., & Howard, A. (2021). Emerging challenges in AI and the need for AI ethics education. *AI and Ethics*, 1(1), 61–65. DOI: 10.1007/s43681-020-00002-7 PMID: 38624388

Chiang, F.-K., Shang, X., & Qiao, L. (2022). Augmented reality in vocational training: A systematic review of research and applications. *Computers in Human Behavior*, 129, 107125. DOI: 10.1016/j.chb.2021.107125

Ghosh, L., & Ravichandran, R. (2024). Emerging technologies in vocational education and training. *Journal of Digital Learning and Education*, 4(1), 41–49. DOI: 10.52562/jdle.v4i1.975

Goertz, L., Hagenhofer, T., & Fehling, C. D. (2021). *Planning the use of augmented and virtual reality for vocational education and training: A practical guide.*

Gonçalves, Y. A., & Vilas Boas. (2012). Overview of Virtual Reality technologies. *Semantic Scholar*. https://api.semanticscholar.org/CorpusID:8120179

Kablitz, D., Conrad, M., & Schumann, S. (2023). Immersive VR-based instruction in vocational schools: Effects on domain-specific knowledge and wellbeing of retail trainees. *Empirical Research in Vocational Education and Training*, 15(9), 9. Advance online publication. DOI: 10.1186/s40461-023-00148-8

Kwiatek, C., Sharif, M., Li, S., Haas, C., & Walbridge, S. (2019). Impact of augmented reality and spatial cognition on assembly in construction. *Automation in Construction*, 108, 102935. DOI: 10.1016/j.autcon.2019.102935

Liu, Y., Zhan, Q., & Zhao, W. (2023). A systematic review of VR/AR applications in vocational education: Models, effects, and performances. *Interactive Learning Environments*, •••, 1–18. DOI: 10.1080/10494820.2023.2263043

Liu, Y., Zhan, Q., & Zhao, W. (2023). A systematic review of VR/AR applications in vocational education: Models, effects, and performances. *Interactive Learning Environments*, 1–18. Advance online publication. DOI: 10.1080/10494820.2023.2263043

Ravichandran, R. R., & Mahapatra, J. (2023). Virtual Reality in vocational education and training: Challenges and possibilities. *Journal of Digital Learning and Education*, 3(1), 25–31. DOI: 10.52562/jdle.v3i1.602

Zouaghi, M. (2019). Augmented Reality (AR) and Virtual Reality (VR): The future of interactive vocational education and training for people with handicaps. *PUPIL: International Journal of Teaching. Education and Learning*, 3(1), 118–129. DOI: 10.20319/pijtel.2019.31.118129

ADDITIONAL READING

Agrawal, R., & Pillai, J. S. (2020, November). Augmented reality application in vocational education: A case of welding training. In *Companion Proceedings of the 2020 Conference on Interactive Surfaces and Spaces* (pp. 23-27). DOI: 10.1145/3380867.3426199

Bacca, J., Baldiris, S., Fabregat, R., & Graf, S. (2015). Mobile augmented reality in vocational education and training. *Procedia Computer Science*, 75, 49–58. DOI: 10.1016/j.procs.2015.12.203

Chiang, F. K., Shang, X., & Qiao, L. (2022). Augmented reality in vocational training: A systematic review of research and applications. *Computers in Human Behavior*, 129, 107125. DOI: 10.1016/j.chb.2021.107125

He, X., & Li, L. (2024). Teaching optimization of virtual reality and augmented reality technology in vocational education. *Journal of Computational Methods in Science and Engineering*, 14727978241297013.

KEY TERMS AND DEFINITIONS

Augmented Reality (AR): A technology that overlays digital information, such as images or animations, onto the physical world, enhancing real-world experiences with interactive elements.

Ethical Concerns: Issues related to privacy, data security, and bias that arise when implementing advanced technologies like VR and AR in education.

Haptic Feedback: A sensory technology that provides tactile responses, such as vibrations, to simulate physical interactions in virtual environments.

Immersive Learning: An educational approach using technologies like VR and AR to create engaging, interactive environments that simulate real-world experiences for deeper understanding.

Mixed Reality (MR): A combination of VR and AR that blends physical and digital elements, allowing users to interact with both simultaneously.

Personalized Learning: Tailoring educational experiences to meet individual learners' needs, abilities, and learning preferences using adaptive technologies.

Simulation Training: The use of VR or AR to replicate real-world scenarios, enabling learners to practice and refine skills in a risk-free setting.

Skill Development: The process of acquiring and refining practical abilities and knowledge essential for performing specific tasks or roles effectively.

Virtual Reality (VR): A fully immersive, computer-generated simulation that allows users to interact with a three-dimensional environment using VR headsets and sensors.

Vocational Education and Training (VET): Programs focused on equipping individuals with specific practical skills and knowledge tailored to particular careers or trades.

Chapter 5
Role of Augmented Reality in Vocational Education and Training: A PRISMA-Compliant Systematic Literature Review

Juhi P. Pathak
https://orcid.org/0000-0002-8028-1556
Amity University, Noida, India

ABSTRACT

Augmented reality (AR) has the potential to revolutionize the field of vocational education and training. AR offers immersive and interactive learning experiences that are especially well-suited to skill-based education by superimposing digital information onto the real world. AR is a perfect tool for improving the teaching and learning process in a variety of vocational disciplines because of the growing complexity of vocational skills and the requirement for practical training. The use of AR in vocational education and training is still in its early phases, despite its promise, and a thorough analysis of the literature is required to comprehend its advantages, disadvantages, and potential future possibilities. Using the PRISMA (Preferred Reporting Items for Systematic Reviews and Meta-Analyses) guidelines, this chapter attempts to conduct a systematic evaluation of the body of research on the application of AR in vocational education and training.

DOI: 10.4018/979-8-3693-8252-3.ch005

INTRODUCTION

Augmented reality (AR) has become a game-changer in recent years and has enormous implications for education, especially for vocational education and training. Historically or traditionally, physical tools, in-person demonstrations, and real-world practice have been key components of vocational education and training, which places an emphasis on practical skills and hands-on experience. Nevertheless, by delivering hitherto unachievable immersive, interactive, and contextually rich learning experiences, the application of AR in this field has the possibility to improve these conventional approaches (Wang et al., 2017; Akçayır & Akçayır, 2017). By superimposing digital content over the real world, augmented reality technology allows students to interact with both virtual and real aspects at the same time. With the ability to practice intricate tasks in a virtual environment that closely mimics real-world settings, students can reduce the risks and expenses associated with traditional training techniques, which makes this capability especially important in vocational education and training (Pantelidis, 2010). For example, augmented reality (AR) can mimic dangerous work settings, giving students the opportunity to practice safety procedures without actually being in risk (Farra et al., 2019).

Numerous industries, including healthcare, engineering, automobile repair, and construction, have investigated the use of augmented reality in vocational education and training (Bacca et al., 2014). Research has demonstrated that augmented reality can enhance students' motivation, engagement, and skill retention, making it an effective tool for vocational education (Garzón & Acevedo, 2019). The use of AR in vocational education and training is still in its infancy, despite these encouraging results, and the corpus of research that has already been done on the subject is dispersed and varied in terms of technique, results, and settings. This chapter provides a PRISMA-compliant systematic literature review in order to methodically evaluate the current state of research on the application of AR in vocational education and training. A thorough and open method for evaluating and synthesizing previous research is offered by the PRISMA (Preferred Reporting Items for Systematic Reviews and Meta-Analyses) framework (Moher et al., 2009). The purpose of this review is to assess the usefulness of augmented reality (AR) in vocational education and training, pinpoint the obstacles and restrictions associated with its application, and draw attention to any gaps in the literature that call for more research.

BACKGROUND

Augmented Reality

Augmented Reality (AR) has evolved significantly over the years, with its definitions reflecting this progression. Augmented Reality is defined as a technology that overlays digital information, such as images, sounds, or other data, onto the physical world, enhancing the user's perception of their environment. AR is defined as a continuum that spans from the real environment to a completely virtual environment, where augmented reality lies near the real-world end of the spectrum. (Milgram and Kishino, 1994) Milgram and Kishino (1994) first positioned AR on a continuum between the real and virtual environments.

AR enables real-time interaction between the user and both the digital and physical elements within their surroundings. AR "allows the user to see the real world, with virtual objects superimposed upon or composited with the real world". Augmented Reality is a system that combines real and virtual objects in a real environment, runs interactively, and in real-time, and registers (aligns) real and virtual objects with each other. This blending of virtual and real-world elements creates an interactive and immersive experience, making AR a powerful tool in various applications, including education and training. (Azuma, 1997)

Later, Cawood & Fiala (2007) described AR as a practical guide to blending the physical and digital worlds, while Dünser et al. (2008) emphasized the integration of digital information with the user's environment in real-time. Papagiannakis et al. (2008) highlighted AR as a medium that merges real and virtual objects for real-time interaction, and Zhou et al. (2008) focused on AR's ability to overlay digital content on the real world, creating an interactive experience. Carmigniani & Furht (2011) defined AR as a technology enhancing user perception by overlaying digital information on physical environments. Craig (2013) described AR as overlaying computer-generated information on the real world to create coexistence between the two, while Billinghurst et al. (2015) noted that AR allows users to see the real world with superimposed virtual objects. Peddie (2017) described AR as a system that overlays real-world environments with computer-generated data and imagery, enhancing users' perceptions.

Vocational Education and Training

Vocational education and training have been defined and understood in various ways over time, reflecting its focus on skill development for specific occupations. Hager & Gonczi (1996) described vocational education and training as the process of developing specific skills and knowledge needed for a particular job, emphasizing practical application. Billett (2001) viewed vocational education and training as learning through work, encompassing practices that directly prepare individuals for the workforce. Grubb & Ryan (1999) defined it as education and training that provides skills required for specific jobs, with a strong emphasis on practical, hands-on experience. Grollmann (2008) emphasized the preparation for the workforce through acquiring technical skills and practical knowledge. Rauner & Maclean (2008) highlighted vocational education and training as education designed to develop occupational competence, combining theoretical and practical components. Mulder (2004) focused on vocational education and training as an approach prioritizing practical skills and competencies necessary for employment. Lucas et al. (2012) described it as education directly related to preparing individuals for work, focusing on skills needed for specific occupations. Lester & Costley (2010) emphasized the combination of theoretical instruction with work-based learning. Paryono (2017) defined vocational education and training as equipping individuals with the technical skills and practical experience needed for specific tasks or jobs. Winch (2013) described it as an educational process that prepares individuals for careers in specific trades or occupations, combining theory with practical application.

MAIN FOCUS OF THE CHAPTER

Issues, Controversies, Problems

Augmented Reality (AR) has been increasingly integrated into vocational education and training, offering innovative ways to enhance learning by merging the physical and digital worlds (Cawood & Fiala, 2007; Carmigniani & Furht, 2011). However, despite its potential, several issues, controversies, and challenges have emerged. One significant issue is the technical limitations of AR, particularly in terms of device performance and user experience. Early AR systems were constrained by the lack of robust tracking and display technologies (Azuma, 1997; Zhou et al., 2008). Although advancements have been made, challenges remain, such as latency, limited field of view, and the computational power required to render AR environments in real-time (Craig, 2013; Peddie, 2017). These technical hurdles can result in a disjointed or less immersive experience, potentially reducing the effectiveness of vocational education and training.

Another controversy revolves around the accessibility and cost of AR technology. High-end AR devices, such as AR glasses or specialized equipment, can be prohibitively expensive for many vocational education and training institutions, particularly in developing countries (Billinghurst et al., 2015). This raises concerns about the digital divide, where only well-funded institutions can afford to incorporate

AR into their training programs, leading to disparities in educational opportunities (Carmigniani & Furht, 2011). Additionally, the integration of AR in vocational education and training raises questions about the balance between virtual and hands-on learning. While AR can simulate real-world scenarios, critics argue that it cannot fully replicate the tactile and sensory experiences of working with actual tools and materials (Dünser et al., 2008; Papagiannakis et al., 2008). This can be particularly problematic in fields where precision and manual dexterity are critical, such as in technical trades or healthcare, where hands-on practice is irreplaceable.

Furthermore, there are concerns regarding the cognitive load imposed by AR environments. The simultaneous processing of real and virtual elements can overwhelm learners, especially those who are less familiar with digital technologies (Milgram & Kishino, 1994). This cognitive strain may hinder the learning process rather than enhance it, potentially leading to lower retention of skills and knowledge (Zhou et al., 2008). Ethical considerations also emerge, particularly in terms of data privacy and the potential misuse of AR in training environments. The technology often requires tracking user movements and interactions, raising concerns about the collection, storage, and use of personal data (Azuma, 1997). As AR becomes more integrated into vocational education and training, ensuring that these technologies are used responsibly, and that learners' privacy is protected becomes increasingly important (Craig, 2013). While AR presents exciting opportunities for enhancing vocational education and training by providing immersive, interactive learning experiences, it also brings significant challenges. These include technical limitations, accessibility issues, the balance between virtual and hands-on learning, cognitive load, and ethical concerns. Addressing these issues is crucial for the effective and equitable implementation of AR in vocational education.

Aims

1. To Provide a Comprehensive Overview of AR in Vocational education and training;
2. To Evaluate the Impact of AR on Learning Outcomes;
3. To evaluate the benefits and challenges of using AR in Vocational education and training;
4. To Discuss Ethical and Practical Considerations

Research Objectives

1. Identify and examine existing literature on Augmented Reality and Vocational education and training

2. Identify dominating themes, concepts and theories in the existing literature on Augmented Reality and Vocational education and training

RESEARCH METHODS

Augmented Reality and Vocational Education and Training

Following the Preferred Reporting Items for Systematic Reviews and Meta-Analyses (PRISMA) guidelines for conducting systematic literature reviews, during August 2024, we performed 3 rounds of selection. First, we searched predetermined keywords in Google Scholar and JSTOR databases. This step generated 57200 results in the Google Scholar database and 1153 results in the JSTOR database. Next, we added filters according to the following inclusion and exclusion criteria

1. Exact phrase of 'Augmented Reality' and 'Vocational Education and Training' anywhere in the article
2. Published between 2014 and 2024

After this we got 9 results in the JSTOR database and 36 results in the Google Scholar database.

Thereafter, according to further inclusion and exclusion criteria of

1. The exact phrase of 'Augmented Reality' and 'Vocational Education and Training' in the Title of the article, we got 0 articles from the JSTOR database and 11 articles from the Google Scholar database.

All the 11 research papers had full-text availability.

Review of Literature

Finally, we screened the full text of the 11 papers ensuring that they met the inclusion or exclusion criteria for 'Augmented Reality and Vocational Education and Training'. Hence, 11 papers were taken as a final sample for analysis (Refer to Table 1).

Table 1. Publication Matrix of selected research papers (author generated)

Sr. No.	Authors	Title	Publication	Volume	Year
1	Chiang, Feng-Kuang; Shang, Xiaojing; Qiao, Lu;	Augmented reality in vocational training: A systematic review of research and applications	Computers in Human Behavior, Elsevier	129	2022
2	Fehling, Christian Dominic; Müller, Andreas; Aehnelt, Mario;	Enhancing vocational training with augmented reality	Proceedings of the 16th international conference on knowledge technologies and data-driven business, ACM Press	N/A	2016
3	Bacca Acosta, Jorge Luis; Navarro, Silvia Margarita Baldiris; Gesa, Ramon Fabregat; Kinshuk, Kinshuk;	Framework for designing motivational augmented reality applications in vocational education and training	Australasian Journal of Educational Technology	35	2019
4	Bacca Acosta, Jorge Luis; Baldiris Navarro, Silvia Margarita; Fabregat Gesa, Ramon; Graf, Sabine;	Mobile augmented reality in vocational education and training	Procedia Computer Science, 2015, Elsevier	75	2015
5	Tan, Bhing-Leet; Guan, Frank Yunqing; Leung, Ivy Mun Wah; Kee, Sharon Yi-May; Devilly, Oran Zane; Medalia, Alice;	A gamified augmented reality vocational training program for adults with intellectual and developmental disabilities: A pilot study on acceptability and effectiveness	Frontiers in psychiatry, Frontiers Media SA	13	2022
6	Lavrentieva, Olena O; Arkhypov, Ihor O; Kuchma, Olexander I; Uchitel, Aleksandr D;	Use of simulators together with virtual and augmented reality in the system of welders' vocational training: past, present, and future	Augmented reality in education: proceedings of the 2nd international workshop (AREdu 2019), Kryvyi Rih, Ukraine, March 22, 2019, CEUR Workshop Proceedings		2020

continued on following page

Table 1. Continued

Sr. No.	Authors	Title	Publication	Volume	Year
7	Mekacher, Leila;	Augmented Reality (AR) and Virtual Reality (VR): The future of interactive vocational education and training for people with handicap	PUPIL: International Journal of Teaching, Education and Learning	3	2019
8	Bacca, Jorge; Baldiris, Silvia; Fabregat, Ramon; Kinshuk;	Insights into the factors influencing student motivation in augmented reality learning experiences in vocational education and training	Frontiers in psychology, Frontiers Media SA	9	2018
9	Sirakaya, Mustafa; Kilic Cakmak, Ebru;	Effects of augmented reality on student achievement and self-efficacy in vocational education and training	International journal for research in vocational education and training, DEU	5	2018
10	Cheung, Hoi Kok; Liu, Sai Lok;	Development of practical vocational training class making use of virtual reality-based simulation system and augmented reality technologies	The 10th International Symposium on Advances in Technology Education, Transactions of ISATE 2016 - ISATE Sendai	N/A	2016
11	Nordin, Siti Zarida Syed; Ismail, Izwah; Mustapa, Asmah; Omar, Politeknik Ungku;	Augmented Reality (AR) Gamification Application in Technical & Vocational Education Training	E-Proceedings of 4th International Conference on Research in TVET Studies (ICOR-TVET 2019)	N/A	2022

DISCUSSION

Impact of Augmented Reality on Vocational Education and Training

Chiang et al. (2022) cite Van Krevelen & Poelman (2010) to highlight the fact that Ivan Sutherland and his students created the first AR system, the Sword of Damocles, at Utah University and Harvard University in the 1960s. According to Caudell & Mizell (1992), Tom Caudell and David Mizell were the first to use 'augmented reality' in a study, as cited by Chiang et al. (2022). In addition, they created the first augmented reality training application to help Boeing Company maintenance work more efficiently and at a lower cost. According to Chiang et al. (2022), the adoption of augmented reality (AR) in vocational and educational training (VET) and on-the-job training (OJT) has been made easier by the availability of AR applications and advancements in hardware equipment. These advancements have been observed in a variety of fields, including medicine (Caudell & Mizell, 1992), the military (Chmielewski et al., 2019), aerospace (Borgen et al., 2021), manufacturing (Forest, 2021), construction (Choi & Park, 2021), agriculture (Yang et al., 2021), and industry (Bogicevic et al., 2021).

Chiang et al. (2022) highlight that AR enhances vocational skills, learning motivation, and academic performance; reduces cognitive load, training time, and operational errors; provides timely feedback, improves participation, and self-regulated learning; and that the AR technology offers innovative alternatives for trainees in vocational education and training. Chiang et al. (2022) classify AR vocational education and training evolution divided into three stages. According to its keyword co-occurrence time zone map of 2004–2021, AR technology was first applied in vocational education and training in 2014. The initial stage was from 2004 – 2007; the development stage was from 2008 – 2015; and the maturity and rise stage was from 2016 – 2021. Chiang et al. (2022) examined eighty studies. Among these, the percentages of each category, going from large to small were Industry (35%), Vocation Education and Training (VET, 26%), Medical (13%), Aviation (9%), Construction (6%), Nuclear (5%), Electric (4%), Agriculture (1%) and Military (1%). Of the 80 studies, 35% identified industrial training as the most common application of AR, followed by vocational education and training (26%), and medicine (13%). The nine AR career training categories are divided into a number of application subclasses.

Fehling et al. (2016) introduced the Social Augmented Learning (SAL) application, which allows Augmented Reality (AR) to be used in scenarios involving vocational education and training and on-the-job training. Azuma et al. (2001) and Milgram (1995) are cited by Fehling et al. (2016) to define augmented reality (AR) as the dynamic, interactive, and appropriately positioned fusion of digital information and data with real objects and surroundings. Fehling et al. (2016) highlight that throughout the industrial-technical vocational education and training process, instruction in the use and upkeep of machinery, from automobiles to industrial plants, is frequently crucial. Not only are these devices becoming increasingly sophisticated, but rising automation makes it impossible to guarantee complete accessibility in every situation, both in terms of location and information. AR may visualize machine elements that are otherwise concealed and make linked processes and cause-and-effect relationships accessible in a systematic context by bridging the media gap between actual and digital training information.

Fehling et al. (2016) cite the work of authors to bring forth the argument that according to some research, augmented reality (AR) can be used to expand traditional learning media with digital content (Grasset et al., 2008) or to construct exploratory learning activities using gamification approaches (Klopfer & Squire, 2008). Situations that would be too costly or risky otherwise can be trained for during vocational education and training and on-the-job training, such as in the automotive industry (Bacca et al., 2015), during the assembly of electronic components (Westerfield et al., 2015), as well as during the simulation of military crisis scenarios (Champney et al., 2015; Fragomeni et al., 2015).

Fehling et al. (2016) argue that AR enhances vocational education and training quality with interactive, collaborative learning opportunities; and that SAL application provides intuitive tools for content creators, teachers, and learners. The author introduces Social Augmented Learning for vocational education and training with AR; describes AR use in training, development, and evaluation of SAL thereby throwing light on the potential for AR in workplace training and learning arrangements. The results can be summarized that SAL application enhances vocational education and training with AR for knowledge-intensive tasks; AR positively impacts learning quality, knowledge transmission, and training efficiency; SAL enables self-regulated learning, content creation, and well-structured lessons; and AR fosters a multimodal learning environment with 3D visualization for trainees.

Bacca et al. (2019) argue that augmented reality boosts student motivation; and that is among its biggest benefits for education. The definition of frameworks to inform and direct the design and development of augmented reality applications that successfully promote student motivation, however, lags behind the research on student motivation in AR. Through the research, the authors analyze a framework for creating AR applications that are motivational in an effort to close that gap. Three theoretical pillars have served as the cornerstone for our framework: co-creation, universal design for learning (UDL), and motivational design. The authors found that the framework not only effectively supports the four dimensions of Keller's (2010) ARCS (attention, relevance, confidence, and satisfaction) model of motivation, but also exhibits exceptional results in the Attention and Confidence dimensions of motivation. The review study involved 58 chemistry students enrolled in the Laboratory Operations vocational education and training (VET) program.

Motivational design is defined as the systemic process of “arranging resources and procedures to bring about changes in people's motivation” by Bacca et al. (2019), citing Keller (2010). The authors define UDL as a validated paradigm for handling student variability, citing Meyer et al. (2014). Its goal is to prevent impediments in the learning process, enabling students to become expert learners. According to Bacca et al. (2019), the UDL framework is founded on current research in cognitive psychology, learning sciences, and neuroscience, which has determined that the human brain is made up of three networks: affective, recognition, and strategic. The three networks serve as the foundation for the three UDL principles, which are to (1) offer various channels for interaction, (2) offer multiple channels for representation, and (3) offer multiple channels for action and expression. These guiding concepts serve as the basis for some of the framework's recommendations. In addition, the authors define co-creation as "any act of collective creativity, i.e., creativity that is shared by two or more people" citing Sanders & Stappers (2008).

Bacca et al. (2015) in another research argue that teachers in vocational education and training (VET) institutions face significant challenges in the teaching process because of the wide range of special educational needs of their students as well as the students' deficiencies in several areas, including motivation, background knowledge, focus, and motivation, as well as an insufficient level of basic competence. Concerning the focus on these elements, numerous research studies have documented the beneficial effects of Augmented Reality (AR) applications in primary, secondary and higher education on student motivation, learning outcomes, teamwork, engagement, learning attitudes, and enjoyment, among other aspects. Bacca et al. (2015) highlight that not much research has been done on the use of augmented reality (AR) in VET or its effects on a wide range of special education needs, including learning disabilities, in students.

The study by Bacca et al. (2015) presents Paint-cAR, a marker-based mobile augmented reality application, to help students learn how to fix paint on cars as part of a vocational education program on car maintenance. The application was created with the Universal Design for Learning (UDL) and the Co-Creation collaborative creation process, which is a methodology for creating mobile augmented reality applications for educational purposes. A cross-sectional assessment study was carried out to verify the Paint-cAR application in an actual setting. In Bacca et al. (2015) a group of Spanish VET students tested the Paint-cAR application, and the Instructional Materials Motivation Survey (IMMS) as cited by Keller (2010) was used to assess students' motivation, specifically in relation to the attention, relevance, confidence, and satisfaction dimensions. The findings demonstrate that the Paint-cAR application was a motivator for the participants. While overall results are encouraging, the dimensions of satisfaction and confidence scored higher. The limitations of the study include that it involves a small sample size and is cross-sectional in nature. The need for longitudinal studies is required to establish clear relationships. Moreover, further studies in other VET fields are needed for concrete generalisations of the impact of AR in VET.

Tan et al. (2022) offered an augmented reality vocational education and training program called Augmented Reality Games to Enhance Vocational Ability of Patients (REAP) which was a skill development initiative within the framework of a mental rehabilitation program. It was put into practice over the course of ten weeks implementing a pretest-posttest mixed-methods study with fifteen disabled persons. It included group exercises that bridged the gap between the classroom and the workplace, as well as gamified augmented reality café training situations. The purpose of this pilot study was to investigate the acceptability and efficacy of the

REAP program when it comes to adults receiving work therapy who have intellectual and developmental disabilities. The pilot study on the REAP program demonstrated that both persons with intellectual and developmental impairments and their vocational rehabilitation trainers could accept and use a gamified augmented reality vocational education and training program. Eight weeks after the program finished, participants on the REAP program continued to demonstrate significant increases in parts of their cognitive performance and vocational abilities when combined with bridging sessions to promote the transfer of learning to the established job therapy.

Tan et al. (2022) cited Ellenkamp et al. (2016) and Meltzer et al. (2020) to highlight that research on assisted employment has demonstrated that individuals with intellectual disabilities face obstacles not just in finding work but also in keeping jobs. Although Tan et al. (2022) have not investigated on the issue, the authors have mentioned that the AR-enabled vocational education and training for clients in supported employment may be used as an additional kind of training to increase job sustainability.

Lavrentieva et al. (2020) have discussed the theory and techniques of simulation, along with its importance in the training of specialists for vocations where a primary qualification is crucial. The most popular VR and AR gear and software solutions for the organization's simulation training of welders have been examined. On the basis of the accomplishments of Fronius, MIMBUS, and Seabery, an evaluation of the software tools and technological infrastructure for the virtual electric welding training and production laboratory has been conducted. It has been demonstrated how to use contemporary equipment to create a virtual simulation of the welding process based on research on the welder's behavioral reactions.

Lavrentieva et al. (2020) discover that the simulators enable the development of neuro-fuzzy logic as well as the design of automated and robotic welding systems, in addition to training. The working unique characteristics of the AR welding simulators have been unveiled. Research indicates that they facilitate the development of fundamental skills necessary for a future expert, including focus, accuracy, and agility. The coaching programs' technical and psychological facets for the training and retraining of certified welders have been demonstrated. Conclusions have been drawn regarding the notable benefits that VR and AR technologies offer over more conventional ones. The evolution of welders' simulation training could go in several directions. Among these, AR technologies have been touted as becoming increasingly popular since they enable the realization of the idea of mass training in basic professional skills. Lavrentieva et al. (2020) cited Gaba (2004) to define simulation. Through the use of an artificially generated scenario that reflects and reproduces real-world problems in an entirely interactive manner, simulation is a technique that can either supplement or enhance a trainee's practical experience. Lavrentieva et al. (2020) also cited Svistunova & Gorshkov (2013) to define the term ‘simulation training’. Through immersion in a particular setting, simulation training is a required part of vocational education and training that applies the professional model to enable everyone to perform tasks efficiently and productively and in accordance with professional standards. The immersive nature of simulation training allows trainees to gain practical experience and skills necessary for their professional activities, ensuring productive outcomes in their respective fields. By incorporating simulation training into vocational education, individuals can enhance their knowledge, accelerate the transfer of skills, and elevate the quality of vocational preparation and retraining, ultimately facilitating a smoother transition to new equipment and technologies.

Lavrentieva et al. (2020) further cited Svistunova & Gorshkov (2013) in the conclusion of their study to highlight that the simulation training technology generally consists of five consecutive steps: Initial testing, Briefing, Work with simulators and simulators, Debriefing, and Summary of work, test control. The initial testing is the first step in simulation training, where the trainee's skills and knowledge are assessed to determine the training route. Briefing follows the initial testing and involves analyzing theoretical material and establishing key provisions for the training session. The third step involves working with simulators and simulators, where trainees engage with computer training devices to practice and enhance their skills. Debriefing is a crucial step where trainees reflect on their performance, receive feedback, and discuss areas for improvement. The final step includes summarizing the work done during the training session and conducting test control to evaluate the trainee's progress and learning outcomes. Lavrentieva et al. (2020) included skill development, better decision-making abilities, enhanced learning, motivation boost, better research opportunities and cost-effectiveness as the advantages of simulation training in VET. Welding simulators combine practical skills training with theoretical study, helping trainees develop both knowledge and hands-on expertise. The simulators prepare trainees for making quality and fast decisions in their professional field. Visualization of educational materials and practical actions improves comprehension and assimilation of information. Built-in gamification increases motivation and emotional engagement among students. Simulators allow for the investigation of human responses during welding, which can be used to develop neuro-fuzzy logic and design automated and robotic welding systems. Despite the high initial cost, simulators can pay for themselves within the first year of use, making them a cost-effective investment over time.

Mekacher (2019) aims to describe the didactic-methodical approach for an interactive virtual vocational education and training program utilizing virtual reality and augmented reality technologies. Being part of a dual VET institution for the disabled, the author’s main concentration is on youth with severe social interaction issues, autism, and special needs. Other target groups can also benefit from the concept highlighted in the study. The learners can engage and experiment with objects and constructions in the virtual environment just as they would in the actual world. The AR-Glasses offer free visualization along with valuable application scenarios for teaching and learning; wherein the wearer is assisted in their activities by additional virtual objects and context-based information. The author's approach is predicated on the learning objectives, trainees' cognitive and psychophysiological characteristics, technology advancements, and goal-oriented teaching pedagogical tactics. Through the study, the author provides instances of how these technologies are being applied in several VET fields, including computer technology, automotive mechatronics engineering, automation and electrotechnology, technical product design, and in-house virtual vocational schooling.

Mekacher (2019) concluded that all students who had access to a smartphone and a VR headgear were able to share their views through a completely new medium and experience the vast array of VR applications. Students have been even more motivated to advance their skills in a professional setting as a result of this enjoyable and educational experience, including in the training labs. The attitude of teachers is greatly influenced by the degree to which students embrace technology. The fact that VR/AR piques students' curiosity about the subject and increases their want to learn more about it is what makes it so effective in technical education. Mekacher (2019) discussed the use of three devices. The first is a virtual reality system, which uses an HTC Vive Pro, an immersive, realistic, and interactive computer-generated experience that takes place in a three-dimensionally replicated environment. The second is Epson Moverio BT-300 which is used to integrate augmented reality or the real-time integration of digital data with the user's surroundings. In contrast to virtual reality, which fabricates an entirely synthetic setting, augmented reality makes use of the current world and superimposes fresh data upon it. The third is Microsoft HoloLens, a head-mounted display and holographic computer that allows users to interact with actual items and holograms in the real world. Another name for this sophisticated augmented reality is "mixed-reality."

Mekacher (2019) emphasized that over the next few years, virtual and augmented reality will also start to affect vocational education and training, citing Fehling, et al. (2016) and other authors. The author cited Freina & Ott (2015) to highlight the importance of VR and cited Akçayır & Akçayır (2017) to stress on the importance of AR in recent times. The author highlights that the lack of didactical models for new technologies presents challenges for educators, requiring them to adapt to rapidly changing technologies and redesign teaching practices to effectively integrate these innovations into the curriculum. Utilizing advanced options in education is essential to enhance teaching effectiveness by providing students with new ways to experience learning, create their own media, gain a deeper understanding of the world, and spark their imagination. Educators must define educational objectives and explore how the integration of Virtual Reality and Augmented Reality can enhance teaching and learning experiences, emphasizing the importance of incorporating these technologies into the curriculum to promote effective teaching strategies.

Bacca et al. (2018) state that studies on Augmented Reality in education have shown that AR programs with a variety of components that increase students' motivation in learning environments. Nevertheless, the authors claim that the majority of the study done up to this point have not clarified exactly what such elements are or how they enhance students' motivation. In order to support the design and development of motivational AR learning experiences for the Vocational Education and Training (VET) level of education, the authors aimed to identify some of the elements that positively promote student motivation in mobile AR learning experiences. A research model built from the literature was empirically validated to identify these components using data from two sources: a self-report measure from the Instructional Materials Motivation Survey (IMMS) and 35 students from four VET institutes interacting with an AR application for learning over a 20-day period. The four aspects of the ARCS model of motivation—attention, relevance, confidence, and satisfaction—are positively found to be connected with the variables like the use of scaffolding, real-time feedback, degree of success, on-task duration, and learning outcomes.

Bacca et al. (2018) cite Santos et al. (2014) to bring forth that the AR learning experiences (ARLEs), or learning experiences supported by AR, have been developed in response to the growing interest in using AR in education. The authors add that a large number of ARLEs have been developed for nearly all educational levels, from early childhood education to higher education. Nevertheless, a majority of studies on student motivation in ARLE are unable to pinpoint the precise elements of AR applications that could help boost motivation in students or provide an explanation for the mechanisms underlying the rise in motivation. Therefore, the authors cited Akçayır and Akçayır (2017) to emphasize that more study on student motivation is required to fully comprehend the benefits of augmented reality in education. In order to aid in the design and development of AR apps that successfully raise motivation (motivating mobile ARLEs), the authors attempt to offer insights into the elements of AR applications that boost student motivation. This study makes two contributions: first, it identifies certain mobile augmented reality application components that may have a positive impact on student motivation at the VET level of education; second, it discusses the implications of these components and the variables they are associated with for the design and development of motivational ARLEs.

Bacca et al. (2018) state the fact that the AR originated in training and maintenance scenarios when Caudell and Mizell (1992) introduced a Head-mounted display for assisting maintenance in the aircraft industry, leading to the concept's inception. The authors cite Azuma (1997) to define AR as a technology that overlays virtual objects onto the real world, allowing users to see a combination of real-world views with digitally generated content. Based on various definitions of Dunleavy et al. (2009), Cuendet et al. (2013), Furió et al. (2013) and Wu et al. (2013), the authors define AR as a technology that integrates real-time physical environments with digital content from computers or mobile devices, enhancing the user's perception of reality. The core essence of AR lies in combining or annotating the real-time view of the physical world with diverse digital content, offering a unique and interactive learning experience for users in educational settings.

Bacca et al. (2018) cite Kourouthanassis et al. (2015) to provide the operational definition of Mobile Augmented Reality (MAR). MAR is distinguished from Desktop Augmented Reality (DAR), the initial generation of AR, by being described as systems that offer AR capabilities through mobile devices like smartphones or tablets. Bacca et al. (2018) concentrate on MAR and marker-based AR in the study. The limitations of the study included limitation of scope and variables among others. The study was conducted in only one VET program (Car's Maintenance) which may restrict the generalizability of the findings to other VET programs. The Paint-cAR application used in the study is a marker-based AR application. As a result, the findings may not apply to other types of AR, such as marker-less or location-based AR. Due to the specific context and technology used, the results need to be interpreted with caution, as they may not be universally applicable. The study considered a specific set of variables represented in the 5-VARLE framework (use of scaffolding, real time feedback, learning outcomes, degree of success and time on task). Other potentially relevant variables were not included, which may limit the discovery of new relationships in similar studies.

Sirakaya & Kilic Cakmak (2018) also cite Azuma (1997) and Caudell and Mizell (1992) to describe AR as a technology that merges real-world visuals with virtual elements in real-time. The purpose of the study was to examine how student achievement and self-efficacy in vocational education and training are affected by the usage of augmented reality (AR). HardwareAR, a marker-based augmented reality program, was created for the conduct of the research. HardwareAR offers details on the properties of ports, assemblies, and hardware parts. Pre- and post-tests were part of the quasi-experimental research design, and a control group was included. 46 undergraduate students taking the Computer Hardware course participated in the study. Data were gathered for the study using an unstructured observation form, a motherboard assembly self-efficacy questionnaire, and an accomplishment test for computer hardware courses. While students in the experimental group utilized the HardwareAR program to learn the same content, the control group used their textbooks (print material) to acquire theoretical and applied knowledge about motherboard assembly.

It was discovered that while the usage of augmented reality (AR) had no effect on students' self-efficacy in relation to theoretical knowledge and assembly abilities, it had a favorable effect on student accomplishment in motherboard assembly. Conversely, using augmented reality (AR) enabled students to finish the assembly process faster and with less assistance. It is concluded that students in the experimental group performed better in computer hardware courses than those in the control group. The outcome of the study demonstrates that applying augmented reality can effectively raise achievement. It was determined that the use of AR applications had no impact on students' theoretical knowledge and skills regarding motherboard assembly. The fact that students possessed high levels of theoretical knowledge and assembly abilities prior to the implementation may have had an impact on this outcome. Based on observations, students were able to construct motherboards faster and with less assistance thanks to the AR application. It is believed that the AR application's simultaneous interaction between virtual objects and the real environment can speed up assembly. Students that used the HardwareAR program to view the procedures and instructions in real time were able to finish the assembly with less assistance. The authors, based on their findings argued that AR presents a significant alternative for subjects requiring learner application and practice because of the simultaneous interaction it allows.

On the lines of Bacca et al. (2018), Sirakaya & Kilic Cakmak (2018) too cited Wu et al. (2013) to claim that while augmented reality (AR) has been around for a while, investigations into its potential and usefulness in educational settings seem to have begun very recently. Sirakaya & Kilic Cakmak (2018) cited various authors to derive at the advantages of AR in Education. The benefits of AR as cited by the authors include increased interest and attention during lessons (Delello, 2014; Perez-Lopez & Contero, 2013; Tomi & Rambli, 2013); enhanced motivation of students (Delello, 2014; Perez-Lopez & Contero, 2013; Tomi & Rambli, 2013); enables the safe creation of environments that cannot be generated in real-world conditions due to various impracticalities (Shelton & Hedley, 2002; Yuen et al., 2011); allows for the safe execution of dangerous experiments in educational settings (Wojciechowski & Cellary, 2013); supports a student-centered learning approach (Delello, 2014); promotes hands-on, experiential learning (Singhal et al., 2012; Wojciechowski & Cellary, 2013); and facilitates the presentation of virtual objects, such as 3D models and abstract concepts, combined with real-world images, making it a valuable tool for teaching tasks that require object manipulation (Westerfield et al., 2015).

The study conducted by Sirakaya & Kilic Cakmak (2018) included 46 students (18 females and 28 males) enrolled at Ahi Evran University's Mucur Vocational School of Higher Education's first year of computer programming. A total of 23 subject pairings were obtained by matching each pair of students based on how similar their pre-test results were in terms of academic achievement and self-efficacy.

Then, it was made sure that every subject pair was equal in terms of factors like overall achievement, prior knowledge, gender, socioeconomic level, experience, and technical expertise. Subsequently, the experimental and control groups, consisting of 23 students each, were formed by randomly assigning the students in the subject pairs to the experimental and control groups.

Sirakaya & Kilic Cakmak (2018) concluded that using AR in vocational education and training enhances student achievement but has no significant impact on self-efficacy in theoretical knowledge or assembly skills. Additionally, AR use reduces the time needed for tasks like motherboard assembly and allows students to work more independently. The findings suggest that AR technology can be an effective tool in applied courses. Future research should explore AR in different fields and with various sample levels. The study also recommends using more suitable devices, such as AR goggles, in future studies to overcome limitations like small smartphone screen sizes. The study conducted in the computer hardware course could be replicated in other courses where students engage in practical, hands-on work. Additionally, while this study focused on students in a Vocational School of Higher Education, similar research could be extended to different sample groups, such as students in Vocational High Schools, where applied teaching methods are widely used.

Cheung & Liu (2016) conducted a research study at the Hong Kong Institute of Vocational Education (IVE) on creating a VR-based simulation system for vocational education and training (VET). Four screens encircle participants in an immersive virtual environment created by the system called the Cave Automatic Virtual Environment (CAVE). This project aims to include augmented reality and virtual reality into real-world training curricula, especially for engineering-related areas. The system is made to mimic different work environments and offers instruction for mechanical and electrical service operations and maintenance. This is especially useful in settings where practical instruction may be hazardous.

Cheung & Liu (2016) cite the works of Cruz-Neira et al. (1992, 1993), and Kuhlen and Hentschel (2014) to define and describe the CAVE system. They explain that CAVE, first introduced by Cruz-Neira and colleagues in 1992 and 1993, offers a broad field of view that significantly enhances the user's sense of presence in a virtual environment. Additionally, they highlight that, unlike other VR systems, CAVE allows users to physically enter the virtual space without relying on a virtual representation of their bodies, thereby greatly enhancing the immersive experience. They also emphasize that the immersive environment provided by CAVE facilitates a faster and more comprehensive understanding of complex spatial relationships and allows users to interact with objects using more natural controllers.

Cheung & Liu (2016) cite several authors to define AR and illustrate its application across various fields. The study cites Milgram et al. (1995) to distinguish between virtual reality and augmented reality, explaining that while VR replaces reality with digital objects, AR overlays digital information on real-world scenes. The authors define AR by citing Azuma et al. (2001), highlighting its key features that include the combination of real and virtual objects, the alignment of these objects in a real environment, and interactive operation in real-time and 3D space. To trace the development and application of AR, the authors cite Sutherland's early work at Harvard University and the University of Utah, where the first AR system was created using a see-through display to present 3D graphics through the research study of Tamura (2002). The authors further mention Caudell and Mizell (1992), who developed an experimental AR system to assist workers in assembling wiring harnesses. The study also cites Feiner et al. (1997) for their mobile AR system, which registered 3D graphical tour guide information with buildings and artefacts. Further, the authors mention the work of Yamabe and Nakajima (2013), who proposed a system framework that augments traditional training environments using AR technologies, emphasizing the importance of maintaining the look and feel of the training environment to closely resemble the real one. The study also cites Van Krevelen and Poelman (2010), who surveyed the state of AR technology and its limitations concerning human factors, and Vera et al. (2014), who explored the application of AR in surgical education. Finally, the authors cite Simon et al. (2014), who proposed an AR-based training program for identifying maintenance tasks necessary for preventive or corrective maintenance.

Nordin et al. (2019) conducted a research study focused on developing a gamification application using augmented reality (AR) specifically designed for Technical & Vocational Education Training (TVET). The study aimed to enhance the learning experience by integrating AR technology into the educational environment. The research leveraged AR to create an interactive and immersive experience for students. The application was designed to overlay computer-generated content onto the real-world environment, directly related to laboratory practices and equipment used in TVET. The application was built on a client/server architecture, where the server side utilized the Easy AR platform. This platform is known for its real-time pattern recognition processing, which allows for the quick creation of AR applications. This setup ensured that the AR application could be efficiently developed and deployed. On the client side, Adobe Animate technology was employed to create a user-friendly and visually appealing graphical interface. The interface was designed to be intuitive, making it easy for students to interact with the application and access the information they needed. The implementation of this AR application aimed to make the learning process more engaging and straightforward. By providing content in an amusing and accessible way, the application was intended to facilitate and enhance students' understanding of the material. The AR application simulated nearly true-to-life environments, which helped attract students' attention and improve their comprehension in the relevant training areas. This simulation aspect made the learning experience more realistic and practical, aligning closely with the hands-on nature of TVET. The study revealed that using AR in this context was effective in engaging students and enhancing their understanding of the subject matter. The nearly true environment simulation provided by the AR application was particularly beneficial in making the learning process more interactive and appealing.

Nordin et al. (2019) noted that AR applications effectively enhanced learning outcomes, particularly in complex subjects like the OSI layer and network topology. The authors highlighted that the finding aligns with previous study of Khan et al. (2019) which reported that AR games made learning more engaging and effective by improving problem-solving, critical thinking, and multitasking skills. While AR games reduced cognitive load for some students, others reported feeling overwhelmed due to the large amount of content and tasks involved, indicating a need for careful design to avoid cognitive overload. The study found that AR-based educational games enhanced motivation by increasing engagement, satisfaction, fun, and enjoyment. The authors cited Chookaew et al. (2017) that described AR learning experiences as joyful and playful, contributing to greater student engagement compared to traditional learning methods; which resonated with the findings of their study. Specific motivational enhancements included increased satisfaction (40%), willingness to learn (38%), attention (38%), confidence (46%), and a positive learning attitude (56%). The study's findings are supported by previous research, underscoring the benefits of AR in making learning more interactive and enjoyable.

Nordin et al. (2019) concluded highlighting the benefits and potential of augmented reality (AR) and gamification in enhancing learning, particularly in Technical and Vocational Education and Training (TVET). The authors argued that AR not only offers novelty but also fosters conversational learning by providing a 3D focal point that encourages group interaction among students, which is especially effective for diploma students who learn better in groups. The study explores how gamification and AR can significantly improve skill development and student engagement in educational settings. However, it also acknowledges the complexity of these technologies, noting that there are both advantages and disadvantages to their use. The conclusion points to future research directions, where the authors plan to investigate how digital media can further elevate gamification in education. They also aim to explore the development of analytical thinking skills through games based on programming concepts, indicating a continued focus on integrating technology to enhance educational outcomes in professional certification environments.

Challenges of Augmented Reality on Vocational Education and Training

The challenges of Augmented Reality (AR) in vocational education and training have been explored by all the authors in our review of literature.

Chiang et al. (2022) discuss several challenges like technological limitations, integration with existing systems, user acceptance and cost among others related to AR in vocational education and training. The study notes that while AR technology offers innovative solutions, it is often constrained by hardware limitations, such as low processing power and inadequate display resolution, which can hinder the overall effectiveness of AR applications. Integrating AR into existing training systems and curricula can be complex and costly. This involves ensuring compatibility with current educational tools and platforms. There may be resistance from both educators and students in adopting new AR technologies, especially if they are not familiar with or comfortable using them. Developing and maintaining AR applications can be expensive, posing a barrier for institutions with limited budgets.

Fehling et al. (2016) highlight the lack of standardization, technical complexity and limited research among the challenges of integrating AR in VET. The absence of standardized AR tools and methodologies can create inconsistencies in training quality and effectiveness across different institutions. AR systems can be technically complex to set up and use, requiring specialized knowledge and training for both instructors and students. There is a need for more empirical research to assess the long-term effectiveness of AR in vocational education and training and to identify best practices for implementation. Bacca et al. (2019) address specific challenges like motivation vs. actual learning, content development and technical issues among others as challenges for AR in VET. While AR can enhance motivation, it does not automatically translate into improved learning outcomes. There is a risk that the novelty of AR might overshadow its educational value if not properly designed. Creating effective AR content that aligns with vocational education and training goals can be challenging. The content needs to be both engaging and educationally relevant. Technical problems, such as software bugs or hardware malfunctions, can disrupt the learning process and impact the effectiveness of AR applications.

Bacca et al. (2015) focus on issues like implementation costs, user training and integration challenges for implementation of AR in VET. The initial setup and ongoing maintenance of AR systems can be costly, which might be a barrier for many vocational education and training institutions. Both educators and students need adequate training to effectively use AR systems. Without proper training, the benefits of AR can be diminished. Integrating AR into existing training frameworks and curricula can be complex and may require significant adjustments. Tan et al. (2022), in concurrence with Chiang et al. (2022) and Bacca et al. (2015) identify similar challenges of user experience apart from technological accessibility and educational effectiveness. Ensuring a smooth and intuitive user experience is crucial, but achieving this can be challenging. Poor user experience can lead to frustration and decreased engagement. Access to the necessary AR hardware and software can be limited, especially in low-resource settings. Measuring the impact of AR on learning outcomes and ensuring that it effectively supports skill development can be difficult.

Lavrentieva et al. (2020) in the lines of Chiang et al. (2022) and Bacca et al. (2015) discuss high costs as the most important challenges of integrating AR in VET apart from complexity of simulation design and the issues of integration into training programs The high cost of VR and AR equipment and software can be a significant barrier, particularly for smaller institutions or those with limited funding. Designing simulations that accurately reflect real-world scenarios and provide meaningful training experiences can be complex and time-consuming. Incorporating AR technologies into existing vocational education and training programs requires careful planning and adaptation. Mekacher (2019) highlights technological adaptation, content relevance and training requirements as the challenges of AR in VET. Adapting new AR technologies to meet the specific needs of students with special needs can be challenging. Ensuring that AR content is relevant and effective for vocational education and training, especially for specialized fields, can be difficult. There is a need for comprehensive training for both educators and students to effectively use AR technologies.

Bacca et al. (2018) focus on motivational aspects, scope limitations and technical issues as main hindrances of AR integration in VET. While AR can increase motivation, it does not always guarantee improved learning outcomes. The design of AR applications must address both motivational and educational needs. The scope of AR applications may be limited by factors such as the type of training and the specific needs of learners. This can affect the generalizability of findings across different contexts. Technical problems, such as software glitches and hardware limitations, can impact the effectiveness of AR applications. Sirakaya & Kilic Cakmak (2018) note the limited impact on theoretical knowledge, cognitive overload, cost and accessibility as the challenges of AR in VET. AR may enhance practical skills but might not significantly affect theoretical understanding or self-efficacy related to theoretical knowledge. AR applications can sometimes overwhelm students with too much information or complex interactions, leading to cognitive overload. The cost of AR technology and its accessibility issues can be barriers for widespread implementation.

Cheung & Liu (2016) mention motion sickness, technical adjustments and integration with real world training as problems of AR in VET in their study. Some users may experience motion sickness or discomfort while using immersive VR systems like CAVE, which can affect their learning experience. Initial design flaws may require ongoing adjustments to the system, such as modifying settings to alleviate user discomfort. Ensuring that AR simulations align closely with real-world training requirements and effectively simulate practical tasks can be challenging. Nordin et al. (2019), in their study, address cognitive overload, content design, cost and resource allocation as problems of AR in VET. AR applications can sometimes lead to cognitive overload if the content and tasks are too complex, affecting students' ability to focus and learn effectively. Designing AR content that is both engaging and educationally effective requires careful consideration to avoid overwhelming students. Developing and implementing AR applications can be resource-intensive, which may pose challenges for institutions with limited budgets.

It can therefore be summarized as while AR holds great promise for enhancing vocational education and training, these studies (Refer to Table 2) highlight significant challenges including high costs, technological limitations, integration difficulties, user acceptance issues, and the need for effective content design. Addressing these challenges requires careful planning, ongoing research, and investment in both technology and training.

Table 2. Challenges of AR in VET Review of Literature matrix (author generated)

Sr. No	Challenges of AR in VET	Review of Literature
1	Technological Limitations	Chiang et al. (2022) Fehling et al. (2016) Bacca et al. (2019) Tan et al. (2022) Lavrentieva et al. (2020) Mekacher (2019) Bacca et al. (2018) Cheung & Liu (2016)
2	Integration with Existing Systems	Chiang et al. (2022) Bacca et al. (2015) Lavrentieva et al. (2020) Cheung & Liu (2016)
3	User Acceptance	Chiang et al. (2022) Bacca et al. (2015) Tan et al. (2022) Mekacher (2019)
4	Cost	Chiang et al. (2022) Bacca et al. (2015) Lavrentieva et al. (2020) Sirakaya & Kilic Cakmak (2018) Nordin et al. (2019)
5	Lack of Standardization	Fehling et al. (2016)
6	Limited Research	Fehling et al. (2016)

continued on following page

Table 2. Continued

Sr. No	Challenges of AR in VET	Review of Literature
7	Motivation vs. Actual Learning	Bacca et al. (2019)
8	Content Development	Bacca et al. (2019) Mekacher (2019) Nordin et al. (2019)
9	Educational Effectiveness	Tan et al. (2022) Sirakaya & Kilic Cakmak (2018)
10	Motivational Aspects	Bacca et al. (2018)
11	Scope Limitations	Bacca et al. (2018)
12	Cognitive Overload	Sirakaya & Kilic Cakmak (2018) Nordin et al. (2019)
13	Motion Sickness	Cheung & Liu (2016)

FUTURE RESEARCH DIRECTIONS

The future research directions highlighted in the review of literature on Augmented Reality (AR) in vocational education and training reflect a broad range of interests and concerns, aiming to address current challenges and explore new opportunities (Refer to Table 3).

Table 3. Future research directions of AR in VET Review of Literature matrix (author generated)

Sr. No	Future Research Directions of AR in VET	Review of Literature
1	Improvement of Technological Integration	Chiang et al. (2022) Fehling et al. (2016) Bacca et al. (2019) Tan et al. (2022) Bacca et al. (2018)
2	User Acceptance and Training	Chiang et al. (2022) Bacca et al. (2015) Tan et al. (2022) Mekacher (2019)
3	Cost-Effectiveness	Chiang et al. (2022) Bacca et al. (2015) Lavrentieva et al. (2020) Sirakaya & Kilic Cakmak (2018)

continued on following page

Table 3. Continued

Sr. No	Future Research Directions of AR in VET	Review of Literature
4	Standardization	Fehling et al. (2016) Lavrentieva et al. (2020)
5	Long-Term Effectiveness	Fehling et al. (2016)
6	Motivational and Educational Balance	Bacca et al. (2019) Tan et al. (2022)
7	Content Development	Bacca et al. (2019) Mekacher (2019)
8	Curriculum Integration	Bacca et al. (2015) Lavrentieva et al. (2020) Cheung & Liu (2016)
9	Simulation Design	Lavrentieva et al. (2020) Cheung & Liu (2016) Nordin et al. (2019)
10	Adaptation for Special Needs	Mekacher (2019)
11	Balancing Motivation and Learning	Bacca et al. (2018)
12	Scope and Generalizability	Bacca et al. (2018)
13	Impact on Theoretical Knowledge	Sirakaya & Kilic Cakmak (2018)
14	Avoiding Cognitive Overload	Sirakaya & Kilic Cakmak (2018) Nordin et al. (2019)
15	Motion Sickness Solutions	Cheung & Liu (2016)
16	Gamification and AR Integration	Nordin et al. (2019)

Chiang et al. (2022) highlight that the future research directions of AR in VET must include improvement of technological integration, user acceptance and training and cost-effectiveness. Fehling et al. (2016) stress on standardization, long-term effectiveness and technical simplicity as future research directions for AR in VET. Bacca et al. (2019) highlight motivational and educational balance, content development and technical enhancements for future research. Bacca et al. (2015) stress on cost reduction, training for educators and students and curriculum integration among others as the prospects for future research. Tan et al. (2022) also include user experience improvement, technological accessibility and educational effectiveness as important areas for future research on use of AR in VET. Lavrentieva et al. (2020) points out areas in creating cost-effective solutions, simulation design and integration strategies where future research can focus on. Mekacher (2019) stresses adaptation for special needs, content relevance and comprehensive training as areas for future research. Bacca et al. (2018) too brings forth future research areas in balancing motivation and learning, technical reliability and investigate how AR applications can be adapted to different vocational contexts and assess their generalizability across various training programs. For Sirakaya & Kilic Cakmak (2018) future research directions would include studying how AR can be used to enhance theoretical knowledge and self-efficacy, in addition to practical skills. Sirakaya & Kilic Cakmak (2018) also highlights looking into research methods to design AR applications that avoid cognitive overload and ensure that content is presented in a manageable and effective manner; and investigate ways to overcome barriers related to the cost and accessibility of AR technology, making it more widely available for vocational education and training. Cheung & Liu (2016) brings forth the need for research in areas that provide solutions to address issues such as motion sickness in immersive VR environments to improve user comfort and learning experience; to conduct research and implement design improvements to the VR systems to address initial flaws and enhance the overall user experience; and also developing methods to ensure that AR simulations closely align with real-world training requirements, providing practical and effective learning experiences. Nordin et al. (2019) highlights the need to study the cognitive load management where studies need to be conducted to investigate strategies for managing cognitive load in AR-based educational games to prevent overwhelming students and ensure effective learning; research best practices for designing AR content that is both engaging and educationally effective, particularly in complex subjects; and explore how gamification can be further integrated with AR to enhance educational outcomes and student engagement in vocational education and training.

From the above discussion, it can be summarized that the future research directions across these studies emphasize improving technology integration, reducing costs, enhancing user experience, and ensuring effective content design. Addressing these areas will help maximize the benefits of AR in vocational education and training and overcome current limitations.

CONCLUSION

This chapter has provided a comprehensive overview of the integration of Augmented Reality (AR) in VET, with a particular focus on its impact, benefits, challenges, and the associated ethical and practical considerations. Through a systematic review guided by the PRISMA guidelines, the chapter critically examined the current body of research and addressed several key aims and objectives. Hence, it can be concluded that Augmented Reality represents a powerful tool with the potential to significantly enhance vocational education and training by providing immersive and interactive learning experiences. While technology offers numerous benefits, including improved engagement and skill development, it also presents challenges that need to be addressed through careful design, implementation, and ethical considerations. The ongoing research and development in this field are essential for optimizing AR applications and fully realizing their potential in vocational education. Future research should focus on refining AR technologies, exploring their impact across different vocational contexts, and addressing the practical and ethical challenges associated with their use.

FUNDING

The author has received no funding for this research.

REFERENCES

Akçayır, M., & Akçayır, G. (2017). Advantages and challenges associated with augmented reality for education: A systematic review of the literature. *Educational Research Review*, 20, 1–11. DOI: 10.1016/j.edurev.2016.11.002

Azuma, R., Baillot, Y., Behringer, R., Feiner, S., Julier, S., & MacIntyre, B. (2001). Recent advances in augmented reality. *IEEE Computer Graphics and Applications*, 21(6), 34–47. DOI: 10.1109/38.963459

Azuma, R. T. (1997). A survey of augmented reality. *Presence (Cambridge, Mass.)*, 6(4), 355–385. DOI: 10.1162/pres.1997.6.4.355

Bacca, J., Baldiris, S., Fabregat, R., & Graf, S., & Kinshuk. (2014). Augmented reality trends in education: A systematic review of research and applications. *Journal of Educational Technology & Society*, 17(4), 133–149.

Bacca, J., Baldiris, S., Fabregat, R., & Kinshuk, . (2018). Insights into the factors influencing student motivation in augmented reality learning experiences in vocational education and training. *Frontiers in Psychology*, 9, 1486. DOI: 10.3389/fpsyg.2018.01486 PMID: 30186196

Bacca Acosta, J. L., Baldiris Navarro, S. M., Fabregat Gesa, R., & Graf, S. (2015). Mobile augmented reality in vocational education and training. *Procedia Computer Science*, 75, 49–58. DOI: 10.1016/j.procs.2015.12.203

Bacca Acosta, J. L., Baldiris Navarro, S. M., Fabregat Gesa, R., & Kinshuk, K. (2019). Framework for designing motivational augmented reality applications in vocational education and training. *Australasian Journal of Educational Technology*, 35(3). Advance online publication. DOI: 10.14742/ajet.4182

Billett, S. (2001). *Learning in the workplace: Strategies for effective practice*. Allen & Unwin.

Billinghurst, M., Clark, A., & Lee, G. (2015). A survey of augmented reality. *Foundations and Trends® in Human–Computer Interaction, 8*(2-3), 73-272.

Bogicevic, V., Liu, S. Q., Seo, S., Kandampully, J., & Rudd, N. A. (2021). Virtual reality is so cool! How technology innovativeness shapes consumer responses to service preview modes. *International Journal of Hospitality Management*, 93, 93. DOI: 10.1016/j.ijhm.2020.102806

Borgen, K. B., Ropp, T. D., & Weldon, W. T. (2021). Assessment of augmented reality technology's impact on speed of learning and task performance in aeronautical engineering technology education. *The International Journal of Aerospace Psychology*, 31(3), 219–229. DOI: 10.1080/24721840.2021.1881403

Carmigniani, J., & Furht, B. (2011). Augmented reality: An overview. In Furht, B. (Ed.), *Handbook of augmented reality* (pp. 3–46). Springer. DOI: 10.1007/978-1-4614-0064-6_1

Caudell, T. P., & Mizell, D. W. (1992). Augmented reality: An application of heads-up display technology to manual manufacturing processes. In *Proceedings of the twenty-fifth Hawaii international conference on system sciences* (Vol. 2, pp. 659–669). Piscataway, NJ. DOI: 10.1109/HICSS.1992.183317

Cawood, S., & Fiala, M. (2007). *Augmented reality: A practical guide*. The Pragmatic Programmers.

Champney, R., Lackey, S. J., Stanney, K., & Quinn, S. (2015). Augmented reality training of military tasks: Reactions from subject matter experts. In *Virtual, Augmented and Mixed Reality: 7th International Conference, VAMR 2015, Held as Part of HCI International 2015, Los Angeles, CA, USA, August 2-7, 2015* [Springer International Publishing.]. *Proceedings*, 7, 251–262.

Cheung, H., & Liu, S. (2016). Development of practical vocational training class making use of virtual reality-based simulation system and augmented reality technologies. *The 10th International Symposium on Advances in Technology Education*, 105-110.

Chiang, F. K., Shang, X., & Qiao, L. (2022). Augmented reality in vocational training: A systematic review of research and applications. *Computers in Human Behavior*, 129, 107125. DOI: 10.1016/j.chb.2021.107125

Chmielewski, M., Sapiejewski, K., & Sobolewski, M. (2019). Application of augmented reality, mobile devices, and sensors for a combat entity quantitative assessment supporting decisions and situational awareness development. *Applied Sciences (Basel, Switzerland)*, 9(21), 4577. DOI: 10.3390/app9214577

Choi, S., & Park, J.-S. (2021). Development of augmented reality system for productivity enhancement in offshore plant construction. *Journal of Marine Science and Engineering*, 9(2), 209. DOI: 10.3390/jmse9020209

Chookaew, S., Howimanporn, S., Sootkaneung, W., & Wongwatkit, C. (2017, July). Motivating pre-service teachers with augmented reality to developing instructional materials through project-based learning approach. In *2017 6th IIAI International Congress on Advanced Applied Informatics (IIAI-AAI)* (pp. 780-784). IEEE. DOI: 10.1109/IIAI-AAI.2017.106

Craig, A. B. (2013). *Understanding augmented reality: Concepts and applications*. Morgan Kaufmann.

Cruz-Neira, C., Sandin, D. J., & DeFanti, T. A. (1993). A 'room' with a 'view'. *IEEE Spectrum*, 30(10), 30–33. DOI: 10.1109/6.237582

Cruz-Neira, C., Sandin, D. J., DeFanti, T. A., Kenyon, R. V., & Hart, J. C. (1992). The CAVE: Audio visual experience automatic virtual environment. *Communications of the ACM*, 35(6), 64–73. DOI: 10.1145/129888.129892

Cuendet, S., Bonnard, Q., Do-Lenh, S., & Dillenbourg, P. (2013). Designing augmented reality for the classroom. *Computers & Education*, 68, 557–569. DOI: 10.1016/j.compedu.2013.02.015

Delello, J. A. (2014). Insights from pre-service teachers using science-based augmented reality. *Journal of Computers in Education*, 1(4), 295–311. DOI: 10.1007/s40692-014-0021-y

Dunleavy, M., Dede, C., & Mitchell, R. (2009). Affordances and limitations of immersive participatory augmented reality simulations for teaching and learning. *Journal of Science Education and Technology*, 18(1), 7–22. DOI: 10.1007/s10956-008-9119-1

Dünser, A., Grasset, R., & Billinghurst, M. (2008). *A survey of evaluation techniques used in augmented reality studies. Human Interface Technology Laboratory New Zealand (HIT Lab NZ)*. University of Canterbury.

Ellenkamp, J. J., Brouwers, E. P., Embregts, P. J., Joosen, M. C., & van Weeghel, J. (2016). Work environment-related factors in obtaining and maintaining work in a competitive employment setting for employees with intellectual disabilities: A systematic review. *Journal of Occupational Rehabilitation*, 26(1), 56–69. DOI: 10.1007/s10926-015-9586-1 PMID: 26112400

Farra, S. L., Miller, E. T., & Timm, N. (2019). Comparison of training methods for mass casualty triage using virtual reality. *Disaster Medicine and Public Health Preparedness*, 13(2), 301–308. DOI: 10.1017/dmp.2018.58 PMID: 30293544

Fehling, C. D., Müller, A., & Aehnelt, M. (2016). Enhancing vocational training with augmented reality. In *Proceedings of the 16th International Conference on Knowledge Technologies and Data-Driven Business*. ACM Press.

Feiner, S., MacIntyre, B., Höllerer, T., & Webster, A. (1997). A touring machine: Prototyping 3D mobile augmented reality systems for exploring the urban environment. *Personal Technologies*, 1(4), 208–217. DOI: 10.1007/BF01682023

Forest, D. D. (2021). Training the next generation of operators: AFPM immersive learning. *Process Safety Progress*, 40(4), 219–223. DOI: 10.1002/prs.12246

Fragomeni, G., Lackey, S. J., Champney, R., Salcedo, J. N., & Serge, S. (2015). Training effectiveness evaluation: Call for fire trainer–augmented virtuality (CFFT-AV). In *Virtual, Augmented and Mixed Reality: 7th International Conference, VAMR 2015, Held as Part of HCI International 2015, Los Angeles, CA, USA, August 2-7, 2015* [Springer International Publishing.]. *Proceedings*, 7, 263–272.

Freina, L., & Ott, M. (2015, April). A literature review on immersive virtual reality in education: state of the art and perspectives. In *The International Scientific Conference E-learning and Software for Education* (Vol. 1, No. 133, pp. 10-1007). DOI: 10.12753/2066-026X-15-020

Furió, D., González-Gancedo, S., Juan, M. C., Seguí, I., & Rando, N. (2013). Evaluation of learning outcomes using an educational iPhone game vs. traditional game. *Computers & Education*, 64, 1–23. DOI: 10.1016/j.compedu.2012.12.001

Gaba, D. M. (2004). The future vision of simulation in health care. *BMJ Quality & Safety*, 13(suppl 1), i2–i10. DOI: 10.1136/qshc.2004.009878 PMID: 15465951

Garzón, J., & Acevedo, J. (2019). Meta-analysis of the impact of augmented reality on students' learning gains. *Educational Research Review*, 27, 244–260. DOI: 10.1016/j.edurev.2019.04.001

Grasset, R., Dünser, A., & Billinghurst, M. (2008, December). Edutainment with a mixed reality book: a visually augmented illustrative childrens' book. In *Proceedings of the 2008 international conference on advances in computer entertainment technology* (pp. 292-295). DOI: 10.1145/1501750.1501819

Grollmann, P. (2008). The quality of vocational teachers: Teacher education, institutional roles and professional reality. *European Educational Research Journal*, 7(4), 535–547. DOI: 10.2304/eerj.2008.7.4.535

Grubb, W. N., & Ryan, P. (1999). *The roles of evaluation for vocational education and training: Plain talk on the field of dreams*. International Labour Organization.

Hager, P., & Gonczi, A. (1996). What is competence? *Medical Teacher*, 18(1), 15–18. DOI: 10.3109/01421599609040255

Keller, J. M. (2010). *Motivational design for learning and performance*. Springer. DOI: 10.1007/978-1-4419-1250-3

Khan, T., Johnston, K., & Ophoff, J. (2019). The impact of an augmented reality application on learning motivation of students. *Advances in Human-Computer Interaction*, 2019(1), 7208494. DOI: 10.1155/2019/7208494

Klopfer, E., & Squire, K. (2008). Environmental Detectives—The development of an augmented reality platform for environmental simulations. *Educational Technology Research and Development*, 56(2), 203–228. DOI: 10.1007/s11423-007-9037-6

Kourouthanassis, P. E., Boletsis, C., & Lekakos, G. (2015). Demystifying the design of mobile augmented reality applications. *Multimedia Tools and Applications*, 74(3), 1045–1066. DOI: 10.1007/s11042-013-1710-7

Kuhlen, T. W., & Hentschel, B. (2014). Quo vadis CAVE: Does immersive visualization still matter? *IEEE Computer Graphics and Applications*, 34(5), 14–21. DOI: 10.1109/MCG.2014.97 PMID: 25248196

Lavrentieva, O. O., Arkhypov, I. O., Kuchma, O. I., & Uchitel, A. D. (2020). Use of simulators together with virtual and augmented reality in the system of welders' vocational training: past, present, and future. In *Augmented reality in education: proceedings of the 2nd international workshop (AREdu 2019), Kryvyi Rih, Ukraine, March 22, 2019* (No. 2547, pp. 201-216). CEUR Workshop Proceedings.

Lester, S., & Costley, C. (2010). Work-based Learning at Higher Education Level: Value, Practice and Critique. *Studies in Higher Education*, 35(5), 561–575. DOI: 10.1080/03075070903216635

Lucas, B., Spencer, E., & Claxton, G. (2012). *How to Teach Vocational Education: A Theory of Vocational Pedagogy*. City & Guilds.

Mekacher, L. (2019). Augmented Reality (AR) and Virtual Reality (VR): The future of interactive vocational education and training for people with handicap. *International Journal of Teaching. Education and Learning*, 3(1), 1–12.

Meltzer, A., Robinson, S., & Fisher, K. R. (2020). Barriers to finding and maintaining open employment for people with intellectual disability in Australia. *Social Policy and Administration*, 54(1), 88–101. DOI: 10.1111/spol.12523

Meyer, A., Rose, D., & Gordon, D. (2014). *Universal design for learning, theory and practice*. CAST Professional Publishing.

Milgram, P., & Kishino, F. (1994). A Taxonomy of Mixed Reality Visual Displays. *IEICE Transactions on Information and Systems*, 77(12), 1321–1329.

Milgram, P., Takemura, H., Utsumi, A., & Kishino, F. (1995, December). Augmented reality: A class of displays on the reality-virtuality continuum. In *Telemanipulator and telepresence technologies* (Vol. 2351, pp. 282–292). Spie. DOI: 10.1117/12.197321

Moher, D., Liberati, A., Tetzlaff, J., & Altman, D. G.The PRISMA Group. (2009). Preferred Reporting Items for Systematic Reviews and Meta-Analyses: The PRISMA Statement. *PLoS Medicine*, 6(7), e1000097. DOI: 10.1371/journal.pmed.1000097 PMID: 19621072

Mulder, M. (2004). Competence-based Vocational Education and Training. In Nijhof, W. J., & Heikkinen, A. (Eds.), *Vocational Education and Training Through Open and Distance Learning* (pp. 65–82). Springer.

Nordin, S. Z. S., Ismail, I., Mustapa, A., & Omar, P. U. (2019) AUGMENTED REALITY (AR) GAMIFICATION APPLICATION IN TECHNICAL & VOCATIONAL EDUCATION TRAINING. *E-Proceedings of 4th International Conference on Research in TVET Studies (ICOR-TVET 2019)*

Pantelidis, V. S. (2010). Reasons to use virtual reality in education and training courses and a model to determine when to use virtual reality. *Themes in Science and Technology Education*, 2(1-2), 59–70.

Papagiannakis, G., Singh, G., & Magnenat-Thalmann, N. (2008). A Survey of Mobile and Wireless Technologies for Augmented Reality Systems. *Computer Animation and Virtual Worlds*, 19(1), 3–22. DOI: 10.1002/cav.221

Paryono. (2017). The Importance of TVET and Its Contribution to Sustainable Development. *The International Education Journal: Comparative Perspectives*, 16(4), 68-87.

Peddie, J. (2017). *Augmented Reality: Where We Will All Live*. Springer. DOI: 10.1007/978-3-319-54502-8

Pérez-López, D., & Contero, M. (2013). Delivering educational multimedia contents through an augmented reality application: A case study on its impact on knowledge acquisition and retention. *Turkish Online Journal of Educational Technology-TOJET*, 12(4), 19–28.

Rauner, F., & Maclean, R. (2008). *Handbook of Technical and Vocational Education and Training Research*. Springer.

Sanders, E., & Stappers, P. (2008). Co-creation and the new landscapes of design. *CoDesign*, 4(1), 5–18. DOI: 10.1080/15710880701875068

Santos, M. E. C., Chen, A., Taketomi, T., Yamamoto, G., Miyazaki, J., & Kato, H. (2013). Augmented reality learning experiences: Survey of prototype design and evaluation. *IEEE Transactions on Learning Technologies*, 7(1), 38–56. DOI: 10.1109/TLT.2013.37

Shelton, B. E., & Hedley, N. R. (2002, September). Using augmented reality for teaching earth-sun relationships to undergraduate geography students. In *The First IEEE International Workshop Agumented Reality Toolkit,* (pp. 8-pp). IEEE. DOI: 10.1109/ART.2002.1106948

Simón, V., Baglee, D., Garfield, S., & Galar, D. (2014). The development of an advanced maintenance training programme utilizing augmented reality.

Singhal, S., Bagga, S., Goyal, P., & Saxena, V. (2012). Augmented chemistry: Interactive education system. *International Journal of Computer Applications*, 49(15), 1–5. DOI: 10.5120/7700-1041

Sirakaya, M., & Kilic Cakmak, E. (2018). Effects of augmented reality on student achievement and self-efficacy in vocational education and training. *International journal for research in vocational education and training, 5*(1), 1-18.

Svistunova, A. A., & Gorshkov, M. D. (2013). *Simuljacionnoe obuchenie v medicine* [Simulation training in medicine]. MGMU im VM Sechenova Publ.

Tamura, H. (2002, November). Steady steps and giant leap toward practical mixed reality systems and applications. In *Proceedings of the International Status Conference on Virtual and Augmented Reality* (pp. 3-12).

Tan, B. L., Guan, F. Y., Leung, I. M. W., Kee, S. Y. M., Devilly, O. Z., & Medalia, A. (2022). A gamified augmented reality vocational training program for adults with intellectual and developmental disabilities: A pilot study on acceptability and effectiveness. *Frontiers in Psychiatry*, 13, 966080. DOI: 10.3389/fpsyt.2022.966080 PMID: 35990062

Tomi, A. B., & Rambli, D. R. A. (2013). An interactive mobile augmented reality magical playbook: Learning number with the thirsty crow. *Procedia Computer Science*, 25, 123–130. DOI: 10.1016/j.procs.2013.11.015

Van Krevelen, D. W. F., & Poelman, R. (2010). A survey of augmented reality technologies, applications and limitations. *The International Journal of Virtual Reality : a Multimedia Publication for Professionals*, 9(2), 1–20. DOI: 10.20870/IJVR.2010.9.2.2767

Vera, A. M., Russo, M., Mohsin, A., & Tsuda, S. (2014). Augmented reality telementoring (ART) platform: A randomized controlled trial to assess the efficacy of a new surgical education technology. *Surgical Endoscopy*, 28(12), 3467–3472. DOI: 10.1007/s00464-014-3625-4 PMID: 24962856

Wang, X., Kim, M. J., Love, P. E., & Kang, S. C. (2017). Augmented Reality in built environment: Classification and implications for future research. *Automation in Construction*, 72, 118–124.

Westerfield, G., Mitrovic, A., & Billinghurst, M. (2015). Intelligent augmented reality training for motherboard assembly. *International Journal of Artificial Intelligence in Education*, 25(1), 157–172. DOI: 10.1007/s40593-014-0032-x

Winch, C. (2013). The Attractiveness of Vocational Education and Training in an Inclusive System. *European Journal of Education*, 48(2), 274–289.

Wojciechowski, R., & Cellary, W. (2013). Evaluation of learners' attitude toward learning in ARIES augmented reality environments. *Computers & Education*, 68, 570–585. DOI: 10.1016/j.compedu.2013.02.014

Wu, H. K., Lee, S. W. Y., Chang, H. Y., & Liang, J. C. (2013). Current status, opportunities and challenges of augmented reality in education. *Computers & Education*, 62, 41–49. DOI: 10.1016/j.compedu.2012.10.024

Yamabe, T., & Nakajima, T. (2013). Playful training with augmented reality games: Case studies towards reality-oriented system design. *Multimedia Tools and Applications*, 62(1), 259–286. DOI: 10.1007/s11042-011-0979-7

Yang, X., Shu, L., Chen, J., Ferrag, M. A., Wu, J., Nurellari, E., & Huang, K. (2021). A survey on smart agriculture: Development modes, technologies, and security and privacy challenges. *IEEE/CAA Journal of Automatica Sinica, 8*(2), 273–302.

Yuen, S. C. Y., Yaoyuneyong, G., & Johnson, E. (2011). Augmented reality: An overview and five directions for AR in education. [JETDE]. *Journal of Educational Technology Development and Exchange*, 4(1), 11. DOI: 10.18785/jetde.0401.10

Zhou, F., Duh, H. B.-L., & Billinghurst, M. (2008). Trends in Augmented Reality Tracking, Interaction and Display: A Review of Ten Years of ISMAR. In *Proceedings of the 7th IEEE/ACM International Symposium on Mixed and Augmented Reality* (pp. 193-202). IEEE.

ADDITIONAL READING

Alves, S., Vaz, J., & Fernandes, A. (2023). Exploring clinical trials to manage firefighters' sleep quality: A PRISMA compliant systematic review. *International Journal of Environmental Research and Public Health*, 20(5), 3862. DOI: 10.3390/ijerph20053862 PMID: 36900873

Khan, A., Sepasgozar, S., Liu, T., & Yu, R. (2021). Integration of BIM and immersive technologies for AEC: A scientometric-SWOT analysis and critical content review. *Buildings*, 11(3), 126. DOI: 10.3390/buildings11030126

Pham, H. T. (2023). Visualizing Contemporary Factors Affecting the Adoption of E-learning: A PRISMA Approach. *TEM Journal*, 12(2), 1056–1068. DOI: 10.18421/TEM122-52

Seyman Guray, T., & Kismet, B. (2023). VR and AR in construction management research: Bibliometric and descriptive analyses. *Smart and Sustainable Built Environment*, 12(3), 635–659. DOI: 10.1108/SASBE-01-2022-0015

KEY TERMS AND DEFINITIONS

Augmented Reality (AR): A technology that overlays digital content such as images or animations onto the physical world, creating an interactive and immersive experience for users.

Gamification: The integration of game-like elements into non-game contexts, such as education, to increase motivation, engagement, and learning effectiveness.

Immersive Learning: A teaching method that uses technologies like AR and VR to create engaging, simulated environments that replicate real-world scenarios for hands-on learning.

Learning Analytics: The process of collecting, analyzing, and interpreting data about learners to improve educational outcomes and personalize training experiences.

Marker-Based AR: An AR approach that uses visual markers, such as QR codes or images, to trigger the display of digital content in real-world environments.

Mixed Reality (MR): A blend of AR and VR that integrates real and virtual elements into one environment, enabling interaction with both.

Motivational Design: A systematic approach to creating educational resources that enhance learner engagement by addressing attention, relevance, confidence, and satisfaction.

Simulation Training: The use of virtual environments to practice and refine skills in a controlled, risk-free setting that mimics real-world tasks.

Universal Design for Learning (UDL): An educational framework that aims to make learning accessible to all students by offering multiple means of engagement, representation, and expression.

Vocational Education and Training (VET): Education programs focused on developing specific practical skills and knowledge for particular jobs or trades.

Chapter 6

Integrating Artificial Intelligence in Police Education: An Analysis of the Top-Down Approach at Taiwan's Central Police University

Leo S. F. Lin
https://orcid.org/0000-0003-3684-5403
Charles Sturt University, Australia

ABSTRACT

This chapter explores the integration of artificial intelligence (AI) in police education by examining the case of Taiwan's Central Police University (CPU). It focuses on the institution's top-down approach to implementing AI technologies within its curriculum and training programs. The findings indicate that as the landscape of law enforcement evolves with rapid technological advancements, CPU has aimed to modernise its educational offerings since 2023 to better prepare future police officers for contemporary challenges. The study highlights the crucial role of institutional leadership in guiding AI adoption among faculty and students, ensuring that educational strategies align with both technological relevance and traditional pedagogical values. By enhancing its capabilities through various projects, conferences, workshops, and guidelines, CPU sets a precedent for other law enforcement vocational education institutions seeking to incorporate AI into their training frameworks.

DOI: 10.4018/979-8-3693-8252-3.ch006

INTRODUCTION

The rapid development of artificial intelligence (AI) has permeated nearly every sector globally, profoundly reshaping industries and professions, from healthcare, finance, manufacturing, retail, education, and crime prevention (Longbing Cao, 2022; Holmes, 2016; L. S. Lin, Aslett, Mekonnen, & Zecevic, 2024a; K. Liu et al., 2022; Noorbakhsh-Sabet, Zand, Zhang, & Abedi, 2019; Oosthuizen, Botha, Robertson, & Montecchi, 2021; Saputra, Astuti, Sayuti, & Kusumastuti, 2023). Law enforcement education, a traditionally structured and conservative field, has also begun to experience this transformation, as vocational, professional, and academic programs increasingly need to incorporate AI tools and methodologies at local, national, and global levels to address the growing threat of cybercrime (L. S. Lin, Aslett, Mekonnen, & Zecevic, 2024b). In Taiwan, the Central Police University (CPU) stands at the forefront of this shift, implementing AI technologies within its vocational education and training (VET) programs. This integration reflects a broader strategic initiative to modernize the training of law enforcement professionals in response to evolving societal needs and the unprecedented rise of digital technologies. As a leading institution for police education, CPU's approach to integrating AI emulates a top-down adoption strategy, wherein institutional directives guide technology implementation within an established teaching and training standards framework. This approach brings institutional challenges and practical considerations, particularly in balancing innovation with the traditional values and goals of police training.

This chapter investigates the strategic initiatives and institutional measures undertaken by CPU in response to the rapid development of AI, examining their influence on the university's curriculum, research capacities, and overarching mission in law enforcement education. Specifically, the study aims to understand how CPU's AI adoption addresses the dual imperatives of technological relevance and vocational specificity in its educational offerings. This chapter uses Rational Choice Institutionalism (RCI) as a theoretical framework that views institutions as structures of incentives and rules where rational actors make strategic, utility-maximizing decisions within constraints. With RCI, the study explores how institutional actors at CPU make strategic, cost-benefit decisions to achieve desired outcomes. RCI suggests that institutions create structured environments to guide individual decisions, aligning choices with immediate objectives and the organization's broader mission.

Taiwan's history of police education provides valuable context for understanding CPU's approach to integrating AI. Formalized police training in Taiwan began in the 27th year of the *Guangxu* era during the Qing Dynasty, laying the groundwork for the structured development of police education. The modern structure of police education was formalized in 1960 with the promulgation of the Police Education Act, which led to the establishment of CPU as a four-year police education institution, elevating police training to the university level. Police education in Taiwan has adopted a two-tiered system with CPU (a higher education institution offering bachelor to doctoral degrees) and the Taiwan Police College (a two-year program providing associate bachelor degrees), creating the foundation for a structured approach to law enforcement training (M. Liu, 1999). Today, police education in Taiwan comprises several categories, each serving distinct functions within the vocational education spectrum. Training education, mandated by Article 85 of Taiwan's ROC Constitution (Newton & Jong, 1989), ensures that civil servant selection is conducted through open competitive examinations, aligning employment with education, training, and evaluation protocols.[1] Promotion education enables career advancement within the police force based on training and evaluation, while professional education provides targeted learning opportunities for specific ranks of police personnel. Advanced education at CPU includes specialized courses for middle to senior police positions and postgraduate programs, underscoring the institution's role in equipping law enforcement professionals with foundational and advanced knowledge as they progress through their careers. By adopting AI into its offerings, CPU is modernizing its curriculum and setting new standards for VET institutions within Taiwan's public sector.

This study is grounded in the research question: *How does Central Police University's top-down approach to AI integration influence the institution's educational model, curriculum, and role in police education and training?* Addressing this question will help elucidate the processes, challenges, and outcomes of adopting AI in a specialized vocational and educational institution. The study examines CPU's experience through the RCI framework, considering the strategic choices made by the institution's leadership and faculty as they balance the benefits of AI with potential challenges, such as ethical concerns, data security, and the preservation of traditional pedagogical values. Integrating AI at the CPU is not only a technological shift but a recalibration of educational objectives, including digital literacy and a critical understanding of AI's role in modern policing. Therefore, this research question seeks to uncover how embedding emerging technologies within an established framework reshapes institutional priorities and examine the implications of these changes for instructors and students in the specialized field of police education.

The contribution of this study lies in its detailed case analysis of AI integration within a prominent, vocationally oriented educational institution. CPU's experience provides valuable insights for other VET institutions seeking to incorporate AI into their curricula and training programs. By focusing on the strategic and practical aspects of AI integration, this study offers concrete examples of how educational institutions can effectively navigate the complexities of adopting innovative technologies. It highlights the essential role of institutional leadership and support in driving successful technological transformation, offering a model that other universities and vocational training centers can adopt. Additionally, the study highlights the broader implications of AI for law enforcement education, particularly in how it might enhance or complicate traditional training practices. These insights are relevant to Taiwan and resonate globally as educational institutions worldwide grapple with how best to incorporate AI while maintaining the integrity of their specialized training programs. In this sense, CPU's endeavor toward AI integration is a microcosm of the broader educational challenges posed by the AI revolution, demonstrating the importance of a strategic and well-supported approach to institutional transformation. This study advances knowledge in this area and contributes to ongoing discussions about the future of AI in vocational education, offering lessons that apply to various national and international contexts.

LITERATURE REVIEW

Artificial Intelligence and Law Enforcement Education and Training

Research on integrating artificial intelligence in police education and vocational training is still sparse, reflecting a major gap in understanding how AI can transform law enforcement education and training environments. The incorporation of AI into policing represents a profound shift, offering opportunities to enhance operational capabilities, situational awareness, and even community safety. Several jurisdictions, particularly in the European Union, have highlighted the need for AI in policing to be human-centered, aligning with values of trust, dignity, and community respect (Sanz-Urquijo, Fosch-Villaronga, & Lopez-Belloso, 2023). This emphasis underscores the importance of ethical AI applications, acknowledging that AI in law enforcement is not merely about efficiency but about supporting a responsible, transparent, and community-focused policing model. AI offers extensive potential uses in policing, with predictive policing standing out as an important area of progress (Kaufmann, 2024). Agencies are adopting predictive policing tools to identify crime patterns preemptively and support more informed decision-making. While AI in predictive policing has shown promise in improving crime mitigation strategies and boosting officers' situational awareness, it also raises questions about balancing technological benefits with ethical considerations (Al Shamsi & Safei, 2023). Recognizing this, the Abu Dhabi Police have combined AI technologies with specialized training for officers, creating collaborative learning environments that prioritize crime prevention and ethical responsibility (Al Shamsi & Safei, 2023). This integration reflects a growing recognition that AI adoption in policing is most effective when paired with robust training that helps officers use these tools responsibly.

Beyond predictive policing, combining augmented reality (AR) with AI is another promising technology to enhance officers' situational awareness (Mojadidi, 2024). Augmented reality applications can provide real-time information overlays in the field, which is especially valuable in high-risk situations where quick, informed responses are crucial (Apostolakis et al., 2022). By embedding AR and AI within training programs, police departments can prepare officers for complex scenarios requiring technical skill and adaptive thinking. This approach meets operational needs and aligns with the shift towards experiential learning in police education, where hands-on training is efficient. Studies have found that officers prefer training that directly applies to their daily duties, fostering engagement and ensuring that training is as relevant as possible to real-world policing (Thomas & Watson, 2017).

An fundamental component of modern police training is mental health and crisis intervention, a growing area of concern given the rise in encounters between law enforcement and individuals experiencing mental health crises (Copsey, 2024). The research underscores the effectiveness of training programs focused on mental health and suicide prevention, which have been shown to improve officers' confidence and skills in managing these sensitive situations (Arensman et al., 2016; Marzano, Smith, Long, Kisby, & Hawton, 2016). Specialized training that equips officers with crisis intervention and de-escalation skills can lead to better outcomes for individuals and officers in crisis, fostering a more compassionate and community-oriented approach to policing (Thomas & Watson, 2017). These types of training complement AI and other technologies by grounding their use in human-centered values. They ensure that while officers gain access to the latest tools, they also prepare to address the social and emotional dimensions of policing.

Integrating AI and enhanced methodologies into police education and training supports a more adaptive, efficient, and empathetic policing model. However, as AI technologies evolve, police education and training programs must pay close attention to ethical considerations, ensuring that AI tools foster community trust rather than erode it. Završnik (2020) and Matulionytė & Hanif (2021) have argued that successful integration of AI in policing requires maintaining a focus on transparency, fairness, and accountability (Matulionyte & Hanif, 2021; Završnik, 2020). As AI becomes more prominent in law enforcement, it is essential to continuously reassess and adapt training programs, ensuring officers are skilled in using AI and attuned to its limitations and ethical implications. The result is a forward-looking police education model that integrates advanced technologies without compromising the foundational values of trust, dignity, and public service.

Taiwan's Police Education

The development of Taiwan's police education system has gradually taken on a uniquely character, shaped by Taiwan's specific social, legal, and cultural context. Over time, a dual-track training structure has emerged, encompassing Central Police University and Taiwan Police College, each playing distinctive roles in preparing future police officers (Liqun Cao & Dai, 2006; Liqun Cao, Huang, & Sun, 2016). Taiwan's police education system has undergone significant transformations in recent years, driven by shifting political dynamics, societal expectations, and the evolving landscape of law enforcement. Integrating evidence-based practices, a strong focus on human rights, and adopting modern technologies are critical in reshaping the training and operational frameworks for police officers in Taiwan.

Evidence-based policing has gained momentum in Taiwan, highlighting the importance of research and data in guiding police practices (Huang & Shih, 2025). Lin et al. (2022) underscore that police receptivity to research is vital for effectively implementing evidence-based strategies (K. Lin, Sidebottom, & Wortley, 2022). Human rights education plays another crucial role in shaping police training in Taiwan. Recent studies reveal that exposure to police education can significantly influence officers' attitudes toward human rights and moral reasoning. A longitudinal study highlighted a troubling trend: increased time spent in police education correlated with a decline in support for human rights and a rise in prejudice among officers (K.-h. Lin, Sidebottom, & Wortley, 2023). This paradox raises critical questions about the content and delivery of police education programs, emphasizing the need to promote ethical standards and a genuine respect for human rights. Trust in the police is fundamental to effective law enforcement. Research indicates that public perceptions of police legitimacy hinge on various factors, such as government responsiveness and experiences with corruption (Sun, Jou, Hou, & Chang, 2014; Wu, Poteyeva, & Sun, 2012). In Taiwan, fostering trust between the police and the community is essential for enhancing cooperation and reducing crime. Educational initiatives focusing on procedural justice and community engagement are vital for building positive relationships between law enforcement and the public, particularly among immigrant populations (Lai, Luo, Kang, & Lo, 2024).

Rational Choice Institutionalism

This chapter defines Rational Choice Institutionalism (RCI) as a theoretical approach within institutional analysis that considers institutions as structures of incentives and rules that constrain and facilitate the actions of rational, utility-maximising actors. Peter Guy identifies four main strands of institutionalism, each offering a different perspective on policy choice and policymaking (Peters, 2019).

First, Normative Institutionalism emphasizes that values, routines, and symbols shape institutions, with individuals adopting and acting according to the values they learn within the institutional framework. This approach highlights the influence of both procedural and substantive values on decision-making. Secondly, Historical Institutionalism argues that policies tend to persist over time unless disrupted by significant forces, and while institutions may be resistant to change, they can evolve gradually without abrupt shifts. Thirdly, Discursive Institutionalism centers on the role of discourse, distinguishing between "coordinative discourse" used within institutions to define their internal identity and "communicative discourse" used to explain the institution's purpose to outsiders. The internal, or coordinative, discourse is often subject to contestation and change, making institutions in this approach more fluid than those in normative institutionalism. Finally, Rational Choice Institutionalism focuses on individual self-interest, where actors within institutions make decisions to maximize their personal goals, viewing institutions as systems of incentives and rules. Unlike normative institutionalists, rational choice scholars believe institutions are more adaptable and more accessible to change.

Rational Choice Institutionalism is a theoretical approach that posits individuals use institutions to maximize their utility, while institutions shape and influence rational behavior (Knight & Sened, 1998). RCI explains the creation of institutions to reduce the transaction costs of collective activities, which would otherwise be higher without them (Williamson, 1985). Institutions persist because they lower uncertainty and facilitate gains from exchange. RCI assumes that political actors have fixed preferences and act instrumentally, using systematic foresight and cost-benefit analysis to maximize their goals (Binder & Rockman, 2005). RCI scholars often define institutions as the "rules of the game." These rules shape actors' incentives, influencing their behavior by outlining available strategies and structuring the sequence of choices they can make. Douglass North considers institutions "the rules of the game in a society or, more formally,...the humanly devised constraints that shape human interaction" (North, 1990). Jack Knight offers a notable definition of institutions in Rational Choice Institutionalism, describes institutions as:

"...sets of rules that structure social interactions in particular ways. These rules (1) provide information about how people are expected to act in particular situations, (2) can be recognized by those who are members of the relevant group as the rules to which others conform in these situations, and (3) structure the strategic choices of actors in such a way as to produce equilibrium outcomes..." (Knight, 1992).

An institution can be seen as a framework that identifies the actors, outlines their available strategies or behaviors, specifies the sequence in which they make choices and details the information they have when making decisions and the outcomes resulting from these choices. When actor preferences, or evaluations of outcomes, are incorporated, this framework transforms into a game (Binder & Rockman, 2005). Actors shape their behavior based on their expectations of how others negotiate, while the institutional environment provides information and enforcement mechanisms that reduce uncertainty (Hall & Taylor, 1996). This "calculus approach" underlines how institutions shape individual behavior and emphasizes the role of strategic interaction in determining policy outcomes.

Rational choice institutionalism views institutions as the outcome of strategic interactions among groups of rational decision-makers (M. Aspinwall & Schneider, 2001; M. D. Aspinwall & Schneider, 2000). In explaining collective decisions, rationalist scholars generally consider three key factors influencing decision-makers behavior and the outcomes they reach: *institutions, interests, and information.* The significance of interest divergence or potential information asymmetries between decision-makers in understanding a specific decision depends on the research question (Schneider & Ershova, 2018). For rational choice scholars, enhancing world knowledge requires linking micro-level interactions to macro-level processes and events (Ferejohn, 2002). This involves examining how individuals make choices within constraints, including anticipating the likely actions of others, to explain equilibrium outcomes or deviations (Levi, 1997).

Rational Choice Institutionalism offers a clear structure with transparent assumptions and systematic arguments. Its cohesive framework allows scholars to build on each other's work, facilitating debate, collaboration, and the accumulation of knowledge. As researchers refine previous models, RCI benefits from collective learning and long-term progress, unlike other approaches that often generate more idiosyncratic theories without a shared foundation (Weyland, 2002). However, an key limitation of RCI lies in its reliance on simplified assumptions, markedly the notion that individuals always act as rational actors driven by self-interest. Such a perspective overlooks important factors such as emotions, social norms, and ethics in decision-making. Furthermore, RCI's conceptual models can detach from real-world complexities, limiting their practical application and potentially overseeing important influences on institutional behaviour.

Discussion of Literature Review

The literature review addresses relevant studies on AI integration into police education and training but could benefit from a more critical examination of existing research gaps to underscore the need for this study. First, while research recognises AI's potential to enhance predictive policing and situational awareness, studies often overlook the complexities of aligning AI applications with law enforcement's ethical and community-focused missions, especially during the stage of police education. Current literature focuses on technological capabilities rather than critically examining the education and training needed to ensure future police officers can use AI responsibly. This gap in understanding the educational requirements for ethical AI use in policing leaves questions about how well AI can truly support community trust and transparency.

Second, even though AI tools like augmented reality can enhance situational awareness, few studies look at how these tools are accepted in education and training, or how to adjust them to meet the needs of police officers. There is little research on how training programs with AR and AI support hands-on learning in police education, which is key for preparing officers for challenging situations that require both tech skills and ethical judgement. Also, combining mental health and crisis intervention skills with AI-focused training is under researched. Few studies explore how AI training can mix well with human-centred skills like crisis management, which is vital for gaining community trust.

Lastly, this study's use of Rational Choice Institutionalism is critical to understanding how schools, like police universities, deal with adding AI to police teaching. RCI provides a straightforward way to see how these schools make smart, cost-based choices when using AI tech that fits their teaching goals and the needs of law enforcement. By seeing police educational institutions as active parts of a more extensive system, RCI allows a look at how certain rewards, limits, and tactics shape what police schools teach, study, and change to meet AI's more prominent role in policing. This method also highlights the ways police schools might adjust to mix new AI tools with the ethical and people-focused needs that are crucial in law enforcement.

METHOD

This study adopts a qualitative single-case approach (Gaya & Smith, 2016; Haugaard Jacobsen, 2007). The case is Central Police University, a unique and suitable case that examines the integration of artificial intelligence into police vocational education in Taiwan. A case study methodology is particularly effective for this research, as it enables an in-depth exploration of complex, context-specific phenomena such as the strategies, challenges, and impacts associated with AI integration within a real-world educational setting. Qualitative approaches are valuable because they allow for a rich, detailed examination of the nuances involved in AI adoption, which cannot be fully captured through quantitative methods. This approach supports a holistic understanding of CPU's initiatives and provides nuanced insights into how these efforts align with broader educational and law enforcement goals.

The study draws from various data sources between January 2023 and October 2024 to provide a comprehensive view of AI integration at CPU. First, the author reviews open-source publications such as academic articles, reports, and relevant policies on AI applications in police education. These sources offer foundational knowledge and a theoretical framework that contextualizes CPU's efforts within the broader landscape of AI education literature. Additionally, official websites reporting on CPU's AI initiatives will be analyzed to explore how these educational reforms resonate with broader societal and institutional contexts, adding depth to the understanding of CPU's strategic directions.

The study draws on multiple data sources from January 2023 to October 2024 to provide a comprehensive view of AI integration at the CPU. First, it includes open-source publications such as academic articles on AI in police education, government reports, and institutional policies on AI applications specific to Taiwan's police training context. Additionally, official CPU websites, institutional announcements, and news reports will be analyzed to understand how CPU's AI reforms resonate with societal and institutional priorities. Key sources include CPU's online event updates, the CPU Journal of Police Science, and various workshop records. These materials capture details of the CPU's strategic priorities and how it communicates AI-related developments.

During the author's tenure at CPU and other institutions in Taiwan from mid-2022 to mid-2024, informal discussions and academic engagements with CPU faculty and leadership provided further context, including access to workshop notes and publicly available speeches by CPU administrators and faculty discussing AI integration. Selected statements and recordings, translated by the author (from Chinese to English), offer direct insights into the strategic motivations behind CPU's AI implementation and faculty priorities in adapting technology for police training.

Finally, the author examines CPU faculty publications and doctoral and master's theses to document AI-driven projects and curriculum advancements. Examples include student research on AI applications recorded in Taiwan's National Digital Library of Theses and Dissertations. These research outputs capture firsthand applications of AI within the CPU's training framework, contributing to a detailed understanding of how the institution operationalizes AI for educational enhancement.

Data analysis will proceed through thematic analysis, allowing for the identification of key patterns and themes within the collected data (Braun & Clarke, 2012; Guest, MacQueen, & Namey, 2011; Maguire & Delahunt, 2017). Initial coding will categorize data into manageable segments, facilitating information organization and revealing recurring themes. Researchers will group these codes into broader themes that reflect core aspects of AI integration at CPU, including pedagogical strategies, technological challenges, ethical concerns, and levels of student engagement. The interpretative analysis will position these thematic findings within the existing literature, providing nuanced insights into how CPU's approach to AI aligns with or diverges from global trends in AI-driven education.

The study also includes a historical overview of Central Police University, tracing its development since its establishment in 1936. This contextual background is essential for understanding CPU's institutional culture and educational evolution, particularly concerning embracing new technologies. Through this qualitative approach, the research aims to offer valuable insights into AI integration at CPU, contributing to the broader discourse on vocational education and law enforcement training.

PROFILING THE CASE

History and Development of Central Police University

Central Police University (CPU) has a rich history that spans over a century and is deeply intertwined with Taiwan's policing evolution. Established in 1901 as the Beijing Police Academy during the Qing Dynasty, the university's foundations were laid in mainland China. Following a series of mergers under the Kuomintang (KMT) government in 1936, the Central Police Academy was created in Nanjing, offering two- and three-year police education programs. However, the Second Sino-Japanese War outbreak forced the academy to relocate to Chongqing, China's wartime capital, in 1937 (Liqun Cao et al., 2016). In 1944, CPU expanded its educational offerings, launching an advanced course for senior police executives. As Taiwan's return to Chinese sovereignty became imminent after World War II, the university began preparing future police leaders, sending top graduates to the United States to study policing techniques and improve Taiwan's standards. Upon Taiwan's post-war reconstruction, CPU's main campus was re-established in Nanjing, and it began to expand its presence, including opening branch campuses in major cities such as Shanghai and Taipei.

The university's stability was disrupted during the Chinese Civil War, leading to multiple relocations. However, by 1954, CPU resumed full operations in Taiwan and eventually gained degree-granting status in 1957, offering a four-year bachelor's program. The institution continued to grow, introducing graduate programs in 1970 and admitting female students in 1974 (Liqun Cao et al., 2016). The 1990s saw CPU expand further, offering doctoral programs and a broader curriculum, including Public Safety, Fire Services, Forensic Science, and Law.

On December 12, 1995, the Legislative Yuan passed CPU's organizational statute, and President Lee Teng-hui formally renamed it Central Police University. A landmark event in CPU's history came in 2013, when it established the College of Police Management and the College of Police Science and Technology, marking its commitment to embracing both academic rigor and technological advancement. Over its 80-year history, CPU has consistently upheld high education standards, continually innovating to meet modern policing needs, and reinforcing its role as a science-driven institution for training Taiwan's future police professionals.[2]

Regarding presidents, CPU's leadership has evolved in response to changing political landscapes and institutional priorities. Initially led by figures like Chiang Kai-shek, the university's leadership reflected the close ties between military and police training. This tradition continued with leaders like Li Shi-zhen and Chen Yu-hui, who emphasized discipline and order during Taiwan's volatile mid-20th-century period. In the 1960s and 1970s, under Mei Ke-wang's leadership, the university shifted toward international academic standards, incorporating a broader educational framework. Mei's tenure signaled the university's emergence as a regional leader in law enforcement education. This direction continues today under recent presidents such as Hou You-yi and Yang Yuan-ming. These leaders have maintained a blend of academic credentials and practical law enforcement experience, ensuring CPU continues preparing students for the evolving challenges of modern policing, including AI integration.

The rise of AI in policing and CPU's efforts to incorporate these technologies into its educational programs can be seen as the next phase in its long history of adapting to modern policing needs. Today, CPU continues its tradition of innovation by integrating AI and addressing contemporary challenges like data security, ethical use of technology, and the development of AI-driven policing strategies. These efforts reflect CPU's enduring mission to balance the legacy of law enforcement training with cutting-edge technological advancements.

Table 1. Key Milestones in the History of the Central Police University

Year	Key Milestone
1936	Established as the Central Police College in Nanjing under the Kuomintang (KMT) government
1937	Relocated to Chongqing during the Second Sino-Japanese War (1937–1945)
1944	Launched training courses for police executives in anticipation of Taiwan's post-war developments
1945	Returned to Nanjing after World War II; expanded its presence nationwide
1954	Resumed operations in Taiwan following the Chinese Civil War and the relocation of the government to Taiwan
1957	Became a degree-granting institution, offering a formal university education in policing

continued on following page

Table 1. Continued

Year	Key Milestone
1970	Launched Taiwan's first graduate program in Police Science
1974	Admitted female students, marking a significant step towards gender equality in police training
1995	Renamed from Central Police College to Central Police University
2013	Established the College of Police Management and the College of Police Science and Technology to expand its academic scope
Present	Incorporating AI into curricula to address modern policing challenges and enhance professional training

Table made by the author

Organizational Structure[3]

The Central Police University is a vital institution under the Ministry of the Interior (MOI), dedicated to advancing policing studies and training professional police personnel. Its leadership structure features a President and a Vice President, both of whom hold senior ranks in the police force. This arrangement ensures that those at the helm possess relevant law enforcement experience, which enhances the institution's ability to address the complexities of policing in Australia. The university houses various departments, including the Department of Academic Affairs and the Department of Student Affairs, each managing specific functions critical to university operations. This clear organizational framework promotes efficiency and effective communication across the institution.

The CPU emphasizes practical training through its Extension Education Training Center, which provides ongoing professional development for in-service officers. This commitment to lifelong learning ensures that current police personnel remain equipped with the latest knowledge and skills necessary for effective law enforcement. The Forensic Science Laboratory also conducts essential scientific research supporting teaching and real-world policing applications. Integrating practical and theoretical learning fosters a comprehensive educational environment, allowing students to apply their knowledge in realistic scenarios.

The CPU establishes its operational regulations to maintain its relevance and adaptability, which require approval from the Ministry of the Interior. This governance structure enables the university to respond promptly to emerging challenges within the policing landscape. Moreover, the university's various committees allow for tailored responses to specific needs, ensuring a dynamic approach to education and administration.

Mission and Goals[4]

The mission and goals of the Central Police University reflect a strong commitment to fostering a well-rounded and dynamic learning environment designed to meet the evolving needs of law enforcement. CPU aspires to strengthen its competitiveness and establish itself as a leading institution in police education, positioning itself among top-tier universities globally. With a clear focus on innovation, it seeks to blend tradition with modernity, offering a unique educational experience that responds to national and international challenges.

At the heart of CPU's mission is the commitment to producing capable and ethical future police professionals. The university balances moral integrity and academic excellence, reflecting honesty and practical action values. This approach is integral to shaping students who excel in technical and theoretical knowledge and uphold the highest standards of conduct in public service. CPU's development goals underscore the importance of nurturing leadership in law enforcement while ensuring that graduates remain prepared to serve the community with dedication and skill.

CPU's development principles are guiding pillars, focusing on strategic foresight, collective action, and efficient administration. The institution recognizes the importance of talent cultivation, resource integration, and maintaining healthy competition among its departments. CPU promotes innovation in academic research and fosters an environment where teaching, discipline, and development integrate seamlessly. This approach aims to provide a comprehensive education that prepares students for the complexities of modern policing.

Furthermore, CPU's development strategies outline the steps required to achieve its ambitious goals. The university commits to strengthening its academic structure, establishing research centers, and continuously enhancing teaching quality. These strategies aim to meet societal needs, improve the learning environment, and motivate staff and students. Through these efforts, the CPU responds to the immediate demands of law enforcement and positions itself as a forward-thinking institution that adapts to the needs of an ever-changing world.

Incumbent president Yang Yuan-ming aims to integrate his extensive practical knowledge with academic instruction. He emphasizes the need for police education to evolve with modern challenges, particularly in the face of increasing cybercrime and technologically advanced criminal activities. Yang's vision for the university involves strengthening the intersection between academic theory and real-world law enforcement, ensuring students grasp the necessary theoretical frameworks and develop practical solid capabilities. His leadership focuses on enhancing emerging technological investigative skills and reinforcing ethical standards, all while nurturing teamwork and a deep commitment to public service, ensuring CPU graduates are well-prepared to meet contemporary challenges in policing.[5]

CPU's University-level Activities Regarding AI in Police Education and Training

Since 2023, Central Police University has been advancing AI integration in Taiwan's police education, focusing on practical skills and ethical considerations. CPU's initiatives address a pressing need identified in global research: the gap between AI's technical capabilities and the training required for its ethical, community-focused application in policing. For instance, recent workshops have introduced essential tools like "Whisper Desktop," an AI speech recognition platform, and "Google NotebookLM," a generative AI Q&A tool tailored to improve communication and expand knowledge for Taiwan's police officers. These tools parallel international trends in AI-enhanced situational awareness. CPU is also taking strides to ensure police students are trained in using these technologies responsibly—a factor often underexplored in other contexts.

Events like the "2024 Smart Technology and Police General Education Academic Conference" align CPU's efforts with global discussions on smart policing and AI's role in law enforcement. This conference encourages an exchange of ideas on how Taiwan's police force can adapt to rapidly changing technological landscapes, similar to the challenges faced by police institutions worldwide. Moreover, CPU's collaboration with international experts, such as Wade Carpenter, President of the International Association of Chiefs of Police, underscores CPU's commitment to learning from international best practices in AI application while addressing Taiwan's unique policing needs.

To sustain and expand these efforts, CPU has launched policies to boost faculty expertise in science and technology education and has plans to establish a "Digital Technology Investigation and Research Centre." These steps reflect CPU's dedication to preparing law enforcement professionals for technical proficiency and the ethical challenges of AI in modern policing, ensuring that Taiwan's approach aligns with global standards while addressing local institutional priorities and societal values.

After reviewing the data, the researcher has identified the following main themes regarding CPU's university-level activities to integrate AI into police education:

A. **Leadership and Strategy:** Top-down leadership and strategy are crucial as institutional leaders set the direction for AI adoption, backed by government support and strategic initiatives that embed AI across educational frameworks.
B. **Faculty Development and Training:** Faculty development and training ensures educators have access to workshops and conferences, empowering them to integrate AI effectively into their teaching.

C. **Curriculum Modernisation and Updates:** Curriculum modernisation reshapes courses to include AI-related content, balancing the benefits of innovative technology with traditional teaching values.
D. **Research and Innovation:** Research and innovation, the planned dedicated AI research centre, fosters creativity and innovation, encouraging ethically sound practices.
E. **Student Engagement and Learning:** Student engagement and learning outcomes benefit from AI tools that enhance critical thinking and analytical skills while guiding students in the ethical use of AI.
F. **Ethics and Challenges:** Challenges and ethical considerations remain central, especially in addressing data privacy and balancing efficiency with public trust in AI applications.
G. **Global Impact and Best Practices:** Global implications and best practices offer insights for vocational education and law enforcement training, sharing lessons learned that can support international standards and collaborative growth.

Table 2. List of CPU University-Level Activities in AI and Police Education and Training (Selected)

#	*Date*	*Title*	*Main Themes*	*Category*
1	October 21, 2024	"AI Speech Recognition Tool Whisper Desktop" Education and Training (https://cc.cpu.edu.tw/p/404-1012-43508.php)	A, B, F	Workshop/ seminar
2	September 29, 2024	"Generative AI Q&A Tool Google NotebookLM" Education and Training (https://cc.cpu.edu.tw/p/404-1012-43447.php)	A, B, D, F	Workshop/ seminar
3	September 24, 2024	2024 Smart Technology and Police General Education Academic Conference (https://gec.cpu.edu.tw/p/404-1027-43391.php)	A, B, D, E, G	Conference
4	September 12, 2024	Official Visit of Wade Carpenter, President of the International Association of Chiefs of Police (https://lib.cpu.edu.tw/p/403-1036-42.php)	A, G	Visit (International exchanges)
5	September 6, 2024	"Strengthen teachers' science and technology teaching functions and health awareness" Education and Training (https://daa.cpu.edu.tw/p/404-1033-43415.php)	A, B	Workshop/ seminar
6	August 20, 2024	"Development and Application of Generative AI" Education and Training (https://child.cpu.edu.tw/p/406-1002-43192,r189.php)	A, B, C, F	Workshop/ seminar
7	August, 2023	Plan to enhance teaching capacity in response to new types of crimes (https://acc.cpu.edu.tw/var/file/8/1008/attach/10/pta_24876_4040058_68189.pdf)	A, B, C, D, E, F, G	Policy/ Guidelines
8	June 29 to July 13, 2024	Project on Strengthening international scientific investigation professional exchange (https://report.nat.gov.tw/ReportFront/ReportDetail/detail?sysId=C11301398)	B, D, G	Project (Faculty International Research)
9	May 14, 2024	2024 Conference on Police Administration and Police Law "Police Service and Smart Policing" (https://pa.cpu.edu.tw/p/406-1014-42521,r21.php)	A, D, E, G	Conference

continued on following page

Table 2. Continued

#	*Date*	*Title*	*Main Themes*	*Category*
10	May 9, 2024	Central Police University's Guide to Using Generative AI Learning Applications (https://daa.cpu.edu.tw/p/406-1033-42663,r772.php)	A, B, C, D, E, F, G	Policy/ Guidelines
11	April, 2024	Plans to establish "Digital Technology Investigation and Research Centre" (https://www.moi.gov.tw/News_Content.aspx?n=4&sms=9009&s=314772)	A, B, D	Project (Research Centre Construction)
12	December 19-21, 2023	2023 AAPS International Symposium on Technological Policing and Criminal Justice (https://www.pbs.npa.gov.tw/ch/app/data/view?module=wg183&id=18740&serno=be016764-6669-4369-9aec-5d3cad6008f5)	A, B, D, E, G	Conference
13	November 24, 2023	Smart Policing Training Workshop (https://daa.cpu.edu.tw/p/406-1033-42016,r36.php)	A, B, D, F	Workshop/ seminar
14	October 2, 2023	AI deep fake technology teacher seminar (https://www.moi.gov.tw/News_Content.aspx?n=10&s=296902)	A, B, D, F	Workshop/ seminar
15	May 11, 2023	Seminar on innovations and challenges of police work in the technological era (https://reurl.cc/WN5aa9)	A, B, D, F, G	Workshop/ seminar

Made by the author

CPU's Currently Policy on the Use of AI

In May 2024, Central Police University released *Guidelines for the Learning and Application of Generative AI.*[6] The guidelines focus on three key areas. The first area is research. Faculty members and researchers are encouraged to use generative AI to assist—not replace—the creative research process. While AI can aid content generation, it cannot replicate essential human skills like creativity, problem-solving, and critical analysis. Researchers should verify AI-generated content for accuracy and source transparency, as AI operates on probabilistic models that may lack citation precision. Academic transparency requires clear disclosure of processes, data sources, and AI collaborations. Researchers must also adhere to developers' terms, copyright laws, and ethics guidelines, ensuring proper citation to uphold research integrity.

The second area is teaching. Instructors should include guidance on AI use in their syllabi, specifying when and how AI tools can assist learning. By diversifying assessment methods—such as incorporating oral exams, practical tasks, and discussions—CPU aims to reduce dependency on AI-generated content and promote independent thought. Students can use AI responses as comparative tools in lessons, encouraging them to critique and refine their analytical skills. Educators should discuss ethical AI usage and evolving AI capabilities, fostering a learning environment that values academic integrity, privacy, and responsible use.

The third area is student learning. Students are encouraged to use generative AI as a supplementary resource to support brainstorming, critical thinking, and literature organization. AI can assist with tasks like language translation and proofreading, but students must review outputs for accuracy, especially in technical contexts. To maintain academic honesty, students should identify AI-generated content and cite sources when applicable. CPU advises students to use AI sparingly as a reference tool, fostering a balanced approach that promotes original analysis and academic integrity.

These guidelines collectively support the ethical, effective, and transparent use of generative AI at CPU, reinforcing academic values across research, teaching, and learning.

RESULTS

Analysis of CPU's AI Integration Efforts in Police Education and Training

Leadership and Strategy

Institutional leadership, underpinned by government policies and support, is pivotal in shaping the AI adoption strategy within CPU's educational framework. The university's leadership ensures that AI integration aligns with Taiwan's law enforcement needs. The 2023 AAPS International Symposium on Technological Policing and Criminal Justice (#12) is one example. The CPU president chaired the event, leveraging both external and internal resources to attract renowned researchers focused on integrating smart technologies, such as AI, into police advanced education. Furthermore, the Official Visit of Wade Carpenter, President of the International Association of Chiefs of Police (#4), demonstrates the importance of international exchanges in aligning CPU's AI adoption strategy with global best practices in law enforcement training. These efforts indicate a strategic approach where leadership is actively engaged in advancing AI in policing education, with international collaborations enhancing this alignment.

Faculty Development and Training

The continuous development of faculty expertise is central to successfully integrating AI into CPU's teaching programs. The university ensures that instructors are equipped to incorporate AI tools while maintaining a solid connection to traditional values in policing. Workshops like the "AI Speech Recognition Tool Whisper

Desktop" (#1) and the "Strengthen Teachers' Science and Technology Teaching Functions and Health Awareness" (#5) reflect the university's commitment to enhancing faculty capacity in the application of AI in education. These workshops help bridge the gap between technology and pedagogy, allowing instructors to teach AI and the core values underpinning law enforcement effectively.

Curriculum Modernisation and Updates

CPU's curriculum is consistently updated to reflect the rapidly evolving landscape of AI and its impact on law enforcement and ensures that police education remains relevant and prepares students for the future of policing. Although CPU is still reviewing how to integrate AI into its curriculum, it has held several workshops for faculty members to support this effort. Examples include the "AI Deep Fake Technology Teacher Seminar" (#14) and the "Seminar on Innovations and Challenges of Police Work in the Technological Era" (#15), which serve as initiatives to incorporate AI and smart policing into the curriculum. These events provide opportunities to keep faculty and students informed of the latest technological advancements while ensuring that the curriculum evolves in response to emerging AI developments.

Research and Innovation

Research and innovation are critical pillars of CPU's strategy to foster a culture of ethical AI use in policing. The university's investments in research centres, such as the Plans to establish the "Digital Technology Investigation and Research Centre" (#11), demonstrate a commitment to creating spaces where new technologies can be explored and developed responsibly. Additionally, the Project on Strengthening International Scientific Investigation Professional Exchange (#8) emphasises the importance of global collaboration in advancing research in AI and law enforcement. By fostering an environment that encourages innovation and ethical research practices, CPU contributes to the broader discourse on AI in policing.

Student Engagement and Learning

AI tools are central to enhancing student engagement and critical thinking, ensuring that future officers are well-equipped to navigate the complexities of AI-driven policing. Events like the Smart Policing Training Workshop (#13) and the AI deep fake technology teacher seminar (#14) provide platforms for teachers to design a model to engage students with AI tools and understand their implications in teaching police students. These events foster technical skills and ethical decision-making, preparing students to apply AI technologies responsibly in their professional roles.

Ethics and Challenges

CPU places significant emphasis on addressing the ethical challenges arising from using AI in policing, particularly about data privacy and public trust. The "Development and Application of Generative AI" (#6) and the 2023 International Symposium on Technological Policing and Criminal Justice (#12) highlight the university's focus on discussing the ethical implications of AI. These events underscore the importance of understanding AI's limitations and risks and how these factors must be managed to maintain public trust and ethical standards in law enforcement practices.

Global Impact and Best Practices

Through engagement with international experts and adopting best practices, CPU ensures that its AI integration efforts are aligned with global trends in smart policing. The Project on Strengthening International Scientific Investigation Professional Exchange (#8) and the Official Visit of Wade Carpenter (#4) are examples to illustrate how CPU actively participates in global dialogues on AI in policing, ensuring that Taiwan's unique challenges are considered in the broader international context. These engagements help CPU stay at the forefront of global developments while adapting practices to local needs and standards.

Institutional Rules and Decision-Making at Central Police University

Key Actors and Their Roles

At Central Police University (CPU), various actors actively shape policies and practices surrounding using artificial intelligence (AI). These stakeholders work together to ensure that AI is integrated ethically, effectively, and aligned with the university's mission and regulatory obligations. Each group has distinct responsibilities that contribute to a balanced approach to AI in research and education.

The administration, led by the university president and academic deans, directs CPU's strategic vision for AI. This group formulates policies on ethical AI use, ensuring compliance with governmental standards while aligning applications with CPU's academic goals. The administration supports the responsible adoption of AI by setting standards and advocating for professional development. For instance, the president has championed workshops to enhance faculty members' AI proficiency, reinforcing the value of staying updated on AI developments in teaching and research.

Faculty members are primary facilitators of AI integration in the classroom and research settings. Tasked with understanding AI's ethical implications, they guide students in responsible use and contribute to developing an AI-enriched curriculum. Faculty also liaise between AI tools and students, finding practical applications that deepen student understanding and improve the learning experience. As part of these efforts, they attend AI workshops organized by the university, which help them understand the benefits and limitations of AI in academia.

Students, as end-users, are expected to develop an ethical understanding of AI tools, particularly their responsible application within academia. Exposure to AI tools like ChatGPT helps students harness technology to support their studies while staying mindful of ethical boundaries. For example, in current teaching environment, instructors encourage students to explore AI applications that can enhance their learning while also training them to assess AI outputs to avoid undue reliance on technology critically.

External experts and collaborators bring valuable perspectives to CPU's AI initiatives. Industry professionals and academic partners provide insights into AI's practical applications, particularly in law enforcement, enriching the academic environment with real-world relevance. CPU regularly hosts workshops where law enforcement experts share their experiences with AI in policing, offering students and faculty a glimpse into practical applications of technology beyond academia.

Institutional Rules Shaping Decisions

Central Police University has set rules to guide using artificial intelligence (AI) in teaching and research. This provides a plan with rules, training, ethics, and teamwork. CPU has created rules for using generative AI in schools, stressing the importance of ethics, rights to ideas, and fairness in teaching and research. By following these rules, CPU helps teachers and researchers make choices about using AI while keeping a balance between new ideas and ethical duties.

CPU's AI rules follow the laws set by the government and school groups that examine AI's ethical and practical use. Following these laws is crucial to CPU's work to reduce risks with AI, showing its promise to good practices. By matching national AI rules, CPU builds a culture of responsibility, ensuring its tech use meets legal and ethical standards.

Ethics are at the heart of CPU's AI approach, guiding the smart use of tech in teaching and research. The school's rules push everyone to think about the ethics of AI in learning, shaping their choices and ways to use it. Teachers and students get regular reminders about their ethical duties when using AI, creating a space of integrity and care. This promise to ethics highlights CPU's aim to keep academic standards while accepting technological changes and shape decisions.

Incentives and Strategic Behaviour at Central Police University

Incentives Driving Actor Behaviour

At Central Police University, various incentives influence the behaviours of key stakeholders, including faculty, researchers, and administrators, in developing and integrating artificial intelligence (AI) education and research. These incentives encourage an initiative-taking approach to AI, emphasising ethical considerations alongside practical applications. The primary incentives shaping CPU behaviour include government policy, professional development, research funding, institutional reputation, student success, and collaboration.

Regarding government policies, CPU follows Taiwan's "AI Smart Island" plan by boosting AI skills among its staff and using the "Digital Police Smart Strategy - S. MART" since 2022. This plan aims to make information safer with stronger rules (Security), change police work with smart support (Mobility), and use AI for better data and case management (AI). It also improves investigation work by allowing access to finance data and mixing real and virtual facts (Resilience) while funding a digital training system with many courses on tech investigations (Training).

Staff growth and skill improvement inspire CPU teachers and staff to better their AI knowledge. As AI grows in importance in education and police work, the university offers regular workshops and talks to help teachers use AI tools in their classes. This push for skill growth increases teacher abilities and keeps them competitive in a fast-changing area. By investing in staff growth, CPU improves its teaching, ensuring students are ready for fundamental work in AI and related jobs.

Research funds and chances are also motivators at CPU. The school uses specific funding plans that encourage innovative ideas in AI for law enforcement. Teachers are invited to do global research in this area, such as in the "Project on Strengthening International Scientific Investigation Professional Exchange." This funding pushes teachers to expand their research, helping academic growth and practical policy solutions. The CPU boosts its academic input by aiding advanced research and helps create smart policing ideas.

Another reason for CPU staff and researchers is to raise the university and personal reputation in the field. Adding AI to the courses and encouraging staff to attend talks and publish papers builds CPU's reputation at home and abroad. This aim for recognition fosters a space where teachers try new methods, work with others, and share their findings.

Lastly, CPU faculty members are responsible for boosting student learning results and job readiness, including AI-related police jobs. By adding AI tools and ideas to their lessons, teachers give students the right skills, both technical and ethical, needed in a tech-focused job market, especially in law enforcement. This focus on student success drives faculty to be creative in their teaching, ensuring graduates are equipped for their careers.

Strategic Choices Made by Actors

In response to these incentives, Central Police University staff, such as teachers, researchers, and leaders, make smart choices about using AI in teaching and studying. These choices reflect the CPU's goal to lead the use of AI for police work. Key choices include adding AI tools to the lessons, working with other fields, investing in teaching training, focusing on safe AI use, working with outside groups, starting new research projects, using feedback, and supporting student-focused learning.

One main choice for faculty members is using AI tools in their lessons. With new policies, they can use generative AI in teaching, helping with creating content, tests, and hands-on learning. Using AI, CPU teachers make lessons more engaging and help students gain real skills for future jobs. Also, CPU teachers collaborate with people from many fields, mixing ideas from tech, law, ethics, and social sciences. This teamwork helps solve tough problems and leads to research that tackles issues in crime prevention and policing.

Staff training remains a top goal for CPU. The school offers workshops and training on AI for teachers and staff. This training helps teachers use AI wisely and well, which improves teaching quality and helps students engage ethically with AI. By giving teachers the right AI skills, CPU helps them guide students effectively, ensuring they adapt to the fast-changing tech world.

Research projects are crucial in the decisions made by the CPU. Faculty members work on novel studies about AI in policing, for example, focusing on big data and deepfake detection. By supporting research, the CPU works to improve AI, which helps improve policing and increases public safety. CPU plans to start the "Digital Technology Investigation and Research Centre" to build skills in tech investigation, digital forensics, and cybersecurity for police, helping keep order and improving case solving.

INFORMATION AND UNCERTAINTY FACING CENTRAL POLICE UNIVERSITY

Information's Impact on Central Police University

Central Police University's leadership believes timely and accurate information is key to its teaching and research success. CPU focuses on complete information to help train students for high-level jobs in law and safety. The right data and tools help CPU build graduates who can face today's and tomorrow's policing challenges. One big plus of this info-rich setup is that it opens more learning paths for students. Data is key to the CPU's research efforts. CPU's research hubs, which deal with digital tech and cybercrime, help by giving a team space to investigate challenging problems.

Ethics are key guidelines to how the CPU manages information. Access to rules and tools about safe AI and digital ethics helps students and staff use technology wisely. This ethical base supports the school's goal of preparing students for the mixed challenges of modern law enforcement, where knowing the new tech's power and moral issues is necessary. The university gathers feedback from students, staff, and industry partners, using this to improve programs. This focus on data-driven checks keeps CPU flexible, changing its plans to meet the new needs of its students and partners.

CPU has an ambition to stay ahead by gathering data on new crimes, online dangers, and tech updates. By equipping students with this knowledge, CPU seeks to ensure its graduates can face future challenges in law enforcement, including the ethical issues tied to digital technology.

Managing Uncertainty at Central Police University

In a fast-changing world, the Central Police University leadership has foreseen future uncertainty. New technology and changing social needs require a flexible approach to teaching and research. To address these changes, the CPU uses different approaches to strengthen itself and prepare for the unknown. First, many faculty members find it hard to update their courses. However, CPU supports them in linking their classes with the newest trends in criminal justice. CPU aims to provide students with a relevant and modern education.

Second, CPU understands that working together across subjects can be challenging, therefore, CPU strives to help its staff and students look at problems from many angles. This teamwork boosts creative solutions and strengthens the university's ability to innovate. Leaders see that changing from old ways of working together to new ones in the AI age takes time and effort.

Third, funding is another challenging issue, and CPU leaders are trying to secure more funds. Investing in research and new ideas is essential for CPU to face uncertainty. The university funds research workshops and seminars on recent problems like cybercrime, AI ethics, and digital evidence. By focusing on research, CPU stays ahead, creating flexible solutions for modern policing. Additionally, CPU's focus on teacher training is vital in dealing with uncertainty. By offering ongoing training for faculty on the latest tools and policing methods, the university ensures its staff can lead in teaching and research.

DISCUSSION

A Top-down Approach

Central Police University has undertaken a continued initiative to embed Artificial Intelligence into its Vocational Education and Training programs, with the effort driven from the top by national policies, including those from the Minister of the Interior, alongside guidance from CPU's leadership. This top-down approach signals a strategic shift in the institution's educational priorities, aiming to enhance the technological competencies of future law enforcement professionals. With AI's rapid advancements, CPU's leadership has underscored the importance of building AI capabilities as foundational to modern law enforcement education. This vision positions AI not as an auxiliary tool but as a core component of academic and operational innovation at CPU. This move has garnered both support and funding for AI-driven projects and resources.

A critical element of CPU's approach involves the comprehensive training of faculty members. To incorporate AI effectively into the curriculum, faculty members participate in specialized training programs and workshops designed to familiarize them with the technical aspects of AI and its practical applications in policing. These training initiatives, which include regular workshops, seminars, and conferences on AI, create a supportive learning environment, fostering the integration of AI into teaching and ensuring that educators can relay up-to-date skills and insights to students. Through these events, CPU supports its staff and facilitates discussions on best practices and innovative pedagogies, helping to strengthen the university's broader commitment to AI-based education.

CPU has secured funding to conduct research and plans to establish a research center that supports this AI-driven shift, funded by Taiwan's Executive Yuan. This research hub underscores CPU's commitment to addressing emerging forms of digital crime, such as cybercrime, ransomware, and deepfake fraud. As a cornerstone of CPU's AI integration strategy, the center aims to provide the institution with research capacity focused on tackling complex digital threats. The center combines digital forensics, cryptocurrency tracking, and cybersecurity expertise to foster innovation that benefits CPU's educational mission and the law enforcement community. The center may contribute to developing methods and technologies essential for modern policing, equipping students with critical skills in digital investigation and crime prevention.

Alongside research advancements, CPU has prioritized AI within its curriculum by introducing coursework that prepares students for the intersection of crime and technology. If everything goes as planned, the curriculum will feature state-of-the-art facilities and equipment, such as cryptocurrency tracking systems and deepfake analysis software, ensuring students can apply their learning in simulated, realistic law enforcement scenarios.

Rational Choice Institutionalism Alignment

CPU's AI approach can be explained by Rational Choice Institutionalism, giving a transparent and fair way to use AI. By setting guidelines, the CPU aims to build a space where AI works ethically and responsibly in schools and labs. These rules are like "game rules," guiding actions by asking for fair use in AI work and forming clear data safety and ownership standards. This RCI-based method cuts down risks linked to AI, helping students and teachers act in line with the values of honesty and safety.

Based on the RCI approach, CPU leadership has planned to make it easier for staff and students to follow AI-related academic and data rules. With RCI's focus on best choices and efficiency, CPU helps students and researchers face issues like data risk and AI limits. The guidelines demonstrate what stakeholders require for academic honesty and privacy, guiding users to make choices that boost learning quality.

CPU has taken steps to manage information flow and ensure rules are followed using RCI ideas in its AI policies. The guidelines share key info on AI's limits, such as risks and biases from too much trust in AI content. Rules are implemented to ensure users state their AI use in university's work, give credit, and follow strict steps when handling sensitive info. These actions boost rule-following, set standards for everyone, and ensure that AI is used properly at the university.

CPU's AI guidelines also demonstrate RCI's approach for balance, blending the good sides of AI with its risks. The guidelines suggest careful, limited AI use, seeing it as support for critical thought and self-learning, not a full replacement. This balance fits personal and school goals, ensuring that individual aims help CPU's bigger goals of keeping academic honesty and data safety. By structuring AI use like this, CPU ensures AI's benefits shine while cutting down risks, helping an environment where AI adds to learning growth.

By applying RCI, the CPU's method to incorporate AI can be seen as an smart choice-making process. RCI helps explain how CPU balances the positive sides of AI with real issues like ethics, resource limits, and school goals. By viewing the CPU, RCI shows how decision-makers at the school think about the pros and cons of new tech, weighing short-term gains against long-term ethical impacts. For example, building a unique AI research centre is not just a technological response but a long-term vision to fit global trends of cybercrime while following to Taiwan's ethical and operational standards in police training and education.

Some Final Considerations

Despite the progress mentioned above, several challenges and limitations lie ahead for the CPU. One of the major obstacles is that some staff and faculty members may be hesitant to adapt this change, which could hinder the successful implementation of new technologies and teaching methods. Also, recruiting faculty specialising in AI and policing is another significant hurdle, as these experts are often in high demand and hard to find. For police students, gathering student feedback is crucial; the CPU should actively monitor learning outcomes to ensure that the integration of AI effectively meets students' educational needs. Resource allocation between departments also raises concerns, as disparities in funding could lead to inequities in support for AI initiatives. Lastly, the implementation of curriculum changes regarding AI will need careful review by the curriculum committee to ensure they align with educational standards and institutional goals. Addressing these challenges is vital for CPU to navigate the complexities of AI integration while fostering a supportive and equitable academic environment.

CONCLUSION

This chapter explores the integration of artificial intelligence into police education, focusing on the leadership of Taiwan's Central Police University in this initiative. Since 2023, Taiwan has pushed to use AI in line with its goals, which have significantly improved police training, teacher skills, and class plans. CPU has ensured its courses meet the new needs of modern policing. This helps officers gain the necessary skills for today's complex, data-driven law enforcement. This forward plan boosts police skills and builds a culture of growth at CPU. The study shows the importance of strong leadership in adding AI to police training. The leaders at CPU have built teamwork between schools, police, and tech firms to help create a complete plan for using AI. This teamwork focuses on ethical issues around AI in police training, stressing fairness, transparency, and responsibility. By exploring these ethical issues, CPU aims to ensure AI tools work well and help create just policing. Though there are challenges from fast tech changes and new societal needs, CPU sets an example for training schools wanting to add AI. This fresh approach marks a key step in police training, proving that a clear, strategic plan can meet law enforcement's new demands. This plan gives teachers and trainees the tools to meet their community's unique needs. Overall, adding AI to police training could assist police work and connect to more extensive discussions on the future of policing in a tech-focused world.

For future study, it's vital to explore a few paths. First, mixed-method studies should be done to see AI's short and long-term effects on police training and effectiveness. This research must examine how AI impacts officers' skills and choices and how they connect with communities. More studies on AI's ethical side are fundamental, especially regarding fairness and privacy. There is also great value in looking at international teamwork for creating AI-driven police training. Research across countries can show the best ways to partner with schools, police, and tech providers, giving a fuller view of AI's use in police training. Another key area is how community input shapes AI-focused classes. Knowing how communities affect AI training can provide insights into AI's social impact, pushing for more community-driven policing.

Finally, a cross-cultural view can offer broader insights into AI's use in police training worldwide. This approach can help find diverse ways in which diverse cultures face the challenges of using AI. By studying how nations manage AI in police education, future research can help build a more effective and fair global police force ready for fast tech changes. With these efforts, AI in police training can shift from a tech update to a huge change that has helped law enforcement and promoted fairness, transparency, and accountability for the future.

REFERENCES

Al Shamsi, H. R. S., & Safei, S. (2023). Artificial Intelligence Adoption in Predictive Policing to Predict Crime Mitigation Performance. *International Journal of Sustainable Construction Engineering and Technology*, 14(3), 289–298. DOI: 10.30880/ijscet.2023.14.03.025

Apostolakis, K. C., Dimitriou, N., Margetis, G., Ntoa, S., Tzovaras, D., & Stephanidis, C. (2022). DARLENE–Improving situational awareness of European law enforcement agents through a combination of augmented reality and artificial intelligence solutions. *Open Research Europe*, 1, 87. DOI: 10.12688/openreseurope.13715.2 PMID: 37645167

Arensman, E., Coffey, C., Griffin, E., Van Audenhove, C., Scheerder, G., Gusmao, R., & Maxwell, M. (2016). Effectiveness of depression–suicidal behaviour gatekeeper training among police officers in three European regions: Outcomes of the Optimising Suicide Prevention Programmes and Their Implementation in Europe (OSPI-Europe) study. *The International Journal of Social Psychiatry*, 62(7), 651–660. DOI: 10.1177/0020764016668907 PMID: 27647606

Aspinwall, M., & Schneider, G. (2001). The rules of integration: Institutionalist approaches to the study of Europe.

Aspinwall, M. D., & Schneider, G. (2000). Same menu, seperate tables: The institutionalist turn in political science and the study of European integration. *European Journal of Political Research*, 38(1), 1–36. DOI: 10.1111/1475-6765.00526

Binder, R. R., & Rockman, B. (2005). Rational Choice Institutionalism.

Braun, V., & Clarke, V. (2012). *Thematic analysis*. American Psychological Association. DOI: 10.1037/13620-004

Cao, L. (2022). Ai in finance: Challenges, techniques, and opportunities. *ACM Computing Surveys*, 55(3), 1–38. DOI: 10.1145/3502289

Cao, L., & Dai, M. (2006). Confidence in the police: Where does Taiwan rank in the world? *Asian Journal of Criminology*, 1(1), 71–84. DOI: 10.1007/s11417-006-9001-0

Cao, L., Huang, L., & Sun, I. (2016). Development and reform of police training and education in Taiwan. *Police Practice and Research*, 17(6), 531–542. DOI: 10.1080/15614263.2015.1086878

Copsey, A. (2024). An Examination of Police Response to Individuals Suffering with Mental Illness.

Ferejohn, J. (2002). Symposium on explanations and social ontology 1: Rational choice theory and social explanation. *Economics and Philosophy*, 18(2), 211–234. DOI: 10.1017/S026626710200202X

Gaya, H., & Smith, E. E. (2016). Developing a qualitative single case study in the strategic management realm: An appropriate research design. *International Journal of Business Management and Economic Research*, 7(2), 529–538.

Guest, G., MacQueen, K. M., & Namey, E. E. (2011). *Applied thematic analysis*. Sage Publications.

Hall, P. A., & Taylor, R. C. (1996). Political science and the three new institutionalisms. *Political Studies*, 44(5), 936–957. DOI: 10.1111/j.1467-9248.1996.tb00343.x

Haugaard Jacobsen, C. (2007). A qualitative single case study of parallel processes. *Counselling & Psychotherapy Research*, 7(1), 26–33. DOI: 10.1080/14733140601140410

Holmes, L. (2016). *Advanced introduction to organised crime*. Edward Elgar Publishing.

Huang, C.-Y., & Shih, C.-H. (2025). *Interviewing vulnerable witnesses and suspects in criminal justice proceedings: Evidence-based development in Taiwan Routledge International Handbook of Investigative Interviewing and Interrogation*. Routledge.

Kaufmann, M. (2024). *AI in policing and law enforcement Handbook on Public Policy and Artificial Intelligence*. Edward Elgar Publishing.

Knight, J. (1992). *Institutions and Social Conflict*. Cambridge University Press. DOI: 10.1017/CBO9780511528170

Knight, J., & Sened, I. (1998). *Explaining social institutions*. University of Michigan Press.

Lai, Y.-L., Luo, F., Kang, C.-C., & Lo, T.-Y. (2024). Exploring Southeast Asian immigrants' attitudes toward the police in Taiwan. *Policing*, 47(2), 199–214. DOI: 10.1108/PIJPSM-12-2022-0150

Levi, M. (1997). *A Model, A Method, and a Map: Rational Choice in Comparative and Historical Analysis. Comparative Politics: Rationality, Culture, and Structure/ Cambridge*. Cambridge Univ. Press.

Lin, K., Sidebottom, A., & Wortley, R. (2022). Evidence-based policing and police receptivity to research: Evidence from Taiwan. *Policing*, 45(5), 860–880. DOI: 10.1108/PIJPSM-04-2022-0050

Lin, K.-h., Sidebottom, A., & Wortley, R. (2023). Police education and democratic policing in Taiwan: A longitudinal quasi-experimental study of the effects of selection and police socialisation on human rights, moral reasoning and prejudice. *Journal of Experimental Criminology*, •••, 1–29.

Lin, L. S., Aslett, D., Mekonnen, G., & Zecevic, M. (2024a). The dangers of voice cloning and how to combat it.

Lin, L. S., Aslett, D., Mekonnen, G., & Zecevic, M. (2024b). The UN Cybercrime Convention: What it Means for Policing and Community Safety in Australia.

Liu, K., Wei, Z., Zhang, C., Shang, Y., Teodorescu, R., & Han, Q.-L. (2022). Towards long lifetime battery: AI-based manufacturing and management. *IEEE/CAA Journal of Automatica Sinica, 9*(7), 1139-1165.

Liu, M. (1999). Review and Strategies for my country's Police Education System.

Maguire, M., & Delahunt, B. (2017). Doing a thematic analysis: A practical, step-by-step guide for learning and teaching scholars. *AISHE-J: The All Ireland Journal of Teaching and Learning in Higher Education, 9*(3).

Marzano, L., Smith, M., Long, M., Kisby, C., & Hawton, K. (2016). Police and suicide prevention. *Crisis*, 37(3), 194–204. DOI: 10.1027/0227-5910/a000381 PMID: 27040129

Matulionyte, R., & Hanif, A. (2021). *A call for more explainable AI in law enforcement.* Paper presented at the 2021 IEEE 25th International Enterprise Distributed Object Computing Workshop (EDOCW). DOI: 10.1109/EDOCW52865.2021.00035

Mojadidi, E. (2024). *Increasing public safety through augmented reality technology utilized by police officers*. Justice Institute of British Columbia, School of Criminal Justice & Security.

Newton, L., & Jong, W. (1989). A Research Guide to Taiwan (ROC) Law. *J. Chinese. L.*, 3, 257.

Noorbakhsh-Sabet, N., Zand, R., Zhang, Y., & Abedi, V. (2019). Artificial intelligence transforms the future of health care. *The American Journal of Medicine*, 132(7), 795–801. DOI: 10.1016/j.amjmed.2019.01.017 PMID: 30710543

North, D. C. (1990). *Institutions, institutional change and economic performance* (Vol. 332). Cambridge university press. DOI: 10.1017/CBO9780511808678

Oosthuizen, K., Botha, E., Robertson, J., & Montecchi, M. (2021). Artificial intelligence in retail: The AI-enabled value chain. *Australasian Marketing Journal*, 29(3), 264–273. DOI: 10.1016/j.ausmj.2020.07.007

Peters, B. G. (2019). *Institutional theory in political science: The new institutionalism.* Edward Elgar Publishing.

Sanz-Urquijo, B., Fosch-Villaronga, E., & Lopez-Belloso, M. (2023). The disconnect between the goals of trustworthy AI for law enforcement and the EU research agenda. *AI and Ethics*, 3(4), 1283–1294. DOI: 10.1007/s43681-022-00235-8

Saputra, I., Astuti, M., Sayuti, M., & Kusumastuti, D. (2023). Integration of Artificial Intelligence in Education: Opportunities, Challenges, Threats and Obstacles. A Literature Review. *The Indonesian Journal of Computer Science*, 12(4). Advance online publication. DOI: 10.33022/ijcs.v12i4.3266

Schneider, G., & Ershova, A. (2018). Rational choice institutionalism and european integration.

Sun, I. Y., Jou, S., Hou, C. C., & Chang, Y. (2014). Public trust in the police in Taiwan: A test of instrumental and expressive models. *Australian and New Zealand Journal of Criminology*, 47(1), 123–140. DOI: 10.1177/0004865813489306

Thomas, S., & Watson, A. (2017). A focus for mental health training for police. *Journal of Criminological Research, Policy and Practice*, 3(2), 93–104. DOI: 10.1108/JCRPP-01-2017-0005

Weyland, K. (2002). Limitations of rational-choice institutionalism for the study of Latin American politics. *Studies in Comparative International Development*, 37(1), 57–85. DOI: 10.1007/BF02686338

Williamson, O. E. (1985). The economic institutions of capitalism. New York: Free Press: Douglas.

Wu, Y., Poteyeva, M., & Sun, I. Y. (2012). Trust in police: A comparison of China and Taiwan. *International Journal of Comparative and Applied Criminal Justice*, 36(3), 189–210. DOI: 10.1080/01924036.2012.699794

Završnik, A. (2020). *Criminal justice, artificial intelligence systems, and human rights.* Paper presented at the ERA forum. DOI: 10.1007/s12027-020-00602-0

KEY TERMS AND DEFINITIONS

Artificial Intelligence in Police Education: The application of artificial intelligence (AI) technologies in police training and education at an institution.

Collaboration in AI Police Education: The cooperative efforts among various stakeholders to improve the effectiveness and relevance of police training and education programs.

Curriculum Integration with AI: Updating and revising police education programs to include new technologies such as artificial intelligence.

Ethical Considerations in AI Police Education: The guidelines and policies for the moral use of artificial intelligence in police education.

Institutional Leadership in AI: The role of individuals in authority within an organisation who command and control the institution's direction, policies, and practices in the context of integrating AI.

Top-Down Approach: A management strategy involving a process where top leadership makes decisions and sets guidelines that guide the implementation of policies and practices at all levels.

Vocational Education and Training (VET): Educational programs aiming to provide individuals with the practical skills and knowledge required for specialised professions.

ENDNOTES

1 See https://law.moj.gov.tw/ENG/LawClass/LawAll.aspx?pcode=A0000001

2 See https://www.cpu.edu.tw/p/412-1000-119.php?Lang=zh-tw

3 See https://law.moj.gov.tw/ENG/LawClass/LawAll.aspx?pcode=D0000022

4 See https://www.cpu.edu.tw/p/412-1000-120.php?Lang=zh-tw

5 See https://www.moi.gov.tw/News_Content.aspx?n=10&s=276317

6 See https://daa.cpu.edu.tw/p/406-1033-42663,r772.php

Chapter 7
AI-Driven Digital Marketing in Kazakhstan: Opportunities and Challenges for Vocational Education and Training

Rajasekhara Mouly Potluri
https://orcid.org/0000-0002-6935-1373
Kazakh-British Technical University, Kazakhstan

Erzhan Bulatovich Mukashev
https://orcid.org/0000-0003-1003-176X
Kazakh-British Technical University, Kazakhstan

Kairzhan S. Abdykhalykov
https://orcid.org/0009-0008-6525-100X
Kazakh-British Technical University, Kazakhstan

Lohith Sekhar Potluri
https://orcid.org/0000-0001-7898-4335
University of California, San Diego, USA

ABSTRACT

This chapter examines Kazakhstan's distinctive digital marketing scene and the transformative potential of artificial intelligence technologies in reshaping vocational education and training. Over the past five years, the rapid evolution of Artificial Intelligence (AI) technology has opened up unprecedented opportunities for vocational education. This book chapter not only explores the promise of artificial intelligence in vocational education through the lens of digital marketing but also emphasizes the transformative power of artificial intelligence. The present artificial intelligence technology introduces innovative application models, such as assisted

DOI: 10.4018/979-8-3693-8252-3.ch007

teaching and learning, which empower teachers to craft personalized instruction and offer real-time support to students. The contemporary artificial intelligence-driven digital marketing for vocational education delivers a hopeful glimpse into the future of vocational education enriched by technology, instilling a sense of optimism and excitement about the possibilities.

INTRODUCTION

Artificial intelligence (AI) technology has introduced rapid changes, leading to swift progress by offering a lifelike experience to its actual users and multiple and unexpected benefits to the marketers' community. For business society, incessantly incorporating new means or methods is essential to maintaining a competitive advantage in their respective businesses—such a continuous demand for creativity yields capital and attention. In the framework of digital marketing, artificial intelligence examines the use of advanced algorithms and machine learning to analyze consumer behavior, predict trends, and automate marketing processes. This application of AI in digital marketing is a way to recognize progressed adeptness, competent understanding of clients, and customization. In the face of it is a viewpoint that emanates from its equitable portion paybacks, noteworthy confrontations occur, such as data privacy concerns, high setup cost, data quality, sourcing skilled personnel, and keeping up successive technological innovations. Modern organizations that bet on artificial intelligence to overcome all these impediments will probably be the most successful in their sectors. AI has influenced digital marketing and offered a wide range of advantages and very few drawbacks to transform the promotional programs of companies by tapping almost all digital avenues to reach the target markets. It is vital to grasp these changes, especially in ensuring companies remain competitive and innovative. The most potent learning type is not being taught what to do but learning how to find a solution independently.

Vocational education, also known as technical or career education, plays a pivotal role in augmenting a nation's economic effectiveness, safeguarding social stability, nurturing technological innovation, and urging national development from the perspective of economic globalization. The status and role of vocational education in society have experienced a significant improvement. It is equally crucial in general higher education and has become an integral component of the national education system and human resource development. Its primary tasks encompass developing diverse talents, transferring technical skills, and encouraging employment and entrepreneurship. It holds paramount significance for the country's and society's development. Vocational education is fabricated so that learners can obtain the intelligence, expertise, and capabilities that are identifiable to a distinct profession, trade, or class of occupations or trades (UNESCO Institute for Statistics, 2024). After successfully completing the educational programs, students competently enter labor markets with the most relevant vocational qualifications and competent skills acknowledged as occupationally oriented by the pertinent state authorities and the labor market. Vocational education is another learning option from the conventional path of the college or university system of education. It is synchronized with the requirements of the labor market and is an integral of the education system. In contrast, traditional college education proffers theoretical or broad-spectrum of different disciplines of knowledge. At the same time, vocational education and training teach students the precise skills and knowledge required to take up a specific craft, technical skill-based job, or trade. Vocational education and training avoid conventional academic studies and instead offer direct expertise and instruction for a particular field or position. This kind of education is exclusively designed to provide competent, pragmatic skills in different technical expertise fields, which are positions that involve hands-on manual work such as data entry operators, electricians, plumbers, piping expertise, two, and four-wheel mechanics, cooking, etc. All these careers are different from college and university education because these programs are treated as non-academic programs. Along with these, vocational education and training programs also educate on managerial skills or job functions, such as computer programming, hotel management courses, entrepreneurship, and small business management. Vocational education is a game changer and a decisive element in transforming the service sector, specifically where front-line employees play a prominent role in influencing customers. The service sector, which incorporates sectors like hospitality, retail, and healthcare, relies heavily on vocational education to equip its workforce with the necessary skills and knowledge beyond textbook learning. It equips them with practical expertise and on-the-job training essential in the fast-paced service sector in different parts of the world. There are two methods for implementing this technology in the educational environment.

First, teachers can be assisted by Artificial Intelligence systems, which function as teachers for each student. Any intelligent technology that provides customized content for each learner is now exclusively used in many classrooms as an intelligent tutoring system (Molenaar, 2021). One alternative use of Artificial Intelligence is to enhance human understanding and assist humans in executing effective and efficient educational programs (Suparyati et al., 2023). Artificial intelligence is bearing a transformative impact on both the labor marketplace and training approaches. Vocational education and training (VET) front-runners play a pivotal role in determining the imminent education through managerial, strategic choices, and policy instructions; without VET leaders, energies to participate in AI into VET risk facing significant barriers to broader uptake (Seufert, 2024). Nimmagadda et al. (2024) emphasized in their book chapter the application of artificial intelligence, even in employee engagement in sectors including education under human resource management departments. Based on the above background and justification, the present book chapter initiated with the core objective of how artificial intelligence-driven digital marketing works for vocational education of the Republic of Kazakhstan and the opportunities and challenges faced in implementing so.

ARTIFICIAL INTELLIGENCE (AI) DRIVEN DIGITAL MARKETING FOR VOCATIONAL EDUCATION

Vocational education and training (VET) programs help people advance in their professional careers with their unique, shorter, and more flexible programs compared to college or university programs. These kinds of programs make it easier for people to return to a learning culture by continuing their education to help them move in their professions. Vocational education and training have some core features, like making a student job-ready and based on competency. Further, this vocational education and training could give a chance to advance to a higher-level position in the same company or field, gain the skills and ken needed to change careers and request higher pay to fit a credential or unique specialty skill (Musseau, 2024). The transformation has taken place in different technologies; in particular, the landscape of artificial intelligence has contributed to the field of digital marketing and has provided numerous benefits, specifically to popularize vocational education and training in different parts of the world. Yen and Yang (2024) highlighted through their extensive research the potential impact of artificial intelligence (AI) and video production skills on workplace development, focusing on the perspective of vocational training. The same authors reiterated that with the rapid growth of artificial intelligence technology, it is essential to investigate how learners attain video production skills under the guidance of artificial intelligence and imagine the possibilities for their future career development. This study examined the process of learning video production skills in the artificial intelligence-dominated era and explored learners' perceptions and expectations of their career development paths. The current research findings indicated that video-making skills are crucial in online marketing, especially vocational education, because of their unique advantages with the introduction of artificial intelligence, which enhances efficiency, and human creativity remains indispensable. Integrating artificial intelligence into vocational education and training can progress learning outcomes with clear recommendations, including emphasizing hands-on experience, personalized learning paths, and collaborative learning. Another research emphasized that vocational education highlights the crucial role played by emerging technologies in shaping pedagogy and skill development by examining cutting-edge innovations such as virtual reality

(VR), augmented reality (AR), artificial intelligence (AI), machine learning (ML), and Internet of Things (IoT), robotics, automation, big data analytics, blockchain, 3D printing, and gamification (Ghosh & Ravichandran, 2024). This study explored the transformative potential of these technologies and suggested solutions like affordable access, educator training programs, and equitable technology distribution. Mandal (2024) stressed that how artificial intelligence can be used in the expansion of vocational education in India and how artificial intelligence can be used efficiently.

Before diving into the core topic, the authors thought that to explain the meaning of the most crucial words of the chapter, i.e., artificial intelligence and digital marketing. Artificial intelligence means the theory and development of computer systems able to perform tasks typically requiring human intelligence, such as visual perception, speech recognition, decision-making, and translation between languages. Digital marketing means promoting brands to connect with potential customers using the internet and other forms of digital communication, including email, social media, and web-based advertising, along with text and multimedia messages as a marketing channel. Artificial intelligence is heavily transforming diverse sectors, including service delivery in vocational education and training. Incorporating artificial intelligence (AI) into vocational education and prospective employee skill development is appropriate and progressively necessary as businesses progress to meet the demands of a technology-driven future. Artificial intelligence can potentially change vocational education by offering more personalized, adaptive, and efficient learning knowledge practices and experiences. Traditional knowledge transformation methods repeatedly follow a one-size-fits-all approach, which can be ineffective and less operative for distinct learning needs. However, artificial intelligence facilitates the conception of tailored vocational education programs that accommodate each learner's identifiable obligations and learning patterns. Through artificial intelligence (AI) powered programs, vocational education can be adapted to review learners' existing skills and recognize gaps that need to be tackled. These technology-based platforms can create altered education programs focusing on the areas where the learners' skill development is concerned, ensuring the knowledge transformation is relevant and practical. This individualized method not only augments the learning experience but also significantly improves the retention and application of new skills in the workplace. As artificial intelligence (AI) incessantly coordinates into manufacturing and service sectors, the demand for prospective employees with AI-related knowledge has significant job opportunities in every country. Even present organizations have to recognize the prominence of upskilling their personnel to remain competitive in an artificial intelligence (AI)-driven world. Developing AI skills among employees is not just about understanding the technology; it involves a comprehensive approach that includes data literacy, problem-solving, and the ability to work with AI systems. Even in this situation, vocational education programs with AI-technology-oriented curricula must be developed based on the requirements of different organizations' specific needs and aspirations to enhance artificial intelligence skills and knowledge. Customized vocational education programs on the basics of artificial intelligence, machine learning, data analysis, and the ethical considerations of artificial intelligence competently enhance the knowledge levels of an organization's employees. Employees must also be equipped with the ability to interpret AI outputs and make informed decisions based on AI-generated insights. By doing so, organizations can ensure that their workforce is proficient in using AI tools and can influence these tools to drive innovation and efficiency. Cela et al. (2025) expounded how the present educational environment is becoming increasingly complex, and the ability to collect, analyze, and act upon data is crucial for institutional improvement. In these highly volatile conditions, all IoT technologies, including artificial intelligence, offer opportunities for educational leaders to optimize various aspects of campus operations, enhance student experiences, and improve administrative efficiency.

Like other educational sectors, artificial intelligence in vocational education is still in its early stages. This is true in pragmatic vocational education fields, where hands-on dexterities require practical, real-world applications. Vocational education stands apart from school and higher education by focusing on pragmatic skills that lead directly to employment. While education systems follow standardized curricula aimed at broad, long-term ken and competencies, and higher education balances academic and research priorities, vocational programs tend to provide hands-on, practical training for definite occupations. Vocational education is rationalized for near-tenure job inclination, predictably persistent to the medium and long-term orientation, mainly just a few months to a couple of years, and contribution targeted education or training connected with the exact requirements of the concerned industry. Artificial intelligence adoption rates are minimal, particularly in developing and underdeveloped worlds, compared to the developed world. In Europe, data on artificial intelligence adoption rates within these traditional vocational programs remains sparse, infrequent, and slow. A recent 2023 survey among Swiss vocational education leaders offered valuable insights into how artificial intelligence is visible in these more conventional sectors (Brighteye Ventures, 2023).

Artificial intelligence (AI) is vital in people's lifetimes, as demonstrated by the cumulative contact between humans and intelligent machines (Kim, 2022; Dang & Liu, 2022). AI comprises structures grounded on machine learning, logical programming, or statistical methods that produce content, create forecasts, deliver endorsements, make choices, or take action based on data analysis (European Commission, 2022, p. 10). Unlike previous rule-based approaches, available AI methods do not simply replicate human rules but make outcomes through optimization and statistical techniques (High-Level Expert Group on AI, 2019). The abilities of this AI application have astonished the global public while also inducing interest in its prospects to take over duties that are conventionally performed by humans (Kasneci et al., 2023). The influence of AI is that it is simultaneously transforming the employment and education systems. On the one hand, the effect of AI on the labor market could be disruptive (Mass-Mann & Hofstetter, 2020; OECD, 2019; Zhang et al., 2021). The perspective for job transposition and new role formation is coupled with modifications in office jobs and concerns (Shiohira 2021). In other ways, the transformative effects of AI could also have an impact on education. AI systems in education offer countless prospects (Miao et al. 2021; Adeshola and Adepoju 2023). These approaches can recognize individual learning needs, design personalized learning pathways, monitor progress, provide real-time feedback, and educate knowledge conclusions. This attempt is remarkably favorable in vocational education and training (VET) structures that need to react to changes in the labor marketplace and business requirements, guaranteeing that the dexterities that are imparted in these organizations are up-to-date and in demand.

ARTIFICIAL INTELLIGENCE (AI) AND DIGITAL MARKETING FOR KAZAKHSTAN VOCATIONAL EDUCATION

The Republic of Kazakhstan, Minister of Science and Higher Education Sayassat Nurbek and Minister of Digital Development, Innovation, and Aerospace Industry Zhaslan Madiyev reported on the development of artificial intelligence (AI) in Kazakhstan and legal regulation of the digital environment. On the instructions of President Kassym-Jomart Tokayev, the above two crucial ministries hectically involved in the development of the concept of artificial intelligence are being implemented, which was announced at an extended Government session on 7th February 2024. In the same meeting, concerned ministers announced that the use of artificial intelligence can increase global GDP by 14% by 2030; 17 universities have already introduced 15 AI specializations, and 2,196 students are studying these programs. His Excellency Prime Minister Olzhas Bektenov said that "by 2029, the number of products using artificial intelligence should grow 5 times. Accordingly, the share of educational programs or disciplines on artificial intelligence should increase. We need qualified specialists in this field. It is important to take into account the opportunities and needs of domestic companies, which will create a multiplier effect on the economy as a whole" (Official Information Source of the Prime Minister of the Republic of Kazakhstan, 2024). Excitingly, in addition to the above, the prime minister instructed the Ministry of Justice to intensify work on improving the legislative framework to regulate the sphere of application of artificial intelligence. The Ministry of Digital Development, Innovation, and Aerospace Industry has set goals until 2029, including training five million people in artificial intelligence skills, 500,000 industry specialists, creating five Kazakh unicorns, increasing IT exports to $5 billion, and implementing at least 25 AI products annually in economic sectors. Based on the best world practices, the Kazakh Ministry of Digital Development, Innovation, and Aerospace Industry and the Mazhilis, the lower house of the Kazakh Parliament, developed a draft law on artificial intelligence (AI) at a July 16 government meeting chaired by Prime Minister Olzhas Bektenov. The draft law follows the instructions of President Kassym-Jomart Tokayev, who stressed the efficient application of artificial intelligence in various sectors such as security, medicine, banking services, logistics, and education (Sakenova, 2024). In the process of developing a competent Kazakhstan digital infrastructure, the government of Kazakhstan has signed a collaborative agreement with the United Arab Emirates (UAE)-based Artificial Intelligence company, Presight, to build a supercomputer and data-processing center (DPC). It's an already burgeoning area-according to Statista, revenue in Kazakhstan's data center market is projected to reach about $417 million by 2028, up from an estimated $320 million this year (BBC StoryWorks, 2024).

Technical and vocational education in Kazakhstan aims to train qualified workers and middle-ranking specialists. It is delivered to academies, colleges, and tertiary colleges based on basic secondary and general secondary education. Kazakhstan's technical and vocational education is offered in 772 organizations, of which 446 are public and 326 are private. The total number of students in these organizations is 517.3 thousand, of which 312 thousand have studied under the state order (Government of Kazakhstan, 2023). Exciting research proved that dual education students are more confident in their demands in the labor market, are more satisfied with the results of their studies, and have higher academic achievement than school-based education students (Doskeyeva et al., 2024). Promoting vocational education in Kazakhstan needs a targeted and strategic approach. By defining your target audience, utilizing digital marketing, offering free trials or demonstrations, creating valuable content, and collaborating with industry partners, the total number of 772 organizations can effectively promote vocational education and help individuals and businesses succeed. Tapping the most accurate digital marketing tool to popularize their vocational education programs by using diverse social media channels can help these institutions get more influencers, which will make these more known in the market. Every institution, specifically in the vocational education sector in Kazakhstan, has to identify social media as an exciting marketing communication tool, social media as a substantial impact on life, social media as a need and efficient media, social media as a free time filler that is constantly growing, and social media is easy to learn. Developing a positive image towards social media and its different channels can be shown as an excellent opportunity for these vocational education institutions to popularize their institutions and their customized programs in the country, which will play a prominent role in supporting the digital marketing strategy. As highlighted in extensive research initiated by Jumasseitova et al. (2024), while introducing any kind of educational institution management, even with the support of technology, should keep in mind achieving environmental, social, and governance (ESG) sustainable initiatives.

ARTIFICIAL INTELLIGENCE (AI) DRIVEN DIGITAL MARKETING FOR VOCATIONAL EDUCATION: OPPORTUNITIES AND CHALLENGES

Artificial intelligence-driven digital marketing has offered numerous benefits to vocational education and training providers. It enhances customer insights, automates routine tasks, facilitates real-time decision-making, and personalizes content. These advancements, however, come with their own set of challenges, including data privacy concerns, high initial investment, dependence on quality data, and skill gaps. Despite these challenges, the benefits of AI-driven digital marketing are substantial and promise to revolutionize vocational education and training. Rongchang et al. (2024) emphasized that with its modular architecture and extensive training, artificial intelligence-based vocation education exhibits vigorous, comprehensive language and generation abilities, which can effectively simulate various virtual roles in different domains, enhancing human-computer interaction. This, in turn, improves the efficiency of teaching and learning while expanding the potential application scenarios in vocational education through expert consultations and virtual tutoring (Fraiwan & Khasawneh, 2023; Grassini, 2023).

Artificial intelligence (AI) facilitates the improvement of teaching efficiency, exclusively in vocational education, where the pragmatic delivery of programs concerns vocational education. The teaching content of vocational education must align with the national and regional development strategies, cater to market demands, and adapt dynamically to technological advancements. The application of artificial intelligence for optimizing teaching content holds significant potential to facilitate vocational education's transformation, intellectualization, and customization. Another artificial intelligence chatbot, ChatGPT, uses natural language processing to create human-like conversational dialogue and formulate better-customized teaching objectives and tasks for these vocational education programs and training facilities. ChatGPT functions as a constructive resource for educators seeking to refine the formulation of precise teaching objectives and create corresponding teaching tasks that harmonize with these objectives (Luo & Tan, 2023). Artificial intelligence (AI) in vocational education proffers diverse opportunities like improving teaching efficiency (evaluation of teaching and learning effectiveness, process assistance, and content optimization), improving learning efficiency (assisting in designing personalized learning content, instant learning support and feedback, opening up new avenues for learning), expand the coverage of vocational education (transforming to remote online, expanding the audience group of vocational education. In the digitalized world's vibrant tapestry, artificial intelligence arises as a formidable string composing transformative configurations.

Artificial intelligence presents its engrained spot in the real world, and marketing is one of its most promising playgrounds. As companies endeavor to connect with consumers more personalized and instinctively, AI's abilities are opening doors to formerly estimated dreadful modernizations. Its appendages are absolutely expanding across numerous aspects of marketing, signaling an era of exceptional transformations and potential. Artificial intelligence offers tremendous support and helps the digital marketing world to create highly attractive and catchy advertisements by analyzing target market customers' data, interests, buying behavior, and spending patterns. Artificial intelligence can determine the best audience and placements for their promotional mix elements, facilitating the design and introducing more pertinent and less wasted promotional programs. Artificial intelligence supports the design and creates influential content that is targeted uniquely based on the personalized requirements of the target market for recommending products and messaging for each customer. With great confidence, most artificial intelligence tools can analyze consumers' and their influencers' interests and habits to determine what exact content is suitable and influence their buying behavior. Artificial intelligence improves analytics and insights and offers a deeper understanding of the company's customers and campaigns, can detect patterns and correlations in large datasets, and provides insights to optimize marketing strategies. Artificial intelligence systematizes companies' campaign management and can support automating routine tasks like budget allocation, promotional program placement, and bidding. This technological giant also suggests improvements to the campaign structure and helps boost performance. Without diminishing the human marketer's role, artificial intelligence excels in analysis, automation, and optimization; human creativity, empathy, and judgment are still the most significant. By synchronizing the efforts of humans and artificial intelligence, digital marketers can shape their future promotional programs.

The rise of artificial intelligence brings challenges along with the discussed opportunities. Based on the opportunities this technology offers, the digital marketing industry has a chance to leverage AI to gain valuable insights, increase efficiency, improve performance, and craft incredibly personalized experiences for the target market customers by expecting a bright future. Along with the extensive opportunities related to artificial intelligence in vocational education discussed above, these technologies also provide crucial challenges regarding their security and reliability. These are primarily concerned with data privacy (protecting user data privacy, data isolation, and access control), algorithm bias (building balanced samples, bias detection tools, and policies and regulations), and technology dependencies (independent thinking, critical thinking, and independent cooperation and joint response)(Rongchang et al., 2024). The industry faces the most pressing challenges as they integrate artificial intelligence into their strategies. These are accuracy and precision and over-reliance on automation. While artificial intelligence can personalize marketing campaigns through digitalization based on user behavior, especially vocational education service providers, there is always a risk of misinterpreting data. Automated digital marketing campaigns can provide an expected level of awareness and popularity to vocational education and training providers in different parts of the world. Applying artificial intelligence in digital marketing comes with encounters that marketers must be aware of. As advanced as AI has become, it still has limitations.

Understanding these challenges is an imperative situation for vocational education service providers to find productive ways to attract prospective customers. These challenges are lack of emotional intelligence, bias and unfairness, job disruption, and lack of transparency (Holinex Digital, 2024). Çela et al. (2024) stressed the significance of artificial intelligence's role in transforming the education sector by offering unprecedented opportunities to increase learning experiences and outcomes. The same study indicated no substantial difference in critical thinking skills between students with prior exposure to artificial intelligence tools and those without. However, a statistically significant negative correlation exists between reliance on AI tools for assignments and students' problem-solving skills, suggesting that excessive dependence on AI can hinder the development of independent problem-solving abilities.

On the contrary, a robust positive correlation was initiated between the frequency of AI tool usage and students' perceptions of academic performance and assignment efficiency, highlighting the potential benefits of AI in enhancing these aspects of the educational experience. These results highlight the need for a balanced integration of AI tools in education to ensure they complement rather than replace traditional learning methods. The study's findings have significant implications for educators and policymakers, suggesting that while AI can enhance specific educational outcomes, addressing its potential risks to promote the development of fundamental cognitive skills is essential. To overcome these challenges, especially in vocational education, marketers need to choose artificial intelligence solutions carefully, focus on human strengths, and work to develop competent, transparent, and fair artificial intelligence models. With a considerate, human-centered approach, marketers can tackle the power of artificial intelligence (AI) while preventing the consequences. The future of artificial intelligence in digital marketing is an intelligent technological tool as long as the company is inclined to face the challenges head-on.

CONCLUSION

This book chapter thoroughly examines the extensive potential of artificial intelligence in vocational education, with the backup of digital marketing. Leveraging the robust digital marketing capabilities to popularize their customized programs and services in the present day's highly competitive labor market, these technologies offer a wide range of teaching aids and help the teaching community in designing personalized and tailored teaching content and processes, enabling the accomplishment of precise vocational educational objectives, expanding educational coverage, and enhancing teaching and learning efficiency. At the same time, these technologies can propose the required answer support and practicing exercises to create a pragmatic approach to learning in the quickest possible time. Artificial intelligence (AI) in today's technology world has been offering a range of experiences with its rapid progress and creating a sensation in every field, including digital marketing through which vocational education and training field also wholly changed its conventional method of delivery of service to technology-based service with ever-expected satisfaction to their learners' community from the curriculum development to transformation, evaluation, and enhancing their skills, knowledge, and their dexterities. For these service providers, artificial intelligence-driven digital marketing persistently assimilates novel tools and approaches that have been presenting an exclusive competitive advantage in their business. With these new tools and techniques, there would be a chance to generate constant demand for creativity stretches in their delivery of service with a wide range of vocational programs from the traditional to advanced and contemporary fields of interest in the labor market. In conclusion, artificial intelligence embodies a precious and applicable tool for achieving modernization, intelligence, and personalization in vocational education. However, it is vital to remain aware of the consequences of its implementation. Rapidly developing appropriate guidelines and protocols, instituting risk prevention and control mechanisms, modifying technological dependence, and encouraging students' standalone intellectual capabilities are critical. By advancing collaborative efforts among various stakeholders, governments and service providers can simplify the judicious application of artificial intelligence in vocational education, thereby accomplishing a harmonious association between humans and technology.

REFERENCES

Adeshola, I., & Adepoju, A. P. (2023). The opportunities and challenges of ChatGPT in education. *Interactive Learning Environments*, •••, 1–14. DOI: 10.1080/10494820.2023.2253858

BBC StoryWorks. (2024). Harnessing the power of AI with a distinctively Kazakh touch. https://www.bbc.com/storyworks/kazakhstan-connection/harnessing-the-power-of-ai-with-a-distinctively-kazakh-touch

Çela, E., Fonkam, M. M., & Potluri, R. M. (2024). Risks of AI-assisted learning on student critical thinking: A case study of Albania. [IJRCM]. *International Journal of Risk and Contingency Management*, 12(1), 1–19. DOI: 10.4018/IJRCM.350185

Çela, E., Potluri, R. M., & Vajjhala, N. R. (2025). A Comprehensive Meta-Analysis of IoT Integration for Data-Driven Decision Making in Education. *Designing Sustainable Internet of Things Solutions for Smart Industries*, 27-50.

Dang, J., & Liu, L. (2022). Implicit theories of the human mind predict competitive and cooperative responses to AI robots. *Computers in Human Behavior*, 134, 107300. DOI: 10.1016/j.chb.2022.107300

Digital, H. (2024). The rise of AI in digital marketing: Challenges and opportunities for marketers. https://holinex.com/the-rise-of-ai-in-digital-marketing-challenges-and-opportunities-for-marketers/

Doskeyeva, G. Z., Kuzembekova, R. A., Umirzakov, S. Y., Beimisheva, A. S., & Salimbayeva, R. A. (2024). How can dual education in technical and vocational institutions improve students' academic achievements and mitigate youth unemployment in Kazakhstan? *Community College Journal of Research and Practice*, •••, 1–16. DOI: 10.1080/10668926.2023.2295472

European Commission. (2020). On Artificial Intelligence—A European approach to excellence and trust [White Paper], https://commission.europa.eu/system/files/2020-02/commission-white-paper-artificial-intelligence-feb2020_en.pdf

Fraiwan, M., & Khasawneh, N. (2023). A review of ChatGPT applications in education, marketing, software engineering, and healthcare: Benefits, drawbacks, and research directions. *arXiv preprint arXiv:2305.00237*.

Garden, T. (2023). The dawn of AI in digital marketing: Opportunities and challenges. Digital Skills Academy. https://blog.talentgarden.com/en/blog/marketing/the-dawn-of-ai-in-digital-marketing-opportunities-and-challenges

Ghosh, L., & Ravichandran, R. (2024). Emerging Technologies in Vocational Education and Training. *Journal of Digital Learning and Education*, 4(1), 41–49. DOI: 10.52562/jdle.v4i1.975

Government of Kazakhstan. (2023). Education in Kazakhstan. https://www.gov.kz/article/128171?lang=en

Grassini, S. (2023). Shaping the future of education: Exploring the potential and consequences of AI and ChatGPT in educational settings. *Education Sciences*, 13(7), 692. DOI: 10.3390/educsci13070692

High-Level Expert Group on Artificial Intelligence. (2019). A definition of AI: Main capabilities and disciplines. European Commission. https://www.aepd.es/sites/default/files/2019-12/ai-definition.pdf

Joseph, J. (2024). AI and digital marketing: Most common opportunities and challenges. https://jeromejoseph.com/ai-digital-marketing-common-opportunities-challenges/

Jumasseitova, A. K., Potluri, R. M., & Smolyakova, E. (2024). Strategic role of alumni associations of Kazakhstan higher educational institutions in achieving sustainable development goals. [IJABIM]. *International Journal of Asian Business and Information Management*, 15(1), 1–21. DOI: 10.4018/IJABIM.351246

Kasneci, E., Seßler, K., Küchemann, S., Bannert, M., Dementieva, D., Fischer, F., & Kasneci, G. (2023). ChatGPT for good? On opportunities and challenges of large language models for education. *Learning and Individual Differences*, 103, 102274. DOI: 10.1016/j.lindif.2023.102274

Kim, S. (2022). Working with robots: Human resource development considerations in human-robot interaction. *Human Resource Development Review*, 21(1), 48–74. DOI: 10.1177/15344843211068810

Luo, S., & Tan, A. (2023). The logical transformation and practical path of educational development in the context of ChatGPT application. *Journal of Chongqing University of Technology (Social Sciences)*, 1-13.

Mandal, P. (2024). Artificial intelligence and future of education: An analytical study in the lens of vocational development. *International Journal of Multidisciplinary Educational Research*, 13(1), 98–105.

Massmann, C., & Hofstetter, A. (2020). AI-pocalypse now? Herausforderungen Künstlicher Intelligenz für Bildungssystem, Unternehmen und die Workforce der Zukunft. *Digitale Bildung und Künstliche Intelligenz in Deutschland: Nachhaltige Wettbewerbsfähigkeit und Zukunftsagenda*, 167-220.

Miao, F., Holmes, W., Huang, R., & Zhang, H. (2021). *AI and education: A guidance for policymakers*. UNESCO Publishing.

Molenaar, I. (2021). Personalization of learning: Towards hybrid human-AI learning technologies. *Blockchain, and Robots*, June 08, 57-77.

Musseau, A. (2024). What is vocational education? EHL Insights. https://hospitalityinsights.ehl.edu/what-is-vocational-education

Nimmagadda, S., Surapaneni, R., & Mouly Potluri, R. (2024). Artificial Intelligence in HR: Employee Engagement Using Chatbots. In Singh, R., Khan, S., Kumar, A., & Kumar, V. (Eds.), *Artificial Intelligence Enabled Management: An Emerging Economy Perspective* (pp. 147–162). De Gruyter., DOI: 10.1515/9783111172408-010

OECD. (2019). Transformative competencies for 2030. Conceptual Learning Framework. https://www.oecd.org/education/2030-project/teaching-and-learning/learning/transformative-competencies/Transformative_Competencies_for_2030_concept_note.pdf

Official Information Source of the Prime Minister of the Republic of Kazakhstan. (2024). Concept for artificial intelligence development for 2024-2029 adopted by government. https://primeminister.kz/en/news/concept-for-artificial-intelligence-development-for-2024-2029-adopted-by-government-28786

Prihantoro, C. R. (2023). Outcome-based education (OBE) based vocational education model in the era of artificial intelligence. *Education Quarterly Eeview*, 6(1), 228–240. DOI: 10.31014/aior.1993.06.01.701

Rongchang, J., Yonghong, C., Yi, P., Shijie, X., & Dandan, Q. (2024). Opportunities and Challenges of AI in Vocational Education. *International Journal of Learning and Teaching*, 10(5), 590–596.

Sakenova, S. (2024). Kazakhstan focuses on precision AI development with new law and committee. *The Astana Times,* 16 July, https://astanatimes.com/2024/07/kazakhstan-focuses-on-precision-ai-development-with-new-law-and-committee/

Seufert, S. (2024). Artificial intelligence in vocational education and training (VET): Evaluating VET leaders' acceptance of AI in Switzerland. DOI: 10.21203/rs.3.rs-4628645/v1

Shiohira, K. (2021). Understanding the Impact of Artificial Intelligence on Skills Development. [*UNESCO-UNEVOC International Centre for Technical and Vocational Education and Training.*]. *Education*, •••, 2030.

Suparyati, A., Widiastuti, I., Saputro, I. N., & Pambudi, N. A. (2023). The role of artificial intelligence (AI) in vocational education. *JIPTEK: Jurnal Ilmiah Pendidikan Teknik dan Kejuruan, 17*(1), 1-20.

UNESCO Institute for Statistics. (2024). Vocational education: Definition. https://uis.unesco.org/en/glossary-term/vocational-education

Ventures, B. (2023). AI's growing role in vocational education. https://www.brighteyevc.com/post/ai-s-growing-role-in-vocational-education

Yen, C. S., & Yang, S. C. (2024). The Integration of Artificial Intelligence and Video Production Skills in Workplace Development: A Study from the Perspective of Vocational Training. *The Review of Socionetwork Strategies*, 18(2), 1–14. DOI: 10.1007/s12626-024-00162-6

Zhang, D., Mishra, S., Brynjolfsson, E., Etchemendy, J., Ganguli, D., Grosz, B., Lyons, T., Manyika, J., Niebles, J. C., Sellitto, M., Shoham, Y., Clark, J., & Perrault, R. (2021). The AI Index 2021 Annual Report. AI Index Steering Committee. Human-Centered AI Institute, Stanford University, CA. https://aiindex.stanford.edu/wp-content/uploads/2021/11/2021-AI-Index-Report_Master.pdf

ADDITIONAL READING

Jakubakynov, B., Tolegenuly, N., Naribai, R., Nurzhanova, Z., Shcherban, T., & Nebelenchuk, I. (2024). Innovative technologies in higher education: Developing international cooperation in professional training. *Globalisation, Societies and Education*, •••, 1–14. DOI: 10.1080/14767724.2024.2339309

Kusmoldayeva, Z., Spanov, M., Mukhamediyeva, G., Baimbetova, A., & Sugirova, G. (2024). Managing healthcare innovation activities in Kazakhstan for optimal effectiveness. *Journal of the International Council for Small Business*, 1-18.

Rakisheva, G., Lepeshev, D., Zakhlebayeva, V., Abibulayeva, A., & Alkhatova, T. (2024). Youth Work in the Republic of Kazakhstan: State and Prospects of Development. *Child and Youth Services*, •••, 1–21. DOI: 10.1080/0145935X.2024.2427918

Zhaksylyk, A., Togtarbay, B., Auyesbay, K., Shoiymbekova, B., & Tolemissova, Z. (2024). Development and problems of the national journalistic model of Kazakhstan, considering social, ethical, managerial, and marketing mechanisms of the media environment. *Atlantic Journal of Communication*, •••, 1–14. DOI: 10.1080/15456870.2024.2386428

KEY TERMS AND DEFINITIONS

Artificial Intelligence (AI): The simulation of human intelligence processes by machines, enabling tasks such as decision-making, visual perception, and language processing.

Augmented Reality (AR): Technology that overlays digital content onto the real world to create interactive and engaging experiences, increasingly used in education and marketing.

Data Privacy: The practice of safeguarding personal data from unauthorized access or misuse, particularly in AI-driven educational and marketing systems.

Digital Marketing: The use of digital channels, such as social media, email, and websites, to promote products or services and connect with target audiences.

Gamification: The integration of game elements into non-game contexts, such as education or marketing, to enhance engagement and motivation.

Internet: of Things (IoT): A network of interconnected devices that collect and exchange data, often used to enhance decision-making in marketing and education.

Machine Learning (ML): A subset of AI focused on developing algorithms that allow systems to learn and improve from data without explicit programming.

Personalized Learning: Tailoring educational experiences to the individual needs and abilities of learners, often achieved using AI-driven tools.

Vocational Education and Training (VET): Education programs focused on equipping individuals with practical skills and knowledge tailored to specific careers or trades.

Workforce Readiness: The development of skills and competencies necessary to meet the demands of modern jobs, particularly in AI-driven and technology-oriented industries.

Chapter 8
Artificial Intelligence Shaping the Future of Vocational Education and Training:
Roles, Impacts, and Insights

Melissa Li Sa Liow
https://orcid.org/0000-0003-3794-733X
University Partnership – Coventry University, PSB Academy, Singapore

ABSTRACT

This chapter analyzes the artificial intelligence (AI)'s role in vocational education and training (VET). First, the chapter reviews existing literature on AI's role and effects in VET, synthesizing findings to offer a comprehensive overview. Second, gathering insights from experts, lecturers, and commercial apprentices. This approach provides practical perspectives on AI's use in VET settings and its impact on educational practices and industry needs. A research framework is developed that identifies key areas for development and proposes research questions for future exploration. The final section provides practical recommendations to mitigate the negative impacts of AI in VET, including strategies for bridging user gaps, overcoming AI's limitations, and ensuring AI tools contribute positively to VET goals.

DOI: 10.4018/979-8-3693-8252-3.ch008

INTRODUCTION

This book chapter addresses a gap in current literature by focusing on the applications and effects of Artificial Intelligence (AI) in Vocational Education and Training (VET), which has been underexplored compared to K-12 and tertiary education. The chapter provides a detailed analysis of how AI technologies can enhance VET by bridging the gap between theoretical research and practical application. Rosyadi et al. (2023) conducted a systematic literature review on AI in vocational education, revealing a lack of studies on AI's impact on VET's future, highlighting the need for further research.

The chapter will draw on insights from experts, lecturers, and apprentices at the Swiss Federal University for Vocational Education and Training (SFUVET) and review existing literature to offer a comprehensive overview of AI's role and effects in VET. It will explore AI applications such as personalized learning, adaptive assessments, and AI-driven career guidance, assessing both positive impacts and challenges like equity, data privacy, and job displacement. A research framework will be developed to outline effective strategies for AI integration in VET, providing practical recommendations to mitigate negative impacts and ensure AI tools enhance training outcomes.

Ultimately, this chapter aims to be a valuable resource for educators, policymakers, industry leaders, and researchers by offering an in-depth exploration of AI's potential in advancing VET. It will provide insights into forming effective partnerships between educational institutions and industries, creating robust internship programs, and aligning graduates with modern workplace demands, contributing to the ongoing discussion about the future of VET in a digital world.

BACKGROUND

Foundation Models of AI

Foundation models are large-scale AI systems pre-trained on extensive datasets that can be fine-tuned for specific applications, facilitating the rapid development of innovative AI products across various industries (Teubner et al., 2023). These models exhibit remarkable capabilities in generating and adapting content across diverse fields such as creative work (Chen et al., 2023), software debugging (Sobania et al., 2023), and text-to-image generation (Ramesh et al., 2021, July). As these models scale, foundation models expand their applicability to tasks beyond their initial training without needing additional data (Brown et al., 2020), and their performance can be further refined with cost-effective fine-tuning and prompt engineering (Liu et al., 2023). As these models become foundational to AI, it can challenge existing governance structures and require organizations to find new ways to differentiate their AI solutions in a landscape where versatile, high-performance models are increasingly accessible (Schneider et al., 2024).

VET Education Systems

The integration of VET into secondary school curricula reflects an increased awareness of students' diverse needs and the changing demands of the global economy. VET, or Career and Technical Education (CTE), prepares learners for specific trades and vocations through practical, hands-on experiences rather than traditional academic learning (AICTE). Originating from early apprenticeship systems and guilds, VET gained significance in the 20th century with industrialization and societal changes and is now a key element of global education policy (Dey & Srivastava, 2022). VET focuses on practical application and hands-on learning, incorporating internships, apprenticeships, and work-based opportunities to build industry connections and enhance both work productivity and personal development (Vats & Malik, 2024).

VET plays a vital role in global education systems, with 44 percent of upper-secondary students in OECD countries enrolled in vocational programs, and up to 70 percent in countries like Austria, Finland, and the Netherlands (OECD, 2023a). VET programs typically blend classroom learning with workplace training, a model prevalent in Denmark and Germany, where apprenticeships are common (OECD, 2023b). VET qualifications often lead to better early career employment outcomes compared to general qualifications, although these benefits may diminish for older age groups due to fewer job advancement opportunities (OECD, 2024). VET also supports lifelong learning by offering upskilling and reskilling opportunities, crucial for adapting to digital and green transitions (OECD, n.d). Effective VET depends on skilled teachers with both theoretical and practical expertise and attracting industry professionals can help address teacher shortages and enhance education-workplace connections. Work-based learning is further supported by in-company trainers who are often required to have specific training (OECD, n.d).

Background of AI in VET

AI, while not a new concept, has become a prominent topic in educational settings, including VET, with research on its potential dating back to the 1980s (Aleksander et al., 1988; Bound, 2011; Katsikas et al., 2016; Lipson, 1984; Vitale et al., 2016; Weigel et al., 2007; Winters et al., 2009). The focus on AI has intensified with discussions of the Fourth Industrial Revolution (Avis, 2018), highlighting the need for technological skills across various industries (Jagannathan et al., 2019). Early studies suggest that educators often have a basic understanding of AI, indicating a need for more comprehensive training programs to effectively integrate AI into teaching (Lindner et al., 2019; Kim et al., 2022; Petridou & Lao, 2024; Singh, 2024). AI, including technologies like machine learning and natural language processing, is increasingly used in education for creating learning materials, personalizing instruction, and solving problems (Khosrow-Pour, 2018; Shinde & Shah, 2018). Its integration in VET promises to enhance learning experiences, skills development, and job market readiness by providing personalized learning, relevant curricula, and tailored career guidance (Lim and Lee, 2024). However, ethical considerations, such as data privacy and bias, must be addressed to ensure responsible AI implementation (Jackaria et al., 2024; Li et al., 2021).

Constructivism Approach

The integration of AI in VET emphasizes the inter-subjective and contextual nature of knowledge, highlighting the inductive process of deriving facts and themes related to users' research queries within AI educational tools. Sharma (2023) associates constructivism with the philosophy of interpretivism. Constructivism focuses on the collaborative production of knowledge among teachers, students, and AI education tools, while interpretivism is concerned with understanding shared perspectives and creating meaning. Constructivists view reality from the individual's perspective, aiming to present multiple viewpoints within a social context. This approach facilitates meaningful teaching and learning experiences for both teachers and students in a safe, self-paced environment.

LITERATURE REVIEW

AI with New VET Requirements

The integration of AI in education, including VET, is reshaping workforce reskilling and the commercial sector. While AI in education (AIEd) offers personalized and adaptive learning tools for both teachers and students, addressing both content and emotional aspects of learning, its effective application requires substantial investment and a deep integration into real-world contexts (Luckin and Holmes, 2016). The fourth industrial revolution, driven by AI, is transforming work processes across industries, necessitating a shift in skill requirements and roles for workers (Schwab, 2017; Petropoulos, 2018). This shift demands not only the creation of new AI-related job profiles but also the enhancement of existing training programs with AI skills (Avis, 2018). Research highlights the need for continuous employee upskilling through personalized training approaches, such as micro-learning, to adapt to technological changes (Maity, 2019). However, a fully digitalized work environment driven by AI remains a future goal, presenting challenges for training young professionals for roles that are not yet fully defined (Attwell et al., 2020). There is a growing recognition of the need to incorporate AI into VET curricula and to enhance the AI knowledge and skills of both students and educators (Chao et al., 2021; Poquet & De Laat, 2021). Investment in AI training is crucial for all ages, including older workers, to prepare for AI-driven work environments and address the current scarcity of AI-focused courses and skilled instructors (Kong et al., 2021; Cazzaniga et al., 2024).

Role of AI in Shaping Future VET Graduates

AI is defined as the creation of systems that replicate human-like behaviors such as perception, reasoning, and learning (Ma, 2019, May). Its development has progressed through three stages: the 1960s focused on knowledge representation, the 1970s saw advancements in device capabilities, and the late 20th century introduced big data and cognitive intelligence, leading to significant breakthroughs in deep learning (Ma, 2019, May). Increased automation in production is reshaping job requirements, necessitating digital skills and proficiency with new technologies (Ma, 2019, May). Guggemos and Seufert (2021) highlight that greater automation presents challenges such as understanding complex interfaces and performing data analysis, while AI enhances distance learning through technologies like voice recognition and augmented reality. Ganga (2021, June) notes that as AI evolves, it increasingly integrates with educational innovations, affecting the pace of digital adoption influenced by various factors including business models and employee training (Bhushan, 2022). Rosyadi et al. (2023) emphasize AI's transformative impact on vocational education by offering personalized learning through technologies like Virtual Compression Testing Machines (VCTMs), immersive learning tools, and virtual assistants, which enhance student engagement and support. Successful AI implementation in education requires targeted teacher training and investment in technology infrastructure, underscoring the importance of digital transformation for preparing a skilled workforce (Rosyadi et al., 2023).

Modern AI Applications in Forms of VET

Current research by Shu and Gu (2023) provides empirical evidence that intelligent education models, empowered by the Edu-Metaverse, significantly enhance learning outcomes compared to traditional methods. The Edu-Metaverse's ecological teaching environment, multimodal resources, and intelligent pedagogy improve student learning and engagement while fostering a better value orientation. Yusro et al. (2024) note that AI technology is increasingly integrated into industrial education, with various countries implementing policies to promote its application in innovative teaching and campus management. The use of technology intelligence in education is deemed essential for future progress. Augmented and virtual reality further transform education by expanding spatial imagination and offering immersive learning experiences (Martin et al., 2018). Companies like Google, Facebook, and Alchemy VR are collaborating with institutions to create realistic virtual reality educational content, enhancing the scope and effectiveness of educational environments (Huttar & BrintzenhofeSzoc, 2020).

Challenges of AI in VET

Luck and Aylett (2000) address the challenge of resource constraints in AI environments, noting that certain physical modeling techniques, such as simulating fish behavior, require substantial computational power due to their complex analytical needs. They suggest that alternatives like local computations, artificial life techniques, or qualitative physics could offer broader accuracy while reducing computational demands. They also emphasize the importance of achieving real-time rendering for continuous interaction, though this may not be necessary for all applications, especially those focused on offline media. The field of intelligent virtual environments, though innovative, still lacks universally applicable tools and frameworks. Despite advancements such as VRML'97, current standards remain inadequate for some applications (Luck & Aylett, 2000).

Gratsiouni et al. (2016) highlight the significance of assessing educational quality and effectiveness, proposing various teaching models and standards for evaluation. Guggemos and Seufert (2021) suggest that as AI-based technology becomes recognized as intelligent machinery, teachers need to effectively learn and utilize it. They argue that digitalization should extend beyond just technological integration to include educational reflection that enhances the learning process. Windelband (2023) outlines key challenges in vocational education, such as adapting to virtual systems, managing data, and integrating new technologies.

Education systems face difficulties in keeping up with AI advancements, especially in vocational education. In Germany, AI education has been predominantly focused on universities, with vocational education incorporating AI topics more recently. Tailoring AI content to meet the needs of apprentices, who differ from university students, is crucial, and feedback from teachers is essential for effective implementation (Rott et al., 2022). The OECD (n.d) stresses the importance of having skilled VET teachers who possess both theoretical and practical knowledge.

Recruiting and retaining qualified VET teachers remains a challenge, but involving industry professionals in teaching can help bridge this gap.

Slimi and Carballid (2023) discuss several risks associated with AI integration in education. Key concerns include algorithmic bias and discrimination, as AI systems may perpetuate biases present in training data, impacting admissions and grading. Strategies to mitigate these risks involve improving transparency, accountability, and employing bias detection techniques (Malik & Aslam, 2024). Adapting AI to diverse educational contexts is also challenging and requires flexible implementation approaches (Malik & Aslam, 2024). Additionally, over-dependence on AI might undermine essential human aspects of education, such as creativity and empathy (Malik & Aslam, 2024). Data privacy and security issues further complicate AI integration, necessitating strict measures and adherence to regulations (Salloum, 2024; Proton AG., 2024; UNCTAD, n.d.). Proper training for educators is also crucial to effectively integrate AI into teaching (Walter, 2024; Gaur et al., 2024).

Bailey (2023) and Ditta and Aslam (2024) address the risks of non-authenticity due to GenAI content in educational settings. GenAI's ability to generate content similar to human-created material poses challenges for validating educational resources and assessments, affecting academic integrity while posing digital divide risks due to non-affordability and non-accessibility by the VET community. For managing these risks, enhancing digital literacy, implementing clear policies, and using technological solutions like digital signatures to verify content authenticity are essential (Alier et al., 2024).

Ethical concerns related to algorithmic bias remain significant in AI integration, with potential to reinforce existing inequalities (Donlon & Tiernan, 2023). Developers need to focus on creating fair algorithms and promoting diversity in data collection to address these issues (Ditta & Aslam, 2024; Malik & Aslam, 2024). Establishing ethical guidelines and regulatory frameworks for responsible AI use in education requires collaboration among policymakers, educators, and developers (Kayyali, 2024; Malik & Aslam, 2024).

Opportunities of AI in VET

Despite these shortcomings, there are marked opportunities for rapid progress. Fisher and Fraser (1998) suggest that fostering closer interaction between research in virtual reality, AI, and artificial life could lead to greater understanding and agreement on critical issues, potentially accelerating the development of new applications using intelligent virtual environments.

The findings by Ameershi et al. (2014) highlight key insights into machine learning during a period when AI had not yet reached its current level of sophistication. First, they present interactive machine learning as an alternative approach to traditional machine learning, emphasizing more dynamic, rapid, and incremental interaction cycles. This approach allows for a closer relationship between the user and the learning system, leading to a more collaborative process where user input and feedback continuously shape the learning model. However, this perspective reflects a time when machine learning models were simpler and more dependent on direct human input for tuning and improvement, contrasting with the present era where advanced AI models often learn from large datasets with minimal human intervention.

Ameershi et al. (2014) argue that understanding user needs and behaviors through formative studies could lead to better system design and user interfaces. This highlights an era when the field was still exploring how humans and machines could effectively interact, as opposed to today's AI landscape, where models increasingly aim for autonomy and less direct human interaction. The challenges identified in 2014 remain relevant, but today, there is a stronger emphasis on user experience in AI-driven applications like chatbots, virtual assistants, and recommendation systems.

Holmes et al. (2022) report that AI has rapidly achieved remarkable success, significantly enhancing performance in manufacturing and service sectors, and making notable impacts in education as well. Jing et al. (2022) observe that with advancements in sustainable manufacturing technology, there is an increasing demand for talent capable of producing diverse and complex intelligent products.

Scholars such as Saxena et al. (2023), and Kot and Nykyporets (2024) highlight AI's significant advancement in education through personalization. AI-driven VET systems can enhance learning by modeling and adapting to individual student needs, improving adaptability and efficiency. By recognizing unique learning preferences and knowledge gaps, AI allows for curriculum customization, which can reduce the need for standardized courses and enable students to advance at their own pace. Research by Fazil et al. (2024) demonstrates that AI can effectively measure student engagement and performance, showing a correlation between participation levels and assessment scores. This capability helps educators identify and support students needing additional assistance. Additionally, AI integration in VET systems can manage administrative queries similarly to virtual assistants in banking and e-commerce, potentially saving institutions money by reducing the need for large administrative staff and allowing them to focus on more critical student services (Aithal & Aithal, 2023).

AI Integration in VET system

Given that AI as an additional qualification is relatively new and the use of digital and adaptive learning content—which allows apprentices to learn at their own pace—is uncommon in dual training, getting insights from experts, lecturers, and commercial apprentices are crucial for implementing this strategy.

The Swiss Federal University for Vocational Education and Training SFUVET (2024) serves as Switzerland's leading authority on vocational education and training. SFUVET provides foundational and advanced training for VET professionals, engages in VET research, aids in the development of various professions, and supports international collaboration in vocational and professional education and training.

The objective is for apprentices to gain vocational competence through additional qualifications, which should be achieved through action-oriented teaching (Tramm & Naeve-Stoß, 2020). This teaching method, grounded in constructivist learning theory, encourages learners to engage in problem-solving situations actively (Herkner & Pahl, 2020). Constructivism posits that knowledge is acquired through realistic problem-solving (Das & Mitra, 2024). In action-oriented classes, learners work in groups to solve, discuss, and evaluate problems, which helps illustrate and explain theoretical principles (Asrifan et al., 2024). Addressing real-world problems aids in developing vocational competence gradually (Christiansen & Even, 2024).

Excerpts from Experts in SFUVET on AI Integration in VET

Following is the narration of the experts from the SFUVET, and they have shared their perspectives on the impact of AI on VET via YouTube (Eidgenössische Hochschule für Berufsbildung EHB, May 17, 2024a).

Serge Chobaz, Head of Sector at the Center for the Development of Occupations, highlights that AI can enhance VET by supporting apprenticeships, identifying apprentice needs, and providing adaptive training. This approach is particularly useful in advanced education tailored to individual backgrounds and documented needs, such as those in portfolios. AI can streamline training content and reduce administrative tasks for teachers, allowing them to focus more on their expertise and the specific needs of learners. Teachers are increasingly using tools like ChatGPT to prepare lessons and integrate multimedia content, which allows them to address the context and needs of their students more effectively.

Siegfried Alberton, Regional Head of Continuing Education, believes that AI has the potential to transform learning methods dramatically. Educators can tailor courses for schools, businesses, and corporate training. As AI becomes integral to many industries, it will be a key topic in VET. Future employees will need to manipulate or program AI, as noted by Dr. Christopher Keller, Senior Researcher on education technologies at SFUVET. Prof. Dr. Antje Barabasch, Head of Research in Teaching and Learning within the VPET system, points out that AI is driving significant changes in fields like medicine and agriculture. Apprentices in these areas will need to adapt to new technologies, such as chatbots, which may alter the roles of commercial employees. Although AI can handle certain tasks, essential human skills like communication, creativity, and collaboration remain crucial.

Dr. Francesca Amenduni, Senior Researcher on education technologies, observes that AI's impact on learning can be both positive and negative. Over-reliance on AI may be detrimental, while using AI to foster critical thinking can be beneficial. Prof. Dr. Lorenzo Bonoli, Head of Master of Science in VET and Senior Researcher, notes that AI can assist with knowledge transfer, practical exercises, and information management. However, the role of human tutors remains vital, especially in situations where apprentices are less physically present. This may necessitate the development of new training models and dual training approaches.

Excerpts from Experts, Lecturer and Commercial Apprentices in SFUVET on Future of AI in VET

Another YouTube topic discussed by the SFUVET group was the future of AI in VET (Eidgenössische Hochschule für Berufsbildung EHB, May 17, 2024b).

Dr. Christopher Keller believes that AI should not be ignored but rather discussed and integrated into curricula to equip the next generation with AI skills. Lynda Fuchs, an e-learning expert, encourages the VET community to embrace AI without fear. Prof. Dr. Jurg Schweri, Senior Researcher on education technologies at SFUVET, acknowledges both the ethical risks and opportunities presented by AI, noting that while AI can enhance efficiency, its use must be carefully regulated. Siegfried Alberton, Regional Head of Continuing Education, asserts that AI, like other technologies, should be utilized during its development and encourages the VET community to learn about its benefits and limitations. Prof. Dr. Antje Barabasch adopts a more critical stance, suggesting that while AI is beneficial in industrial contexts, learners should first acquire fundamental skills and social competencies through traditional methods before engaging with advanced tools.

Greta Agnello, a commercial apprentice, views AI as a promising future tool that must be used ethically to maintain quality. Barbara Da Silva Santos, another apprentice, feels that the VET community needs to improve its understanding of AI. Teachers should guide apprentices and students in using AI effectively across various contexts. Rene Hasler, a lecturer, emphasizes the importance of young people understanding AI and the functioning of neural networks, which often operate as “black boxes.” He suggests that, with proper caution, AI can be beneficial in learning and everyday life, but learners need expert knowledge to evaluate AI-generated results.

Gaby Walker, a scientific advisor for educational technologies in VET, stresses the need to remain open to new technologies while critically assessing their relevance and potential for discontinuation. Serge Chobaz points out that AI excels in data collection and information retrieval, making it a superior tool in these areas. However, establishing clear, flexible, and agile regulations for AI remains a significant challenge. Some technical colleges are developing their own AI systems to mitigate potential issues with market-available AI. Prof. Dr. Lukas Graf, Head of the Swiss Observatory for VET OBS SFUVET, notes current uncertainty about AI's implications for VET and the workplace. He advocates for using AI to handle detailed or repetitive tasks, allowing human workers to focus on more creative and meaningful aspects of their roles.

Summary Table and Research Framework

Table 1 encapsulates the diverse aspects of AI's influence on VET, from its benefits and drawbacks to the gaps in user understanding and the limitations inherent in AI technology.

Table 1. Four AI Aspects on VET

Positive AI Impacts in VET		
Aspect	**Description**	**Experts**
Support for Apprenticeships	AI aids in supporting apprenticeships by determining needs and providing adaptive training.	Serge Chobaz, Dr. Christopher Keller
Administrative Efficiency	Reduces administrative tasks for teachers, allowing them to focus on teaching and student support.	Serge Chobaz, Prof. Dr. Lorenzo Bonoli
Enhanced Lesson Preparation	Facilitates lesson preparation with AI tools, integrating multimedia tailored to learner needs.	Serge Chobaz
Adaptation to Learning Needs	Customizes learning content based on individual educational backgrounds and needs.	Serge Chobaz
Integration in Courses	AI becomes integral in various business contexts, preparing students for future AI-related roles.	Siegfried Alberton, Dr. Christopher Keller
Knowledge Transfer and Storage	Enhances knowledge transfer, information storage, and management of large data sets.	Prof. Dr. Lorenzo Bonoli
Future Skills Preparation	Encourages inclusion of AI skills in curricula to prepare students for future demands.	Dr. Christopher Keller, Lynda Fuchs
Improved Work Meaningfulness	AI handles repetitive tasks, enabling focus on creative and meaningful work.	Prof. Dr. Lukas Graf
Negative AI Impacts in VET		
Aspect	**Description**	**Experts**

continued on following page

Table 1. Continued

Positive AI Impacts in VET		
Aspect	**Description**	**Experts**
Over-Reliance on AI	Excessive dependence on AI may reduce critical thinking and problem-solving skills.	Dr. Francesca Amenduni
Reduction of Human Interaction	AI's role might lessen the importance of human interaction, impacting skills like communication and collaboration.	Prof. Dr. Antje Barabasch, Dr. Francesca Amenduni
Ethical Risks	AI introduces ethical challenges requiring regulation to prevent misuse and ensure responsible use.	Prof. Dr. Jurg Schweri
Potential Job Displacement	AI might lead to job redundancy in some roles, altering employment landscapes.	Prof. Dr. Lukas Graf
Caution with AI Usage	Risk of inappropriate or misunderstood use of AI, leading to ineffective or harmful applications.	Rene Hasler, Gaby Walker
User Gaps in AI Applications in VET		
Aspect	**Description**	**Experts**
Lack of AI Knowledge	Insufficient understanding of AI's benefits, limitations, and effective use in VET.	Greta Agnello, Barbara Da Silva Santos
Need for AI Training	Necessity for improved education on how to use AI tools in teaching and learning environments.	Greta Agnello, Barbara Da Silva Santos
Understanding Neural Networks	Need for comprehension of AI neural networks and their workings to critically evaluate AI outputs.	Rene Hasler
Ethical Use of AI	Requirement for clear guidelines on ethical AI use and its impact on education.	Gaby Walker
Inherent AI Disabilities in VET		
Aspect	**Description**	**Experts**
Limited Human-like Competence	AI lacks the ability to fully replicate human qualities such as creativity, empathy, and complex interpersonal skills.	Prof. Dr. Antje Barabasch, Prof. Dr. Lorenzo Bonoli
Dependence on Data Quality	AI effectiveness is contingent upon the quality and relevance of input data, with poor data leading to biased or inaccurate results.	Prof. Dr. Lorenzo Bonoli
Complexity and Transparency Issues	AI systems, especially neural networks, can be opaque, making it challenging to understand how decisions are made or to trust results.	Rene Hasler, Gaby Walker
Regulatory Challenges	Challenges in establishing clear, flexible, and effective regulations for managing AI applications in VET.	Serge Chobaz, Prof. Dr. Jurg Schweri

Adapted from Eidgenössische Hochschule für Berufsbildung EHB (May 17, 2024 a,b)

Here is a research framework model summarizing the positive and negative impacts of AI in VET that would be impacted by two moderating variables - user gaps, and inherent AI disabilities based on the perspectives of experts, lecturer and commercial apprentice from SFUVET. The two moderating variables would either increase or decrease the positive and negative impacts of AI in VET which in turn impact the level of achieving the VET goals such as meeting the learning outcomes and the level of work readiness with the necessary knowledge, skills and abilities.

Figure 1. Research Framework

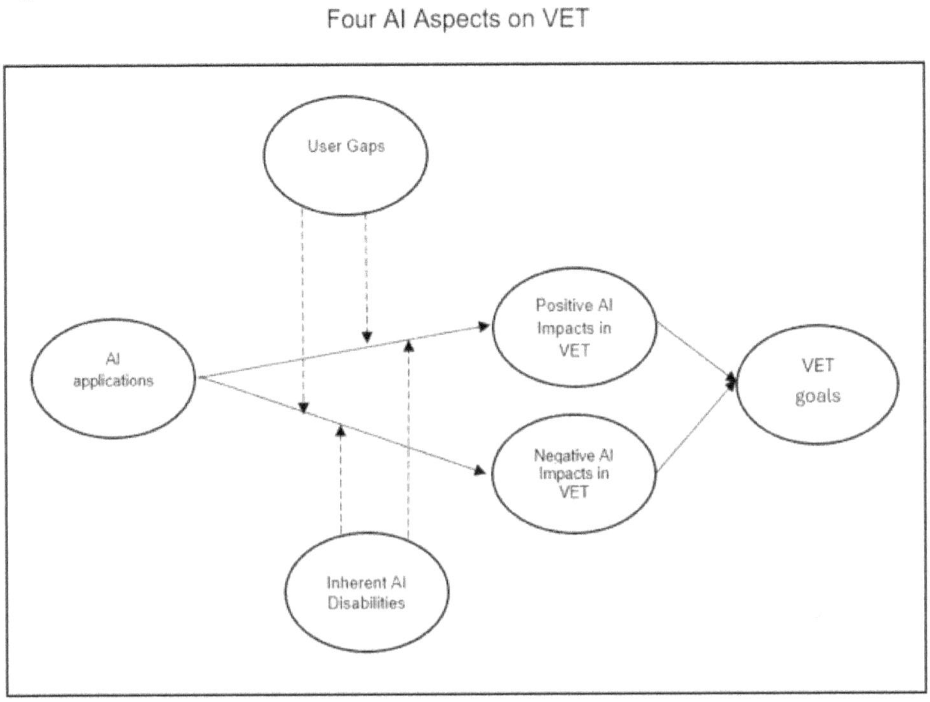

Source: Author

CONCLUSIONS AND RECOMMENDATIONS

In the digital age, where technological advancements occur rapidly, VET must align with national strategies to support both social and economic development. VET must navigate the challenges and opportunities presented by AI and embrace a proactive approach to transformation and growth. It is essential for VET to develop skills that leverage human strengths in the digital era, while effectively utilizing AI technology to produce competent graduates. This involves implementing policies that enhance the abilities of VET educators, using AI technology to innovate, creating AI-based products, upgrading educational facilities and infrastructure to keep pace with technological advancements, and fostering partnerships between vocational education institutions and the industry, both domestically and internationally.

To mitigate these ethical risks, Ditta and Aslam (2024) recommend that developers of AI driven VET systems implement recourse mechanisms to address errors, biases, or unintended outcomes resulting from AI use in VET. This includes promoting diversity and inclusivity in data collection through strategies like data augmentation, diverse sampling methods, and bias mitigation algorithms, particularly in the under-resourced VET institutions. Malik and Aslam (May 2024) emphasize the need for collaboration between policymakers and educators to establish ethical guidelines, accountability measures, and regulatory frameworks that ensure the responsible use of AIEPs and minimize the risks of algorithmic bias.

To ensure effective integration of AI and foster collaboration among the VET community—including educators, school administrators, and students—it is crucial for AI users to undergo comprehensive training and professional development. Educators need to be equipped with the knowledge, tools, and skills necessary to effectively utilize AI technologies in their teaching and continually evaluate their impact on student learning outcomes. There are innovative AI tools for educators to be trained in such as Canva Magic Studio, ChatGPT, MagicSchool.ai, Google Gemini and Learnt.ai (Panda Education and Training, 2024). However, there is a risk of over-reliance on automation and technology, which could undermine the human-centered aspects of education. Therefore, achieving a balance between human-centric pedagogy and AI-driven innovation in VET is vital. Integrating generative AI should align with fostering creativity, critical thinking, enhanced collaboration, and adhering to educational values and goals among educators, administrators, and students.

AI integration in VET presents several important considerations. AI has the potential to significantly enhance the learning experience through technologies such as ChatGPT, augmented reality, and virtual reality, which can make learning more engaging and interactive by allowing students to virtually assess tasks like predicting concrete strength. Additionally, AI supports personalized learning, adapting to the specific needs of each student, and boosts teaching efficiency through AI-powered question-and-answer systems and self-tests that provide immediate feedback. Despite these benefits, challenges such as limited practical experience and diverse teacher perceptions of AI's effectiveness must be addressed to fully harness AI's potential in VET. AI's positive impacts include greater accessibility and flexibility, especially in supporting students' development of problem-solving skills and creative decision-making. However, there is a continuous need for improved teacher training and more specialized research on AI's impact within vocational education. The findings also emphasize the critical need to further integrate Information and Communication Technology (ICT) into VET to build a digitally skilled workforce, which involves enhancing infrastructure, curriculum, and teacher training to meet modern job market demands (Rosyadi et al., 2023, p. 257).

This chapter contributes a theoretical framework that examines the positive and negative impacts of AI in VET while considering user gaps and the limitations of AI, based on the constructionist theory of learning, to prepare VET graduates to be future-ready. AI enables innovative and interactive teaching methods, such as immersive game-based learning and virtual simulations, which boost student motivation and engagement. It also offers personalized guidance through virtual assistants or chatbots that provide quick and precise answers to student questions, tutoring support, and immediate feedback. Successful implementation of these technologies requires a focus on teacher training, developing communication skills, and investing in technological infrastructure. Additionally, this book chapter highlights the significance of digital transformation in VET and its impact on preparing a technologically skilled workforce. In an increasingly complex work environment, adapting and evolving VET is essential. This chapter encourages practical change and adaptation in VET to ensure students are well-prepared to compete in a dynamic job market, potentially leading to increased employment opportunities and improved personal incomes.

The chapter also offers insights into the expectations, concerns, and aspirations of experts, lecturers, and commercial apprentices regarding AI-related additional training. When it comes to the didactic design and content of additional AI qualification programs, there is a need for more development, as expectations and ideas vary among teachers and apprentices. It may be challenging for teachers to adopt a student-centered didactic approach, while apprentices may prefer more teacher-centered instruction. A blended-learning approach could effectively merge both perspectives by allowing apprentices to learn independently through software while maintaining in-person class activities for adequate teacher support. The study also indicates that linking all content with practical examples is crucial for a high-quality training program. Both teachers and apprentices tend to agree more on content design and learning software. Overall, the learning content should encompass basic theoretical concepts of AI, tailored to the apprentices' level. Lastly, both groups concurred that learning software could best support the apprentices' learning process with explanatory videos and various practice options.

Based on the structured discussion in this section, Table 2 presents a set of recommendations categorized by different aspects pertinent to AI training in VET.

Table 2. Recommendations on AI training in VET

Aspect	Description	Recommendations
Expectations and Design	Teachers and apprentices have differing preferences for didactic design; teachers prefer student-oriented, apprentices prefer teacher-centered.	Implement a blended-learning approach to balance student autonomy with teacher support. Include practical examples throughout the content to make it more relatable and engaging.
Content and Learning Software	Both teachers and apprentices agree on the need for theoretical AI concepts adapted to apprentices' levels. They also favor explanatory videos and exercise options.	Develop AI training content that includes foundational theoretical concepts and adapts to the apprentices' skill levels. Ensure the learning software features explanatory videos and ample practice exercises to support diverse learning needs.
Apprentice Readiness and Interest	There's a disparity between teachers' and apprentices' views on prerequisites for AI training; apprentices show high interest regardless of academic performance.	Investigate the balance between academic performance and interest in AI for successful participation. Consider providing AI training programs that cater to varying levels of prior academic achievement and focus on fostering engagement and motivation.
Employer Perspective	The study did not cover employer perspectives on future skill requirements and the relevance of AI training.	Future research should include employer views to align AI training programs with industry needs. Understand employers' expectations to ensure that training programs meet future job market demands and support the development of relevant skills.
Negative AI Impacts	Over-reliance on AI, reduced human interaction, ethical risks, and potential job displacement are concerns.	Develop strategies to mitigate negative impacts such as promoting critical thinking, maintaining human interaction, establishing ethical guidelines, and addressing potential job displacement through reskilling programs.
User Gaps in AI Applications	Users lack knowledge of AI benefits and limitations, need for AI training, understanding neural networks, and ethical use of AI.	Provide comprehensive training on AI tools and their effective use, including insights into neural networks. Establish clear ethical guidelines for AI usage in education to address gaps in understanding and application.
Inherent AI Disabilities	AI lacks human-like competence, depends on data quality, faces complexity and transparency issues, and regulatory challenges.	Address AI limitations by focusing on areas where AI falls short, such as creativity and empathy. Ensure high-quality data input and strive for transparency in AI processes. Develop clear regulations and guidelines to manage AI applications effectively.

From: Author (2024)

Future Research Directions

The limitations of this book chapter primarily stem from its focus on reviewing literature from 1998 to 2024 on the integration of AI in VET systems, and from its reliance on narratives sourced solely from within the SFUVET institution. It does not explore how AI content is shared across different devices, such as mobile phones and laptops, nor does it delve into collaborations with other VET institutions, such as research-led projects or collaborative online learning initiatives involving students. Future research could benefit from a dedicated framework that examines the perspectives of different stakeholders—educators, school administrators, and students—individually. This is crucial, as each group may have unique needs and expectations regarding AI integration. If feasible, future studies could employ a longitudinal Structural Equation Modeling (SEM) design to evaluate the direction of causality and gather empirical evidence for potential hypotheses outlined in the research framework of Figure 1. Additionally, a comparative study across different countries could yield valuable insights, as the exposure to and acceptance of AI in VET varies based on socio-economic contexts and technology acceptance levels.

Looking ahead, future research in VET should continue to explore the prerequisites that apprentices need for effective participation in advanced AI qualification programs. The current finding that teachers believe high-performing apprentices with higher education entrance qualifications are the most suitable for AI training does not align with the apprentices' own assessments. Apprentices, regardless of their academic performance or school qualifications, show strong interest in additional AI qualifications. Thus, further research could investigate whether academic performance or genuine interest in participation is more crucial for successful engagement in AI qualifications. This book chapter has narrowly focused on AI training in VET and incorporating employer perspectives might be a fruitful avenue for future research. Understanding the expectations and future needs of employers regarding the skills of their professionals is vital not only for gaining employer support for such training programs and enhance the teachers' AI literacy but also for encouraging employers to reflect on their organization's future development and the skill sets required for their workforce.

Future research on AI's role in VET should prioritize evaluating the effectiveness of AI implementations including the logistics, infrastructure and cost effectiveness through investment or financial aid by public-private partnerships, the importance of teacher training for adopting AI technology, and the impact of AI use on students' problem-solving and decision-making skills in under-resourced VET institutions. Further studies should explore how AI can enhance the overall learning experience for students and its influence on their readiness for careers customized for VET like SFUVET planning to develop and improve their own VET systems. There are other commercial AI driven solutions for VET provided by IBM SkillsBuild platform that runs the Coursera and Singapore Ministry of Education including Ngee Ann Polytechnic have been forefront in personalizing learning experiences using AI tools (TVET Trainer, 2024). Additionally, it is crucial to examine how the integration of AI and Information and Communication Technology (ICT) in VET affects the accessibility and scalability of vocational education in a responsible and ethical manner and students' ability to meet current labor market needs. Such research on developing networks for VET would provide valuable insights for educators, policymakers, industry leaders, and researchers, enabling them to understand better how AI can transform vocational education while protecting sensitive data, enhance the quality of learning, and prepare students more effectively for a complex and evolving job market.

Furthermore, research should delve into the comparative impact of AI integration on VET across different socio-economic contexts, considering the diversity in technology adoption and acceptance levels. It should also investigate the factors that contribute to successful AI-driven pedagogies, including blended learning models that balance AI tools with human interaction. Research could explore the effectiveness of various AI tools, such as virtual simulations and AI-driven feedback systems, in fostering critical thinking and creativity among VET students. This would help identify best practices and scalable models that other institutions can adopt.

Lastly, future studies could also benefit from a multi-stakeholder approach by involving employers, students, educators, and policy makers to create a holistic understanding of AI's role in VET. This would help in developing comprehensive policies and curricula that are aligned with the needs of both the industry and the learners, ensuring that AI not only enhances learning experiences but also meets future job market requirements effectively.

REFERENCES

Aithal, P. S., & Aithal, S. (2023). How to increase emotional infrastructure of higher education institutions. [IJMTS]. *International Journal of Management, Technology, and Social Sciences*, 8(3), 356–394. DOI: 10.47992/IJMTS.2581.6012.0307

Aleksander, I., Vivet, M., Kerr, D., Gillingham, J., Fernandez de Castro, M. I., Diaz de Ilarraza Sanchez, A., Felisa Vordejo Maillo, M., & Lees, P. (1988). *Artificial intelligence and its potential as an aid to vocational training and education*. CEDEFOP. https://eric. ed.gov/?id=ED316734

Alier, M., García-Peñalvo, F., & Camba, J. D. (2024). Generative Artificial Intelligence in Education: From Deceptive to Disruptive. *International Journal of Interactive Multimedia and Artificial Intelligence, Special issue on Generative Artificial Intelligence in Education, 5*, 5-14. DOI: 10.9781/ijimai.2024.02.011

Amershi, S., Cakmak, M., Knox, W. B., & Kulesza, T. (2014). Power to the people: The role of humans in interactive machine learning. *AI Magazine*, 35(4), 105–120. DOI: 10.1609/aimag.v35i4.2513

Asrifan, A., Hamid, R. J., Syawal, S., & Muthmainnah, M. (2024). Tech-Enhanced Early Learning: Harnessing the Power of Persuasive Educational Technologies. *Power of Persuasive Educational Technologies in Enhancing Learning*, IGI Global, 63-96.

Avis, J. (2018). Socio-technical imaginary of the fourth industrial revolution and its implications for vocational education and training: A literature review. *Journal of Vocational Education and Training*, 70(3), 337–363. DOI: 10.1080/13636820.2018.1498907

Bailey, J. (2023). AI in Education: The leap into a new era of machine intelligence carries risks and challenges, but also plenty of promise. *Education Next*, 23(4), 29–36.

Bhushan, P. (2022). Recent Used and Future Application of Artificial Intelligent (AI). [IJSREM]. *International Journal of Scientific Research in Engineering and Management*, 6(11). Advance online publication. DOI: 10.55041/SREM16966

Bound, H. (2011). Vocational education and training teacher professional development: Tensions and context. *Studies in Continuing Education*, 33(2), 107–119. DOI: 10.1080/0158037X.2011.554176

Brown, P. (2020). Some observations on the race to higher education, digital technologies and the future of work. *Journal of Education and Work*, 33(7–8), 491–499. DOI: 10.1080/13639080.2020.1852500

Brown, T. B. (2020). Language models are few-shot learners. *arXiv preprint arXiv:2005.14165.*

Cazzaniga, M., Jaumotte, M. F., Li, L., Melina, M. G., Panton, A. J., Pizzinelli, C., & Tavares, M. M. M. (2024). *Gen-AI: Artificial intelligence and the future of work.* International Monetary Fund. DOI: 10.5089/9798400262548.006

Chao, P. J., Hsu, T. H., Liu, T. P., & Cheng, Y. H. (2021). Knowledge of and competence in artificial intelligence: Perspectives of Vietnamese digital-native students. *IEEE Access : Practical Innovations, Open Solutions*, 9, 75751–75760. DOI: 10.1109/ACCESS.2021.3081749

Chen, L., Sun, L., & Han, J. (2023). A comparison study of human and machine-generated creativity. *Journal of Computing and Information Science in Engineering*, 23(5), 051012. Advance online publication. DOI: 10.1115/1.4062232

Christiansen, B., & Even, A. M. (Eds.). (2024). *Advancing Student Employability Through Higher Education.* IGI Global. DOI: 10.4018/979-8-3693-0517-1

Das, S., & Mitra, A. (2024). Enhancing Logic and Problem-Solving Skills in the Digital Age. In *Revolutionizing Curricula Through Computational Thinking, Logic, and Problem Solving* (pp. 40-59). IGI Global. DOI: 10.4018/979-8-3693-1974-1.ch003

Dey, S., & Srivastava, A. (2022). Reimagining Technical and Vocational Education and Training in India: Prospects and Challenges. *University News*, 60(20), 3–8.

Ditta, A., & Aslam, M. U. (2024). *Education in the AI Age: Navigating Challenges of Generative AI Integration.* https://www.researchgate.net/publication/380364982

Donlon, E., & Tiernan, P. (2023). Chatbots and Citations: An experiment in academic writing with Generative AI. *Irish Journal of Technology Enhanced Learning*, 7(2), 75–87. DOI: 10.22554/ijtel.v7i2.125

Eidgenössische Hochschule für Berufsbildung EHB. (May 17, 2024a). *AI in VET: 4/12 How does AI impact vocational and professional training?* YouTube. https://www.youtube.com/watch?v=uv09fKJMHMk

Eidgenössische Hochschule für Berufsbildung EHB. (May 17, 2024b). YouTube. *AI in VET: 12/12 How do you see the future of AI in vocational education and training?*https://www.youtube.com/watch?v=R4pEl5KlprU

Fazil, A. W., Hakimi, M., Shahidzay, A. K., & Hasas, A. (2024). Exploring the Broad Impact of AI Technologies on Student Engagement and Academic Performance in University Settings in Afghanistan. *RIGGS: Journal of Artificial Intelligence and Digital Business*, 2(2), 56–63. DOI: 10.31004/riggs.v2i2.268

Fraser, G., & Fisher, S. S. (1998). Intelligent virtual worlds continue to develop. *Computer Graphics*, 32(3), 15–19. DOI: 10.1145/281278.281285

Ganga, X. (2021, June). Educational Artificial Intelligence (EAI) Connotation, Key Technology and Application Trend-Interpretation and analysis of the two reports entitled "Preparing for the Future of Artificial Intelligence" and "The National Artificial Intelligence Research and Development Strategic Plan". In *2021 International Conference on Intelligent Computing, Automation and Applications (ICAA)* (pp. 219-223). IEEE. DOI: 10.1109/ICAA53760.2021.00046

Gaur, A. S., Sharan, H. O., & Kumar, R. (2024). AI in Education: Ethical Challenges and Opportunities. *The Ethical Frontier of AI and Data Analysis*, IGI Global, 39-54.

Gocen, A., & Aydemir, F. (2020). Artificial intelligence in education and schools. *Research on Education and Media*, 12(1), 13–21. DOI: 10.2478/rem-2020-0003

Gratsiouni, D., Koutsouba, M., Venetsanou, F., & Tyrovola, V. (2016). Learning and digital environment of dance–the case of Greek traditional dance in YouTube. *European Journal of Open, Distance and E-learning*, 19(2), 80–95. DOI: 10.1515/eurodl-2016-0009

Guggemos, J., & Seufert, S. (2021). Teaching with and teaching about technology–Evidence for professional development of in-service teachers. *Computers in Human Behavior*, 115, 106613. Advance online publication. DOI: 10.1016/j.chb.2020.106613

Herkner, V., & Pahl, J. P. (2020). Handlungsorientierung in der Berufsbildung. *Handbuch Berufsbildung*, 189-203. https://doi.org/DOI: 10.1007/978-3-658-19312-6_17

Holmes, W., Porayska-Pomsta, K., Holstein, K., Sutherland, E., Baker, T., Shum, S. B., Santos, O. C., Rodrigo, M. T., Cukurova, M., Bittencourt, I. I., & Koedinger, K. R. (2022). Ethics of AI in education: Towards a community-wide framework. *International Journal of Artificial Intelligence in Education*, 32(3), 1–23. DOI: 10.1007/s40593-021-00239-1

Huttar, C. M., & BrintzenhofeSzoc, K. (2020). Virtual reality and computer simulation in social work education: A systematic review. *Journal of Social Work Education*, 56(1), 131–141. DOI: 10.1080/10437797.2019.1648221

Jackaria, P. M., Hajan, B. H., Mastul, A. R. H., & Sali, F. Z. (2024). Generation AI in a Reimagined Classroom: Challenges, Opportunities and Implications to Education. *Exploring Youth Studies in the Age of AI*, IGI Global, 174-185.

Jagannathan, S., Ra, S., & Maclean, R. (2019). Dominant recent trends impacting on jobs and labor markets - an overview. *International Journal of Training Research*, 17(sup1), 1–11. DOI: 10.1080/14480220.2019.1641292

Jing, X., Zhu, R., Lin, J., Yu, B., & Lu, M. (2022). Education sustainability for intelligent manufacturing in the context of the new generation of artificial intelligence. *Sustainability (Basel)*, 14(21), 14148. Advance online publication. DOI: 10.3390/su142114148

Kayyali, M. (2024). Future possibilities and challenges of AI in education. In *Transforming education with generative AI: Prompt engineering and synthetic content creation* (pp. 118–137). IGI Global. DOI: 10.4018/979-8-3693-1351-0.ch006

Khosrow-Pour, D. B. A. (Ed.). (2018). *Advanced Methodologies and Technologies in Artificial Intelligence, Computer Simulation, and Human-Computer Interaction*. IGI Global.

Kim, J., Lee, H., & Cho, Y. H. (2022). Learning design to support student-AI collaboration: Perspectives of leading teachers for AI in education. *Education and Information Technologies*, 27(5), 1–36. DOI: 10.1007/s10639-021-10831-6

Kong, S. C., Cheung, W. M. Y., & Zhang, G. (2021). Evaluation of an artificial intelligence literacy course for university students with diverse study backgrounds. *Computers and Education: Artificial Intelligence, 2*, Article 100026.

Kot, S. O., & Nykyporets, S. S. (2024). *Utilization of artificial intelligence in enhancing English language proficiency in tertiary education. Science and Education in the Third Millennium: Information Technology*. Education, Law, Psychology, Social Sphere, Management.

Kotsifakos, D., Adamopoulos, P., & Douligeris, C. (2016, September). Design and development of a learning management system for vocational education. In *Proceedings of the SouthEast European Design Automation, Computer Engineering,Computer Networks and Social Media Conference* (pp. 110-117). https://doi.org/DOI: 10.1145/2984393.2984413

Li, T., Song, W. N., & Zhou, J. H. (2021, May). Research on Artificial Intelligence Industrial Big Data Platform for Industrial Internet Applications. In *2021 IEEE 4th International Conference on Electronics Technology (ICET)* (pp. 955-959). IEEE. DOI: 10.1109/ICET51757.2021.9450991

Lim, S. C. J., & Lee, M. F. (2024). Rethinking education in the era of artificial intelligence (AI): Towards future workforce competitiveness and business success. In *Emerging Technologies in Business: Innovation Strategies for Competitive Advantage* (pp. 151–166). Springer Nature Singapore. DOI: 10.1007/978-981-97-2211-2_7

Lipson, J. I. (1984). In Voc (Ed.), *Educational technology*. Information Series 268 https://eric.ed.gov/?id=ED240385

Liu, P., Yuan, W., Fu, J., Jiang, Z., Hayashi, H., & Neubig, G. (2023). Pre-train, prompt, and predict: A systematic survey of prompting methods in natural language processing. *ACM Computing Surveys*, 55(9), 1–35. DOI: 10.1145/3560815

Luck, M., & Aylett, R. (2000). Applying artificial intelligence to virtual reality: Intelligent virtual environments. *Applied Artificial Intelligence*, 14(1), 3–32. DOI: 10.1080/088395100117142

Luckin, R., & Holmes, W. (2016). Intelligence unleashed: An argument for AI in education. https://discovery.ucl.ac.uk/id/eprint/1475756

Ma, J. (2019, May). The challenge and development of vocational education under the background of artificial intelligence. In *2019 5th International Conference on Humanities and Social Science Research (ICHSSR 2019)* (pp. 522-525). Atlantis Press. DOI: 10.2991/ichssr-19.2019.102

Maity, S. (2019). Identifying opportunities for artificial intelligence in the evolution of training and development practices. *Journal of Management Development*, 38(8), 651–663. DOI: 10.1108/JMD-03-2019-0069

Malik, A., & Aslam, M. U. (2024). *Reimagining Teaching: Exploring Challenges of Generative AI Integration in Education.*https://www.researchgate.net/publication/380365121

OECD. (2023a). Enrolment rates of 15–19-year-olds and 20-24 year-olds, by level of education (2021): Students enrolled in full-time and part-time programmes in both public and private institutions. In *Education at a Glance 2023: OECD Indicators*. OECD Publishing., DOI: 10.1787/85f3d55d-

OECD. (2023b). *Profile of students enrolled in vocational programmes (2021) in Education at a Glance 2023: OECD Indicators*. OECD Publishing., DOI: 10.1787/88a34fe2-

OECD. (2024). *Educational attainment and labour-force status*. https://data-explorer.oecd.org (database) OECD (n.d). *Vocational education and training (VET), Key Messages*. https://www.oecd.org/en/topics/sub-issues/vocational-education-and-training-vet.html

Panda Training and Education. (2024). *12+ Incredible AI Tools for Educators*. https://pandaeducation.co.uk/blog/incredible-ai-tools-for-trainers/

Petridou, E., & Lao, L. (2024). Identifying challenges and best practices for implementing AI additional qualifications in vocational and continuing education: A mixed methods analysis. *International Journal of Lifelong Education*, 43(4), 1–16. DOI: 10.1080/02601370.2024.2351076

Petropoulos, G. (2018). The impact of artificial intelligence on employment. In Neufeind, A., O'Reilly, J., & Ranft, F. (Eds.), *Work in the digital age – challenges of the fourth industrial revolution* (pp. 119–132). Rowman & Littlefield International.

Poquet, O., & De Laat, M. (2021). Developing capabilities: Lifelong learning in the age of AI. *British Journal of Educational Technology*, 52(4), 1695–1708. DOI: 10.1111/bjet.13123

Proton, A. G. (2024). *What is GDPR, the EU's new data protection law?*https://gdpr.eu/what-is-gdpr/

Ramesh, A., Pavlov, M., Goh, G., Gray, S., Voss, C., Radford, A., & Sutskever, I. (2021, July). Zero-shot text-to-image generation. In *International conference on machine learning* (pp. 8821-8831). Pmlr.

Rosyadi, M. I., Kustiawan, I., Tetehfio, E. O., & Joshua, Q. (2023). The Role of AI In Vocational Education: A Systematic Literature Review. *Journal of Vocational Education Studies*, 6(2), 244–263. DOI: 10.12928/joves.v6i2.9032

Rott, K. J., Lao, L., Petridou, E., & Schmidt-Hertha, B. (2022). Needs and requirements for an additional AI qualification during dual vocational training: Results from studies of apprentices and teachers. *Computers and education. Artificial Intelligence*, 3, 100102. Advance online publication. DOI: 10.1016/j.caeai.2022.100102

Salloum, S. A. (2024). AI Perils in Education: Exploring Ethical Concerns. *Artificial Intelligence in Education: The Power and Dangers of ChatGPT in the Classroom*, 669-675.

Saxena, A. K., García, V., Amin, M. R., Salazar, J. M. R., & Dey, S. (2023). Structure, Objectives, and Operational Framework for Ethical Integration of Artificial Intelligence in Educational. *Sage Science Review of Educational Technology, 6*(1), 88-100. https://journals.sagescience.org/index.php/ssret/article/view/139

Schneider, J., Meske, C., & Kuss, P. (2024). Foundation models: A new paradigm for artificial intelligence. *Business & Information Systems Engineering*, 66(2), 1–11. DOI: 10.1007/s12599-024-00851-0

Schwab, K. (2017). *The fourth industrial revolution*. Crown Currency.

Sharma, A. (2023). *Potential of technology supported competence development for Maritime Education and Training*. [doctoral dissertation]. University of South-Eastern Norway, Notodden, Norway.

Shinde, P. P., & Shah, S. (2018, August). A review of machine learning and deep learning applications. In *2018 Fourth international conference on computing communication control and automation (ICCUBEA)* (pp. 1-6). IEEE. https://doi.org/ DOI: 10.1109/ICCUBEA.2018.8697857

Shu, X., & Gu, X. (2023). An empirical study of A smart education model enabled by the edu-metaverse to enhance better learning outcomes for students. *Systems*, 11(2), 75. Advance online publication. DOI: 10.3390/systems11020075

Singh, A. R. (2024). The Future of Vocational Learning in India: How Artificial Intelligence and Creativity Will Shape Learning of Skills in 2030. In *Educational Perspectives on Digital Technologies in Modeling and Management* (pp. 293–304). IGI Global. DOI: 10.4018/979-8-3693-2314-4.ch015

Slimi, Z., & Carballido, B. V. (2023). Navigating the Ethical Challenges of Artificial Intelligence in Higher Education: An Analysis of Seven Global AI Ethics Policies. *TEM Journal, 12*(2). https://www.ceeol.com/search/article-detail?id=1122977

Sobania, D., Briesch, M., Hanna, C., & Petke, J. (2023). An analysis of the automatic bug fixing performance of chatgpt. In *2023 IEEE/ACM International Workshop on Automated Program Repair (APR)* (pp. 23-30). IEEE. DOI: 10.1109/APR59189.2023.00012

Swiss Federal University for Vocational Education and Training SFUVET. (2024). *About SFUVET*. https://www.sfuvet.swiss/sfuvet/about-sfuvet

Teubner, T., Flath, C. M., Weinhardt, C., van der Aalst, W., & Hinz, O. (2023). Welcome to the Era of ChatGPT et al. *Business & Information Systems Engineering*, 65(2), 95–101. DOI: 10.1007/s12599-023-00795-x

Trainer, T. V. E. T. (2024). *Case Studies and Examples*. https://tvettrainer.com/ai-powered-personalised-learning-for-vocational-education-and-training-vet/

Tramm, T., & Naeve-Stoß, N. (2020). Curricula für die berufliche Bildung–Lernfeldstruktur zwischen Situations-und Fächerorientierung. *Handbuch Berufsbildung*, 309-324. https://doi.org/DOI: 10.1007/978-3-658-19312-6_26

UNCTAD. (n.d.). *Data Protection and Privacy Legislation Worldwide*. https://unctad.org/page/data-protection-and-privacy-legislation-worldwide

Vats, S., & Malik, N. A. (2024). Comprehensive Review of Vocational Education and Training (VET) in Secondary School. *International Journal of Research Publication and Reviews*, 5(6), 5812–5818. DOI: 10.55248/gengpi.5.0624.1612

Vitale, G., Bonarini, A., Matteucci, M., & Bascetta, L. (2016). Toward vocational robotics: An experience in post-secondary school education and job training through robotics. *IEEE Robotics & Automation Magazine*, 23(4), 73–81. DOI: 10.1109/MRA.2016.2571998

Walter, Y. (2024). Embracing the future of Artificial Intelligence in the classroom: The relevance of AI literacy, prompt engineering, and critical thinking in modern education. *International Journal of Educational Technology in Higher Education*, 21(1), 15. Advance online publication. DOI: 10.1186/s41239-024-00448-3

Weigel, T., Mulder, M., & Collins, K. (2007). The concept of competence in the development of vocational education and training in selected EU member states. *Journal of Vocational Education and Training*, 59(1), 53–66. DOI: 10.1080/13636820601145549

Windelband, L. (2023). Artificial intelligence and assistance systems for technical vocational education and training–Opportunities and risks. In *New Digital Work: Digital Sovereignty at the Workplace* (pp. 195–213). Springer International Publishing. DOI: 10.1007/978-3-031-26490-0_12

Winters, A., Meijers, F., Kuijpers, M., & Baert, H. (2009). What are vocational training conversations about? Analysis of vocational training conversations in Dutch vocational education from a career learning perspective. *Journal of Vocational Education and Training*, 61(3), 247–266. DOI: 10.1080/13636820903194690

KEY TERMS AND DEFINITIONS

Adaptive Learning: It is a delivery of custom learning experiences that employs computer algorithms and artificial intelligence (AI) to manage interactions with learners through just-in-time feedback, pathways, and resources (rather than providing a one-size-fits-all learning experience).

Artificial Intelligence in Education (AIEd): The application of AI (Artificial Intelligence) technologies or software in educational environments to support teaching, learning, or decision-making processes.

Augmented Reality: An immersive technology that enriches the real world by adding computer-generated perceptual elements. Through the use of software, apps, and devices like AR glasses, AR projects digital content onto actual environments and objects, enhancing the user's interaction with the physical world.

Chatbots: A computer program that mimics and processes human conversation, whether written or spoken, enabling humans to interact with digital devices as though they were talking to a real person.

Constructivism: The theory proposing that learners actively build their own understanding of knowledge, rather than simply absorbing information passively. Through their experiences and subsequent reflection, individuals create personal representations and integrate new information into their existing knowledge frameworks (schemas).

Fourth industrial revolution: The incorporation of advanced digital technologies into manufacturing and industrial operations involves a range of innovations, such as industrial IoT networks, artificial intelligence (AI), Big Data, robotics, and automation.

GenAI: A type of artificial intelligence (AI) technology capable of creating diverse forms of content, such as audio, images, synthetic data and text.

Machine learning: A field within artificial intelligence (AI) and computer science that emphasizes using data and algorithms to enable AI to mimic human learning and progressively enhance its accuracy. It involves creating and utilizing computer systems that can learn and adapt independently, employing algorithms and statistical models to analyze data patterns and make inferences.

Preferred Reporting Items for Systematic Reviews and Meta-Analyses (PRISMA): A 27-item checklist used to improve transparency in systematic reviews. These items cover all aspects of the manuscript, including title, abstract, introduction, methods, results, discussion, and funding.

Structural equation modeling (SEM): A set of techniques that aims to express hypotheses regarding the means, variances, and covariances of observed data using a reduced number of 'structural' parameters. These parameters are specified by an assumed underlying conceptual or theoretical framework.

Virtual Reality: A computer-generated environment that simulates real-world scenes and objects, creating the sensation of immersion for the user. This virtual space is experienced through a device called a Virtual Reality headset or helmet.

Vocational and Educational Training: All types and levels of education that deliver knowledge and skills relevant to occupations across different economic and social sectors, utilizing formal, non-formal, and informal learning approaches in both school-based and work-based settings.

Chapter 9
Transformation of Quality Education Through E-Learning for Sustainable Development

Sumit Pathak
Sharda University, India

Vishal Jain
https://orcid.org/0000-0003-1126-7424
Sharda University, India

ABSTRACT

Education is already hovering on the edge of the Education 4.0 revolution fueled by technology integration and student participation. Therefore, Education 4.0 eliminates rigid structures, lectures and focuses on teachers as Education 4.0 is meant for digital generation providing a flexible learning process that is continuous. Central to this shift is the Smart Hybrid Learning System, which brings together models such as the Challenge Based learning and the Case Based learning in dynamic online environments. Enhancing learning solution; online learning platforms, LMS, AI, IoT provide rich engagement solutions. Today's school structures fail to capture such changing needs, which puts emphasis on old fashioned approaches. Such classroom practices as the flipped and smart classroom helps overcome these gaps but issues with implementation is still an issue with issues to do with infrastructure and digital divide. Education 4.0 is the strategic direction towards mass, choice and flexibility for learning in the era of volatility.

DOI: 10.4018/979-8-3693-8252-3.ch009

1. INTRODUCTION

1.1 Overview of e-Learning in Education

E-learning has revolutionized the overall process of knowledge transmission or acquisition, changing the face of education altogether (Allen & Seaman, 2017; Christensen, Horn, & Johnson, 2011). It interacts with a digital approach in offering flexible and accessible learning experiences that are interactive through technology (Anderson & Dron, 2018; Dziuban, Graham, Moskal, Norberg, & Sicilia, 2018). E-learning has terminated geography and time barriers and democratized education for a greater number than was ever conceived previously (Bonk & Graham, 2012; Huang et al., 2020).

E-learning simply refers to a wide range of quite different digital tools and platforms that can support learning. Such digital tools and platforms may include online courses, virtual classes, education apps, and so on (Bates, 2019; Garrison, 2017). Since e-learning provides much more flexibility, it therefore offers much better chances for pupils by catering to different learning styles and paces, consequently providing more personable learning experiences compared to the classroom setting (Hrastinski, 2019; Martin & Bolliger, 2018; Sun et al., 2008).

1.2 Evolution of Digital Learning Platforms

The strides of digital learning platforms have been characterized by high-tech development and academic paradigm shifts (Castañeda & Selwyn, 2018; Redecker, 2017). From mere computer-based training modules, it has journeyed to being highly sophisticated and AI-driven learning ecosystems (Gašević, Dawson, & Siemens, 2015; Kizilcec et al., 2020).

Early digital learning environments were characteristically about the presentation of content—the computer-based version of the paper-based textbook (Bates, 2019; Clark & Mayer, 2016). Over time, these systems have included interactive content, multimedia, and assessments. Learning Management Systems (LMS) are an environment that could be described as being developed primarily in the late 1990s and early 2000s—a central place for managing a course and a way to engage students (Bonk & Graham, 2012; Moore, Dickson-Deane, & Galyen, 2011).

MOOCs, or massive open online courses, that came forth in the 2010s also changed the e-learning landscape because it became possible to access high-class educational resources from top-ranked institutions across the world for free or at low cost (Joksimović et al., 2018; Reich & Ruipérez-Valiente, 2019). Last but not least, adaptive learning technologies and AI only recently made it possible to have real personalized learning experiences whereby content and pace can be tailored to meet the individual needs of learners (Chen et al., 2020; Veletsianos & Shepherdson, 2016).

Figure 1. Graph for the transformation of quality education through e-learning for sustainable development from 2020 -24[Chen et al., 2020; Veletsianos & Shepherdson, 2016]

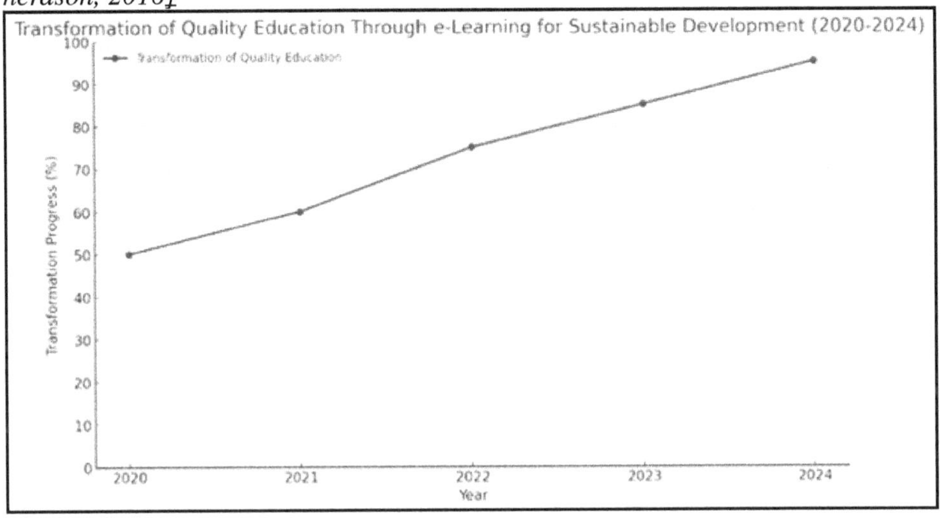

1.3 Introduction to Sustainable Development in Education

Thus, educational practices and systems that sustain development aim at catering to the needs of today's generation yet ensuring that the same generation can provide for its own needs when time passes (Tait, 2018; Zawacki-Richter & Qayyum, 2019). This idea is quite in tandem with what the United Nations Sustainable Development Goals have stipulated, especially SDG 4, which states that "there must be an inclusive and equitable quality education which should promote lifelong learning possibilities for everyone" (United Nations, 2015).

It is in this regard that education finds its link to sustainability in the dimensions of economics, human, and environmental factors (Redecker, 2017; Selwyn, 2016). Certainly, this sustainability refers to accessibility, adaptability, and responsiveness by the educational systems towards changing societal needs without losing their quality standards (Veletsianos & Shepherdson, 2016; Weller, 2020).

1.4 Significance of Quality Education Through e-Learning

The greatest advantage of e-learning is its integration into educational frameworks due to its huge potential for the quality and reach of education. Quality education through e-learning is important in several ways:

- **Accessibility**: E-learning overthrows geographical and socioeconomic barriers so that quality education is accessible worldwide regardless of where the learner is located (Bonk & Graham, 2012; Guri-Rosenblit, 2018).
- **Flexibility**: The learner can access learning material on his or her schedule without regard to circumstance, which is a significant benefit for nontraditional learners or those balancing other commitments (Dabbagh, Benson, & Denham, 2015; Tait, 2018).
- **Personalization**: Advanced levels of an e-learning framework can tailor content and learning paths, making learning more engaging and suited to individual needs (Anderson & Dron, 2018; Picciano, 2017).
- **Resource Efficiency**: E-learning is often greener than traditional teaching because digital updates are easily made and widely distributed, reducing the need for physical resources and environmental impacts associated with printed materials (Redecker, 2017; Slade & Prinsloo, 2013).
- **Skill Development**: E-learning promotes digital literacy skills as technologies increasingly become essential to modern life (Gašević, Dawson, & Siemens, 2015; Veletsianos & Shepherdson, 2016).
- **Lifelong Learning**: Continuing education is supported by e-learning, which makes access to a rich package of courses and resources hassle-free, contributing to continuous learning (Laurillard, 2013; Weller, 2020).

1.5 Objectives and Scope of the Chapter

This chapter seeks to examine the transformative potential of e-learning in achieving quality education in terms of sustainable development (Guri-Rosenblit, 2018; Redecker, 2017). Toward this end, the objectives of this chapter include the following:

- Analyzing the state of play of e-learning technologies and their impact on educational quality (Bernard, Borokhovski, Schmid, Tamim, & Abrami, 2014; Bates, 2019).
- Exploring the roles of e-learning technologies in sustainable development goals for education (Panigrahi, Srivastava, & Sharma, 2018; Weller, 2020).

- Best practices and innovative approaches for implementing e-learning in quality education (Veletsianos & Shepherdson, 2016; Dabbagh, Benson, & Denham, 2015).
- Discussing the challenges of scaling up e-learning initiatives in relation to sustainability for development (Kizilcec et al., 2020; Tait, 2018).
- Examining future trends and prospects for e-learning that would enhance both the quality and sustainability of education (Laurillard, 2013; Siemens, 2014).

This chapter spans from technical changes to pedagogical proposals in order to explain the scope of e-learning (Clark & Mayer, 2016; Koehler, Mishra, & Cain, 2013). It will expand from primary education up to tertiary levels, as well as professional development and lifelong learning (Bonk & Graham, 2012; Chao, 2019). The context in which this happens is global, reflecting opportunities and challenges related to the implementation of e-learning solutions across diverse socioeconomic and cultural realities (Castañeda & Selwyn, 2018; Zawacki-Richter & Qayyum, 2019).

2. FUNDAMENTALS OF E-LEARNING FOR QUALITY EDUCATION

2.1 Key Concepts in Digital Learning

The basic ideas regarding these concepts relate to the general structure and skeleton of an e-learning system. The knowledge of the concepts discussed below forms the essential elements of developing and implementing a workable strategy for e-learning:

- **Asynchronous vs. Synchronous Learning**: Online learning processes provide students with the opportunity to read materials and complete coursework at their convenience, supporting self-paced learning (Hrastinski, 2019; Moore, Dickson-Deane, & Galyen, 2011). In contrast, synchronous learning involves instructor-led, time-dependent interaction between instructors and learners, fostering real-time engagement (Martin & Bolliger, 2018). Both have unique advantages and can be integrated to form a cohesive learning process (Kearney, Schuck, Burden, & Aubusson, 2012).
- **Blended Learning**: This teaching method combines live face-to-face instruction with online components, leveraging the strengths of both methods to enhance the learning experience (Dziuban et al., 2018; Bernard et al., 2014).

- **Adaptive Learning**: Adaptive learning systems adjust content and pacing to meet individual learners' needs, creating personalized learning paths through AI and machine learning algorithms (Chen, Zou, Cheng, & Xie, 2020; Picciano, 2017).
- **Microlearning**: This approach segments learning material into smaller, focused pieces that can be quickly reviewed and easily absorbed, catering to modern attention spans and busy schedules (Redecker, 2017; Huang et al., 2020).
- **Gamification**: Gamification involves adding game design elements and mechanics to a non-game context to enhance learner engagement and motivation (Anderson & Dron, 2018; Chao, 2019).
- **Learning Analytics:** Teachers measuring, collecting data, analyzing, and reporting on their learners or learning contexts about how people learn or how to optimize the learning environment.

2.2 Technological Infrastructure for e-Learning

Any practical e-learning system will depend on some technological infrastructures (Redecker, 2017; Veletsianos & Shepherdson, 2016). Some of the lists include:

- **Learning Management Systems (LMS):** These are central platforms where online learning activities can be created, reported, and tracked, with examples like Moodle, Canvas, and Blackboard (Anderson & Dron, 2018; Martin & Bolliger, 2018).
- **Content Management Systems (CMS):** A set of tools enabling the production, management, and distribution of e-learning content across media types (Chen et al., 2020; Garrison, 2017).
- **Video Conferencing Tools:** These are essential for synchronous learning, allowing real-time discussion with learners and vice versa. Common tools include Zoom, Microsoft Teams, and Google Meet (Hrastinski, 2019; Moore, Dickson-Deane, & Galyen, 2011).
- **Cloud Computing:** This tool offers scalable, flexible storage for learning resources and access to data, an essential component in modern e-learning systems (Dabbagh, Benson, & Denham, 2015; Kizilcec et al., 2020).
- **Mobile Learning Platforms:** With widespread smartphone and tablet use, mobile-friendly learning platforms are key for accessibility and usability (Kearney et al., 2012; Castañeda & Selwyn, 2018).
- **Virtual and Augmented Reality (VR/AR):** These technologies support interactive, hands-on learning through practice and visualization, especially

beneficial in subjects requiring visualization or simulation (Bonk & Graham, 2012; Huang et al., 2020).

2.3 Integration of Sustainability in e-Learning Practices

Some major domains of engagement in integrating sustainability into e-learning practices are:

- **Energy Efficient Technologies**: Using energy-efficient hardware and optimizing software to shrink the carbon footprint of e-learning systems (Bates, 2019; Weller, 2020).
- **Digital Resource Management**: Implementing strategies to create, use, and recycle digital learning resources effectively, with minimal digital waste (Redecker, 2017; Guri-Rosenblit, 2018).
- **Content Development for Sustainability**: Developing content that raises awareness of sustainability issues and encourages learners toward sustainable practices (Castañeda & Selwyn, 2018; Laurillard, 2013).
- **Inclusive Design**: Ensuring that e-learning interfaces and resources are accessible to as many students as possible, including learners with disabilities, contributes to social sustainability (Chen et al., 2020; Dede & Richards, 2012).
- **Long-term Viability**: E-learning is designed to be long-lasting, and e-learning systems and content can be easily updated and adapted according to changing requirements (Dabbagh, Benson, & Denham, 2015; Major, 2015).

2.4 Role of AI and Big Data in Enhancing e-Learning

The AI and Big Data analytics revolution will bring significant developments into the approach to e-learning. Most importantly, AI algorithms are now analyzing learner data, recommending customized content and adaptive learning pathways (Chen et al., 2020; Gašević, Dawson, & Siemens, 2015). Intelligent tutoring systems would be another advance, offering one-on-one human-like tutoring customized for every individual learner's particular needs (Clark & Mayer, 2016; Dede & Richards, 2012). With AI, automated grading and feedback improve, allowing grading of assignments, immediate feedback on student activity, and identification of patterns in learner errors to inform instructional responses (Guri-Rosenblit, 2018; Kizilcec et al., 2020).

Predictive analytics utilizes large datasets to help educational institutions predict student performance, reveal at-risk learners, and provide interventions before students fall behind (Slade & Prinsloo, 2013; Joksimović et al., 2018). With NLP, learners can interact more naturally with the e-learning environment, including the use of voice commands and chatbots (Hrastinski, 2019; Kearney et al., 2012). Moreover, content optimization is enhanced because the analysis of Big Data regarding successful learning materials and methodology helps update the e-learning content with those techniques (Veletsianos & Shepherdson, 2016; Picciano, 2017).

Figure 2. Role of AI and Big Data in Enhancing e-Learning [google search engine]

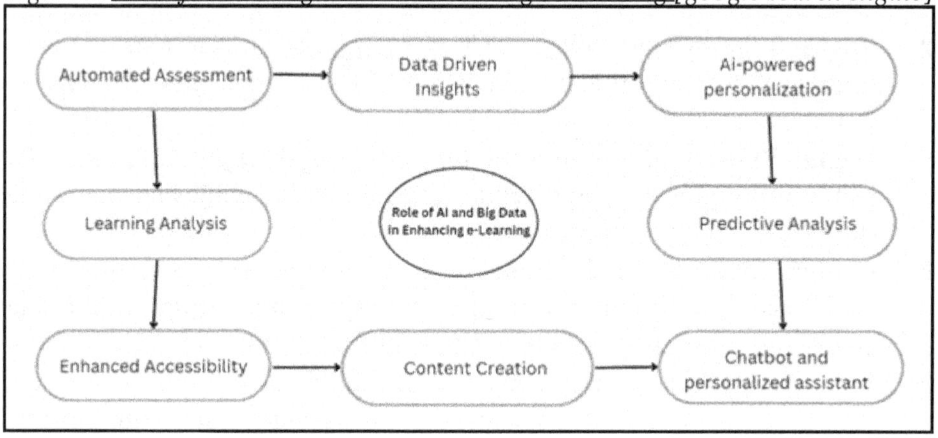

2.5 Ethical and Legal Considerations in e-Learning

E-learning, consequently, is raising various ethical and legal issues. Primary among these issues is data privacy and security assurance to protect learner data and ensure conformity with pertinent data protection regulations such as the General Data Protection Regulation (GDPR) while following best cyber-security practices (Gašević, Dawson, & Siemens, 2015; Slade & Prinsloo, 2013). The other key consideration in this regard is the rights intellectual property, where proper licensing and accreditation of the digital learning resources are done, with copyrights respected in content creation and distribution (Bates, 2019; Selwyn, 2016). Digital equitability also, as all the e-learning resources and technologies have to be accessible to everybody irrespective of socio-economic status or location (Redecker, 2017; Dabbagh, Benson, & Denham, 2015). Academic integrity will be maintained by making sure that there is no cheating and plagiarism in online assessments while ensuring the privacy of the learner (Hrastinski, 2019; Martin & Bolliger, 2018). Accessibility compliance is critical with many requirements now put on e-learning platforms and content for accessibility and compliance against the Web Content Accessibility Guidelines (WCAG) (Bonk & Graham, 2012; Guri-Rosenblit, 2018). Ethical use of AI in learning calls for algorithms applied to the e-learning process to be less biased, and clear decision-making by AI (Chen, Zou, Cheng, & Xie, 2020; Kizilcec et al., 2020). Cross-border education will be problematic at different levels with an understanding of complex legal issues and diverse regulations, laws, and norms in each country or territory involved in providing e-learning courses (Tait, 2018; Zawacki-Richter & Qayyum, 2019). All these concerns addressed to the design and delivery of e-learning would achieve quality education while contributing to sustainability and ensuring ethical practices in the digital age (Anderson & Dron, 2018; Garrison, 2017).

3. LITERATURE REVIEW

Table 1. Table for Literature Survey

Author(s) & Year	Title	Research Focus	Key Findings	Relevance to e-Learning & Sustainable Development
Williams & Jones (2024)	Blended Learning for Resilient Educational Systems	Exploring blended learning models for sustainable education	Blended learning (online + face-to-face) provides flexible, scalable education solutions.	Encourages resilient education systems, promoting lifelong learning and flexibility, aligned with SDG 4.
Kumar & Ali (2024)	Overcoming Barriers to E-Learning in Developing Countries	Examining infrastructure challenges in e-learning adoption	Mobile learning helps bridge gaps in education access in regions with limited infrastructure.	Promotes inclusive education by overcoming digital divides, supporting SDG 4 and reducing inequalities.
Johnson et al. (2024)	The Role of Open Educational Resources (OER) in Sustainable Education	Investigating OER's contribution to sustainable education	OERs increase access to quality education while reducing costs and environmental impact.	Supports both SDG 4 and SDG 12 by promoting accessible education and sustainable resource use.
Rivera (2024)	Designing E-Learning Platforms for Student Well-being	Exploring the relationship between e-learning design and mental health	Thoughtful e-learning design reduces student stress and enhances mental well-being.	Promotes SDG 3 (Good Health and Well-being) by creating more balanced educational experiences.

continued on following page

Table 1. Continued

Author(s) & Year	Title	Research Focus	Key Findings	Relevance to e-Learning & Sustainable Development
Garcia et al. (2024)	Digital Literacy as a Driver of E-Learning Success	Investigating the role of digital literacy in e-learning outcomes	Higher digital literacy correlates with better e-learning success and retention rates.	Improves ability to use e-learning tools for lifelong learning, supporting SDG 4 and overall digital inclusion.
Zhang et al. (2023)	E-Learning for Environmental Awareness and Action	Investigating the role of e-learning in sustainability education	E-learning on environmental topics increases awareness of climate change and promotes ecological literacy.	Supports SDG 13 (Climate Action) by fostering knowledge on environmental sustainability.
Hernandez (2023)	AI-Powered Personalized Learning for Skill Development	Exploring the role of AI in adaptive e-learning systems	AI-driven systems personalize learning experiences, improving skill acquisition and learning outcomes.	Contributes to equitable education by offering personalized learning paths, supporting lifelong learning.
Smith et al. (2023)	The Impact of Digital Tools on Educational Quality	Investigating how e-learning tools impact student outcomes	E-learning tools improve student engagement and knowledge retention, particularly in diverse settings.	Enhances accessibility and inclusivity in education, supporting SDG 4 (Quality Education).
Zhao & Kemp (2021)	E-Learning: Opportunities for Global Education	Investigates how e-learning platforms provide opportunities for global access to education	Concludes that e-learning bridges educational gaps, particularly in developing regions, aligning with SDG 4	Supports the global dissemination of quality education through e-learning as a tool for sustainable development
Bates (2021)	Education for Sustainable Development: A Roadmap	Provides an overview of global strategies for integrating sustainable development in education systems	Emphasizes the role of digital tools and online platforms in scaling sustainable education practices globally	Links policy recommendations with the use of e-learning as a strategic enabler for sustainable education

continued on following page

Table 1. Continued

Author(s) & Year	Title	Research Focus	Key Findings	Relevance to e-Learning & Sustainable Development
Azevedo et al. (2020)	E-Learning and Sustainable Development	Examines how e-learning can contribute to achieving sustainable development goals (SDGs)	E-learning facilitates access to quality education, promotes lifelong learning, and reduces the environmental impact by minimizing the need for physical infrastructure	Demonstrates the direct impact of e-learning on SDG 4 (Quality Education) and other related goals such as reducing inequalities (SDG 10)
Jisc (2020)	Technology for Good: Sustainable Practices in Education	Evaluates technology's role in making education sustainable	Highlights that digital learning reduces environmental impacts, supports social equity, and improves educational outreach	Directly links the benefits of technology-enhanced learning to sustainable practices in education
Garrison & Vaughan (2019)	Blended Learning in Higher Education	Discusses the effectiveness of blended learning models for improving educational outcomes	Indicates that blended learning is essential in providing flexible and inclusive education options, which align with sustainable development initiatives	Demonstrates the potential of blended learning models in achieving sustainability by expanding education access while reducing physical resource use
Singh & Thurman (2019)	Impact of Online Learning on Educational Quality	Analyzes the impact of online learning on student outcomes and educational quality	Found that e-learning can enhance learning experiences when designed with active and collaborative elements	Connects online learning quality with long-term sustainable educational outcomes
Anderson & Dron (2018)	Learning Design for Sustainability	Explores pedagogical models for integrating e-learning with sustainable practices	Emphasizes blended and fully online models as effective methods to reach diverse student populations and incorporate sustainability content	Highlights how e-learning can be a tool for promoting education for sustainable development (ESD)

4. CURRENT STATE OF E-LEARNING AND QUALITY EDUCATION

4.1 Overview of Current e-Learning Systems

The landscape of e-learning has changed and diversified tremendously, with many systems and platforms competing to dominate the world of digital education (Anderson & Dron, 2018; Weller, 2020). The present systems of e-learning can be broadly categorized into a few:

a) **LMS**: As is true for most institutionally driven efforts at e-learning, LMS providers such as Canvas, Moodle, and Blackboard continue to provide the lion's share of learning management systems. The maturity of LMS has greatly improved, making the system friendlier to user interfaces and providing mobile access as well as hooks that allow third-party learning tools to be readily connected with others. Some of the new features of the systems are analytics, adaptive paths, and the collaborative environment for peer-to-peer communication (Bates, 2019; Dabbagh, Benson, & Denham, 2015).
b) **MOOCs**: Coursera, edX, and FutureLearn are democratizing access to higher education content. Developments have recently led to the offer of micro-credentials and full online degrees, blurring boundaries between traditional and online learning (Reich & Ruipérez-Valiente, 2019; Veletsianos & Shepherdson, 2016).
c) **Microlearning Platforms**: Duolingo, Grovo, and many others have responded to the increasing demand for bite-sized, just-in-time learning. Specialized in delivering content that may be devoured quickly, many of the devices applied use gamification to heighten engagement (Picciano, 2017; Redecker, 2017).
d) **Adaptive Learning Systems**: Emerging from AI and machine learning, even tools like Knewton and ALEKS personalize the learner's experience to each learner's individual needs. Their algorithms continually evaluate and thus adapt content to different learner performance levels and paces (Chen et al., 2020; Guri-Rosenblit, 2018).
e) **Virtual and Augmented Reality Learning Environments**: Recently, there is a trend in building e-learning environments about spatial understandings or practical training that engages immersive technologies. Examples include Labster for virtual laboratories and Google Expeditions for virtual field trips (Dede & Richards, 2012; Huang et al., 2020).

f) **Social Learning Networks**: From the belief that social interaction is valuable in learning, there exists Edmodo and Brainly, a model that assumes social learning, so that students can share sources of knowledge and share their opinions with one another (Gašević, Dawson, & Siemens, 2015; Kahu & Nelson, 2018).

4.2 Impact of e-Learning on Student Engagement and Outcomes

E-learning is extremely widely studied for its influence on student engagement and results, as it has very deep implications, with many positive outcomes but also areas needing improvement (Dziuban et al., 2018; Bernard et al., 2014). Among the most important strengths of e-learning is that it encourages more engagement. More interactive elements, such as the utilization of multimedia content and gamification, often make engagement factors far higher than in traditional lecture-based teaching (Bonk & Graham, 2012; Chao, 2019). For example, a report from the Research Institute of America indicated that retention increased by 25-60% while using e-learning. However, in traditional learning, only 8-10% retention was reported (Bates, 2019). Besides improved retention, learning outcomes have also been enhanced. A meta-analysis by the U.S. Department of Education indicated that students who learned online performed moderately better compared to those receiving face-to-face instruction (Chen et al., 2020; Martin & Bolliger, 2018). E-learning encourages more personalized, self-paced learning, allowing students to learn at their own pace, which supports better understanding and retention of content, especially for lower-performing students in traditional class settings (Redecker, 2017; Sun et al., 2008). Additionally, engaging in e-learning environments exposes students to digital literacy skills, preparing them for a more technologically driven workforce (Gašević, Dawson, & Siemens, 2015; Veletsianos & Shepherdson, 2016).

E-learning has its drawbacks too. First, it requires more self-motivation to fully benefit from its flexibility. Some students struggle to meet this requirement, leading to higher dropout rates in fully online courses compared to traditional ones (Rovai & Downey, 2010; Panigrahi, Srivastava, & Sharma, 2018). Another challenge relates to collaborative skills. Although e-learning tools provide collaborative functionality, they cannot fully replicate the spontaneous interactions and social learning that occur in a real classroom (Selwyn, 2016; Kahu & Nelson, 2018).

4.3 Case Studies: Successful e-Learning Implementations

Several institutions and organizations have successfully implemented e-learning initiatives, demonstrating the potential of digital education (Bates, 2019; Christensen, Horn, & Johnson, 2011):

a) **Arizona State University (ASU) Online**: ASU has been a pioneer in online education, offering over 200 degree programs fully online. Their adaptive learning system has shown significant improvements in student success rates, particularly in challenging STEM courses (Garrison, 2017; Picciano, 2017).
b) **Western Governors University (WGU)**: WGU's competency-based education model, delivered entirely online, has shown high student satisfaction rates and strong employment outcomes for graduates (Anderson & Dron, 2018; Tait, 2018).
c) **Coursera's Degree Programs**: Coursera's partnership with top universities to offer full online degrees has shown promising results. For instance, the University of Illinois' online MBA program on Coursera has seen completion rates of over 80%, comparable to on-campus programs (Reich & Ruipérez-Valiente, 2019; Veletsianos & Shepherdson, 2016).
d) **Khan Academy**: This non-profit organization has successfully provided free, high-quality education to millions worldwide. Their mastery learning approach, coupled with data analytics, has shown significant improvements in student performance, particularly in mathematics (Gašević, Dawson, & Siemens, 2015; Martin & Bolliger, 2018).
e) **Corporate e-Learning: IBM's Digital Learning Platform**: IBM's comprehensive e-learning platform for employee training and development has led to significant cost savings and improved skill development across the organization (Clark & Mayer, 2016; Redecker, 2017).

4.4 Challenges and Limitations in e-Learning Adoption

While it promises much, e-learning also faces huge challenges before it may popularize:

a. **Digital Divide**: This has continued to be an important barrier; unequal access to technology and high-speed internet has led many countries to struggle with maintaining this gap (Castañeda & Selwyn, 2018; Huang et al., 2020).
b. **Technology Literacy**: In the absence of literacy skills on the part of students and educators, low levels of adoption and effectiveness are contributory factors (Gašević, Dawson, & Siemens, 2015; Kearney et al., 2012).
c. **Quality Control**: Maintaining quality is challenging in e-learning curricula because of the vast number of online courses now flooding the market (Dabbagh, Benson, & Denham, 2015; Moore, Dickson-Deane, & Galyen, 2011).

d. **Resistance to Change**: Traditional educational structures and many teachers resist change and may feel an aversion to e-learning methods, often due to perceived job security threats or doubts about their effectiveness (Guri-Rosenblit, 2018; Rovai & Downey, 2010).
e. **Alienation of Students**: Many e-learning programs lack sufficient interaction between teacher and student, leading to feelings of alienation and potential demotivation or decreased mental engagement among students (Hrastinski, 2019; Kahu & Nelson, 2018).
f. **Reliability of Testing**: Online assignments are easily susceptible to cheating, creating challenges in ensuring academic integrity in e-learning assessments (Slade & Prinsloo, 2013; Panigrahi, Srivastava, & Sharma, 2018).
g. **The Cost of Making High-Quality Content**: Developing high-quality content for e-learning requires significant time and financial resources, making it prohibitively expensive for sensitive or niche topics (Bates, 2019; Clark & Mayer, 2016).

4.5 Accessibility and Inclusivity in Digital Education

Accessibility and inclusiveness are two of the important factors to ensure that e-learning is equitably implemented (Redecker, 2017; Tait, 2018). Besides, web content accessibility guidelines consider features such as alternative text for images, keyboard navigation, or videos with closed captions (Huang et al., 2020; Gašević, Dawson, & Siemens, 2015). Universal Design for Learning principles are also critical to ensure that e-learning content can be accessed by learners with diverse needs and styles of learning (Bates, 2019; Kearney et al., 2012). Provision for multilingual support can be made through the offering of content in different languages and tools that help translate, thereby enhancing inclusivity for non-native speakers (Picciano, 2017; Veletsianos & Shepherdson, 2016). Cultural sensitivity in the design of content is necessary when targeting diverse student populations worldwide. Materials should, therefore, be relevant as well as respectful (Castañeda & Selwyn, 2018; Kahu & Nelson, 2018). Adaptive technologies, such as screen readers, voice recognition software, and alternative input devices, are essential to enhance accessibility for students with multiple disabilities (Guri-Rosenblit, 2018; Slade & Prinsloo, 2013). Optimization for mobile learning in e-learning platforms is also important, as it allows online learning access for learners who do not possess personal computers, with support from affordable access initiatives, partnerships with telecom companies, government subsidies, low-cost devices, and internet access (Dede & Richards, 2012; Weller, 2020).

In this respect, e-learning definitely has great potential to change the face of education, as there have been notable successes in its implementation, positively impacting student engagement and outcomes (Hrastinski, 2019; Martin & Bolliger, 2018). However, challenges remain, such as accessibility, maintaining quality, and equal adoption. Thus, ensuring that solutions are provided to address these challenges is one way of unlocking the full impact of e-learning in reaching the ideals of quality education and sustainable development (Anderson & Dron, 2018; Selwyn, 2016).

5. TECHNOLOGICAL ADVANCEMENTS IN E-LEARNING FOR SUSTAINABLE DEVELOPMENT

5.1 AI-driven Learning Platforms

Art has opened new dimensions for e-learning platforms that attain personalization and effectiveness. The Intelligent Tutoring Systems (ITS), to which Carnegie Learning's MATHia comes in addition, have been offering personalized guidance suited to the specific needs of individual learners as well as their pace and style of learning (Clark & Mayer, 2016; Garrison, 2017). It adapts and changes the levels of difficulty dynamically based on the performance of a student, thus providing a customized learning experience to support the better outcome for students (Chen, Zou, Cheng, & Xie, 2020; Redecker, 2017). It also propels e-learning with strategic contributions of NLP, such as in ETS's e-rater. E-rater is an essay grader that awards marks while it delivers instant feedback (Dziuban, Graham, Moskal, Norberg, & Sicilia, 2018; Anderson & Dron, 2018). Even platforms like Duolingo use NLP to judge pronunciation and grammar in real-time. AI-powered chatbots like Georgia State University's "Pounce" assist 24/7 at fingertips without much paperwork (Kahu & Nelson, 2018; Veletsianos & Shepherdson, 2016).

AI is also making the entire process of developing content for education a lot more streamlined. Tools like Quillbot, which summarizes texts in self-mode, are assisting in presenting complicated texts succinctly to help the student prepare concise study materials (Bonk & Graham, 2012; Laurillard, 2013). Similarly, other applications like Cerego rely on AI algorithms that may be able to suggest the best time to review to optimize student learning (Picciano, 2017; Panigrahi, Srivastava, & Sharma, 2018). Automating parts of the development of such contents or controlling the learning management enables AI to boost the effectiveness of e-learning systems, hence making them more responsive to individual needs for learning (Bernard, Borokhovski, Schmid, Tamim, & Abrami, 2014; Moore, Dickson-Deane, & Galyen, 2011).

Predictive analytics, AI claims, analyze humongous amounts of student data and will therefore accurately forecast future performance as well as identify students in danger so that interventions are possible at the right time (Siemens, 2014; Gašević, Dawson, & Siemens, 2015). For instance, one example is Purdue University's Course Signals system. For the first time in the history of any institution, Purdue University's Course Signals has presented evidence of raising retention rates considerably through predictive analysis (Christensen, Horn, & Johnson, 2011; Reich & Ruipérez-Valiente, 2019). Another very exciting application concerns adaptive assessments with platforms such as Knewton, where questions change up the difficulty based on students' responses in order to better measure knowledge and skills (Weller, 2020; Sun, Tsai, Finger, Chen, & Yeh, 2008). Collectively, all these innovations form the underpinning of AI directed toward the optimization of outcomes and engagement toward making e-learning more efficient and personalized (Dabbagh, Benson, & Denham, 2015; Koehler, Mishra, & Cain, 2013).

5.2 Real-time Data Analytics and Personalized Learning

Adding real-time data analytics to e-learning is where personalization of learning experiences improves to a great extent (Gašević, Dawson, & Siemens, 2015; Picciano, 2017). Learning analytics dashboards, which include elements like Blackboard Analytics for Learn, give educators real-time insight into learning activities and engagement, thereby becoming tools to improve performance and eliminate potential problems at an early stage (Dziuban, Graham, Moskal, Norberg, & Sicilia, 2018; Gašević et al., 2015). Yet another important innovation is adaptive learning pathways. DreamBox Learning, for example, uses real-time data to continually personalize the learning pathway for every single student, challenging all students appropriately and maximizing outcomes (Kizilcec et al., 2020; Martin & Bolliger, 2018).

Competency-Based Education also leverages Data Analytics. Such analytics have been applied in institutions like the Western Governors University where students can progress based on demonstrated mastery rather than time spent and, therefore, making the learning process more efficient and personalized (Christensen, Horn, & Johnson, 2011; Garrison, 2017). To track the mood within the students and their engagement level, online sentiment analysis helps instructors filter out the sentiments coming from forums and discussion boards (Slade & Prinsloo, 2013; Chen, Zou, Cheng, & Xie, 2020). The new trend is resource allocation predictive modeling, and hence Arizona State University uses data analytics for course demand prediction and correlation with the right allocation of courses (Anderson & Dron, 2018; Reich & Ruipérez-Valiente, 2019).

An example of this is the Learning Experience Platform or LXP. In the LXP, formal and informal learning resources are aggregated so that an individualized learning experience around the needs and personal preferences can be provided (Redecker, 2017; Veletsianos & Shepherdson, 2016). Such LXPs offer extensive approaches to learning as they integrate all these sources together as educational and training materials for making learning more personalized and effective (Bonk & Graham, 2012; Bates, 2019).

5.3 IoT-enabled Classrooms and Smart Learning Environments

Most of the learning spaces were renovated, both physical and virtual, through the internet of things (IoT). Different technologies which exist in a smart classroom environment make learning processes much more comfortable and effective (Dziuban et al., 2018; Anderson & Dron, 2018). For example, Google Jamboard enables instant sharing of content to facilitate the collaborative learning of students (Castañeda & Selwyn, 2018; Redecker, 2017). These sensors continually monitor the environmental aspect to include temperature, air quality, or lighting levels so as to optimize the physical setting of learning for better engagement and comfort (Hrastinski, 2019; Huang et al., 2020). In addition, most systems for attendance tracking have RFID or Bluetooth technology so as to enable automation of attendance collection. This would save time and increase efficiency in the process (Gašević, Dawson, & Siemens, 2015; Picciano, 2017).

Neither are exempt from usage in teaching. For instance, while exercising and training in physical education, smartwatches and fitness trackers track the students' activity and health data while making pupils have a healthier attitude towards learning (Kearney, Schuck, Burden, & Aubusson, 2012; Martin & Bolliger, 2018). VR and AR headsets, among them the Microsoft HoloLens, deliver an immersive learning experience, especially with subjects like anatomy or engineering where pupils explore complex concepts in an interactive manner (Bonk & Graham, 2012; Bates, 2019).

With IoT, distance learning becomes enhanced because, with the use of IoT, learners may access lab experiments from a distance and thus be able to conduct physical experiments directly central to learning in the STEM fields (Chen, Zou, Cheng, & Xie, 2020; Garrison, 2017). Here, smart home learning environments apply smart speakers and smart displays—in the form of the Amazon Echo Show—to 'animate' learning spaces around the home (Dede & Richards, 2012; Veletsianos & Shepherdson, 2016). Also, IoT devices help in gathering considerable sets of learning behavior and outcomes that may turn out of high value for research studies and policy in education (Siemens, 2014; Gašević, Dawson, & Siemens, 2015). Thirdly, IoT-based energy management systems help educational institutions to be responsible towards the carbon footprint for sustainability goals and assist in encouraging responsible and environmentally friendly practices within the learning environment (Huang et al., 2020; Tait, 2018).

Figure 3. Amount of use of IoT-enabled classrooms and smart learning environments by category. Data retrieved from [Huang et al., 2020Tait, 2018].

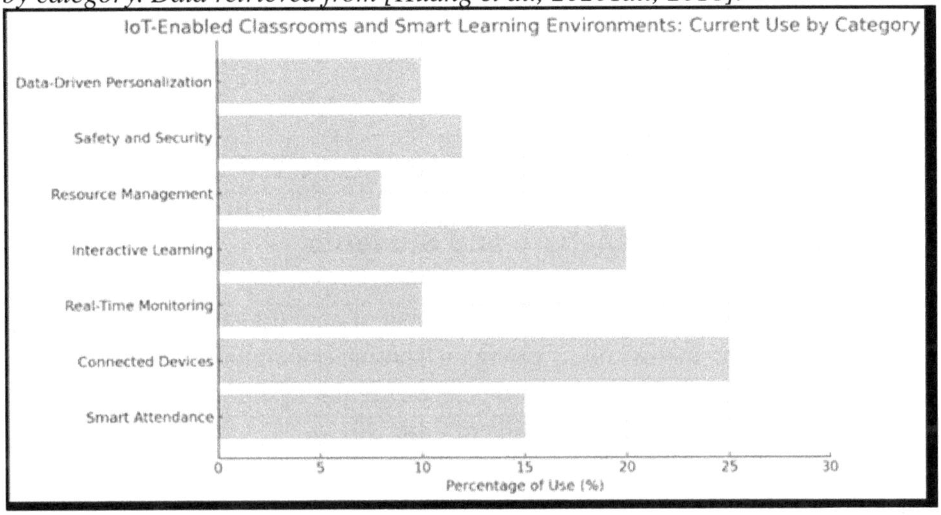

5.4 Remote Learning Technologies and Virtual Classrooms

Table 2. Remote Learning Technologies and Virtual Classrooms

Technology Category	Examples	Features and Applications
Advanced Video Conferencing Tools	Zoom, Microsoft Teams	Education-specific features such as Breakout rooms, Virtual hand-raising, real-time polls, and integration of whiteboard functionalities.
Virtual Reality (VR) Classrooms	Engage, Spatial	Enables 3D interactions and collaborations in virtual classrooms for an immersive learning experience.
Virtual Learning with AR	Google Expeditions	Provides interactive 3D models and field tours, allowing students to learn from home.
Asynchronous Learning Platforms	Loom, Screencastify	Allows instructors to create and share video courses that students can access at any time.
Online Proctored Solutions	ProctorU, Examity	Uses AI and human proctors to monitor and prevent academic dishonesty during online assessments.

continued on following page

Table 2. Continued

Technology Category	Examples	Features and Applications
Cooperative Learning Tools	Miro, Padlet	Provides an open space for collaborative projects and brainstorming among students.
Mobile Apps	Kahoot, Quizlet	Gamifies the learning process and enables assessment through interactive quizzes and speed-based activities.

6. SKILL DEVELOPMENT AND TRAINING IN THE DIGITAL AGE

6.1 Digital Skills for Teachers and Students

There is a grave need for critical development of core digital skills by both the instructor and learner in this rapidly changing landscape of digital education. Within this section, you will learn about the competencies required and strategies to achieve them (Redecker, 2017; Koehler, Mishra, & Cain, 2013).

For Educators:

Teachers will need a foundational understanding of the following:

- **Technological Competency:** The use of LMSs such as Canvas or Moodle in courses, assignments, and tracking student progress should be well known to teachers. Video conferencing, skills in Zoom, and content creation applications, like Adobe Creative Suite, contribute to creating an interactive online class setting (Garrison, 2017; Bonk & Graham, 2012).
- **Online Pedagogy:** Developing pedagogical accommodations for the online learning context is essential. Knowledge about instructional design principles, strategies for facilitating students' engagement in virtual classes, and managing online group work are key aspects (Anderson & Dron, 2018; Laurillard, 2013).
- **Data Literacy:** The successful teacher should monitor student performance and engagement, as dashboards and analytics have become indispensable parts of educational technology tools. Knowledge of data privacy principles also helps ensure proper use of educational technology (Gašević, Dawson, & Siemens, 2015; Slade & Prinsloo, 2013).
- **Digital Assessment Techniques:** Faculty must employ digital assessments using a mixed mode and be aware of strategies to sustain academic integrity.

Awareness of AI-based assessment tools and their limitations is also essential (Chen et al., 2020; Kizilcec et al., 2020).

For Students:

The students will acquire digital competencies in these areas:

- **Digital Literacy:** Basic skills, including word processing, spreadsheets, presentations, and general problem-solving skills, are fundamental (Clark & Mayer, 2016; Martin & Bolliger, 2018).
- **Information Literacy:** Students should learn to evaluate credible online sources, conduct research using academic databases, and understand copyright, fair use, and citation rules (Panigrahi, Srivastava, & Sharma, 2018; Selwyn, 2016).
- **Online Communication and Collaboration:** Mastery of online discussion forums, video conference etiquette, and shared tools, such as Google Docs, is crucial for collaboration (Hrastinski, 2019; Kahu & Nelson, 2018).
- **Digital Citizenship:** Teaching students about online privacy, managing digital footprints, and understanding the ethics of online behavior is essential (Dabbagh, Benson, & Denham, 2015; Castañeda & Selwyn, 2018).
- **Adaptive Learning Skills:** Students should practice self-directed learning strategies and time management skills in asynchronous environments and apply metacognitive learning strategies to enhance their online learning experience (Christensen, Horn, & Johnson, 2011; Dziuban et al., 2018).

Skill Development Strategies:

- **Curriculum Integration:** Digital skills are integrated with subject areas, so they are learned as part of a broader learning process rather than in isolation (Bates, 2019; Guri-Rosenblit, 2018).
- **Micro-credentialing:** Awarding badges or certificates for developing specific digital skills encourages continuous learning and skill development (Reich & Ruipérez-Valiente, 2019; Weller, 2020).
- **Peer-to-Peer Learning:** Providing students and instructors with opportunities to engage as peers in learning fosters the sharing of best practices and digital competencies (Kearney et al., 2012; Major, 2015).
- **Hands-on Experience in Workshops:** Training in workshop sessions gives students and instructors practical experience by mimicking real-life classroom interactions (Veletsianos & Shepherdson, 2016; Moore, Dickson-Deane, & Galyen, 2011).

- **Web-based Resources and Tutorials:** Self-paced, easy-to-access resources support further skill development for users (Sun et al., 2008; Tait, 2018).

6.2 AI-Assisted Skill Assessment and Improvement

This new scenario changes the way of testing and enhancing skills within the digital environment of learning by a wide array of innovative tools and methods. Among them is auto skill gap analysis wherein algorithms judge the performance of learners in order to capture the skill gap in depth accuracy (Koehler, Mishra, & Cain, 2013; Dziuban et al., 2018). Personal skill profiles through platforms like Coursera and LinkedIn Learning make course recommendations based on NLP for analyzing written work, machine learning for patterns by learning behavior, and comparative analysis against industry-standard frameworks (Bonk & Graham, 2012; Kizilcec et al., 2020).

The other good thing about the assessment using AI is that the pathways of learning are tailored to each student. Adaptive platforms like Knewton and ALEKS offer real-time individualized learning experiences (Clark & Mayer, 2016; Martin & Bolliger, 2018). AI-powered recommendation systems adapt the delivery of resources and courses accordingly to meet individual needs, aiming to better deliver an outcome (Hrastinski, 2019; Dabbagh et al., 2015). AI systems also provide instant feedback, and sometimes even coaching within skills – resources such as Grammarly suggest correct sentence structures, LeetCode offers instant coding evaluations, and Duolingo uses speech recognition to evaluate pronunciation (Anderson & Dron, 2018; Chen et al., 2020).

More evidence of predictive analytics is in the ability to develop skills, predict demand for skills, and track learning outcomes on platforms like Faethm AI, which predicts industry-specific skills in demand (Joksimović et al., 2018; Reich & Ruipérez-Valiente, 2019). Immersive learning experiences are created by AI-enabled Virtual Reality and Augmented Reality environments (Laurillard, 2013; Weller, 2020). Further, advanced AI systems measure other skills critical to humans, such as emotional intelligence and soft skills, using tools like sentiment analysis and facial recognition (Panigrahi, Srivastava, & Sharma, 2018; Castañeda & Selwyn, 2018). Project management tools coupled with AI and customer service training offered from platforms ensure the process of continuous skills assessment in a professional environment (Guri-Rosenblit, 2018; Veletsianos & Shepherdson, 2016). Among all these applications, however, there are problems to be solved, such as bias and data privacy issues, tendency to over-rely on AI capabilities, and adaptability to various learning styles so proper assessment is made (Siemens, 2014; Slade & Prinsloo, 2013).

6.3 Continuous Professional Development for Educators

In the 21st-century context, such type of knowledge can be described as continuous professional development (CPD), which is very crucial to support educational innovations (Redecker, 2017; Guri-Rosenblit, 2018). Sites like Edmodo and LinkedIn's Education Hub promote sharing of ideas around the world, whereas sites like FutureLearn and Google for Education offer guided online courses and various micro-credentials (Dede & Richards, 2012; Koehler, Mishra, & Cain, 2013). The use of digital badges has been found 73% effective with education professionals for recognition as these are verified (Anderson & Dron, 2018; Chen, Zou, Cheng, & Xie, 2020). Innovative tools for practice-based professional development, such as SimSchool or TeachLivE, enable detailed, virtual action-research with 82% teacher improvement (Laurillard, 2013; Martin & Bolliger, 2018). For instance, IBM Watson Education helps learners navigate skill development based on performance data (Siemens, 2014; Bates, 2019).

A total of 68% of online PD activity is made available by Coursera and edX MOOCs for convenient access to material from the world's best learning institutions (Joksimović et al., 2018; Reich & Ruipérez-Valiente, 2019). The importance of using online forums, such as networking and Q&A, has been realized since over 90% of learners and attendees of ISTE's virtual conference benefited from this aspect (Bonk & Graham, 2012; Tait, 2018). Positive feedback in mentoring through reflective practice platforms, such as eTwinning and AI-assisted tools like BetterUp, has also indicated a 60% improvement with continuous practice (Christensen, Horn, & Johnson, 2011; Kizilcec et al., 2020). Nevertheless, 74% of educators report difficulties such as time constraints, availability of technological resources, and implementation in the classroom (Panigrahi, Srivastava, & Sharma, 2018; Selwyn, 2016). In general, all these CPD tools help raise teaching standards while at the same time serving as exemplars of continuous professionalism (Dabbagh, Benson, & Denham, 2015; Garrison, 2017).

6.4 Challenges in Digital Literacy and Skill Training

It is thus no wonder that embracing digital transformation poses numerous challenges in developing digital literacy and skills by both educators and learners and institutions around the world (Redecker, 2017; Dabbagh, Benson, & Denham, 2015). One significant issue is the so-called digital divide, which sets limits to access and use of technologies through differences in infrastructures, economic reasons, and inequalities around the world (Selwyn, 2016; Castañeda & Selwyn, 2018). Rural regions usually do not have good high-speed internet access and just enough usable devices, while poor communities also undergo expenses for devices and internet subscriptions (Bates, 2019; Panigrahi, Srivastava, & Sharma, 2018). This way, imbalances lead to inequality in access to practical skills development and provoke social cleavages. Solutions could be broadband access everywhere, equitable distribution of devices in schools, and the creation of learning resources that would not demand internet access (Kearney, Schuck, Burden, & Aubusson, 2012).

The challenges also include rapid technological changes wherein there is always an update required in software and hardware, which complicates curriculum relevance and results in the obsolescence of skills (Anderson & Dron, 2018; Laurillard, 2013). Emphasis on transferable digital skills and agile curricula, and variable levels of digital proficiency among learners and educators, cause difficulty in the conceptualization of an inclusive program strategy (Redecker, 2017; Tait, 2018). Adaptive learning systems and peer mentoring may be employed to accommodate diverse needs (Hrastinski, 2019; Kahu & Nelson, 2018).

Information overload and digital wellbeing are yet another problems born of this constant connection (Veletsianos & Shepherdson, 2016; Kizilcec et al., 2020). Further information literacy skills—filtering out credible information from misinformation—are therefore necessary to draw out credible sources from misinformation (Garrison, 2017; Sun, Tsai, Finger, Chen, & Yeh, 2008). Practices that encourage mindful technology use and promote critical thinking abilities in curricula are therefore necessary to deal with such issues (Chen, Zou, Cheng, & Xie, 2020; Christensen, Horn, & Johnson, 2011). Other complexities of increased digital activity include privacy and security threats such as data breaches and student privacy challenges. Training individuals on cybersecurity and ethical frameworks for the use of data, for example, is how managers of the problems tackle these issues (Slade & Prinsloo, 2013; Gašević, Dawson, & Siemens, 2015).

Issues with the assessment and certification of digital skills include standardizing continually changing skills and authenticating online tests (Martin & Bolliger, 2018; Chao, 2019). Performance-based assessments and industry collaboration in validation can be used as counterbalances. Good teacher training and support are also crucial because varying levels of digital proficiency alongside scarce professional development resources expose teachers to challenges in their teaching (Major, 2015; Dziuban, Graham, Moskal, Norberg, & Sicilia, 2018). Ongoing professional development and supporting networks can help keep educators abreast of the pace with which technology is changing (Weller, 2020; Guri-Rosenblit, 2018).

Necessary for solving the online dilemmas and to understand the impacts of technologies on societies is also teaching ethical and critical thinking in digital contexts (Koehler, Mishra, & Cain, 2013; Laurillard, 2013). Teaching skills in that way, by using case studies and interdisciplinary approaches, integrates ethical thinking into the development of digital skills (Clark & Mayer, 2016; Dede & Richards, 2012). Therefore, solving these challenges requires cooperation among educators, policymakers, tech developers, and learners, which results in more inclusive and effective digital literacy programs (Anderson & Dron, 2018; Zawacki-Richter & Qayyum, 2019).

7. ECONOMIC AND SOCIETAL IMPACT OF E-LEARNING

E-learning's rise has significantly influenced economic, educational, and societal landscapes. This section delves into the costs, benefits, and broader impacts of implementing e-learning, examining global education accessibility and workforce development.

7.1 Cost Analysis of e-Learning Implementations

This involves short-term initial costs and long-term benefits to institutions, governments, and learners.

Initial Costs:

- **Infrastructure:** High investments in hard infrastructure (servers, networking), as well as software licenses, including Learning Management Systems and video conferencing tools (Bates, 2019; Dabbagh, Benson, & Denham, 2015). This can reach universities up to a range of $500K and $2M (Allen & Seaman, 2017).
- **Development of Content:** Creating digital courses will run from $10K to $50K for a course, but reusable content has the possibility of saving on a long-term run (Bonk & Graham, 2012; Major, 2015).
- **Training:** The average institutions train faculties, and they usually cost 5-10% of an annual e-learning budget (Christensen, Horn, & Johnson, 2011; Moore, Dickson-Deane, & Galyen, 2011).
- **Technical Support:** Maintenance costs normally weigh between 15-20% of a one-time setup every year (Hrastinski, 2019; Tait, 2018).

Long-term Concerns:

- E-learning is flexible in scale, ensuring that the higher education distribution shall reach much more students, without scaling costs proportionally. This is what Georgia Tech's online programs reveal (Martin & Bolliger, 2018; Veletsianos & Shepherdson, 2016). Savings in costs from brick-and-mortar infrastructure can be devoted to investing in technology (Guri-Rosenblit,

2018; Rovai & Downey, 2010). Savings from travel and tuition are passed on to students, and low-cost online education options are presented by the Western Governors University, for example. E-learning also improves workforce productivity with continuous learning without the interruption of careers (Panigrahi, Srivastava, & Sharma, 2018; Weller, 2020).

Return on Investment:

- **Institutional ROI:** Initiation costs are quite high, but savings and efficiency usually balance this out in 3-5 years; for example, in an appropriately redesigned program, overall costs fall 37% (Castañeda & Selwyn, 2018; Garrison, 2017).
- **Societal ROI:** Increased access to education increases the workforce's skills and decreases environmental degradation (Dede & Richards, 2012; Redecker, 2017).
- **Individual ROI:** Increased access to education increases the potential for more money and keeps it within an affordable and flexible reach (Clark & Mayer, 2016; Slade & Prinsloo, 2013).

Challenges

- Other issues are left unsolved, such as the digital divide wherein not everyone has equal availability of technology, cost of lowering education quality, technological obsolescence, and sometimes unacknowledged cost in terms of data security and licensing (Anderson & Dron, 2018; Kizilcec et al., 2020; Siemens, 2014).

Case Studies:

- Arizona State University invested $100M worth of its digital infrastructure. Now it serves 38,000 online students (Hrastinski, 2019; Reich & Ruipérez-Valiente, 2019).
- The Open University in the UK serves 170,000 students at 30% lower costs compared to traditional universities (Joksimović et al., 2018; Picciano, 2017).
- edX offers more than 3,000 courses to support global-scale learning (Kahu & Nelson, 2018; Chen, Zou, Cheng, & Xie, 2020).
- From the cost analysis, it can be evident that the investment in e-learning is not just about knowing how much money is being invested but also that such implementations have returns (Garrison, 2017; Kearney, Schuck, Burden, & Aubusson, 2012).

Figure 4. Cost analysis of e-Learning implementation in the present time for each category [Data retrieved from Google database]

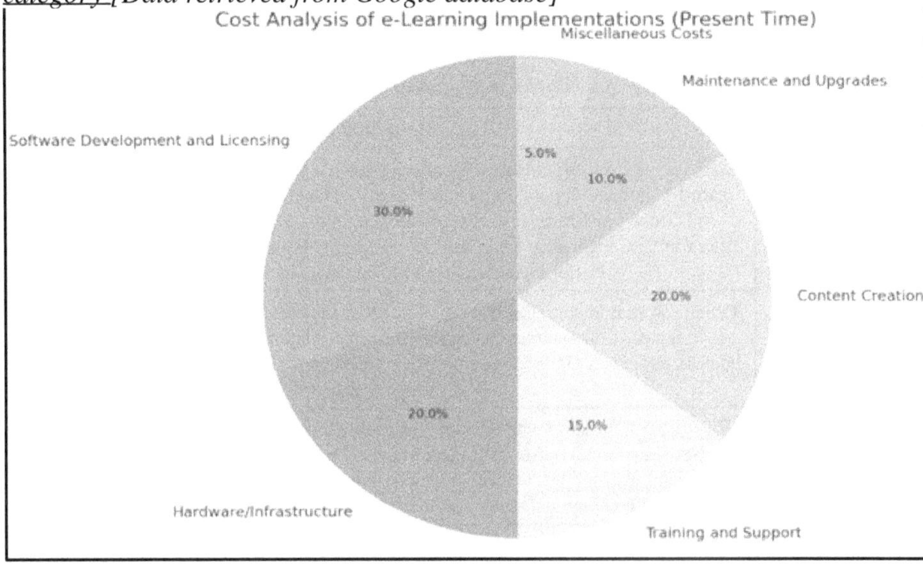

7.2 Impact on Global Education Accessibility

Table 3. Table showing impact on global education accessibility

Aspect	Description
Global Extensions in Higher Education	MOOCs (like Coursera) democratize learning, providing access to millions globally. Institutions like the University of the People offer fully online programs, reaching over 75,000 students. Micro-credentials address specific skill gaps through short, focused courses.
Reducing Education Gap in Developing Countries	Mobile learning uses common mobile phones to make education accessible on screens, while Kolibri services offer digital products without needing the internet. Localization efforts, e.g., by Khan Academy, ensure content is available in various languages for diverse learners.
Promoting Life-Long Learning	Asynchronous courses support adult learners balancing work and education. E-learning also aids corporate professional development. Adaptive technologies (e.g., Blackboard Ally) and AI tools create individualized learning paths. VR offers accessibility for physically challenged learners.
Global Collaboration	Virtual classrooms facilitate international learning and cross-cultural projects, enhancing intercultural student participation.
Restrictions	E-learning faces challenges such as digital divides, unequal tech access, lack of online degree recognition, cultural insensitivity in content, and varied digital literacy. Equal access to infrastructure, devices, and the internet remains a critical area of improvement.

7.3 Influence on Workforce Development and Employment

Table 4. Table for Influence on Workforce Development and Employment

Key Area	Description
Closing Skills Gaps	E-learning addresses skills gaps by offering job-specific training in collaboration with industry partners. Examples include Udacity's Nanodegrees in AI and data science, and Grovo's just-in-time workplace skills training. Major companies like Google offer Career Certificates, while IBM saved $200 million using e-learning for training. Platforms like Degreed provide custom training paths.
Impact on Employment Patterns	Remote work is encouraged by e-learning, with LinkedIn Learning seeing an increase in remote work courses during the pandemic. Platforms like Fiverr Learn and bootcamps such as General Assembly help freelancers and professionals pivot towards tech careers.
Overcoming Employment Obstacles	E-learning addresses youth unemployment through initiatives like the World Bank's New Economy Workforce Project in Lebanon, which focuses on digital skills. Programs also support women in male-dominated fields and provide accessibility-focused learning paths, such as Microsoft's initiative for disabled individuals.
Trend Incidence and Future Scenario	AI and automation will impact all industries, increasing the need for continuous learning. Programs like Coursera's "AI for Everyone" are aimed at non-technical professionals. Platforms like MindTools enhance critical soft skills, while AT&T's Future Ready promotes reskilling and lifelong learning.
Challenges and Considerations	Despite e-learning advantages, a digital literacy gap remains a challenge. Google's Applied Digital Skills program is a free solution aimed at bridging this gap. Digital credentials like Open Badges can help verify skills. Pluralsight monitors emerging tech skills to keep courses relevant.

Conclusion

E-learning is a powerful force in workforce development, bridging skills gaps, and helping as many people as possible to transition into new careers. However, to unleash its full potential, it is important to address its challenges issues such as digital literacy and credential recognition. As the technology continues to evolve, so too will e-learning shape a skilled adaptable global workforce.

7.4 Student Perception and Acceptance of e-Learning

The effectiveness of e-learning largely depends on the perception and acceptance levels of the students, driven by a host of factors and the significant global events that recently occurred, such as the COVID-19 pandemic (Huang et al., 2020; Reich & Ruipérez-Valiente, 2019).

- **Important Factors Influencing Student Perception:** The advantage of e-learning is flexibility, ensuring ease and convenience when it comes to learning. Most students prefer self-paced learning (Bonk & Graham, 2012; Bernard et al., 2014). Indeed, aside from conceptions of both content and instructor engagement, students' comfort with technology also relates to their learning experience (Martin & Bolliger, 2018). Platforms that support a social network and encourage collaboration increase engagement while allowing for adaptability in e-learning, catering to personal learning styles (Garrison, 2017; Kahu & Nelson, 2018). Cultural and socioeconomic factors, including infrastructure restrictions, might also affect the perception of the quality of online education (Panigrahi, Srivastava, & Sharma, 2018; Kizilcec et al., 2020).
- **Evolution of Perception:** E-learning was mostly preferred for the flexibility it offered, but regarding quality, there were serious issues that had to be addressed (Clark & Mayer, 2016). However, through increased exposure during the pandemic, many students reported a preference for the blended model of learning afterward (Dziuban et al., 2018; Tait, 2018).
- **Challenge of Acceptability Among Students:** While e-learning provides numerous advantages, it does not eliminate the problem of a digital divide in access to technology (Castañeda & Selwyn, 2018; Veletsianos & Shepherdson, 2016). Reluctance and lack of self-discipline tend to inhibit learners in asynchronous learning environments, and students may feel isolated due to a lack of face-to-face contact and technical glitches (Koehler, Mishra, & Cain, 2013; Picciano, 2017). Concerns with regard to online assessment integrity complicate the ease of acceptance (Chen et al., 2020; Sun et al., 2008).
- **Improving Mechanisms:** Institutions can improve acceptance by making courses highly interactive through gamification and other appealing features (Weller, 2020; Redecker, 2017). Adaptive technologies can provide experiences tailored to individual learners, leading to better results (Hrastinski, 2019). Better support infrastructures, such as technical support and mentoring services, can better position students for success (Allen & Seaman, 2017). Focusing on training students in digital literacy can improve their experience and make them more adept at using e-learning systems (Laurillard, 2013). Using blended models of learning, which combine online learning and face-to-face instruction, may be associated with increased satisfaction (Major, 2015; Anderson & Dron, 2018).

In conclusion, student attitudes toward e-learning depend heavily on flexibility, quality of learning content, and available support systems. While the COVID-19 epidemic encouraged swift acceptance, motivations and digital access remain pertinent concerns. Institutional focus on personalization and support should lead to maximally enhanced student outcomes in e-learning environments (Dabbagh, Benson, & Denham, 2015; Bates, 2019).

7.5 Policy and Regulatory Considerations

The growth of e-learning necessitates policies to ensure quality, accessibility, and equity (Guri-Rosenblit, 2018; Moore, Dickson-Deane, & Galyen, 2011). Some of these policies are discussed below:

Institutional Policies:

- **Academic Integrity:** There should be guidelines about online proctoring or plagiarism detection (Dabbagh, Benson, & Denham, 2015; Redecker, 2017).
- **Ownership of Course Material:** Clear rules regarding ownership should be established for online course materials (Koehler, Mishra, & Cain, 2013).
- **Faculty Development:** Professional development is essential to uphold standards in online teaching (Bates, 2019; Allen & Seaman, 2017).
- **Data Privacy:** Compliance with data protection laws is necessary to safeguard student information (Slade & Prinsloo, 2013; Gašević, Dawson, & Siemens, 2015).

National Policies and Regulations:

- **Accreditation:** Online programs are formulating new accreditation standards (Picciano, 2017).
- **Access and Funding:** Governments are securing funding to advance mass digital learning and ensure access for disabled learners (Bonk & Graham, 2012; Weller, 2020).
- **Acceptance of Online Credentials:** Structures for micro-credential acceptance are being established (Reich & Ruipérez-Valiente, 2019).

Cross-Border Education/International Policies:

- **Cross-Border Education:** UNESCO's Global Convention addresses issues of qualification recognition across borders (Anderson & Dron, 2018).

- **Protection of Data:** The General Data Protection Regulation requires e-learning entities worldwide to maintain privacy (Selwyn, 2016).
- **OER/Open Educational Resources:** Policies encourage the sharing of free educational resources globally (Veletsianos & Shepherdson, 2016; Huang et al., 2020).

Emerging Policy Challenges:

- **AI in Education:** Ethical policies are essential for managing AI applications in e-learning environments (Kizilcec et al., 2020; Siemens, 2014).
- **Cybersecurity:** Strong policies must be developed to prevent cyber-attacks (Clark & Mayer, 2016).
- **Sustainability:** New regulations promote ecological e-learning practices (Laurillard, 2013).

In conclusion, the developing landscape of e-learning policy emphasizes access, privacy, and digital infrastructure. Policymakers must modernize as new technologies evolve, ensuring quality and innovation while consulting internationally (Chen et al., 2020; Tait, 2018).

8. FUTURE DIRECTIONS AND INNOVATIONS IN E-LEARNING

8.1 Emerging Technologies and Their Potential in Education

Modern technologies have begun to penetrate the core of the education system. Virtual and augmented reality offer students immersive platforms to not only view but also explore complex ideas in three dimensions (Kearney, Schuck, Burden, & Aubusson, 2012; Dede & Richards, 2012). Blockchain technology is also under consideration for its potential to provide a secure and verifiable credentialing system (Chen et al., 2020). The Internet of Things (IoT) is transforming learning into a "smart campus" experience by connecting devices to create an integrated learning environment (Weller, 2020).

8.2 Personalized and Adaptive Learning Solutions

Advances in data analytics and machine learning now enable truly personalized learning experiences, adapting in real-time based on student performance, learning styles, and preferences (Martin & Bolliger, 2018). Intelligent tutoring systems offer tailored guidance and support, bringing e-learning closer to an optimized educational journey for each learner (Christensen, Horn, & Johnson, 2011; Major, 2015).

8.3 Role of AI in Predictive and Preventive Models of Education

Artificial intelligence is transforming educational models by introducing predictive and preventive capabilities. AI algorithms can analyze large datasets to identify student challenges early on, potentially preventing declines in performance or dropouts (Guri-Rosenblit, 2018; Kizilcec et al., 2020). Additionally, AI can forecast future skills needs, allowing educational offerings to adapt to shifting workforce demands (Siemens, 2014).

8.4 Collaboration between Teachers and Technology

As e-learning grows, teachers and technology increasingly collaborate, integrating human expertise with advanced technological tools. Teachers can work alongside AI systems to enhance instructional techniques and deliver more personalized student services (Hrastinski, 2019; Clark & Mayer, 2016). This synergy enables new approaches that blend human intuition with technological precision, enriching the learning experience (Panigrahi, Srivastava, & Sharma, 2018).

8.5 Visions for the Future: Autonomous and Immersive Learning

In this vision for the future, learning could become more autonomous and immersive. AI-driven tutors may independently guide learners through flexible curricula that adjust in real-time to each student's needs (Anderson & Dron, 2018; Picciano, 2017). Virtual reality, meanwhile, could make educational experiences in history or science remarkably lifelike, redefining learning for students (Castañeda & Selwyn, 2018). In a rapidly evolving knowledge economy, adaptive lifelong learning might become standard worldwide, further blurring the line between formal education and continuous learning (Laurillard, 2013; Redecker, 2017).

9. CONCLUSION

E-learning today stands at an unprecedented position in education. It has brought knowledge to people's lives in the form of a customized experience that is truly effective. Originating in the electronics world, evolving into its recent form as a state of art - AI-driven state of e-learning - it has given thoroughly shaped and advanced opportunities in education. All of these-advances in AI, data analytics, IoT, VR, and AR-make it now possible to create learning environments that might not otherwise be possible.

For instance, apart from influencing technology, e-learning promotes democratization of education worldwide and has very positive influences on workforce development. However, there is this digital divide and concern for the quality of education, and also data privacy concerns associated with AI applications of education-all issues which will require constant attention through the policy frameworks that will provide opportunities equitably while ensuring that distance education is not tampered with.

The horizon for e-learning seems pretty limitless in the near future. On this front, the interaction of AI and immersive technologies with adaptive learning talks of increasingly personalized yet engaging experiences for education. As we step into this exciting new pathway, the challenge would be to move these developments forward without letting education lose its touch of humanity, equity, or keeping in line with other social goals. All these changes, challenges, and opportunities of this increasingly digital and interconnected world would remain part of the future evolution of e-learning, taking learners through all.

REFERENCES

Allen, I. E., & Seaman, J. (2017). *Digital learning compass: Distance education enrollment report 2017*. Babson Survey Research Group.

Anderson, T., & Dron, J. (2018). Learning technology through three generations of technology enhanced distance education pedagogy. European Journal of Open. *Distance and E-Learning*, 21(2), 1–17.

Bates, A. W. (2019). *Teaching in a digital age: Guidelines for designing teaching and learning*. Tony Bates Associates Ltd.

Bernard, R. M., Borokhovski, E., Schmid, R. F., Tamim, R. M., & Abrami, P. C. (2014). A meta-analysis of blended learning and technology use in higher education: From the general to the applied. *Journal of Computing in Higher Education*, 26(1), 87–122. DOI: 10.1007/s12528-013-9077-3

Bonk, C. J., & Graham, C. R. (2012). *The handbook of blended learning: Global perspectives, local designs*. John Wiley & Sons.

Castañeda, L., & Selwyn, N. (2018). More than tools? Making sense of the ongoing digitizations of higher education. *International Journal of Educational Technology in Higher Education*, 15(1), 22. DOI: 10.1186/s41239-018-0109-y

Chao, R. Y. (2019). Propensity score matching in massive open online courses. *British Journal of Educational Technology*, 50(2), 652–668.

Chen, X., Zou, D., Cheng, G., & Xie, H. (2020). Detecting latent topics and trends in educational technologies over four decades using structural topic modeling: A retrospective of all volumes of Computers & Education. *Computers & Education*, 151, 103855. DOI: 10.1016/j.compedu.2020.103855

Christensen, C. M., Horn, M. B., & Johnson, C. W. (2011). *Disrupting class: How disruptive innovation will change the way the world learns*. McGraw-Hill.

Clark, R. C., & Mayer, R. E. (2016). *E-learning and the science of instruction: Proven guidelines for consumers and designers of multimedia learning*. John Wiley & Sons. DOI: 10.1002/9781119239086

Dabbagh, N., Benson, A. D., & Denham, A. (2015). Instructional strategies and models for e-learning. Handbook of Research on Educational Communications and Technology, 281-294.

Dede, C., & Richards, J. (2012). *Digital teaching platforms: Customizing classroom learning for each student*. Teachers College Press.

Dziuban, C., Graham, C. R., Moskal, P. D., Norberg, A., & Sicilia, N. (2018). Blended learning: The new normal and emerging technologies. *International Journal of Educational Technology in Higher Education*, 15(1), 3. DOI: 10.1186/s41239-017-0087-5

. Garrison, D. R. (2017). E-learning in the 21st century: A community of inquiry framework for research and practice. Routledge.

Gašević, D., Dawson, S., & Siemens, G. (2015). Let's not forget: Learning analytics are about learning. *TechTrends*, 59(1), 64–71. DOI: 10.1007/s11528-014-0822-x

Guri-Rosenblit, S. (2018). E-Teaching in Higher Education: An Essential Prerequisite for E-Learning. *Journal of New Approaches in Educational Research*, 7(2), 93–97. DOI: 10.7821/naer.2018.7.298

Hrastinski, S. (2019). What do we mean by blended learning? *TechTrends*, 63(5), 564–569. DOI: 10.1007/s11528-019-00375-5

Huang, R. H., Liu, D. J., Tlili, A., Yang, J. F., & Wang, H. H. (2020). *Handbook on facilitating flexible learning during educational disruption: The Chinese experience in maintaining undisrupted learning in COVID-19 outbreak*. Smart Learning Institute of Beijing Normal University.

Joksimović, S., Poquet, O., Kovanović, V., Dowell, N., Mills, C., Gašević, D., Dawson, S., Graesser, A. C., & Brooks, C. (2018). How do we model learning at scale? A systematic review of research on MOOCs. *Review of Educational Research*, 88(1), 43–86. DOI: 10.3102/0034654317740335

Kahu, E. R., & Nelson, K. (2018). Student engagement in the educational interface: Understanding the mechanisms of student success. *Higher Education Research & Development*, 37(1), 58–71. DOI: 10.1080/07294360.2017.1344197

Kearney, M., Schuck, S., Burden, K., & Aubusson, P. (2012). Viewing mobile learning from a pedagogical perspective. *Research in Learning Technology*, 20(1), 20. DOI: 10.3402/rlt.v20i0.14406

Kizilcec, R. F., Reich, J., Yeomans, M., Dann, C., Brunskill, E., Lopez, G., Turkay, S., Williams, J. J., & Tingley, D. (2020). Scaling up behavioral science interventions in online education. *Proceedings of the National Academy of Sciences of the United States of America*, 117(26), 14900–14905. DOI: 10.1073/pnas.1921417117 PMID: 32541050

Koehler, M. J., Mishra, P., & Cain, W. (2013). What is technological pedagogical content knowledge (TPACK)? *Journal of Education*, 193(3), 13–19. DOI: 10.1177/002205741319300303

Laurillard, D. (2013). *Rethinking university teaching: A conversational framework for the effective use of learning technologies*. Routledge. DOI: 10.4324/9781315012940

Major, C. H. (2015). *Teaching online: A guide to theory, research, and practice*. JHU Press. DOI: 10.1353/book.38784

Martin, F., & Bolliger, D. U. (2018). Engagement matters: Student perceptions on the importance of engagement strategies in the online learning environment. *Online Learning : the Official Journal of the Online Learning Consortium*, 22(1), 205–222. DOI: 10.24059/olj.v22i1.1092

Moore, J. L., Dickson-Deane, C., & Galyen, K. (2011). e-Learning, online learning, and distance learning environments: Are they the same? *The Internet and Higher Education*, 14(2), 129–135. DOI: 10.1016/j.iheduc.2010.10.001

Panigrahi, R., Srivastava, P. R., & Sharma, D. (2018). Online learning: Adoption, continuance, and learning outcome—A review of literature. *International Journal of Information Management*, 43, 1–14. DOI: 10.1016/j.ijinfomgt.2018.05.005

Picciano, A. G. (2017). Theories and frameworks for online education: Seeking an integrated model. *Online Learning : the Official Journal of the Online Learning Consortium*, 21(3), 166–190. DOI: 10.24059/olj.v21i3.1225

. Redecker, C. (2017). European framework for the digital competence of educators: DigCompEdu. Joint Research Centre (Seville site).

Reich, J., & Ruipérez-Valiente, J. A. (2019). The MOOC pivot. *Science*, 363(6423), 130–131. DOI: 10.1126/science.aav7958 PMID: 30630920

Rovai, A. P., & Downey, J. R. (2010). Why some distance education programs fail while others succeed in a global environment. *The Internet and Higher Education*, 13(3), 141–147. DOI: 10.1016/j.iheduc.2009.07.001

Selwyn, N. (2016). *Is technology good for education?* John Wiley & Sons.

Siemens, G. (2014). Connectivism: A learning theory for the digital age. *International Journal of Instructional Technology and Distance Learning*, 2(1), 3–10.

Slade, S., & Prinsloo, P. (2013). Learning analytics: Ethical issues and dilemmas. *The American Behavioral Scientist*, 57(10), 1510–1529. DOI: 10.1177/0002764213479366

Sun, P. C., Tsai, R. J., Finger, G., Chen, Y. Y., & Yeh, D. (2008). What drives a successful e-Learning? An empirical investigation of the critical factors influencing learner satisfaction. *Computers & Education*, 50(4), 1183–1202. DOI: 10.1016/j.compedu.2006.11.007

Tait, A. (2018). Open Universities: The next phase. *Asian Association of Open Universities Journal*, 13(1), 13–23. DOI: 10.1108/AAOUJ-12-2017-0040

Veletsianos, G., & Shepherdson, P. (2016). A systematic analysis and synthesis of the empirical MOOC literature published in 2013–2015. *International Review of Research in Open and Distance Learning*, 17(2). Advance online publication. DOI: 10.19173/irrodl.v17i2.2448

Weller, M. (2020). 25 Years of Ed Tech. Athabasca University Press.

Zawacki-Richter, O., & Qayyum, A. (Eds.). (2019). *Open and distance education in Asia, Africa and the Middle East: National perspectives in a digital age*. Springer. DOI: 10.1007/978-981-13-5787-9

Compilation of References

Abduljabbar, R., Dia, H., Liyanage, S., & Bagloee, S. A. (2019, January 2). Applications of Artificial Intelligence in Transport: An Overview. *Sustainability (Basel)*, 11(1), 189–189. DOI: 10.3390/su11010189

Abràmoff, M. D., Tarver, M. E., Loyo-Berríos, N., Trujillo, S., Char, D., Obermeyer, Z., Eydelman, M., & Maisel, W. H. (2023, September 12). Considerations for addressing bias in artificial intelligence for health equity. *NPJ Digital Medicine*, 6(1), 170. Advance online publication. DOI: 10.1038/s41746-023-00913-9 PMID: 37700029

Adeshola, I., & Adepoju, A. P. (2023). The opportunities and challenges of ChatGPT in education. *Interactive Learning Environments*, •••, 1–14. DOI: 10.1080/10494820.2023.2253858

Adiguzel, T., Kaya, M. H., & Cansu, F. K. (2023). Revolutionizing education with AI: Exploring the transformative potential of ChatGPT. [Online]. *Contemporary Educational Technology*, 15(3), ep429. Advance online publication. DOI: 10.30935/cedtech/13152

Ahanin, E., Sade, A. B., & Tat, H. H. (2022, December 19). Applications of Artificial Intelligence and Voice Assistant in Healthcare. *International Journal of Academic Research in Business & Social Sciences*, 12(12). Advance online publication. DOI: 10.6007/IJARBSS/v12-i12/16048

Ahmed, U. (2014) Remarks by Usman Ahmed. Proceedings of the ASIL Annual Meeting. [Online]. Available: http://dx.doi.org/DOI: 10.5305/procannmeetasil.108.0348

Aithal, P. S., & Aithal, S. (2023). How to increase emotional infrastructure of higher education institutions. [IJMTS]. *International Journal of Management, Technology, and Social Sciences*, 8(3), 356–394. DOI: 10.47992/IJMTS.2581.6012.0307

Akçayır, M., & Akçayır, G. (2017). Advantages and challenges associated with augmented reality for education: A systematic review of the literature. *Educational Research Review*, 20, 1–11. DOI: 10.1016/j.edurev.2016.11.002

Akgun, S., & Greenhow, C. (2022). Artificial intelligence in education: Addressing ethical challenges in K-12 settings. *AI and Ethics*, 2(3), 431–440. DOI: 10.1007/s43681-021-00096-7 PMID: 34790956

Al Shamsi, H. R. S., & Safei, S. (2023). Artificial Intelligence Adoption in Predictive Policing to Predict Crime Mitigation Performance. *International Journal of Sustainable Construction Engineering and Technology*, 14(3), 289–298. DOI: 10.30880/ijscet.2023.14.03.025

Al-Ansi, A. M., Jaboob, M., Garad, A., & Al-Ansi, A. (2023). Analyzing augmented reality (AR) and virtual reality (VR) recent development in education. *Social Sciences & Humanities Open*, 8(1), 100532. DOI: 10.1016/j.ssaho.2023.100532

Aleksander, I., Vivet, M., Kerr, D., Gillingham, J., Fernandez de Castro, M. I., Diaz de Ilarraza Sanchez, A., Felisa Vordejo Maillo, M., & Lees, P. (1988). *Artificial intelligence and its potential as an aid to vocational training and education.* CEDEFOP. https://eric. ed.gov/?id=ED316734

Alekseeva, L., Azar, J., Giné, M., Samila, S., & Taska, B. (2021, May 18). The demand for AI skills in the labor market. Elsevier BV, 71, 102002-102002. DOI: 10.1016/j.labeco.2021.102002

Aliabadi, R., Singh, A., & Wilson, J E. (2023, January 1). Transdisciplinary AI Education: The Confluence of Curricular and Community Needs in the Instruction of Artificial Intelligence. Springer International Publishing, 137-151. DOI: 10.1007/978-981-99-7947-9_11

Alier, M., García-Peñalvo, F., & Camba, J. D. (2024). Generative Artificial Intelligence in Education: From Deceptive to Disruptive. *International Journal of Interactive Multimedia and Artificial Intelligence, Special issue on Generative Artificial Intelligence in Education, 5*, 5-14. DOI: 10.9781/ijimai.2024.02.011

Allen, I. E., & Seaman, J. (2017). *Digital learning compass: Distance education enrollment report 2017*. Babson Survey Research Group.

Alqahtani, T., Badreldin, H. A., Alrashed, M., Alshaya, A. I., Alghamdi, S. S., bin Saleh, K., Alowais, S. A., Alshaya, O. A., Rahman, I., Al Yami, M. S., & Albekairy, A. M. (2023, August). bin Saleh, K., Alowais, S. A., Alshaya, O. A., Rahman, I., Al Yami, M. S. and Albekairy, A. M. (2023) The emergent role of artificial intelligence, natural learning processing, and large language models in higher education and research. [Online]. *Research in Social & Administrative Pharmacy*, 19(8), 1236–1242. Advance online publication. DOI: 10.1016/j.sapharm.2023.05.016 PMID: 37321925

Amershi, S., Cakmak, M., Knox, W. B., & Kulesza, T. (2014). Power to the people: The role of humans in interactive machine learning. *AI Magazine*, 35(4), 105–120. DOI: 10.1609/aimag.v35i4.2513

Amer-Yahia, S. (2022) Towards AI-powered data-driven education. Proceedings of the VLDB Endowment. [Online]. Available: http://dx.doi.org/DOI: 10.14778/3554821.3554900

Anderson, T., & Dron, J. (2018). Learning technology through three generations of technology enhanced distance education pedagogy. European Journal of Open. *Distance and E-Learning*, 21(2), 1–17.

Apostolakis, K. C., Dimitriou, N., Margetis, G., Ntoa, S., Tzovaras, D., & Stephanidis, C. (2022). DARLENE–Improving situational awareness of European law enforcement agents through a combination of augmented reality and artificial intelligence solutions. *Open Research Europe*, 1, 87. DOI: 10.12688/openreseurope.13715.2 PMID: 37645167

Arensman, E., Coffey, C., Griffin, E., Van Audenhove, C., Scheerder, G., Gusmao, R., & Maxwell, M. (2016). Effectiveness of depression–suicidal behaviour gatekeeper training among police officers in three European regions: Outcomes of the Optimising Suicide Prevention Programmes and Their Implementation in Europe (OSPI-Europe) study. *The International Journal of Social Psychiatry*, 62(7), 651–660. DOI: 10.1177/0020764016668907 PMID: 27647606

Arief, U. M., Wibawanto, H., & Nastiti, A. L. (2023). Augmented reality technology for vocational education. *Advances in Social Science, Education and Humanities Research (ASSEHR)*, 201. Atlantis Press. https://www.atlantis-press.com/article/25903467.pdf

Aspinwall, M., & Schneider, G. (2001). The rules of integration: Institutionalist approaches to the study of Europe.

Aspinwall, M. D., & Schneider, G. (2000). Same menu, seperate tables: The institutionalist turn in political science and the study of European integration. *European Journal of Political Research*, 38(1), 1–36. DOI: 10.1111/1475-6765.00526

Asrifan, A., Hamid, R. J., Syawal, S., & Muthmainnah, M. (2024). Tech-Enhanced Early Learning: Harnessing the Power of Persuasive Educational Technologies. *Power of Persuasive Educational Technologies in Enhancing Learning*, IGI Global, 63-96.

Attwell, G., Deitmer, L., Tūtlys, V., Roppertz, S., & Perini, M. (2020). Digitalisation, artificial intelligence and vocational occupations and skills: What are the needs for training teachers and trainers? DOI: 10.5281/ZENODO.4005713

Autor, D., & Dorn, D. (2013, August 1). The Growth of Low-Skill Service Jobs and the Polarization of the US Labor Market. *The American Economic Review*, 103(5), 1553–1597. DOI: 10.1257/aer.103.5.1553

Avis, J. (2018). Socio-technical imaginary of the fourth industrial revolution and its implications for vocational education and training: A literature review. *Journal of Vocational Education and Training*, 70(3), 337–363. DOI: 10.1080/13636820.2018.1498907

Azuma, R. T. (1997). A survey of augmented reality. *Presence (Cambridge, Mass.)*, 6(4), 355–385. DOI: 10.1162/pres.1997.6.4.355

Azuma, R., Baillot, Y., Behringer, R., Feiner, S., Julier, S., & MacIntyre, B. (2001). Recent advances in augmented reality. *IEEE Computer Graphics and Applications*, 21(6), 34–47. DOI: 10.1109/38.963459

Bacca Acosta, J. L., Baldiris Navarro, S. M., Fabregat Gesa, R., & Graf, S. (2015). Mobile augmented reality in vocational education and training. *Procedia Computer Science*, 75, 49–58. DOI: 10.1016/j.procs.2015.12.203

Bacca Acosta, J. L., Baldiris Navarro, S. M., Fabregat Gesa, R., & Kinshuk, K. (2019). Framework for designing motivational augmented reality applications in vocational education and training. *Australasian Journal of Educational Technology*, 35(3). Advance online publication. DOI: 10.14742/ajet.4182

Bacca, J., Baldiris, S., Fabregat, R., & Graf, S., & Kinshuk. (2014). Augmented reality trends in education: A systematic review of research and applications. *Journal of Educational Technology & Society*, 17(4), 133–149.

Bacca, J., Baldiris, S., Fabregat, R., & Kinshuk, . (2018). Insights into the factors influencing student motivation in augmented reality learning experiences in vocational education and training. *Frontiers in Psychology*, 9, 1486. DOI: 10.3389/fpsyg.2018.01486 PMID: 30186196

Bailey, J. (2023). AI in Education: The leap into a new era of machine intelligence carries risks and challenges, but also plenty of promise. *Education Next*, 23(4), 29–36.

Bates, A. W. (2019). *Teaching in a digital age: Guidelines for designing teaching and learning*. Tony Bates Associates Ltd.

BBC StoryWorks. (2024). Harnessing the power of AI with a distinctively Kazakh touch. https://www.bbc.com/storyworks/kazakhstan-connection/harnessing-the-power-of-ai-with-a-distinctively-kazakh-touch

Bengio, Y., Hinton, G. E., Yao, A. C., Song, D., Abbeel, P., Darrell, T., Harari, Y. N., Zhang, Y., Lan, X., Shalev-Shwartz, S., Hadfield, G. K., Clune, J., Maharaj, T., Hutter, F., Baydin, A. G., McIlraith, S. A., Gao, Q., Acharya, A., Krueger, D., & Mindermann, S. (2024, May 20). Managing extreme AI risks amid rapid progress. *Science*, 384(6698), 842–845. DOI: 10.1126/science.adn0117 PMID: 38768279

Bernard, R. M., Borokhovski, E., Schmid, R. F., Tamim, R. M., & Abrami, P. C. (2014). A meta-analysis of blended learning and technology use in higher education: From the general to the applied. *Journal of Computing in Higher Education*, 26(1), 87–122. DOI: 10.1007/s12528-013-9077-3

Berretta, S., Tausch, A., Peifer, C., & Kluge, A. (2023, May 23). The Job Perception Inventory: Considering human factors and needs in the design of human–AI work. *Frontiers of Medicine*, 14, 1128945. Advance online publication. DOI: 10.3389/fpsyg.2023.1128945 PMID: 37287772

Bewersdorff, A., Zhai, X., Roberts, J., & Nerdel, C. (2023, January 1). Myths, mis- and preconceptions of artificial intelligence: A review of the literature. Elsevier BV, 4, 100143-100143. DOI: 10.1016/j.caeai.2023.100143

Bhushan, P. (2022). Recent Used and Future Application of Artificial Intelligent (AI). [IJSREM]. *International Journal of Scientific Research in Engineering and Management*, 6(11). Advance online publication. DOI: 10.55041/SREM16966

Bhutoria, A. (2022). Personalized education and Artificial Intelligence in the United States, China, and India: A systematic review using a Human-In-The-Loop model. Computers and Education [Online]. *Artificial Intelligence*, 3, 100068. Advance online publication. DOI: 10.1016/j.caeai.2022.100068

Billett, S. (2001). *Learning in the workplace: Strategies for effective practice*. Allen & Unwin.

Billinghurst, M., Clark, A., & Lee, G. (2015). A survey of augmented reality. *Foundations and Trends® in Human–Computer Interaction, 8*(2-3), 73-272.

Binder, R. R., & Rockman, B. (2005). Rational Choice Institutionalism.

Bini, S A. (2018, February 27). Artificial Intelligence, Machine Learning, Deep Learning, and Cognitive Computing: What Do These Terms Mean and How Will They Impact Health Care?. Elsevier BV, 33(8), 2358-2361. DOI: 10.1016/j.arth.2018.02.067

Bizzo, B. C., Dasegowda, G., Bridge, C., Miller, B., Hillis, J. M., Kalra, M. K., Durniak, K., Stout, M., Schultz, T., Alkasab, T., & Dreyer, K. J. (2023). Addressing the Challenges of Implementing Artificial Intelligence Tools in Clinical Practice: Principles From Experience. [Online]. *Journal of the American College of Radiology*, 20(3), 352–360. Advance online publication. DOI: 10.1016/j.jacr.2023.01.002 PMID: 36922109

Blasí, D E., Anastasopoulos, A., & Neubig, G. (2022, January 1). Systematic Inequalities in Language Technology Performance across the World's Languages. DOI: 10.18653/v1/2022.acl-long.376

Bogicevic, V., Liu, S. Q., Seo, S., Kandampully, J., & Rudd, N. A. (2021). Virtual reality is so cool! How technology innovativeness shapes consumer responses to service preview modes. *International Journal of Hospitality Management*, 93, 93. DOI: 10.1016/j.ijhm.2020.102806

Bohr, A., & Memarzadeh, K. (2020, January 1). The rise of artificial intelligence in healthcare applications. Elsevier BV, 25-60. DOI: 10.1016/B978-0-12-818438-7.00002-2

Bonk, C. J., & Graham, C. R. (2012). *The handbook of blended learning: Global perspectives, local designs*. John Wiley & Sons.

Borenstein, J., & Howard, A. (2020, September 13). Emerging challenges in AI and the need for AI ethics education. *AI and Ethics*, 1(1), 61–65. DOI: 10.1007/s43681-020-00002-7 PMID: 38624388

Borgen, K. B., Ropp, T. D., & Weldon, W. T. (2021). Assessment of augmented reality technology's impact on speed of learning and task performance in aeronautical engineering technology education. *The International Journal of Aerospace Psychology*, 31(3), 219–229. DOI: 10.1080/24721840.2021.1881403

Bound, H. (2011). Vocational education and training teacher professional development: Tensions and context. *Studies in Continuing Education*, 33(2), 107–119. DOI: 10.1080/0158037X.2011.554176

Bowman, S. (2022, January 1). The Dangers of Underclaiming: Reasons for Caution When Reporting How NLP Systems Fail. DOI: 10.18653/v1/2022.acl-long.516

Braganza, A., Chen, W., Canhoto, A I., & Sap, S. (2020, August 18). Productive employment and decent work: The impact of AI adoption on psychological contracts, job engagement and employee trust. Elsevier BV, 131, 485-494. DOI: 10.1016/j.jbusres.2020.08.018

Braiki, B. A., Harous, S., Zaki, N., & Alnajjar, F. (2020, August 25). Artificial intelligence in education and assessment methods. [IAES]. *Institute of Advanced Engineering and Science*, 9(5), 1998–2007. DOI: 10.11591/eei.v9i5.1984

Braun, V., & Clarke, V. (2012). *Thematic analysis.* American Psychological Association. DOI: 10.1037/13620-004

Brown, T. B. (2020). Language models are few-shot learners. *arXiv preprint arXiv:2005.14165.*

Brown, P. (2020). Some observations on the race to higher education, digital technologies and the future of work. *Journal of Education and Work*, 33(7–8), 491–499. DOI: 10.1080/13639080.2020.1852500

Buttazzo, G. (2023, August 25). Rise of artificial general intelligence: Risks and opportunities. *Frontiers of Medicine*, 6, 1226990. Advance online publication. DOI: 10.3389/frai.2023.1226990 PMID: 37693010

Butz, M V. (2021, February 26). Towards Strong AI. Springer Science+Business Media, 35(1), 91-101. DOI: 10.1007/s13218-021-00705-x

Camarda, J., Lee, S. J., & Lee, J. (2021, January 1). The AI Displacement Risk. *Springer Nature*, 67-71, 67–71. Advance online publication. DOI: 10.1007/978-3-030-77271-0_7

Cao, X. (2023) Case Study of China-s Compulsory Education System: AI Apps and Extracurricular Dance Learning. International Journal of Human-€"Computer Interaction. [Online]. Available: http://dx.doi.org/.DOI: 10.1080/10447318.2023.2188539

Cao, L. (2022). Ai in finance: Challenges, techniques, and opportunities. *ACM Computing Surveys*, 55(3), 1–38. DOI: 10.1145/3502289

Cao, L., & Dai, M. (2006). Confidence in the police: Where does Taiwan rank in the world? *Asian Journal of Criminology*, 1(1), 71–84. DOI: 10.1007/s11417-006-9001-0

Cao, L., Huang, L., & Sun, I. (2016). Development and reform of police training and education in Taiwan. *Police Practice and Research*, 17(6), 531–542. DOI: 10.1080/15614263.2015.1086878

Carmigniani, J., & Furht, B. (2011). Augmented reality: An overview. In Furht, B. (Ed.), *Handbook of augmented reality* (pp. 3–46). Springer. DOI: 10.1007/978-1-4614-0064-6_1

Cassidy, D., Borgne, Y. L., Bellas, F., Vuorikari, R., Rondin, E., Sharma, M., Niewint-Gori, J., Gröpler, J., Gilleran, A., & Kralj, L. (2023, January 1). Use Scenarios & Practical Examples of AI Use in Education. Cornell University. https://doi.org/DOI: 10.48550/arXiv.2309

Castañeda, L., & Selwyn, N. (2018). More than tools? Making sense of the ongoing digitizations of higher education. *International Journal of Educational Technology in Higher Education*, 15(1), 22. DOI: 10.1186/s41239-018-0109-y

Caudell, T. P., & Mizell, D. W. (1992). Augmented reality: An application of heads-up display technology to manual manufacturing processes. In *Proceedings of the twenty-fifth Hawaii international conference on system sciences* (Vol. 2, pp. 659–669). Piscataway, NJ. DOI: 10.1109/HICSS.1992.183317

Cawood, S., & Fiala, M. (2007). *Augmented reality: A practical guide*. The Pragmatic Programmers.

Cazzaniga, M., Jaumotte, M. F., Li, L., Melina, M. G., Panton, A. J., Pizzinelli, C., & Tavares, M. M. M. (2024). *Gen-AI: Artificial intelligence and the future of work*. International Monetary Fund. DOI: 10.5089/9798400262548.006

Çela, E., Potluri, R. M., & Vajjhala, N. R. (2025). A Comprehensive Meta-Analysis of IoT Integration for Data-Driven Decision Making in Education. *Designing Sustainable Internet of Things Solutions for Smart Industries*, 27-50.

Çela, E., Fonkam, M. M., & Potluri, R. M. (2024). Risks of AI-assisted learning on student critical thinking: A case study of Albania. [IJRCM]. *International Journal of Risk and Contingency Management*, 12(1), 1–19. DOI: 10.4018/IJRCM.350185

Cerit, J., Dindarian, A., & Norel, N C. (2020, April 1). Women, AI, and the Power of Supporting Communities: A Digital Gender-Support Partnership. Elsevier BV, 1(1), 100009-100009. DOI: 10.1016/j.patter.2020.100009

Champney, R., Lackey, S. J., Stanney, K., & Quinn, S. (2015). Augmented reality training of military tasks: Reactions from subject matter experts. In *Virtual, Augmented and Mixed Reality: 7th International Conference, VAMR 2015, Held as Part of HCI International 2015, Los Angeles, CA, USA, August 2-7, 2015* [Springer International Publishing.]. *Proceedings*, 7, 251–262.

Chan, C. K. Y. (2023). A comprehensive AI policy education framework for university teaching and learning. [Online]. *International Journal of Educational Technology in Higher Education*, 20(1), 38. Advance online publication. DOI: 10.1186/s41239-023-00408-3

Chao, P. J., Hsu, T. H., Liu, T. P., & Cheng, Y. H. (2021). Knowledge of and competence in artificial intelligence: Perspectives of Vietnamese digital-native students. *IEEE Access : Practical Innovations, Open Solutions*, 9, 75751–75760. DOI: 10.1109/ACCESS.2021.3081749

Chao, R. Y. (2019). Propensity score matching in massive open online courses. *British Journal of Educational Technology*, 50(2), 652–668.

Chaudhry, M. A., & Kazim, E. (2021, July 7). Artificial Intelligence in Education (AIEd): A high-level academic and industry note 2021. *SSRN*, 2(1), 157–165. DOI: 10.2139/ssrn.3833583 PMID: 34790953

Cheng, L., Varshney, K. R., & Liu, H. (2021, August 28). Socially Responsible AI Algorithms: Issues, Purposes, and Challenges. *Journal of Artificial Intelligence Research*, 71, 1137–1181. DOI: 10.1613/jair.1.12814

Chen, L., Sun, L., & Han, J. (2023). A comparison study of human and machine-generated creativity. *Journal of Computing and Information Science in Engineering*, 23(5), 051012. Advance online publication. DOI: 10.1115/1.4062232

Chen, X., Zou, D., Cheng, G., & Xie, H. (2020). Detecting latent topics and trends in educational technologies over four decades using structural topic modeling: A retrospective of all volumes of Computers & Education. *Computers & Education*, 151, 103855. DOI: 10.1016/j.compedu.2020.103855

Chernov, A., Chernova, V A., & Komarova, T. (2020, January 1). The Usage of Artificial Intelligence in Strategic Decision Making in Terms of Fourth Industrial Revolution. DOI: 10.2991/aebmr.k.200201.005

Cheung, H., & Liu, S. (2016). Development of practical vocational training class making use of virtual reality-based simulation system and augmented reality technologies. *The 10th International Symposium on Advances in Technology Education*, 105-110.

Chiang, F.-K., Shang, X., & Qiao, L. (2022). Augmented reality in vocational training: A systematic review of research and applications. *Computers in Human Behavior*, 129, 107125. DOI: 10.1016/j.chb.2021.107125

Chmielewski, M., Sapiejewski, K., & Sobolewski, M. (2019). Application of augmented reality, mobile devices, and sensors for a combat entity quantitative assessment supporting decisions and situational awareness development. *Applied Sciences (Basel, Switzerland)*, 9(21), 4577. DOI: 10.3390/app9214577

Choi, S., & Park, J.-S. (2021). Development of augmented reality system for productivity enhancement in offshore plant construction. *Journal of Marine Science and Engineering*, 9(2), 209. DOI: 10.3390/jmse9020209

Choithani, T., Chowdhury, A., Patel, S., Patel, P., Patel, D., & Shah, M. (2022, September 2). A Comprehensive Study of Artificial Intelligence and Cybersecurity on Bitcoin, Crypto Currency and Banking System. Springer Science+Business Media, 11(1), 103-135. DOI: 10.1007/s40745-022-00433-5

Chookaew, S., Howimanporn, S., Sootkaneung, W., & Wongwatkit, C. (2017, July). Motivating pre-service teachers with augmented reality to developing instructional materials through project-based learning approach. In *2017 6th IIAI International Congress on Advanced Applied Informatics (IIAI-AAI)* (pp. 780-784). IEEE. DOI: 10.1109/IIAI-AAI.2017.106

Chowdhury, S., & Nath, A. (2021, December 15). Trends In Natural Language Processing: Scope And Challenges., 393-401. DOI: 10.32628/CSEIT217698

Christensen, C. M., Horn, M. B., & Johnson, C. W. (2011). *Disrupting class: How disruptive innovation will change the way the world learns*. McGraw-Hill.

Christiansen, B., & Even, A. M. (Eds.). (2024). *Advancing Student Employability Through Higher Education*. IGI Global. DOI: 10.4018/979-8-3693-0517-1

Clark, R. C., & Mayer, R. E. (2016). *E-learning and the science of instruction: Proven guidelines for consumers and designers of multimedia learning*. John Wiley & Sons. DOI: 10.1002/9781119239086

Cohen, E. B., & Gordon, I. K. (2022). First, do no harm. Ethical and legal issues of artificial intelligence and machine learning in veterinary radiology and radiation oncology. Veterinary Radiology &amp [Online]. *Ultrasound*, 63(S1), 840–850. Advance online publication. DOI: 10.1111/vru.13171 PMID: 36514231

Copsey, A. (2024). An Examination of Police Response to Individuals Suffering with Mental Illness.

Corsini, A. (2022). *Welcome to European Atherosclerosis Journal, a new Open Access Journal: European Atherosclerosis Journal, a new Open Access Journal*. European Atherosclerosis Journal. [Online], DOI: 10.56095/eaj.v1i1.6

Craig, A. B. (2013). *Understanding augmented reality: Concepts and applications*. Morgan Kaufmann.

Crigger, E., Reinbold, K., Hanson, C., Kao, A., Blake, K., & Irons, M. (2022, January 12). Trustworthy Augmented Intelligence in Health Care. Springer Science+Business Media, 46(2). DOI: 10.1007/s10916-021-01790-z

Cruz-Neira, C., Sandin, D. J., & DeFanti, T. A. (1993). A 'room' with a 'view'. *IEEE Spectrum*, 30(10), 30–33. DOI: 10.1109/6.237582

Cruz-Neira, C., Sandin, D. J., DeFanti, T. A., Kenyon, R. V., & Hart, J. C. (1992). The CAVE: Audio visual experience automatic virtual environment. *Communications of the ACM*, 35(6), 64–73. DOI: 10.1145/129888.129892

Cuendet, S., Bonnard, Q., Do-Lenh, S., & Dillenbourg, P. (2013). Designing augmented reality for the classroom. *Computers & Education*, 68, 557–569. DOI: 10.1016/j.compedu.2013.02.015

Currie, G., Hespel, A., & Carstens, A. (2023). Australian perspectives on artificial intelligence in veterinary practice. Veterinary Radiology &amp [Online]. *Ultrasound*, 64(3), 473–483. Advance online publication. DOI: 10.1111/vru.13234 PMID: 37022301

Dabbagh, N., Benson, A. D., & Denham, A. (2015). Instructional strategies and models for e-learning. Handbook of Research on Educational Communications and Technology, 281-294.

Dai, Y., Chai, C. S., Lin, P., Jong, M. S., Guo, Y., & Jian-jun, Q. (2020, August 14). Promoting Students' Well-Being by Developing Their Readiness for the Artificial Intelligence Age. *Sustainability (Basel)*, 12(16), 6597–6597. DOI: 10.3390/su12166597

Dang, J., & Liu, L. (2022). Implicit theories of the human mind predict competitive and cooperative responses to AI robots. *Computers in Human Behavior*, 134, 107300. DOI: 10.1016/j.chb.2022.107300

Das, S., & Mitra, A. (2024). Enhancing Logic and Problem-Solving Skills in the Digital Age. In *Revolutionizing Curricula Through Computational Thinking, Logic, and Problem Solving* (pp. 40-59). IGI Global. DOI: 10.4018/979-8-3693-1974-1.ch003

Dede, C., & Richards, J. (2012). *Digital teaching platforms: Customizing classroom learning for each student*. Teachers College Press.

Delello, J. A. (2014). Insights from pre-service teachers using science-based augmented reality. *Journal of Computers in Education*, 1(4), 295–311. DOI: 10.1007/s40692-014-0021-y

Denny, P., Becker, B. A., Leinonen, J., & Prather, J. (2023) Chat Overflow: Artificially Intelligent Models for Computing Education - renAIssance or apocAIypse? *Proceedings of the 2023 Conference on Innovation and Technology in Computer Science Education* V. 1. [Online]. Available: DOI: 10.1145/3587102.3588773

Dey, S., & Srivastava, A. (2022). Reimagining Technical and Vocational Education and Training in India: Prospects and Challenges. *University News*, 60(20), 3–8.

Díaz-Rodríguez, N., Ser, J D., Coeckelbergh, M., Prado, M L D., Herrera-Viedma, E., & Herrera, F. (2023, June 24). Connecting the dots in trustworthy Artificial Intelligence: From AI principles, ethics, and key requirements to responsible AI systems and regulation. Elsevier BV, 99, 101896-101896. DOI: 10.1016/j.inffus.2023.101896

Dieterle, E., Dede, C., & Walker, M E. (2022, September 27). The cyclical ethical effects of using artificial intelligence in education. Springer Nature. DOI: 10.1007/s00146-022-01497-w

Digital, H. (2024). The rise of AI in digital marketing: Challenges and opportunities for marketers. https://holinex.com/the-rise-of-ai-in-digital-marketing-challenges-and-opportunities-for-marketers/

Ditta, A., & Aslam, M. U. (2024). *Education in the AI Age: Navigating Challenges of Generative AI Integration*. https://www.researchgate.net/publication/380364982

Donlon, E., & Tiernan, P. (2023). Chatbots and Citations: An experiment in academic writing with Generative AI. *Irish Journal of Technology Enhanced Learning*, 7(2), 75–87. DOI: 10.22554/ijtel.v7i2.125

Doskeyeva, G. Z., Kuzembekova, R. A., Umirzakov, S. Y., Beimisheva, A. S., & Salimbayeva, R. A. (2024). How can dual education in technical and vocational institutions improve students' academic achievements and mitigate youth unemployment in Kazakhstan? *Community College Journal of Research and Practice*, •••, 1–16. DOI: 10.1080/10668926.2023.2295472

Dunleavy, M., Dede, C., & Mitchell, R. (2009). Affordances and limitations of immersive participatory augmented reality simulations for teaching and learning. *Journal of Science Education and Technology*, 18(1), 7–22. DOI: 10.1007/s10956-008-9119-1

Dünser, A., Grasset, R., & Billinghurst, M. (2008). *A survey of evaluation techniques used in augmented reality studies. Human Interface Technology Laboratory New Zealand (HIT Lab NZ)*. University of Canterbury.

Dziuban, C., Graham, C. R., Moskal, P. D., Norberg, A., & Sicilia, N. (2018). Blended learning: The new normal and emerging technologies. *International Journal of Educational Technology in Higher Education*, 15(1), 3. DOI: 10.1186/s41239-017-0087-5

Eguchi, A., Okada, H., & Muto, Y. (2021, June 1). Contextualizing AI Education for K-12 Students to Enhance Their Learning of AI Literacy Through Culturally Responsive Approaches. Springer Science+Business Media, 35(2), 153-161. DOI: 10.1007/s13218-021-00737-3

Eidgenössische Hochschule für Berufsbildung EHB. (May 17, 2024a). *AI in VET: 4/12 How does AI impact vocational and professional training?* YouTube. https://www.youtube.com/watch?v=uv09fKJMHMk

Eidgenössische Hochschule für Berufsbildung EHB. (May 17, 2024b). YouTube. *AI in VET: 12/12 How do you see the future of AI in vocational education and training?*https://www.youtube.com/watch?v=R4pEl5KlprU

Elder, A., Ring, C., Heitmiller, K., Gabriel, Z., & Saedi, N. (2020, November 5). The role of artificial intelligence in cosmetic dermatology—Current, upcoming, and future trends. Wiley, 20(1), 48-52. DOI: 10.1111/jocd.13797

Ellenkamp, J. J., Brouwers, E. P., Embregts, P. J., Joosen, M. C., & van Weeghel, J. (2016). Work environment-related factors in obtaining and maintaining work in a competitive employment setting for employees with intellectual disabilities: A systematic review. *Journal of Occupational Rehabilitation*, 26(1), 56–69. DOI: 10.1007/s10926-015-9586-1 PMID: 26112400

Elliott, K., Price, R M., Shaw, P., Spiliotopoulos, T., Ng, M., Coopamootoo, K., & Moorsel, A V. (2021, June 1). Towards an Equitable Digital Society: Artificial Intelligence (AI) and Corporate Digital Responsibility (CDR). Springer Science+Business Media, 58(3), 179-188. DOI: 10.1007/s12115-021-00594-8

Emmert-Streib, F., Yli-Harja, O., & Dehmer, M. (2020, December 23). Artificial Intelligence: A Clarification of Misconceptions, Myths and Desired Status. *Frontiers of Medicine*, 3, 524339. Advance online publication. DOI: 10.3389/frai.2020.524339 PMID: 33733197

European Commission. (2020). On Artificial Intelligence—A European approach to excellence and trust [White Paper], https://commission.europa.eu/system/files/2020-02/commission-white-paper-artificial-intelligence-feb2020_en.pdf

Faishal, M., Mathew, S., Neikha, K., Pusa, K., & Zhimomi, T. (2023, June 16). The future of work: AI, automation, and the changing dynamics of developed economies. *GSC Online Press*, 18(3), 620–629. DOI: 10.30574/wjarr.2023.18.3.1086

Farra, S. L., Miller, E. T., & Timm, N. (2019). Comparison of training methods for mass casualty triage using virtual reality. *Disaster Medicine and Public Health Preparedness*, 13(2), 301–308. DOI: 10.1017/dmp.2018.58 PMID: 30293544

Fazil, A. W., Hakimi, M., Shahidzay, A. K., & Hasas, A. (2024). Exploring the Broad Impact of AI Technologies on Student Engagement and Academic Performance in University Settings in Afghanistan. *RIGGS: Journal of Artificial Intelligence and Digital Business*, 2(2), 56–63. DOI: 10.31004/riggs.v2i2.268

Feeney, B., Zuccarini, M., Singh, T., Aldewereld, H., Marrone, S., & Quille, K. (2022) Developing a Human Centred AI Masters. *Proceedings of the 27th ACM Conference on on Innovation and Technology in Computer Science Education* Vol. 2. [Online]. Available: DOI: 10.1145/3502717.3532120

Fehling, C. D., Müller, A., & Aehnelt, M. (2016). Enhancing vocational training with augmented reality. In *Proceedings of the 16th International Conference on Knowledge Technologies and Data-Driven Business*. ACM Press.

Feiner, S., MacIntyre, B., Höllerer, T., & Webster, A. (1997). A touring machine: Prototyping 3D mobile augmented reality systems for exploring the urban environment. *Personal Technologies*, 1(4), 208–217. DOI: 10.1007/BF01682023

Ferejohn, J. (2002). Symposium on explanations and social ontology 1: Rational choice theory and social explanation. *Economics and Philosophy*, 18(2), 211–234. DOI: 10.1017/S026626710200202X

Fernández, P. (2016, July 4). "Through the looking glass: envisioning new library technologies" how artificial intelligence will impact libraries. Emerald Publishing Limited, 33(5), 5-8. DOI: 10.1108/LHTN-05-2016-0024

Fikri, M A., Abdullah, S C., & Ramli, M H M. (2014, January 1). Arm Exoskeleton for Rehabilitation Following Stroke by Learning Algorithm Prediction. Elsevier BV, 42, 357-364. DOI: 10.1016/j.procs.2014.11.074

Floridi, L., & Taddeo, M. (2016, November 15). What is data ethics? *Philosophical Transactions. Series A, Mathematical, Physical, and Engineering Sciences*, 374(2083), 20160360–20160360. DOI: 10.1098/rsta.2016.0360 PMID: 28336805

Ford, S., & Minshall, T. (2019). Where and how 3D printing is used in teaching and education. DOI: 10.17863/CAM.35360

Forest, D. D. (2021). Training the next generation of operators: AFPM immersive learning. *Process Safety Progress*, 40(4), 219–223. DOI: 10.1002/prs.12246

Fragomeni, G., Lackey, S. J., Champney, R., Salcedo, J. N., & Serge, S. (2015). Training effectiveness evaluation: Call for fire trainer–augmented virtuality (CFFT-AV). In *Virtual, Augmented and Mixed Reality: 7th International Conference, VAMR 2015, Held as Part of HCI International 2015, Los Angeles, CA, USA, August 2-7, 2015* [Springer International Publishing.]. *Proceedings*, 7, 263–272.

Fraiwan, M., & Khasawneh, N. (2023). A review of ChatGPT applications in education, marketing, software engineering, and healthcare: Benefits, drawbacks, and research directions. *arXiv preprint arXiv:2305.00237.*

Fraser, G., & Fisher, S. S. (1998). Intelligent virtual worlds continue to develop. *Computer Graphics*, 32(3), 15–19. DOI: 10.1145/281278.281285

Frehywot, S., & Vovides, Y. (2023). An equitable and sustainable community of practice framework to address the use of artificial intelligence for global health workforce training. [Online]. *Human Resources for Health*, 21(1), 45. Advance online publication. DOI: 10.1186/s12960-023-00833-5 PMID: 37312214

Freina, L., & Ott, M. (2015, April). A literature review on immersive virtual reality in education: state of the art and perspectives. In *The International Scientific Conference E-learning and Software for Education* (Vol. 1, No. 133, pp. 10-1007). DOI: 10.12753/2066-026X-15-020

Furió, D., González-Gancedo, S., Juan, M. C., Seguí, I., & Rando, N. (2013). Evaluation of learning outcomes using an educational iPhone game vs. traditional game. *Computers & Education*, 64, 1–23. DOI: 10.1016/j.compedu.2012.12.001

Gaba, D. M. (2004). The future vision of simulation in health care. *BMJ Quality & Safety*, 13(suppl 1), i2–i10. DOI: 10.1136/qshc.2004.009878 PMID: 15465951

Ganga, X. (2021, June). Educational Artificial Intelligence (EAI) Connotation, Key Technology and Application Trend-Interpretation and analysis of the two reports entitled "Preparing for the Future of Artificial Intelligence" and "The National Artificial Intelligence Research and Development Strategic Plan". In *2021 International Conference on Intelligent Computing, Automation and Applications (ICAA)* (pp. 219-223). IEEE. DOI: 10.1109/ICAA53760.2021.00046

Garden, T. (2023). The dawn of AI in digital marketing: Opportunities and challenges. Digital Skills Academy. https://blog.talentgarden.com/en/blog/marketing/the-dawn-of-ai-in-digital-marketing-opportunities-and-challenges

Garzón, J., & Acevedo, J. (2019). Meta-analysis of the impact of augmented reality on students' learning gains. *Educational Research Review*, 27, 244–260. DOI: 10.1016/j.edurev.2019.04.001

Gašević, D., Dawson, S., & Siemens, G. (2015). Let's not forget: Learning analytics are about learning. *TechTrends*, 59(1), 64–71. DOI: 10.1007/s11528-014-0822-x

Gaskins, N R. (2022, September 19). Interrogating Algorithmic Bias: From Speculative Fiction to Liberatory Design. Springer Science+Business Media, 67(3), 417-425. DOI: 10.1007/s11528-022-00783-0

Gasser, U., & Almeida, V. (2017, November 1). A Layered Model for AI Governance. *IEEE Internet Computing*, 21(6), 58–62. DOI: 10.1109/MIC.2017.4180835

Gaur, A. S., Sharan, H. O., & Kumar, R. (2024). AI in Education: Ethical Challenges and Opportunities. *The Ethical Frontier of AI and Data Analysis*, IGI Global, 39-54.

Gaya, H., & Smith, E. E. (2016). Developing a qualitative single case study in the strategic management realm: An appropriate research design. *International Journal of Business Management and Economic Research*, 7(2), 529–538.

Gehlhaus, D., Koslosky, L., Goode, K., & Perkins, C. (2021, October 1). U.S. AI Workforce: Policy Recommendations. DOI: 10.51593/20200087

Ghosh, L., & Ravichandran, R. (2024). Emerging technologies in vocational education and training. *Journal of Digital Learning and Education*, 4(1), 41–49. DOI: 10.52562/jdle.v4i1.975

Gibbons, E. (2021, March 1). Toward a More Equal World: The Human Rights Approach to Extending the Benefits of Artificial Intelligence. *IEEE Technology and Society Magazine*, 40(1), 25–30. DOI: 10.1109/MTS.2021.3056295

Gibson, D., Kovanovic, V., Ifenthaler, D., Dexter, S., & Feng, S. (2023). Learning theories for artificial intelligence promoting learning processes. [Online]. *British Journal of Educational Technology*, 54(5), 1125–1146. Advance online publication. DOI: 10.1111/bjet.13341

Gocen, A., & Aydemir, F. (2020). Artificial intelligence in education and schools. *Research on Education and Media*, 12(1), 13–21. DOI: 10.2478/rem-2020-0003

Goertz, L., Hagenhofer, T., & Fehling, C. D. (2021). *Planning the use of augmented and virtual reality for vocational education and training: A practical guide.*

Gonçalves, Y. A., & Vilas Boas. (2012). Overview of Virtual Reality technologies. *Semantic Scholar*. https://api.semanticscholar.org/CorpusID:8120179

Government of Kazakhstan. (2023). Education in Kazakhstan. https://www.gov.kz/article/128171?lang=en

Grasset, R., Dünser, A., & Billinghurst, M. (2008, December). Edutainment with a mixed reality book: a visually augmented illustrative childrens' book. In *Proceedings of the 2008 international conference on advances in computer entertainment technology* (pp. 292-295). DOI: 10.1145/1501750.1501819

Grassini, S. (2023). Shaping the future of education: Exploring the potential and consequences of AI and ChatGPT in educational settings. *Education Sciences*, 13(7), 692. DOI: 10.3390/educsci13070692

Gratsiouni, D., Koutsouba, M., Venetsanou, F., & Tyrovola, V. (2016). Learning and digital environment of dance–the case of Greek traditional dance in YouTube. *European Journal of Open, Distance and E-learning*, 19(2), 80–95. DOI: 10.1515/eurodl-2016-0009

Grieve, R., Woodley, J., Hunt, S E., & McKay, A B. (2021, July 15). Student fears of oral presentations and public speaking in higher education: a qualitative survey. Routledge, 45(9), 1281-1293. DOI: 10.1080/0309877X.2021.1948509

Grollmann, P. (2008). The quality of vocational teachers: Teacher education, institutional roles and professional reality. *European Educational Research Journal*, 7(4), 535–547. DOI: 10.2304/eerj.2008.7.4.535

Grubb, W. N., & Ryan, P. (1999). *The roles of evaluation for vocational education and training: Plain talk on the field of dreams*. International Labour Organization.

Guest, G., MacQueen, K. M., & Namey, E. E. (2011). *Applied thematic analysis*. Sage Publications.

Guggemos, J., & Seufert, S. (2021). Teaching with and teaching about technology–Evidence for professional development of in-service teachers. *Computers in Human Behavior*, 115, 106613. Advance online publication. DOI: 10.1016/j.chb.2020.106613

Guleria, P., & Sood, M. (2022). Explainable AI and machine learning: Performance evaluation and explainability of classifiers on educational data mining inspired career counseling. [Online]. *Education and Information Technologies*. Advance online publication. DOI: 10.1007/s10639-022-11221-2 PMID: 35875826

Guri-Rosenblit, S. (2018). E-Teaching in Higher Education: An Essential Prerequisite for E-Learning. *Journal of New Approaches in Educational Research*, 7(2), 93–97. DOI: 10.7821/naer.2018.7.298

GurriarÃ¡n, R. (2007) Alejandro Otero. Ãlbum de Galicia. [Online]. Available: .DOI: 10.17075/adg.2007.22182

Guzman, A L. (2018, August 9). Voices in and of the machine: Source orientation toward mobile virtual assistants. Elsevier BV, 90, 343-350. DOI: 10.1016/j.chb.2018.08.009

Hager, P., & Gonczi, A. (1996). What is competence? *Medical Teacher*, 18(1), 15–18. DOI: 10.3109/01421599609040255

Haldorai, A., Murugan, S., & Ramu, A. (2020, February 29). Evolution, challenges, and application of intelligent ICT education: An overview. Wiley, 29(3), 562-571. DOI: 10.1002/cae.22217

Hall, P. A., & Taylor, R. C. (1996). Political science and the three new institutionalisms. *Political Studies*, 44(5), 936–957. DOI: 10.1111/j.1467-9248.1996.tb00343.x

Haugaard Jacobsen, C. (2007). A qualitative single case study of parallel processes. *Counselling & Psychotherapy Research*, 7(1), 26–33. DOI: 10.1080/14733140601140410

Herkner, V., & Pahl, J. P. (2020). Handlungsorientierung in der Berufsbildung. *Handbuch Berufsbildung*, 189-203. https://doi.org/DOI: 10.1007/978-3-658-19312-6_17

High-Level Expert Group on Artificial Intelligence. (2019). A definition of AI: Main capabilities and disciplines. European Commission. https://www.aepd.es/sites/default/files/2019-12/ai-definition.pdf

Holmes, L. (2016). *Advanced introduction to organised crime*. Edward Elgar Publishing.

Holmes, W., Porayska-Pomsta, K., Holstein, K., Sutherland, E., Baker, T., Shum, S. B., Santos, O. C., Rodrigo, M. T., Cukurova, M., Bittencourt, I. I., & Koedinger, K. R. (2022). Ethics of AI in education: Towards a community-wide framework. *International Journal of Artificial Intelligence in Education*, 32(3), 1–23. DOI: 10.1007/s40593-021-00239-1

Hoy, M B. (2018, January 2). Alexa, Siri, Cortana, and More: An Introduction to Voice Assistants. Taylor & Francis, 37(1), 81-88. DOI: 10.1080/02763869.2018.1404391

Hrastinski, S. (2019). What do we mean by blended learning? *TechTrends*, 63(5), 564–569. DOI: 10.1007/s11528-019-00375-5

Huang, C.-Y., & Shih, C.-H. (2025). *Interviewing vulnerable witnesses and suspects in criminal justice proceedings: Evidence-based development in Taiwan Routledge International Handbook of Investigative Interviewing and Interrogation*. Routledge.

Huang, R. H., Liu, D. J., Tlili, A., Yang, J. F., & Wang, H. H. (2020). *Handbook on facilitating flexible learning during educational disruption: The Chinese experience in maintaining undisrupted learning in COVID-19 outbreak*. Smart Learning Institute of Beijing Normal University.

Hughes, C., Robert, L., Frady, K., & Arroyos, A. (2019, July 10). Managing Technology and Middle- and Low-skilled Employees. DOI: 10.1108/9781789730777

Huttar, C. M., & BrintzenhofeSzoc, K. (2020). Virtual reality and computer simulation in social work education: A systematic review. *Journal of Social Work Education*, 56(1), 131–141. DOI: 10.1080/10437797.2019.1648221

Ifenthaler, D., & Schumacher, C. (2023). Reciprocal issues of artificial and human intelligence inÂ education. [Online]. *Journal of Research on Technology in Education*, 55(1), 1–6. Advance online publication. DOI: 10.1080/15391523.2022.2154511

Ifraheem, S., Rasheed, M., & Siddiqui, A. (2024). Transforming education through artificial intelligence: Personalization, engagement and predictive analytics. *Journal of Asian Development Studies*, 13(2), 250–266. DOI: 10.62345/jads.2024.13.2.22

Ioni ă, S. (2017, October 1). Autonomous vehicles: From paradigms to technology. *IOP Conference Series. Materials Science and Engineering*, 252, 012098–012098. DOI: 10.1088/1757-899X/252/1/012098

Iqbal, S., Ahmad, S., Akkour, K., Wafa, A. N. A., AlMutairi, H. M., & Aldhufairi, A. M. (2021). Review article: Impact of Artificial Intelligence in Medical Education. [Online]. *MedEdPublish*, 10(1). Advance online publication. DOI: 10.15694/mep.2021.000041.1

Jackaria, P. M., Hajan, B. H., Mastul, A. R. H., & Sali, F. Z. (2024). Generation AI in a Reimagined Classroom: Challenges, Opportunities and Implications to Education. *Exploring Youth Studies in the Age of AI*, IGI Global, 174-185.

Jagannathan, S., Ra, S., & Maclean, R. (2019). Dominant recent trends impacting on jobs and labor markets - an overview. *International Journal of Training Research*, 17(sup1), 1–11. DOI: 10.1080/14480220.2019.1641292

Jaimovich, N., Saporta-Eksten, I., Siu, H., & Yedid-Levi, Y. (2021, July 8). The macroeconomics of automation: Data, theory, and policy analysis. Elsevier BV, 122, 1-16. DOI: 10.1016/j.jmoneco.2021.06.004

Jiang, R., Chen, Y., Peng, Y., Xie, S., & Qu, D. (2024). Opportunities and challenges of AI in vocational education. *International Journal of Learning and Teaching*, 10(5), 590–596. DOI: 10.18178/ijlt.10.5.590-596

Jing, X., Zhu, R., Lin, J., Yu, B., & Lu, M. (2022). Education sustainability for intelligent manufacturing in the context of the new generation of artificial intelligence. *Sustainability (Basel)*, 14(21), 14148. Advance online publication. DOI: 10.3390/su142114148

Johnson, G M. (2020, June 20). Algorithmic bias: on the implicit biases of social technology. Springer Science+Business Media, 198(10), 9941-9961. DOI: 10.1007/s11229-020-02696-y

Joksimović, S., Poquet, O., Kovanović, V., Dowell, N., Mills, C., Gašević, D., Dawson, S., Graesser, A. C., & Brooks, C. (2018). How do we model learning at scale? A systematic review of research on MOOCs. *Review of Educational Research*, 88(1), 43–86. DOI: 10.3102/0034654317740335

Joseph, J. (2024). AI and digital marketing: Most common opportunities and challenges. https://jeromejoseph.com/ai-digital-marketing-common-opportunities-challenges/

Joslyn, S., & Alexander, K. (2022). Evaluating artificial intelligence algorithms for use in veterinary radiology. Veterinary Radiology &amp [Online]. *Ultrasound*, 63(S1), 871–879. Advance online publication. DOI: 10.1111/vru.13159 PMID: 36514228

Jumasseitova, A. K., Potluri, R. M., & Smolyakova, E. (2024). Strategic role of alumni associations of Kazakhstan higher educational institutions in achieving sustainable development goals. [IJABIM]. *International Journal of Asian Business and Information Management*, 15(1), 1–21. DOI: 10.4018/IJABIM.351246

Kablitz, D., Conrad, M., & Schumann, S. (2023). Immersive VR-based instruction in vocational schools: Effects on domain-specific knowledge and wellbeing of retail trainees. *Empirical Research in Vocational Education and Training*, 15(9), 9. Advance online publication. DOI: 10.1186/s40461-023-00148-8

Kahu, E. R., & Nelson, K. (2018). Student engagement in the educational interface: Understanding the mechanisms of student success. *Higher Education Research & Development*, 37(1), 58–71. DOI: 10.1080/07294360.2017.1344197

Kamalov, F., Calonge, D. S., & Gurrib, I. (2023, August 16). New Era of Artificial Intelligence in Education: Towards a Sustainable Multifaceted Revolution. *Sustainability (Basel)*, 15(16), 12451–12451. DOI: 10.3390/su151612451

Kasneci, E., Seßler, K., Küchemann, S., Bannert, M., Dementieva, D., Fischer, F., & Kasneci, G. (2023). ChatGPT for good? On opportunities and challenges of large language models for education. *Learning and Individual Differences*, 103, 102274. DOI: 10.1016/j.lindif.2023.102274

Kaufmann, M. (2024). *AI in policing and law enforcement Handbook on Public Policy and Artificial Intelligence*. Edward Elgar Publishing.

Kayyali, M. (2024). Future possibilities and challenges of AI in education. In *Transforming education with generative AI: Prompt engineering and synthetic content creation* (pp. 118–137). IGI Global. DOI: 10.4018/979-8-3693-1351-0.ch006

Kearney, M., Schuck, S., Burden, K., & Aubusson, P. (2012). Viewing mobile learning from a pedagogical perspective. *Research in Learning Technology*, 20(1), 20. DOI: 10.3402/rlt.v20i0.14406

Keaveney, S. G., & Dowling, D. P. (2018). Application of additive manufacturing in design & manufacturing engineering education. In 2018 2nd International Symposium on Small-Scale Intelligent Manufacturing Systems (SIMS) (pp. 1–6). DOI: 10.1109/SIMS.2018.8355289

Keller, J. M. (2010). *Motivational design for learning and performance*. Springer. DOI: 10.1007/978-1-4419-1250-3

Khan, T., Johnston, K., & Ophoff, J. (2019). The impact of an augmented reality application on learning motivation of students. *Advances in Human-Computer Interaction*, 2019(1), 7208494. DOI: 10.1155/2019/7208494

Khosravi, H., Shum, S. B., Chen, G., Conati, C., Tsai, Y.-S., Kay, J., Knight, S., Martinez-Maldonado, R., Sadiq, S., & Gašević, D. (2022). Explainable Artificial Intelligence in education. Computers and Education [Online]. *Artificial Intelligence*, 3, 100074. Advance online publication. DOI: 10.1016/j.caeai.2022.100074

Khosrow-Pour, D. B. A. (Ed.). (2018). *Advanced Methodologies and Technologies in Artificial Intelligence, Computer Simulation, and Human-Computer Interaction*. IGI Global.

Kim, J., Lee, H., & Cho, Y. H. (2022). Learning design to support student-AI collaboration: Perspectives of leading teachers for AI in education. *Education and Information Technologies*, 27(5), 1–36. DOI: 10.1007/s10639-021-10831-6

Kim, S. (2022). Working with robots: Human resource development considerations in human-robot interaction. *Human Resource Development Review*, 21(1), 48–74. DOI: 10.1177/15344843211068810

Kim, S., Jang, Y., Kim, W., Choi, S., Jung, H., Kim, S., & Kim, H. (2021, May 18). Why and What to Teach: AI Curriculum for Elementary School. *Association for the Advancement of Artificial Intelligence*, 35(17), 15569–15576. DOI: 10.1609/aaai.v35i17.17833

Kizilcec, R F. (2023, June 9). To Advance AI Use in Education, Focus on Understanding Educators. Springer Science+Business Media, 34(1), 12-19. DOI: 10.1007/s40593-023-00351-4

Kizilcec, R. F., Reich, J., Yeomans, M., Dann, C., Brunskill, E., Lopez, G., Turkay, S., Williams, J. J., & Tingley, D. (2020). Scaling up behavioral science interventions in online education. *Proceedings of the National Academy of Sciences of the United States of America*, 117(26), 14900–14905. DOI: 10.1073/pnas.1921417117 PMID: 32541050

Klopfer, E., & Squire, K. (2008). Environmental Detectives—The development of an augmented reality platform for environmental simulations. *Educational Technology Research and Development*, 56(2), 203–228. DOI: 10.1007/s11423-007-9037-6

Knight, J. (1992). *Institutions and Social Conflict*. Cambridge University Press. DOI: 10.1017/CBO9780511528170

Knight, J., & Sened, I. (1998). *Explaining social institutions*. University of Michigan Press.

Koehler, M. J., Mishra, P., & Cain, W. (2013). What is technological pedagogical content knowledge (TPACK)? *Journal of Education*, 193(3), 13–19. DOI: 10.1177/002205741319300303

Kong, S. C., Cheung, W. M. Y., & Zhang, G. (2021). Evaluation of an artificial intelligence literacy course for university students with diverse study backgrounds. *Computers and Education: Artificial Intelligence, 2*, Article 100026.

Kot, S. O., & Nykyporets, S. S. (2024). *Utilization of artificial intelligence in enhancing English language proficiency in tertiary education. Science and Education in the Third Millennium: Information Technology*. Education, Law, Psychology, Social Sphere, Management.

Kotsifakos, D., Adamopoulos, P., & Douligeris, C. (2016, September). Design and development of a learning management system for vocational education. In *Proceedings of the SouthEast European Design Automation, Computer Engineering,Computer Networks and Social Media Conference* (pp. 110-117). https://doi.org/DOI: 10.1145/2984393.2984413

Kourouthanassis, P. E., Boletsis, C., & Lekakos, G. (2015). Demystifying the design of mobile augmented reality applications. *Multimedia Tools and Applications*, 74(3), 1045–1066. DOI: 10.1007/s11042-013-1710-7

Kühl, N., Schemmer, M., Goutier, M., & Satzger, G. (2022, November 9). Artificial intelligence and machine learning. Springer Science+Business Media, 32(4), 2235-2244. DOI: 10.1007/s12525-022-00598-0

Kuhlen, T. W., & Hentschel, B. (2014). Quo vadis CAVE: Does immersive visualization still matter? *IEEE Computer Graphics and Applications*, 34(5), 14–21. DOI: 10.1109/MCG.2014.97 PMID: 25248196

Kumar, R., Sexena, A., & Gehlot, A. (2023) Artificial Intelligence in Smart Education and Futuristic Challenges. 2023 International Conference on Disruptive Technologies (ICDT). [Online]. Available: http://dx.doi.org/DOI: 10.1109/ICDT57929.2023.10151129

Kwiatek, C., Sharif, M., Li, S., Haas, C., & Walbridge, S. (2019). Impact of augmented reality and spatial cognition on assembly in construction. *Automation in Construction*, 108, 102935. DOI: 10.1016/j.autcon.2019.102935

Kwiatek, G., Saarno, T., Ader, T., Bluemle, F., Bohnhoff, M., Chendorain, M., Dresen, G., Heikkinen, P., Kukkonen, I., Leary, P., Leonhardt, M., Malin, P., Martínez-Garzón, P., Passmore, K., Passmore, P., Valenzuela, S., & Wollin, C. (2019). Controlling fluid-induced seismicity during a 6.1-km-deep geothermal stimulation in Finland. *Science Advances*, 5(5), eaav7224. Advance online publication. DOI: 10.1126/sciadv.aav7224 PMID: 31049397

Lai, Y.-L., Luo, F., Kang, C.-C., & Lo, T.-Y. (2024). Exploring Southeast Asian immigrants' attitudes toward the police in Taiwan. *Policing*, 47(2), 199–214. DOI: 10.1108/PIJPSM-12-2022-0150

Laurillard, D. (2013). *Rethinking university teaching: A conversational framework for the effective use of learning technologies*. Routledge. DOI: 10.4324/9781315012940

Lavrentieva, O. O., Arkhypov, I. O., Kuchma, O. I., & Uchitel, A. D. (2020). Use of simulators together with virtual and augmented reality in the system of welders' vocational training: past, present, and future. In *Augmented reality in education: proceedings of the 2nd international workshop (AREdu 2019), Kryvyi Rih, Ukraine, March 22, 2019* (No. 2547, pp. 201-216). CEUR Workshop Proceedings.

Lee, I., & Perret, B. (2022, June 28). Preparing High School Teachers to Integrate AI Methods into STEM Classrooms. *Association for the Advancement of Artificial Intelligence*, 36(11), 12783–12791. DOI: 10.1609/aaai.v36i11.21557

Lester, S., & Costley, C. (2010). Work-based Learning at Higher Education Level: Value, Practice and Critique. *Studies in Higher Education*, 35(5), 561–575. DOI: 10.1080/03075070903216635

Levi, M. (1997). *A Model, A Method, and a Map: Rational Choice in Comparative and Historical Analysis. Comparative Politics: Rationality, Culture, and Structure/ Cambridge*. Cambridge Univ. Press.

Li, T., Song, W. N., & Zhou, J. H. (2021, May). Research on Artificial Intelligence Industrial Big Data Platform for Industrial Internet Applications. In *2021 IEEE 4th International Conference on Electronics Technology (ICET)* (pp. 955-959). IEEE. DOI: 10.1109/ICET51757.2021.9450991

Li, M. D., & Little, B. P. (2023). Appropriate Reliance on Artificial Intelligence in Radiology Education. [Online]. *Journal of the American College of Radiology*, 20(11), 1126–1130. Advance online publication. DOI: 10.1016/j.jacr.2023.04.019 PMID: 37392983

Lim, S. C. J., & Lee, M. F. (2024). Rethinking education in the era of artificial intelligence (AI): Towards future workforce competitiveness and business success. In *Emerging Technologies in Business: Innovation Strategies for Competitive Advantage* (pp. 151–166). Springer Nature Singapore. DOI: 10.1007/978-981-97-2211-2_7

Lim, T., Gottipati, S., & Cheong, M. L. F. (2023). Ethical considerations for artificial intelligence in educational assessments. In Keengwe, J. (Ed.), (pp. 32–79). Advances in educational technologies and instructional design. IGI Global., DOI: 10.4018/979-8-3693-0205-7.ch003

Lin, L. S., Aslett, D., Mekonnen, G., & Zecevic, M. (2024a). The dangers of voice cloning and how to combat it.

Lin, L. S., Aslett, D., Mekonnen, G., & Zecevic, M. (2024b). The UN Cybercrime Convention: What it Means for Policing and Community Safety in Australia.

Lin, K.-h., Sidebottom, A., & Wortley, R. (2023). Police education and democratic policing in Taiwan: A longitudinal quasi-experimental study of the effects of selection and police socialisation on human rights, moral reasoning and prejudice. *Journal of Experimental Criminology*, •••, 1–29.

Lin, K., Sidebottom, A., & Wortley, R. (2022). Evidence-based policing and police receptivity to research: Evidence from Taiwan. *Policing*, 45(5), 860–880. DOI: 10.1108/PIJPSM-04-2022-0050

Lipson, J. I. (1984). In Voc (Ed.), *Educational technology*. Information Series 268 https://eric.ed.gov/?id=ED240385

Liu, K., Wei, Z., Zhang, C., Shang, Y., Teodorescu, R., & Han, Q.-L. (2022). Towards long lifetime battery: AI-based manufacturing and management. *IEEE/CAA Journal of Automatica Sinica, 9*(7), 1139-1165.

Liu, M. (1999). Review and Strategies for my country's Police Education System (In Chinese:).

Liu, P., Yuan, W., Fu, J., Jiang, Z., Hayashi, H., & Neubig, G. (2023). Pre-train, prompt, and predict: A systematic survey of prompting methods in natural language processing. *ACM Computing Surveys*, 55(9), 1–35. DOI: 10.1145/3560815

Liu, Y. (2022, January 1). Artificial Intelligence and Its Application in Educational Industry. *Artificial Intelligence and Its Application in Educational Industry.*, 5(6). Advance online publication. DOI: 10.25236/FER.2022.050608

Liu, Y., Zhan, Q., & Zhao, W. (2023). A systematic review of VR/AR applications in vocational education: Models, effects, and performances. *Interactive Learning Environments*, •••, 1–18. DOI: 10.1080/10494820.2023.2263043

Lucas, B., Spencer, E., & Claxton, G. (2012). *How to Teach Vocational Education: A Theory of Vocational Pedagogy*. City & Guilds.

Luckin, R., & Holmes, W. (2016). Intelligence unleashed: An argument for AI in education. https://discovery.ucl.ac.uk/id/eprint/1475756

Luck, M., & Aylett, R. (2000). Applying artificial intelligence to virtual reality: Intelligent virtual environments. *Applied Artificial Intelligence*, 14(1), 3–32. DOI: 10.1080/088395100117142

Luo, S., & Tan, A. (2023). The logical transformation and practical path of educational development in the context of ChatGPT application. *Journal of Chongqing University of Technology (Social Sciences)*, 1-13.

Luo, G., Yuan, Q., Li, J., Wang, S., & Yang, F. (2022, May 1). Artificial Intelligence Powered Mobile Networks: From Cognition to Decision. *IEEE Network*, 36(3), 136–144. DOI: 10.1109/MNET.013.2100087

Ma, J. (2019, May). The challenge and development of vocational education under the background of artificial intelligence. In *2019 5th International Conference on Humanities and Social Science Research (ICHSSR 2019)* (pp. 522-525). Atlantis Press. DOI: 10.2991/ichssr-19.2019.102

Maguire, M., & Delahunt, B. (2017). Doing a thematic analysis: A practical, step-by-step guide for learning and teaching scholars. *AISHE-J: The All Ireland Journal of Teaching and Learning in Higher Education, 9*(3).

Maity, S. (2019). Identifying opportunities for artificial intelligence in the evolution of training and development practices. [Online]. *Journal of Management Development*, 38(8), 651–663. Advance online publication. DOI: 10.1108/JMD-03-2019-0069

Major, C. H. (2015). *Teaching online: A guide to theory, research, and practice*. JHU Press. DOI: 10.1353/book.38784

Malerbi, F. K., Nakayama, L. F., Gayle Dychiao, R., Zago Ribeiro, L., Villanueva, C., Celi, L. A., & Regatieri, C. V. (2023). Digital Education for the Deployment of Artificial Intelligence in Health Care. [Online]. *Journal of Medical Internet Research*, 25, e43333. Advance online publication. DOI: 10.2196/43333 PMID: 37347537

Malik, A., & Aslam, M. U. (2024). *Reimagining Teaching: Exploring Challenges of Generative AI Integration in Education.*https://www.researchgate.net/publication/380365121

Mallik, S., & Gangopadhyay, A. (2023, May 5). Proactive and reactive engagement of artificial intelligence methods for education: A review. *Frontiers of Medicine*, 6, 1151391. Advance online publication. DOI: 10.3389/frai.2023.1151391 PMID: 37215064

Mandal, P. (2024). Artificial intelligence and future of education: An analytical study in the lens of vocational development. *International Journal of Multidisciplinary Educational Research*, 13(1), 98–105.

Martin, F., & Bolliger, D. U. (2018). Engagement matters: Student perceptions on the importance of engagement strategies in the online learning environment. *Online Learning : the Official Journal of the Online Learning Consortium*, 22(1), 205–222. DOI: 10.24059/olj.v22i1.1092

Marzano, L., Smith, M., Long, M., Kisby, C., & Hawton, K. (2016). Police and suicide prevention. *Crisis*, 37(3), 194–204. DOI: 10.1027/0227-5910/a000381 PMID: 27040129

Massmann, C., & Hofstetter, A. (2020). AI-pocalypse now? Herausforderungen Künstlicher Intelligenz für Bildungssystem, Unternehmen und die Workforce der Zukunft. *Digitale Bildung und Künstliche Intelligenz in Deutschland: Nachhaltige Wettbewerbsfähigkeit und Zukunftsagenda*, 167-220.

Matulionyte, R., & Hanif, A. (2021). *A call for more explainable AI in law enforcement.* Paper presented at the 2021 IEEE 25th International Enterprise Distributed Object Computing Workshop (EDOCW). DOI: 10.1109/EDOCW52865.2021.00035

Mekacher, L. (2019). Augmented Reality (AR) and Virtual Reality (VR): The future of interactive vocational education and training for people with handicap. *International Journal of Teaching. Education and Learning*, 3(1), 1–12.

Meltzer, A., Robinson, S., & Fisher, K. R. (2020). Barriers to finding and maintaining open employment for people with intellectual disability in Australia. *Social Policy and Administration*, 54(1), 88–101. DOI: 10.1111/spol.12523

Menekse, M. (2023). Envisioning the future of learning and teaching engineering in the artificial intelligence era: Opportunities and challenges. [Online]. *Journal of Engineering Education*, 112(3), 578–582. Advance online publication. DOI: 10.1002/jee.20539

Mese, I. (2023). The Impact of Artificial Intelligence on Radiology Education in the Wake of Coronavirus Disease 2019. [Online]. *Korean Journal of Radiology*, 24(5), 478. Advance online publication. DOI: 10.3348/kjr.2023.0278 PMID: 37133214

Meyer, A., Rose, D., & Gordon, D. (2014). *Universal design for learning, theory and practice*. CAST Professional Publishing.

Miao, F., Holmes, W., Huang, R., & Zhang, H. (2021). *AI and education: A guidance for policymakers*. UNESCO Publishing.

Milgram, P., & Kishino, F. (1994). A Taxonomy of Mixed Reality Visual Displays. *IEICE Transactions on Information and Systems*, 77(12), 1321–1329.

Milgram, P., Takemura, H., Utsumi, A., & Kishino, F. (1995, December). Augmented reality: A class of displays on the reality-virtuality continuum. In *Telemanipulator and telepresence technologies* (Vol. 2351, pp. 282–292). Spie. DOI: 10.1117/12.197321

Mohammad Aniq Bin Amdan, N., Janius, N., Jasman, M. N. B., & Kasdiah, M. A. H. B. (2024). Advancement of AI tools in learning for technical vocational education and training (TVET) in Malaysia: Empowering students and tutors. *International Journal of Science and Research Archive*, 12(1), 2061–2068. DOI: 10.30574/ijsra.2024.12.1.0971

Mohammadkarimi, E. (2023, July 17). Teachers' reflections on academic dishonesty in EFL students' writings in the era of artificial intelligence. *Canadian Philosophy of Education Society*, 6(2). Advance online publication. DOI: 10.37074/jalt.2023.6.2.10

Moher, D., Liberati, A., Tetzlaff, J., & Altman, D. G.The PRISMA Group. (2009). Preferred Reporting Items for Systematic Reviews and Meta-Analyses: The PRISMA Statement. *PLoS Medicine*, 6(7), e1000097. DOI: 10.1371/journal.pmed.1000097 PMID: 19621072

Mojadidi, E. (2024). *Increasing public safety through augmented reality technology utilized by police officers*. Justice Institute of British Columbia, School of Criminal Justice & Security.

Molenaar, I. (2021). Personalization of learning: Towards hybrid human-AI learning technologies. *Blockchain, and Robots*, June 08, 57-77.

Moore, J. L., Dickson-Deane, C., & Galyen, K. (2011). e-Learning, online learning, and distance learning environments: Are they the same? *The Internet and Higher Education*, 14(2), 129–135. DOI: 10.1016/j.iheduc.2010.10.001

Mulder, M. (2004). Competence-based Vocational Education and Training. In Nijhof, W. J., & Heikkinen, A. (Eds.), *Vocational Education and Training Through Open and Distance Learning* (pp. 65–82). Springer.

Musseau, A. (2024). What is vocational education? EHL Insights. https://hospitalityinsights.ehl.edu/what-is-vocational-education

Nafea, I. T. (2018). Machine learning in educational technology. In Farhadi, H. (Ed.), *Machine learning: Advanced techniques and emerging applications*. InTech., DOI: 10.5772/intechopen.72906

Newton, L., & Jong, W. (1989). A Research Guide to Taiwan (ROC) Law. *J. Chinese. L.*, 3, 257.

Ng, D T K., Leung, J K L., Chu, S K W., & Qiao, S. (2021, January 1). Conceptualizing AI literacy: An exploratory review. Elsevier BV, 2, 100041-100041. DOI: 10.1016/j.caeai.2021.100041

Ng, D T K., Leung, J K L., Su, J., Ng, C W., & Chu, S K W. (2023, February 1). Teachers' AI digital competencies and twenty-first century skills in the post-pandemic world. Springer Science+Business Media, 71(1), 137-161. DOI: 10.1007/s11423-023-10203-6

Nguyen, A., Ngo, H N., Hong, Y., Dang, B., & Nguyen, B T. (2022, October 13). Ethical principles for artificial intelligence in education. Springer Science+Business Media, 28(4), 4221-4241. DOI: 10.1007/s10639-022-11316-w

Nimmagadda, S., Surapaneni, R., & Mouly Potluri, R. (2024). Artificial Intelligence in HR: Employee Engagement Using Chatbots. In Singh, R., Khan, S., Kumar, A., & Kumar, V. (Eds.), *Artificial Intelligence Enabled Management: An Emerging Economy Perspective* (pp. 147–162). De Gruyter., DOI: 10.1515/9783111172408-010

Noorbakhsh-Sabet, N., Zand, R., Zhang, Y., & Abedi, V. (2019). Artificial intelligence transforms the future of health care. *The American Journal of Medicine*, 132(7), 795–801. DOI: 10.1016/j.amjmed.2019.01.017 PMID: 30710543

Nordin, S. Z. S., Ismail, I., Mustapa, A., & Omar, P. U. (2019) AUGMENTED REALITY (AR) GAMIFICATION APPLICATION IN TECHNICAL & VOCATIONAL EDUCATION TRAINING. *E-Proceedings of 4th International Conference on Research in TVET Studies (ICOR-TVET 2019)*

North, D. C. (1990). *Institutions, institutional change and economic performance* (Vol. 332). Cambridge university press. DOI: 10.1017/CBO9780511808678

Noy, S., & Zhang, W. (2023) Experimental Evidence on the Productivity Effects of Generative Artificial Intelligence. SSRN Electronic Journal. [Online]. Available: http://dx.doi.org/DOI: 10.2139/ssrn.4375283

OECD. (2019). Transformative competencies for 2030. Conceptual Learning Framework. https://www.oecd.org/education/2030-project/teaching-and-learning/learning/transformative-competencies/Transformative_Competencies_for_2030_concept_note.pdf

OECD. (2023a). Enrolment rates of 15–19-year-olds and 20-24 year-olds, by level of education (2021): Students enrolled in full-time and part-time programmes in both public and private institutions. In *Education at a Glance 2023: OECD Indicators*. OECD Publishing., DOI: 10.1787/85f3d55d-

OECD. (2023b). *Profile of students enrolled in vocational programmes (2021) in Education at a Glance 2023: OECD Indicators*. OECD Publishing., DOI: 10.1787/88a34fe2-

OECD. (2024). *Educational attainment and labour-force status*. https://data-explorer.oecd.org (database) OECD (n.d). *Vocational education and training (VET), Key Messages*. https://www.oecd.org/en/topics/sub-issues/vocational-education-and-training-vet.html

Official Information Source of the Prime Minister of the Republic of Kazakhstan. (2024). Concept for artificial intelligence development for 2024-2029 adopted by government. https://primeminister.kz/en/news/concept-for-artificial-intelligence-development-for-2024-2029-adopted-by-government-28786

Okolo, C T., Aruleba, K., & Obaido, G. (2022, December 31). Responsible AI in Africa—Challenges and Opportunities. Springer International Publishing, 35-64. DOI: 10.1007/978-3-031-08215-3_3

Oosthuizen, K., Botha, E., Robertson, J., & Montecchi, M. (2021). Artificial intelligence in retail: The AI-enabled value chain. *Australasian Marketing Journal*, 29(3), 264–273. DOI: 10.1016/j.ausmj.2020.07.007

Otero, L C., Catalá, A., Fernández-Morante, C., Taboada, M., López, B C., & Barro, S. (2023, April 19). AI literacy in K-12: a systematic literature review. Springer Science+Business Media, 10(1). DOI: 10.1186/s40594-023-00418-7

Panda Training and Education. (2024). *12+ Incredible AI Tools for Educators*. https://pandaeducation.co.uk/blog/incredible-ai-tools-for-trainers/

Panigrahi, R., Srivastava, P. R., & Sharma, D. (2018). Online learning: Adoption, continuance, and learning outcome—A review of literature. *International Journal of Information Management*, 43, 1–14. DOI: 10.1016/j.ijinfomgt.2018.05.005

Pantelidis, V. S. (2010). Reasons to use virtual reality in education and training courses and a model to determine when to use virtual reality. *Themes in Science and Technology Education*, 2(1-2), 59–70.

Papagiannakis, G., Singh, G., & Magnenat-Thalmann, N. (2008). A Survey of Mobile and Wireless Technologies for Augmented Reality Systems. *Computer Animation and Virtual Worlds*, 19(1), 3–22. DOI: 10.1002/cav.221

Paryono. (2017). The Importance of TVET and Its Contribution to Sustainable Development. *The International Education Journal: Comparative Perspectives*, 16(4), 68-87.

Paul, D., Sanap, G., Shenoy, S., Kalyane, D., Kalia, K., & Tekade, R K. (2020, October 21). Artificial intelligence in drug discovery and development. Elsevier BV, 26(1), 80-93. DOI: 10.1016/j.drudis.2020.10.010

Peddie, J. (2017). *Augmented Reality: Where We Will All Live*. Springer. DOI: 10.1007/978-3-319-54502-8

Pérez-López, D., & Contero, M. (2013). Delivering educational multimedia contents through an augmented reality application: A case study on its impact on knowledge acquisition and retention. *Turkish Online Journal of Educational Technology-TOJET*, 12(4), 19–28.

Peters, T M., & Visser, R W. (2023, January 1). The Importance of Distrust in AI. Springer Science+Business Media, 301-317. DOI: 10.1007/978-3-031-44070-0_15

Peters, B. G. (2019). *Institutional theory in political science: The new institutionalism*. Edward Elgar Publishing.

Petridou, E., & Lao, L. (2024). Identifying challenges and best practices for implementing AI additional qualifications in vocational and continuing education: A mixed methods analysis. *International Journal of Lifelong Education*, 43(4), 1–16. DOI: 10.1080/02601370.2024.2351076

Petropoulos, G. (2018). The impact of artificial intelligence on employment. In Neufeind, A., O'Reilly, J., & Ranft, F. (Eds.), *Work in the digital age – challenges of the fourth industrial revolution* (pp. 119–132). Rowman & Littlefield International.

Phoon, K., & Koh, F. (2017, December 21). Robo-Advisors and Wealth Management. *Journal of Alternative Investments*, 20(3), 79–94. DOI: 10.3905/jai.2018.20.3.079

Picciano, A. G. (2017). Theories and frameworks for online education: Seeking an integrated model. *Online Learning : the Official Journal of the Online Learning Consortium*, 21(3), 166–190. DOI: 10.24059/olj.v21i3.1225

Pizzi, M., Romanoff, M., & Engelhardt, T. (2020, April 1). AI for humanitarian action: Human rights and ethics. Cambridge University Press, 102(913), 145-180. DOI: 10.1017/S1816383121000011

Poquet, O., & De Laat, M. (2021). Developing capabilities: Lifelong learning in the age of AI. *British Journal of Educational Technology*, 52(4), 1695–1708. DOI: 10.1111/bjet.13123

Prihantoro, C. R. (2023). Outcome-based education (OBE) based vocational education model in the era of artificial intelligence. *Education Quarterly Eeview*, 6(1), 228–240. DOI: 10.31014/aior.1993.06.01.701

Proton, A. G. (2024). *What is GDPR, the EU's new data protection law?*https://gdpr.eu/what-is-gdpr/

Rad, H. S., Alipour, R., & Jafarpour, A. (2023). Using artificial intelligence to foster students- writing feedback literacy, engagement, and outcome: A case of Wordtune application. [Online]. *Interactive Learning Environments*. Advance online publication. DOI: 10.1080/10494820.2023.2208170

Ragulina, Y. V., Dubova, Y. I., Litvinova, T. N., & Balashova, N. (2022, June 15). The Environmental AI Economy and its Contribution to Decarbonization and Waste Reduction. *Frontiers in Environmental Science*, 10, 914003. Advance online publication. DOI: 10.3389/fenvs.2022.914003

Ramdhani, F. F., & Mulyanti, B. (2020). Additive manufacturing in education. *IOP Conference Series. Materials Science and Engineering*, 830(4), 042093. DOI: 10.1088/1757-899X/830/4/042093

Ramesh, A., Pavlov, M., Goh, G., Gray, S., Voss, C., Radford, A., & Sutskever, I. (2021, July). Zero-shot text-to-image generation. In *International conference on machine learning* (pp. 8821-8831). Pmlr.

Rauner, F., & Maclean, R. (2008). *Handbook of Technical and Vocational Education and Training Research*. Springer.

Ravichandran, R. R., & Mahapatra, J. (2023). Virtual Reality in vocational education and training: Challenges and possibilities. *Journal of Digital Learning and Education*, 3(1), 25–31. DOI: 10.52562/jdle.v3i1.602

Reich, J., & Ruipérez-Valiente, J. A. (2019). The MOOC pivot. *Science*, 363(6423), 130–131. DOI: 10.1126/science.aav7958 PMID: 30630920

Reinman, S L. (2015, June 30). Open Knowledge Repository. Emerald Publishing Limited, 29(5), 21-22. DOI: 10.1108/RR-05-2015-0113

Riedl, C., & Woolley, A. W. (2016, December 9). Teams vs. Crowds: A Field Test of the Relative Contribution of Incentives, Member Ability, and Emergent Collaboration to Crowd-Based Problem Solving Performance. *Academy of Management Discoveries*, 3(4), 382–403. DOI: 10.5465/amd.2015.0097

Rongchang, J., Yonghong, C., Yi, P., Shijie, X., & Dandan, Q. (2024). Opportunities and Challenges of AI in Vocational Education. *International Journal of Learning and Teaching*, 10(5), 590–596.

Rosyadi, M. I., Kustiawan, I., Tetehfio, E. O., & Joshua, Q. (2023). The Role of AI In Vocational Education: A Systematic Literature Review. *Journal of Vocational Education Studies*, 6(2), 244–263. DOI: 10.12928/joves.v6i2.9032

Rott, K. J., Lao, L., Petridou, E., & Schmidt-Hertha, B. (2022). Needs and requirements for an additional AI qualification during dual vocational training: Results from studies of apprentices and teachers. *Computers and education. Artificial Intelligence*, 3, 100102. Advance online publication. DOI: 10.1016/j.caeai.2022.100102

Rovai, A. P., & Downey, J. R. (2010). Why some distance education programs fail while others succeed in a global environment. *The Internet and Higher Education*, 13(3), 141–147. DOI: 10.1016/j.iheduc.2009.07.001

Sakenova, S. (2024). Kazakhstan focuses on precision AI development with new law and committee. *The Astana Times,* 16 July, https://astanatimes.com/2024/07/kazakhstan-focuses-on-precision-ai-development-with-new-law-and-committee/

Salloum, S. A. (2024). AI Perils in Education: Exploring Ethical Concerns. *Artificial Intelligence in Education: The Power and Dangers of ChatGPT in the Classroom*, 669-675.

Sanders, E., & Stappers, P. (2008). Co-creation and the new landscapes of design. *CoDesign*, 4(1), 5–18. DOI: 10.1080/15710880701875068

Santos, M. E. C., Chen, A., Taketomi, T., Yamamoto, G., Miyazaki, J., & Kato, H. (2013). Augmented reality learning experiences: Survey of prototype design and evaluation. *IEEE Transactions on Learning Technologies*, 7(1), 38–56. DOI: 10.1109/TLT.2013.37

Sanz-Urquijo, B., Fosch-Villaronga, E., & Lopez-Belloso, M. (2023). The disconnect between the goals of trustworthy AI for law enforcement and the EU research agenda. *AI and Ethics*, 3(4), 1283–1294. DOI: 10.1007/s43681-022-00235-8

Saputra, I., Astuti, M., Sayuti, M., & Kusumastuti, D. (2023). Integration of Artificial Intelligence in Education: Opportunities, Challenges, Threats and Obstacles. A Literature Review. *The Indonesian Journal of Computer Science*, 12(4). Advance online publication. DOI: 10.33022/ijcs.v12i4.3266

Saxena, A. K., García, V., Amin, M. R., Salazar, J. M. R., & Dey, S. (2023). Structure, Objectives, and Operational Framework for Ethical Integration of Artificial Intelligence in Educational. *Sage Science Review of Educational Technology, 6*(1), 88-100. https://journals.sagescience.org/index.php/ssret/article/view/139

Schiff, D. (2021). Education for AI, not AI for Education: The Role of Education and Ethics in National AI Policy Strategies. [Online]. *International Journal of Artificial Intelligence in Education*. Advance online publication. DOI: 10.1007/s40593-021-00270-2

Schlögl, S., Postulka, C., Bernsteiner, R., & Ploder, C. (2019, January 1). Artificial Intelligence Tool Penetration in Business: Adoption, Challenges and Fears. Springer Science+Business Media, 259-270. DOI: 10.1007/978-3-030-21451-7_22

Schneider, G., & Ershova, A. (2018). Rational choice institutionalism and european integration.

Schneider, J., Meske, C., & Kuss, P. (2024). Foundation models: A new paradigm for artificial intelligence. *Business & Information Systems Engineering*, 66(2), 1–11. DOI: 10.1007/s12599-024-00851-0

Schwab, K. (2017). *The fourth industrial revolution*. Crown Currency.

Selwyn, N. (2016). *Is technology good for education?* John Wiley & Sons.

Seufert, S. (2024). Artificial intelligence in vocational education and training (VET): Evaluating VET leaders' acceptance of AI in Switzerland. DOI: 10.21203/rs.3.rs-4628645/v1

Shaffer, K J., Gaumer, C J., & Bradley, K P. (2020, February 3). Artificial intelligence products reshape accounting: time to re-train. Emerald Publishing Limited, 34(6), 41-43. DOI: 10.1108/DLO-10-2019-0242

Shankar, V., Kalyanam, K., Setia, P., Golmohammadi, A., Tirunillai, S., Douglass, T., Hennessey, J., Bull, J., & Waddoups, R. (2020, November 10). How Technology is Changing Retail. Elsevier BV, 97(1), 13-27. DOI: 10.1016/j.jretai.2020.10.006

Sharma, A. (2023). *Potential of technology supported competence development for Maritime Education and Training*. [doctoral dissertation]. University of South-Eastern Norway, Notodden, Norway.

Shelton, B. E., & Hedley, N. R. (2002, September). Using augmented reality for teaching earth-sun relationships to undergraduate geography students. In *The First IEEE International Workshop Agumented Reality Toolkit,* (pp. 8-pp). IEEE. DOI: 10.1109/ART.2002.1106948

Sheridan, T. B., & Parasuraman, R. (2005, June 1). Human-Automation Interaction. *Review of Human Factors and Ergonomics*, 1(1), 89–129. DOI: 10.1518/155723405783703082

Shinde, P. P., & Shah, S. (2018, August). A review of machine learning and deep learning applications. In *2018 Fourth international conference on computing communication control and automation (ICCUBEA)* (pp. 1-6). IEEE. https://doi.org/ DOI: 10.1109/ICCUBEA.2018.8697857

Shiohira, K. (2021). Understanding the Impact of Artificial Intelligence on Skills Development. [*UNESCO-UNEVOC International Centre for Technical and Vocational Education and Training.*]. *Education*, •••, 2030.

Shu, X., & Gu, X. (2023). An empirical study of A smart education model enabled by the edu-metaverse to enhance better learning outcomes for students. *Systems*, 11(2), 75. Advance online publication. DOI: 10.3390/systems11020075

Siemens, G. (2014). Connectivism: A learning theory for the digital age. *International Journal of Instructional Technology and Distance Learning*, 2(1), 3–10.

Simón, V., Baglee, D., Garfield, S., & Galar, D. (2014). The development of an advanced maintenance training programme utilizing augmented reality.

Singh, A. R. (2024). The Future of Vocational Learning in India: How Artificial Intelligence and Creativity Will Shape Learning of Skills in 2030. In *Educational Perspectives on Digital Technologies in Modeling and Management* (pp. 293–304). IGI Global. DOI: 10.4018/979-8-3693-2314-4.ch015

Singhal, S., Bagga, S., Goyal, P., & Saxena, V. (2012). Augmented chemistry: Interactive education system. *International Journal of Computer Applications*, 49(15), 1–5. DOI: 10.5120/7700-1041

Sirakaya, M., & Kilic Cakmak, E. (2018). Effects of augmented reality on student achievement and self-efficacy in vocational education and training. *International journal for research in vocational education and training, 5*(1), 1-18.

Slade, S., & Prinsloo, P. (2013). Learning analytics: Ethical issues and dilemmas. *The American Behavioral Scientist*, 57(10), 1510–1529. DOI: 10.1177/0002764213479366

Slimi, Z., & Carballido, B. V. (2023). Navigating the Ethical Challenges of Artificial Intelligence in Higher Education: An Analysis of Seven Global AI Ethics Policies. *TEM Journal, 12*(2). https://www.ceeol.com/search/article-detail?id=1122977

Sloane, M., Danks, D., & Moss, E. (2024, April 24). Tackling AI Hyping. Springer Nature. DOI: 10.1007/s43681-024-00481-y

Sobania, D., Briesch, M., Hanna, C., & Petke, J. (2023). An analysis of the automatic bug fixing performance of chatgpt. In *2023 IEEE/ACM International Workshop on Automated Program Repair (APR)* (pp. 23-30). IEEE. DOI: 10.1109/APR59189.2023.00012

Sousa, M. L. (2023) Santos, Manuel Pimentel Pereira dos. DicionÃ¡rio BiogrÃ¡fico de Cientistas, Engenheiros e MÃ©dicos em Portugal. [Online]. Available: http://dx.doi.org/.DOI: 10.58277/SUFF8895

Srinivasan, V., & Murthy, H. (2021, January 1). Improving reading and comprehension in K-12: Evidence from a large-scale AI technology intervention in India. Elsevier BV, 2, 100019-100019. DOI: 10.1016/j.caeai.2021.100019

Stahl, B C. (2021, January 1). Ethical Issues of AI. Springer International Publishing, 35-53. DOI: 10.1007/978-3-030-69978-9_4

Statti, A., & Torres, K M. (2020, March 14). The Forgotten Minority: Exploring Deficiencies in Access to Education and Technology in Rural America. Taylor & Francis, 95(2), 173-182. DOI: 10.1080/0161956X.2020.1745608

Sun, I. Y., Jou, S., Hou, C. C., & Chang, Y. (2014). Public trust in the police in Taiwan: A test of instrumental and expressive models. *Australian and New Zealand Journal of Criminology*, 47(1), 123–140. DOI: 10.1177/0004865813489306

Sun, P. C., Tsai, R. J., Finger, G., Chen, Y. Y., & Yeh, D. (2008). What drives a successful e-Learning? An empirical investigation of the critical factors influencing learner satisfaction. *Computers & Education*, 50(4), 1183–1202. DOI: 10.1016/j.compedu.2006.11.007

Suparyati, A., Widiastuti, I., Saputro, I. N., & Pambudi, N. A. (2023). The role of artificial intelligence (AI) in vocational education. *JIPTEK: Jurnal Ilmiah Pendidikan Teknik dan Kejuruan, 17*(1), 1-20.

Suzuki, K. (2020). AI: A New Open Access Journal for Artificial Intelligence. [Online]. *AI*, 1(2), 141–142. Advance online publication. DOI: 10.3390/ai1020007

Svistunova, A. A., & Gorshkov, M. D. (2013). *Simuljacionnoe obuchenie v medicine* [Simulation training in medicine]. MGMU im VM Sechenova Publ.

Swiss Federal University for Vocational Education and Training SFUVET. (2024). *About SFUVET*. https://www.sfuvet.swiss/sfuvet/about-sfuvet

Tait, A. (2018). Open Universities: The next phase. *Asian Association of Open Universities Journal*, 13(1), 13–23. DOI: 10.1108/AAOUJ-12-2017-0040

Tamura, H. (2002, November). Steady steps and giant leap toward practical mixed reality systems and applications. In *Proceedings of the International Status Conference on Virtual and Augmented Reality* (pp. 3-12).

Tan, B. L., Guan, F. Y., Leung, I. M. W., Kee, S. Y. M., Devilly, O. Z., & Medalia, A. (2022). A gamified augmented reality vocational training program for adults with intellectual and developmental disabilities: A pilot study on acceptability and effectiveness. *Frontiers in Psychiatry*, 13, 966080. DOI: 10.3389/fpsyt.2022.966080 PMID: 35990062

Tanveer, M., Hassan, S., & Bhaumik, A. (2020). Academic Policy Regarding Sustainability and Artificial Intelligence (AI). [Online]. *Sustainability (Basel)*, 12(22), 9435. Advance online publication. DOI: 10.3390/su12229435

Tavakoli, M., Faraji, A., Vrolijk, J., Molavi, M., Mol, S. T., & Kismih, Ã. (2022, April). [3]k, G. (2022) An AI-based open recommender system for personalized labor market driven education. [Online]. *Advanced Engineering Informatics*, 52, 101508. Advance online publication. DOI: 10.1016/j.aei.2021.101508

Teubner, T., Flath, C. M., Weinhardt, C., van der Aalst, W., & Hinz, O. (2023). Welcome to the Era of ChatGPT et al. *Business & Information Systems Engineering*, 65(2), 95–101. DOI: 10.1007/s12599-023-00795-x

Thomas, V L., & Fowler, K. (2020, September 11). Close Encounters of the AI Kind: Use of AI Influencers As Brand Endorsers. Taylor & Francis, 50(1), 11-25. DOI: 10.1080/00913367.2020.1810595

Thomas, S., & Watson, A. (2017). A focus for mental health training for police. *Journal of Criminological Research, Policy and Practice*, 3(2), 93–104. DOI: 10.1108/JCRPP-01-2017-0005

Tomi, A. B., & Rambli, D. R. A. (2013). An interactive mobile augmented reality magical playbook: Learning number with the thirsty crow. *Procedia Computer Science*, 25, 123–130. DOI: 10.1016/j.procs.2013.11.015

Trainer, T. V. E. T. (2024). *Case Studies and Examples*. https://tvettrainer.com/ai-powered-personalised-learning-for-vocational-education-and-training-vet/

Tramm, T., & Naeve-Stoß, N. (2020). Curricula für die berufliche Bildung–Lernfeldstruktur zwischen Situations-und Fächerorientierung. *Handbuch Berufsbildung*, 309-324. https://doi.org/DOI: 10.1007/978-3-658-19312-6_26

Triguero, I., Molina, D., Poyatos, J., Ser, J D., & Herrera, F. (2023, November 8). General Purpose Artificial Intelligence Systems (GPAIS): Properties, definition, taxonomy, societal implications and responsible governance. Elsevier BV, 103, 102135-102135. DOI: 10.1016/j.inffus.2023.102135

UNCTAD. (n.d.). *Data Protection and Privacy Legislation Worldwide*. https://unctad.org/page/data-protection-and-privacy-legislation-worldwide

UNESCO Institute for Statistics. (2024). Vocational education: Definition. https://uis.unesco.org/en/glossary-term/vocational-education

Van Krevelen, D. W. F., & Poelman, R. (2010). A survey of augmented reality technologies, applications and limitations. *The International Journal of Virtual Reality : a Multimedia Publication for Professionals*, 9(2), 1–20. DOI: 10.20870/IJVR.2010.9.2.2767

Varnosfaderani, S. M., & Forouzanfar, M. (2024, March 29). The Role of AI in Hospitals and Clinics: Transforming Healthcare in the 21st Century. *Bioengineering (Basel, Switzerland)*, 11(4), 337–337. DOI: 10.3390/bioengineering11040337 PMID: 38671759

Vats, S., & Malik, N. A. (2024). Comprehensive Review of Vocational Education and Training (VET) in Secondary School. *International Journal of Research Publication and Reviews*, 5(6), 5812–5818. DOI: 10.55248/gengpi.5.0624.1612

Veletsianos, G., & Shepherdson, P. (2016). A systematic analysis and synthesis of the empirical MOOC literature published in 2013–2015. *International Review of Research in Open and Distance Learning*, 17(2). Advance online publication. DOI: 10.19173/irrodl.v17i2.2448

Ventures, B. (2023). AI's growing role in vocational education. https://www.brighteyevc.com/post/ai-s-growing-role-in-vocational-education

Vera, A. M., Russo, M., Mohsin, A., & Tsuda, S. (2014). Augmented reality telementoring (ART) platform: A randomized controlled trial to assess the efficacy of a new surgical education technology. *Surgical Endoscopy*, 28(12), 3467–3472. DOI: 10.1007/s00464-014-3625-4 PMID: 24962856

Vitale, G., Bonarini, A., Matteucci, M., & Bascetta, L. (2016). Toward vocational robotics: An experience in post-secondary school education and job training through robotics. *IEEE Robotics & Automation Magazine*, 23(4), 73–81. DOI: 10.1109/MRA.2016.2571998

Walter, Y. (2024). Embracing the future of Artificial Intelligence in the classroom: The relevance of AI literacy, prompt engineering, and critical thinking in modern education. *International Journal of Educational Technology in Higher Education*, 21(1), 15. Advance online publication. DOI: 10.1186/s41239-024-00448-3

Wang, N., & Lester, J C. (2023, June 1). K-12 Education in the Age of AI: A Call to Action for K-12 AI Literacy. Springer Science+Business Media, 33(2), 228-232. DOI: 10.1007/s40593-023-00358-x

Wang, Y. (2020, March 18). When artificial intelligence meets educational leaders' data-informed decision-making: A cautionary tale. Elsevier BV, 69, 100872-100872. DOI: 10.1016/j.stueduc.2020.100872

Wang, C., Zhu, H., Wang, P., Zhu, C., Zhang, X., Chen, E., & Xiong, H. (2021). Personalized and Explainable Employee Training Course Recommendations: A Bayesian Variational Approach. [Online]. *ACM Transactions on Information Systems*. Advance online publication. DOI: 10.1145/3490476

Wang, X., Kim, M. J., Love, P. E., & Kang, S. C. (2017). Augmented Reality in built environment: Classification and implications for future research. *Automation in Construction*, 72, 118–124.

Watson, G., Desouza, K C., Ribière, V., & Lindič, J. (2021, February 4). Will AI ever sit at the C-suite table? The future of senior leadership. Elsevier BV, 64(4), 465-474. DOI: 10.1016/j.bushor.2021.02.011

Weigel, T., Mulder, M., & Collins, K. (2007). The concept of competence in the development of vocational education and training in selected EU member states. *Journal of Vocational Education and Training*, 59(1), 53–66. DOI: 10.1080/13636820601145549

Weller, M. (2020). 25 Years of Ed Tech. Athabasca University Press.

Westerfield, G., Mitrovic, A., & Billinghurst, M. (2015). Intelligent augmented reality training for motherboard assembly. *International Journal of Artificial Intelligence in Education*, 25(1), 157–172. DOI: 10.1007/s40593-014-0032-x

Weyland, K. (2002). Limitations of rational-choice institutionalism for the study of Latin American politics. *Studies in Comparative International Development*, 37(1), 57–85. DOI: 10.1007/BF02686338

Williamson, O. E. (1985). The economic institutions of capitalism. New York: Free Press: Douglas.

Winch, C. (2013). The Attractiveness of Vocational Education and Training in an Inclusive System. *European Journal of Education*, 48(2), 274–289.

Windelband, L. (2023). Artificial intelligence and assistance systems for technical vocational education and training–Opportunities and risks. In *New Digital Work: Digital Sovereignty at the Workplace* (pp. 195–213). Springer International Publishing. DOI: 10.1007/978-3-031-26490-0_12

Winters, A., Meijers, F., Kuijpers, M., & Baert, H. (2009). What are vocational training conversations about? Analysis of vocational training conversations in Dutch vocational education from a career learning perspective. *Journal of Vocational Education and Training*, 61(3), 247–266. DOI: 10.1080/13636820903194690

Wojciechowski, R., & Cellary, W. (2013). Evaluation of learners' attitude toward learning in ARIES augmented reality environments. *Computers & Education*, 68, 570–585. DOI: 10.1016/j.compedu.2013.02.014

Wright, S A., & Schultz, A E. (2018, September 17). The rising tide of artificial intelligence and business automation: Developing an ethical framework. Elsevier BV, 61(6), 823-832. DOI: 10.1016/j.bushor.2018.07.001

Wu, H. K., Lee, S. W. Y., Chang, H. Y., & Liang, J. C. (2013). Current status, opportunities and challenges of augmented reality in education. *Computers & Education*, 62, 41–49. DOI: 10.1016/j.compedu.2012.10.024

Wu, Y., Poteyeva, M., & Sun, I. Y. (2012). Trust in police: A comparison of China and Taiwan. *International Journal of Comparative and Applied Criminal Justice*, 36(3), 189–210. DOI: 10.1080/01924036.2012.699794

Xu, J. J., & Babaian, T. (2021). Artificial intelligence in business curriculum: The pedagogy and learning outcomes. [Online]. *International Journal of Management Education*, 19(3), 100550. Advance online publication. DOI: 10.1016/j.ijme.2021.100550

Xu, W., & Ouyang, F. (2021). A systematic review of AI role in the educational system based on a proposed conceptual framework. [Online]. *Education and Information Technologies*. Advance online publication. DOI: 10.1007/s10639-021-10774-y

Yamabe, T., & Nakajima, T. (2013). Playful training with augmented reality games: Case studies towards reality-oriented system design. *Multimedia Tools and Applications*, 62(1), 259–286. DOI: 10.1007/s11042-011-0979-7

Yang, L., Tian, M., Duan, X., Cheng, Q., & Zheng, J. (2024, May 31). AI-driven anonymization: Protecting personal data privacy while leveraging machine learning., 67(1), 256-262. DOI: 10.54254/2755-2721/67/2024MA0053

Yang, X., Shu, L., Chen, J., Ferrag, M. A., Wu, J., Nurellari, E., & Huang, K. (2021). A survey on smart agriculture: Development modes, technologies, and security and privacy challenges. *IEEE/CAA Journal of Automatica Sinica, 8*(2), 273–302.

Yarger, L., Payton, F C., & Neupane, B. (2019, December 17). Algorithmic equity in the hiring of underrepresented IT job candidates. Emerald Publishing Limited, 44(2), 383-395. DOI: 10.1108/OIR-10-2018-0334

Yen, C. S., & Yang, S. C. (2024). The Integration of Artificial Intelligence and Video Production Skills in Workplace Development: A Study from the Perspective of Vocational Training. *The Review of Socionetwork Strategies*, 18(2), 1–14. DOI: 10.1007/s12626-024-00162-6

Yilmaz, R., Bakhaidar, M., Alsayegh, A., & Del Maestro, R. (2023). O022 Real-time artificial intelligence instructor vs expert instruction in teaching of expert level tumour resection skills - a randomized controlled trial. [Online]. *British Journal of Surgery*, 110(Supplement_3), znad101.022. Advance online publication. DOI: 10.1093/bjs/znad101.022

Yim, I H Y., & Su, J. (2024, January 6). Artificial intelligence (AI) learning tools in K-12 education: A scoping review. Springer Science+Business Media. DOI: 10.1007/s40692-023-00304-9

You, Y., Chen, Y., You, Y., Zhang, Q., & Cao, Q. (2023). Evolutionary Game Analysis of Artificial Intelligence Such as the Generative Pre-Trained Transformer in Future Eduscation. [Online]. *Sustainability (Basel)*, 15(12), 9355. Advance online publication. DOI: 10.3390/su15129355

Yuen, S. C. Y., Yaoyuneyong, G., & Johnson, E. (2011). Augmented reality: An overview and five directions for AR in education. [JETDE]. *Journal of Educational Technology Development and Exchange*, 4(1), 11. DOI: 10.18785/jetde.0401.10

Zador, A. M., Escola, G. S., Richards, B. A., Ölveczky, B. P., Bengio, Y., Boahen, K., Botvinick, M., Chklovskii, D. B., Churchland, A. K., Clopath, C., DiCarlo, J. J., Ganguli, S., Hawkins, J., Körding, K., Koulakov, A. A., LeCun, Y., Lillicrap, T., Marblestone, A., Olshausen, B. A., & Tsao, D. Y. (2023, March 22). Catalyzing next-generation Artificial Intelligence through NeuroAI. *Nature Communications*, 14(1), 1597. Advance online publication. DOI: 10.1038/s41467-023-37180-x PMID: 36949048

Završnik, A. (2020). *Criminal justice, artificial intelligence systems, and human rights.* Paper presented at the ERA forum. DOI: 10.1007/s12027-020-00602-0

Zawacki-Richter, O., & Qayyum, A. (Eds.). (2019). *Open and distance education in Asia, Africa and the Middle East: National perspectives in a digital age*. Springer. DOI: 10.1007/978-981-13-5787-9

Zhang, D., Mishra, S., Brynjolfsson, E., Etchemendy, J., Ganguli, D., Grosz, B., Lyons, T., Manyika, J., Niebles, J. C., Sellitto, M., Shoham, Y., Clark, J., & Perrault, R. (2021). The AI Index 2021 Annual Report. AI Index Steering Committee. Human-Centered AI Institute, Stanford University, CA. https://aiindex.stanford.edu/wp-content/uploads/2021/11/2021-AI-Index-Report_Master.pdf

Zhang, K., & Aslan, A. B. (2021, January 1). AI technologies for education: Recent research & future directions. https://www.sciencedirect.com/science/article/pii/S2666920X21000199

Zhang, S., Fu, D., Liang, W., Zhang, Z., Yu, B., Cai, P., & Yao, B. (2024, March 14). TrafficGPT: Viewing, processing and interacting with traffic foundation models. Elsevier BV, 150, 95-105. https://doi.org/DOI: 10.1016/j.tranpol.2024.03.006

Zhou, F., Duh, H. B.-L., & Billinghurst, M. (2008). Trends in Augmented Reality Tracking, Interaction and Display: A Review of Ten Years of ISMAR. In *Proceedings of the 7th IEEE/ACM International Symposium on Mixed and Augmented Reality* (pp. 193-202). IEEE.

Zouaghi, M. (2019). Augmented Reality (AR) and Virtual Reality (VR): The future of interactive vocational education and training for people with handicaps. *PUPIL: International Journal of Teaching. Education and Learning*, 3(1), 118–129. DOI: 10.20319/pijtel.2019.31.118129

About the Contributors

Eriona Çela is a distinguished academic currently serving as a Full-Time Professor at the University of New York Tirana, where she is a member of the Faculty of Law and Social Sciences in the Department of Psychology. She earned her Ph.D. in Teaching Methodology of English for Specific Purposes (ESP) from the University of Bari "Aldo Moro" in Italy, enhancing her extensive background in language education, which includes earlier degrees in English Language and Law from the University of Tirana and Business Academy College in Albania. Dr. Çela's research interests are broad and interdisciplinary, focusing on Business English, Teaching Methodology, ESP, Academic Writing, Higher Education, Plagiarism, and European Integration among others. She is well-versed in teaching a range of subjects including Academic Writing, ESL, Business English, and Legal English. She also has significant expertise in translating legal, business, and educational documents. Her academic experience spans several respected institutions, including previous roles as an Assistant Professor at the University of Luarasi, University of Elbasan "Aleksandër Xhuvani", University of Tirana, and University of Durrës "Aleksandër Moisiu". In addition to her academic roles, Dr. Çela has held significant administrative positions within the Albanian Ministry of Education and Sport, where she contributed to integration, coordination, and project feasibility. Dr. Çela is active in the academic community as a member and managing editor of various editorial boards, including those for the European Journal of Arts, Humanities and Social Sciences, and the International Journal of Risk and Contingency Management. Her contributions to conferences and scholarly journals are numerous, underscoring her commitment to advancing research and practice in her fields of expertise. She also brings practical insights into her teaching and research from her experiences as a trainer and higher education expert involved in quality assurance and educational reforms in Albania. This rich background informs her ongoing contributions to academic discussions and policy-making in education, both in Albania and internationally.

Narasimha Rao Vajjhala currently serves as the Dean of the Faculty of Engineering and Architecture at the University of New York Tirana in Albania. He previously held the position of Chair for the Computer Science and Software Engineering programs at the American University of Nigeria. Dr. Vajjhala is a senior member of both the ACM and IEEE. He is the Editor-in-Chief of the International Journal of Risk and Contingency Management (IJRCM) and a member of the Risk Management Society (RIMS) and the Project Management Institute (PMI). With over 23 years of experience, Dr. Vajjhala has taught programming and database-related courses across Europe and Africa at both graduate and undergraduate levels. He has also worked as a consultant for technology firms in Europe and participated in EU-funded projects. Dr. Vajjhala holds a Doctorate in Information Systems and Technology from the United States, a Master of Science in Computer Science and Applications from India, and a Master of Business Administration specializing in Information Systems from Switzerland.

Rajasekhara Mouly Potluri is an accomplished professor of management and marketing at Kazakh British Technical University, Kazakhstan, with thirty years of industry and teaching experience. His research interests cover the fields of Marketing, CSR, HRM, Organizational Behavior and Entrepreneurship. He has published and presented 90+ research articles, book chapters, case studies, and talks in peer-reviewed journals indexed in Scopus, ABDC, SSCI, and KCI and at international conferences. He has won 11 Best Research Paper Awards and ten Academic Service Excellence Awards at conference presentations in Egypt, South Korea, Malaysia, and UAE. He earned his Ph.D. degree in management and marketing from Shivaji University and holds four master's degrees in business administration (marketing), commerce (banking), philosophy (human resources), and an MBA in Islamic marketing from the International Islamic Marketing Association in the UK.

Philip Eappen is an assistant professor of Healthcare Management and Director of Clinical Services and Transition to Community at the Breton Ability Center. at Cape Breton University, Canada. Before joining Cape Breton University, he taught at the University of Toronto, the Southern Alberta Institute of Technology, and Fanshawe College. He previously worked as a director of health services and chief administrator of healthcare operations at the American University of Nigeria. His fields of research interest include teaching methodology innovations, the use of technology to enhance education, and healthcare informatics. He has authored several books, book chapters and journal articles. He holds a Bachelor of Nursing from (institute, country), a Master of Business Administration in Health Care Management (institute, country), and a Doctorate in Healthcare Administration from Central Michigan University, USA.

***

Kairzhan Abdykhalykov is a Vice-Dean and Assistant Professor of the School of Business at the Kazakh-British Technical University of Kazakhstan and holds a Ph.D. in International Economic Relations. He is an extensive researcher with a decade and a half of experience and has published many research papers, book chapters, and international conference presentations in his area of specialization. His universal exposure and vast experience in a multicultural work environment proffers numerous benefits to the organization where he works. Dr. Kairzhan's research interests are international economic relations, macroeconomics, project management, entrepreneurship, and small business management.

Andi Asrifan, S.Pd, M.Pd, a distinguished figure in the realm of education, particularly in English Language Education, has made significant contributions through his extensive research, teaching, and leadership roles. As the Head of the Institute for Cooperation and International Affairs at Universitas Muhammadiyah Sidenreng Rappang and now a lecturer in Universitas Negeri Makassar (UNM), Dr. Asrifan's academic journey is marked by a rich tapestry of achievements, including a Doctor of Education in English Language Education. His work spans various facets of education, language, and technology, reflecting the diverse topics covered in his publications and research endeavors. These include, but are not limited to, the impact of the COVID-19 pandemic on educational practices, methodologies in English as a Foreign Language (EFL) classrooms, and the integration of technology in teaching and learning processes. Dr. Asrifan's commitment to advancing educational standards and practices is further evidenced by his active participation in international conferences, webinars, and workshops across countries like India, the Philippines, and Pakistan. These events, organized by various institutions and associations, underscore his role as a global educator and thought leader. His dedication to professional development is also highlighted through his involvement in numerous courses and certifications in personal branding, public speaking, and literacy teaching. Moreover, Dr. Asrifan's leadership extends beyond academia into organizational and educational development, where he has served in various capacities, including as an external examiner for Ph.D. dissertations and a reviewer for scientific journals. His accolades, memberships in professional organizations, and roles as an ambassador for international associations speak volumes of his influence and commitment to fostering educational excellence and sustainable development goals globally.

Abhijit Banerjee is a researcher in the Department of Electronics & Communication Engineering at Dr. B.C. Roy Engineering College, Durgapur, with expertise spanning Telecommunications Engineering, Industrial Organization, Game Theory, and Supply Chain Management. His work focuses on optimization, decision analysis, and mathematical programming, utilizing advanced modeling techniques to address real-world challenges in telecommunications and supply chains. Abhijit's skills include Analytic Hierarchy Process (AHP), decision analysis, multicriteria analysis, operations management, and heuristics. He is proficient in optimization methods such as linear and mathematical programming, combining theoretical rigor with practical applications. His most recent publication, *Repulsion-Propulsion Firefly Algorithm with Fast Convergence to Solve Highly Multi-Modal Problems*, highlights his innovative approach to heuristic algorithm development and optimization in complex problem-solving scenarios. Abhijit's interdisciplinary research bridges theory and practice, contributing significantly to both academic knowledge and industry solutions.

Rajiv Iyer serves as an Associate Professor in the Department of Computer Science and Engineering at Amity University, Mumbai. Holding a Ph.D. in the field of the Internet of Things (IoT), Dr. Iyer has amassed 14 years of distinguished experience in academia. He is a registered Patent Agent (IN/PA3625) and holds certifications as an educator for AWS and Celonis. Additionally, he contributes as a Google Facilitator for Machine Learning and serves as a mentor and advisor for the Kaggle BIPOC program, reflecting his commitment to advancing innovation and education in emerging technologies.

Vishal Jain is presently working as a Professor at the Department of Computer Science and Engineering, School of Engineering and Technology, Sharda University, Greater Noida, India. Before that, he worked for several years as an Associate Professor at Bharati Vidyapeeths Institute of Computer Applications and Management (BVICAM), New Delhi. He has more than 18 years of experience in the academics. He has earned degrees: Ph.D (CSE), M.Tech (CSE), MBA (HR), MCA, MCP, and CCNA. He has more than 1900 research citations with Google Scholar (h-index score 21 and i-10 index 49) and has authored more than 150 research papers in professional journals and conferences. He has authored and edited more than 60 books (most of them are indexed at the Scopus) with various reputed publishers, including Elsevier, Springer, IET, Apple Academic Press, CRC, Taylor and Francis Group, Scrivener, Wiley, Emerald, NOVA Science, River Publishers, IGI-Global and Bentham Science. He has more than 160 Scopus publications. He is the book series editor of 10 book series with the reputed international publishers. His research areas include machine learning, information retrieval, semantic web, ontology engineering, data mining, ad hoc networks, sensor networks and network security. He received a Young Active Member Award for the year 2012–13 from the Computer Society of India, and Best Faculty Award for the year 2017 and Best Researcher Award for the year 2019 from BVICAM, New Delhi.

Juvrianto Chrissunday Jakob is a dedicated English lecturer at the Civil Engineering Department of Ambon State Polytechnic, Indonesia. With a strong academic background and a passion for education, his areas of expertise encompass Teaching English as a Foreign Language (TEFL), integrating Technology in Language Learning, Discourse Analysis, and English for Specific Purposes (ESP). These fields reflect his commitment to equipping students with language skills tailored to their professional and academic needs. Juvrianto holds a master's degree in English Education from Universitas Negeri Makassar, Indonesia, where he honed his skills in pedagogy and research. His scholarly pursuits focus on exploring innovative teaching methodologies and the application of modern tools in language instruction, ensuring his teaching methods align with the evolving demands of education in the digital era. Beyond his role as a lecturer, Juvrianto is an active contributor to academic communities. He serves as a tutor and language instructor, helping learners enhance their English proficiency. His dedication to academic excellence is further evident in his role as a reviewer for several local and international journals, where he evaluates and supports the dissemination of research in his field. Juvrianto's professional journey is driven by his belief in lifelong learning and his desire to foster effective communication skills in students and professionals alike. His contributions to the intersection of language, technology, and education underscore his impact as an educator and scholar.

Leo S. F. Lin is a Senior Lecturer at the School of Policing Studies, Charles Sturt University, Australia. Before joining Charles Sturt University, he was an assistant professor of Criminal Justice and Security Management at Ming Chuan University and an adjunct assistant professor at Central Police University, Taiwan. He also served as a visiting lecturer at the University of Malaya, Malaysia, and an affiliated lecturer at the University of Glasgow, UK.

Melissa Liow Li Sa presently serves as the Assistant Director (Academic) at PSB Academy, where she collaborates with a team of Course Directors to oversee both undergraduate and postgraduate Business courses offered in partnership with Coventry University. Dr. Liow graduated with a Bachelor of Business Degree from University of Technology Sydney (UTS), Masters in Business Administration from University of Wales (UOW) and PhD in Business from International University of Malaya-Wales (IUMW). Dr Liow has taught subjects in the Business Venturing, Management, Marketing, Tourism and Hospitality Management disciplines at the undergraduate and postgraduate level. She has provided supervision to Masters and

Doctoral candidates specialising in the fields of Entrepreneurship, Human Resource Management and Marketing. She actively participates as a reviewer for esteemed publications including the International Journal of Contemporary Hospitality Management, Tourism and Hospitality Management, Journal of Global Hospitality and Tourism, ASEAN Journal on Hospitality and Tourism, as well as book chapters for IGI Global.

Poornima Mahesh is a distinguished academic professional with a strong background in the Electronics and Telecommunication field. She holds a B.Tech., MTech., and Ph.D. and has extensive experience of 21 years in academia. Dr. Poornima currently serves as in charge Principal in a College affiliated to the University of Mumbai. She is Six Sigma Yellow belt, and SCRUM Fundamentals certified Professional. Dr. Poornima has made significant contributions to research with a strong publication record of 23 papers in national and international journals and conferences, along with two books published in the field of electronics and telecommunications. She is also a dedicated educator and has taught a wide range of courses at various levels and is known for her passion for teaching and her ability to inspire and mentor students. She played a pivotal role in organizing various international conferences, workshops, and training programs. Dr. Poornima has expertise in wireless communication, antenna, internet of things, robotics, Google cloud, Electronics devices and artificial intelligence.

Vedprakash Maralapalle holds a Ph.D. in Civil Engineering from NMIMS University, Mumbai, and brings over a decade of academic experience to his role as an Assistant Professor in the Department of Civil Engineering at ASET, Amity University, Mumbai. As a licensed structural engineer with the Mumbai Municipal Corporation, Dr. Maralapalle combines academic rigor with practical expertise. His innovative contributions to the field are reflected in his impressive portfolio of eight patent filings, six of which have been granted, with others under review. Dr. Maralapalle has an extensive scholarly record, including five publications in internationally recognized, peer-reviewed journals indexed in SCI/Scopus, as well as six presentations at national and international conferences. Additionally, he is the author of two published books, further establishing his authority in civil engineering. A dedicated academician, he also serves as a reviewer for six international journals and is committed to student engagement through workshops and seminars. Dr. Maralapalle's career exemplifies a blend of innovation, research, and education, making him a distinguished figure in the field of civil engineering.

Uswah Mujahidah Rasuna Said is a committed academic and researcher with a strong foundation in Arabic Language Education, holding a Bachelor's degree from the State University of Makassar, where she graduated with a GPA of 3.83. Recognized for her academic excellence, she was awarded the Bidik Misi scholarship for underprivileged students with exceptional potential. Currently, she is pursuing advanced studies at the Indonesia University of Education as a recipient of the esteemed LPDP scholarship under the Ministry of Finance, Republic of Indonesia. Her research interests include Arabic vocabulary acquisition strategies, speech act analysis during conflict, and pedagogical modernization in the Middle East. Notable research projects include the development of educational tools, such as a mobile application to facilitate Quranic memorization, and investigations into the impact of linguistic politeness in war communication. She has presented her findings at international conferences, receiving accolades such as the Best Presenter Award for her transformative research. Beyond academia, Uswah has demonstrated exceptional leadership skills, serving in various capacities, including Chair of the Research and Strategic Studies Commission and Treasurer of the Sulawesi Lamacca Community. Her work extends to community empowerment, particularly through initiatives that enhance education in remote areas and provide disaster relief across Indonesia. She has played a vital role in projects involving education infrastructure improvements and trauma healing programs for disaster-affected communities. Fluent in Indonesian and proficient in English and Arabic, Uswah combines her linguistic abilities with expertise in public speaking and academic writing. Her commitment to education, research, and community development underscores her passion for advancing knowledge and fostering social impact. With her extensive experience, she continues to contribute to the academic community while championing initiatives that bridge education and humanitarian efforts.

Erzhan Mukashev is a Dean and Associate Professor of the School of Business at the Kazakh-British Technical University of Kazakhstan and holds a Ph.D. in Economics from the University of Maryland, USA. He is a voracious researcher with more than two decades of experience and has published many research papers, book chapters, and international conference presentations in his area of specialization. His global exposure and extensive experience in multicultural and multi-ethnic work environments greatly benefit the organizations he works for in achieving global collaborations and flawless administration. Dr. Erzhan's research interests are comparative institutional economics, macroeconomics, project management, entrepreneurship, and small business management.

Juhi P. Pathak is an Associate Professor at the Amity School of Communication, Amity University, Noida (Uttar Pradesh), and a Post-Doctoral Research Fellow at Manipur International University (Manipur), India. With over 12 years of experience in teaching and research and 5 years of industry experience, Dr. Pathak has authored six books and actively contributes as a social worker. A TEDxYouth motivational speaker, she is also affiliated with several national and international media organizations. Her work has earned her numerous awards, honors, and letters of appreciation from prestigious government bodies and research institutions worldwide.

Sumit Pathak is a B.Tech student in Computer Science and Engineering at Sharda University, Greater Noida, Uttar Pradesh. Since beginning his studies in 2022, he has demonstrated a keen interest in advancing his knowledge and skills in computer science, preparing for a dynamic career in technology and innovation.

Lohith Sekhar Potluri is a full-time Data Scientist at the School of Medicine of the University of California San Diego, San Diego, USA. Mr. Potluri completed his Master's in data science and is a voracious researcher in his field of interest. He has published several research articles, book chapters, and conference paper presentations, mostly in data science, machine learning, artificial intelligence, and statistics, with his command over R Language R Studio, SQL, and SaaS. Mr. Potluri won four Best Paper and Academic Excellence awards at international conferences and is working on three research projects.

Paramita Sarkar completed her Ph.D. research at the IT Department, AKCSIT, University of Calcutta, India, under the joint supervision of Professor Dr. Rituparna Chaki (University of Calcutta) and Professor Dr. Agostino Cortesi (Ca' Foscari University, Italy). Her thesis, titled *Improved Resource Management Using Concepts of Nurse Scheduling*, focused on developing optimization strategies for resource management. She holds a Master of Engineering in Computer Science and Engineering from West Bengal University of Technology (In-House), India, and a Bachelor of Technology in Computer Science and Engineering from Kalyani University, India. Dr. Sarkar is currently a full-time Assistant Professor in the Computer Science and Engineering Department at JIS University. Prior to this, she served for 17 years as a full-time Assistant Professor in the Computer Science and Engineering Department at Calcutta Institute of Engineering and Management, Kolkata, India, amassing a total of 18.5 years of teaching experience. As part of her professional growth, she participated in the prestigious “Biometrics-Intelligent Solution” training under the SPINAKER project at Bialystok University of Technology, Poland, gaining valuable expertise in biometrics and intelligent systems during a two-month on-site program. Her research interests include designing resource scheduling optimization algorithms, developing intelligent search methods, and applying AI and machine learning techniques to detect plant diseases. Dr. Sarkar seeks challenging roles as an AI/ML Engineer and resource optimizer in cloud computing, leveraging her expertise in experimental design, data analysis, and algorithm development. Proficient in literature reviews, research methodologies, and statistical software, she is dedicated to advancing knowledge in her field through innovative research and impactful scientific contributions.

Gour Sundar Mitra Thakur is an accomplished academic and AI enthusiast with 16 years of teaching and research experience in Computer Science and Engineering. He earned his B.Tech and M.Tech degrees in Computer Science and Engineering, followed by a PhD from the National Institute of Technology Durgapur, India. His doctoral research, titled "Intelligent Systems in Manifold Decision Making," underscores his expertise in developing advanced computational methodologies for complex problem-solving. Currently serving as an Associate Professor in the Department of Computer Science and Engineering (AIML) at Dr. B. C. Roy Engineering College, Durgapur, Dr. Thakur has contributed extensively to the academic community, publishing 22 research articles in reputed international journals, conferences, and book chapters. He is also an active reviewer for prestigious journals such as Knowledge-Based Systems, Applied Soft Computing, International Journal of Fuzzy Systems, and Frontiers in Oncology. Dr. Thakur's research interests lie in the application of AI, machine learning (ML), and deep learning (DL) algorithms to address real-world challenges in diverse domains such as biology, agriculture, environmental sustainability, and manufacturing. With expertise in TensorFlow and PyTorch, he has developed cutting-edge ML/DL models and designed robust ML pipelines for solving complex problems. A strong advocate for ethical AI, Dr. Thakur is committed to building systems that are fair, transparent, and unbiased. He excels in interdisciplinary collaboration, leveraging insights from various fields to achieve innovative solutions. His passion for advancing AI technologies drives his continuous pursuit of impactful research and applications.

Alexey Vedishchev is an experienced IT professional and educator with over 12 years of expertise in computer science education. He holds an MSc in Information Technology and Business from Altay State Technical University in Russia, where he also completed specialized training in information management for higher education. Since 2014, he has been an instructor at the American University of Nigeria, where he teaches various programming, database, and software development courses. Aleksei's teaching style emphasizes research, project-based learning, and diverse instructional methods. His professional background includes roles in IT support and management at organizations like Russian Post and Quanteq LTD, focusing on product support, IT policy development, and infrastructure planning.

Risman Wanci is a dedicated English lecturer at Famika University in Makassar, Indonesia, where he inspires students to develop their language proficiency and academic skills. With a strong academic foundation, he obtained his Master's degree in Linguistics from Hasanuddin University, where he delved into the complexities of language structure, meaning, and use. His passion for advancing education led him to pursue and earn his doctoral degree in English Education from the State University of Makassar. This achievement underscores his commitment to both theoretical and practical aspects of English language teaching. Risman's expertise spans a wide range of topics, including linguistics, pedagogy, and curriculum development. His doctoral research focused on innovative methods to enhance the teaching and learning process, contributing valuable insights to the field of English education. These accomplishments reflect his dedication to improving the quality of language instruction, particularly in the Indonesian context. In addition to his teaching responsibilities, Risman actively engages in academic research and professional development. His work often explores the intersection of linguistics and education, emphasizing the role of language in shaping effective communication and understanding in diverse settings. He is also a frequent contributor to seminars and conferences, sharing his knowledge and collaborating with fellow educators and researchers. Risman's unwavering commitment to academic excellence and his passion for language education make him a respected figure in his field. His work continues to impact students and educators alike, fostering a deeper appreciation for the power of language in education and beyond.

Index

A

B

C

D

E

G

H

I

K

L

M

O

P

R

S

T

V

W

www.ingramcontent.com/pod-product-compliance
Lightning Source LLC
LaVergne TN
LVHW081248011026
849162LV00004BA/894